JIRA Development Cookbook

Develop and customize plugins, program workflows, work
on custom fields, master JQL functions, and more – to
effectively customize, manage, and extend JIRA

Jobin Kuruvilla

BIRMINGHAM - MUMBAI

JIRA Development Cookbook

First published: November 2011

Production Reference: 1161111

Published by Packt Publishing Ltd.
Livery Place
35 Livery Street
Birmingham B3 2PB, UK

ISBN 978-1-84968-180-3

www.packtpub.com

Cover Image by Sandeep Babu (sandyjb@gmail.com)

Credits

Author

Jobin Kuruvilla

Reviewers

Fidel Castro Armario

Justin Koke

Dawid Kowalski

Sergey Markovich

Marcin Zręda

Acquisition Editor

Amey Kanse

Development Editor

Alina Lewis

Technical Editors

Sakina Kaydawala

Mohd. Sahil

Copy Editors

Leonard D'Silva

Brandt D'Mello

Laxmi Subramanian

Project Coordinator

Leena Purkait

Proofreader

Lesley Harrison

Indexer

Tejal Daruwale

Graphics

Valentina D'Silva

Production Coordinator

Aparna Bhagat

Cover Work

Aparna Bhagat

About the Author

Jobin Kuruvilla is an Atlassian Consultant who is experienced in customizing JIRA and writing JIRA plugins for various customers. He is working with Go2group, a premier Atlassian partner and is involved in managing Atlassian products for big enterprises to small starter license installations.

Jobin had started his career as a Java/J2EE Developer in one of the biggest IT companies in India. After spending the initial years in the SOA world, he got hooked into this amazing product called JIRA, which he came across during the evaluation of third-party products for a requirements management solution. Soon Jobin realized the power of JIRA and pledged to spread the word. He has been doing it ever since, and reckons there is a long way to go!

Jobin runs a website named "J Tricks – Little JIRA Tricks" (http://www.j-tricks.com). He has written numerous tutorials to help the developer community, who he thinks has contributed immensely to his personal development. It is indeed those tutorials that sowed the first seeds for this book.

Acknowledgment

No book is the product of just the author – he just happens to be the one with his name on the cover.

A number of people contributed to the success of this book, and it would take more space than I have to thank each one individually.

First of all, thanks to the Almighty God for helping me to sail through the difficulties in this short life and for making my life as wonderful as it is now.

The next biggest thanks go to my Acquisition editor, Amey Kanse, who patiently explained to me every single doubt I threw at him and made me feel at home through the entire process of writing this book. Thank you, Amey, for believing in me and for being a wonderful guide through this process. Special thanks should go to Mary Nadar, who recognized the author in me, Leena Purkait, the Project coordinator for this book, and Alina Lewis, the Development editor of the book. Also thanks to the entire Packt Publishing team for working so diligently to help bring out a high quality product.

It is amazing to work with a team of talented developers and technical geeks. I am fortunate to work with such teams throughout my career, and it just makes you fall in love with the work. In particular, thanks are due to each and every member of the 'STORM team', 'PD&B team', and 'RAMP team'. Your encouragement and support were invaluable to me – you guys rock!

I must also thank the talented JIRA community who are instrumental in helping each other, sharing solutions, being active on the forums, running user groups, and what not. I am just one of the many who benefited.

Before I wind up, thank you, Atlassian, for giving us JIRA and a set of other wonderful products. You don't realize how much easier you are making our lives!

Last, but not least, a big thank you to the Go2group for the reception that you have given, the support extended in writing this book, and for believing in my capabilities.

About the Reviewers

Fidel Castro Armario has been working for Spanish Public Administration (Junta de Andalucía) since 2000 as a Consultant and Software Engineer. During his career, he specialized in business process design, implementation and optimization, and software QA. Since 2008, he is focused on designing and implementing a whole system of processes based on JIRA for IT departments management, IT services outsourcing, and CRM implementation.

He has a passion for designing highly detailed and accurate workflows, with self-explanatory interfaces, which are teamwork-oriented and aimed for work efficiency. He employs for his work a self-developed methodology, enabling implementation of high complexity processes, keeping maintenance and administration cost at low levels.

JIRA Workflow Toolbox plugin is a comprehensive workflow extension developed by Fidel as support for his work and is available at the Atlassian Plugin Exchange site.

My deepest gratitude goes to so many people who have trusted me and supported my efforts. Without them, I couldn't have carried out any of my projects on JIRA.

I would like to dedicate my work to my wife, Carmen, and my son, Felipe, for their support and understanding for the many hours I devoted to review this book.

Dawid Kowalski is a third year student at Poznań University of Technology in Poland. He is currently employed at Wolters Kluwer as a Software Developer and works on JIRA-related projects. He is ambitious, hard-working, and organized. He is active in the scientific club and works there on optimization problems. He is also the captain of the Imagine Cup 2010 and 2011 semi-finalist team.

> I would like to thank my closest friends and family for continuous support and encouragement.

Sergey Markovich is currently a co-founder of Plugenta Labs, a company focusing on the development of add-ons to enterprise software and an independent Atlassian JIRA and Confluence contractor.

In the past, a code wizard in several multinational corporations and startups and a Bachelor in Computer Science.

> I want to thank my mom and dad for giving me birth and growing me up the way you did it. Everything I have in my life I it owe to you.
>
> I also want to say warm words to everybody involved with Plugenta Labs. It's a real pleasure to work with you and I keep learning from you every day.

Marcin Zręda specializes in Business Analysis and Quality Assurance. He has many years of experience as a programmer and designer. He is the author of many articles on JIRA and the owner of the `http://www.testandtry.com` blog. He has implemented JIRA for many departments for more than 600 employees. He is currently directing the department of business analysis for a large international company.

www.PacktPub.com

Support files, eBooks, discount offers and more

You might want to visit www.PacktPub.com for support files and downloads related to your book.

Did you know that Packt offers eBook versions of every book published, with PDF and ePub files available? You can upgrade to the eBook version at www.PacktPub.com and as a print book customer, you are entitled to a discount on the eBook copy. Get in touch with us at service@packtpub.com for more details.

At www.PacktPub.com, you can also read a collection of free technical articles, sign up for a range of free newsletters and receive exclusive discounts and offers on Packt books and eBooks.

http://PacktLib.PacktPub.com

Do you need instant solutions to your IT questions? PacktLib is Packt's online digital book library. Here, you can access, read and search across Packt's entire library of books.

Why Subscribe?

- ▶ Fully searchable across every book published by Packt
- ▶ Copy and paste, print and bookmark content
- ▶ On demand and accessible via web browser

Free Access for Packt account holders

If you have an account with Packt at www.PacktPub.com, you can use this to access PacktLib today and view nine entirely free books. Simply use your login credentials for immediate access.

Instant Updates on New Packt Books

Get notified! Find out when new books are published by following @PacktEnterprise on Twitter, or the Packt Enterprise Facebook page.

This book is dedicated to

My wife Anumol, the joy of my heart, my best friend for years who even chose to give up her career for the company of this mortal. Anu, I wouldn't be in this place if not for your unconditional love and care.

My sweet little daughter Anna, the light of my world. I am sure you will read this one day and understand what I was doing all night scratching my head in front of the laptop instead of changing your nappies!

My parents, Alice and Kuruvilla, who brought me up in a village not many people have heard of. Nothing beats the pain and suffering they have undergone in the process

My sister, Juby Sara, the best sister in the world. It is a privilege watching you follow my footsteps outshining me all the way!

My friends from TKM and JNV Kottayam who dared me to dream and then helped me to achieve them. You guys are the best.

This book would not have been possible without your love and understanding.

A big thank you from the bottom of my heart. I have nothing to give back, but my love and prayers.

Table of Contents

Preface

This book is your one-stop resource for mastering JIRA extension and customization. You will learn how to create your own JIRA plugins, customize the look-and-feel of your JIRA UI, work with workflows, issues, custom fields, and much more.

The book starts with recipes on simplifying the plugin development process followed by a complete chapter dedicated to the plugin framework to master plugins in JIRA.

Then we will move on to writing custom field plugins to create new field types or custom searchers. We then learn how to program and customize workflows to transform JIRA into a user-friendly system.

We will then look at customizing the various searching aspects of JIRA such as JQL, searching in plugins, managing filters, and so on.

Then the book steers towards programming issues; that is, creating/editing/deleting issues, creating new issue operations, managing the other various operations available on issues using the JIRA APIs, and so on.

In the latter half of the book, you will learn how to customize JIRA by adding new tabs, menus, and web items, communicate with JIRA using the REST, SOAP, or XML/RPC interfaces, and work with the JIRA database.

The book ends with a chapter on useful and general JIRA recipes.

What this book covers

Chapter 1, Plugin Development Process, covers the fundamentals of JIRA plugin development process. It covers, in detail, the setting up of a development environment, creating a plugin, deploying it, and testing it.

Chapter 2, Understanding Plugin Framework, covers, in detail, the JIRA architecture and looks at the various plugin points. It also looks at how to build JIRA from source and extend or override the existing JIRA functionalities.

Chapter 3, Working with Custom Fields, looks at programmatically creating custom fields in JIRA, writing custom field searchers, and various other useful recipes related to custom fields.

Chapter 4, Programming Workflows, looks at the various ways of programming the JIRA workflows. It includes writing new conditions, validators, post functions, and so on, and contains related recipes that are useful in extending the workflows.

Chapter 5, Gadgets and Reporting in JIRA, covers the reporting capabilities of JIRA. It looks at writing reports, dashboard gadgets, among others in detail.

Chapter 6, The Power of JIRA Searching, covers the searching capabilities of JIRA and how it can be extended using the JIRA APIs.

Chapter 7, Programming Issues, looks at the various APIs and methods used for managing issues programmatically. It covers the CRUD operations, working with attachments, programming change logs and issue links, time tracking, among others.

Chapter 8, Customizing the UI, looks at the various ways of extending and modifying the JIRA user interface.

Chapter 9, Remote Access to JIRA, looks at the remote capabilities of JIRA – REST, SOAP, and XML/RPC, and the ways of extending them.

Chapter 10, Dealing with the Database, looks at the database architecture of JIRA and covers the major tables in detail. It also covers the different ways to extend the storage and access or modify the data from plugins.

Chapter 11, Useful Recipes, covers a selected list of useful recipes which do not belong in the preceding categories, but are powerful enough to get your attention! Read away!!

What you need for this book

This book focuses on JIRA development. You will need the following software as a bare minimum:

- ▶ JIRA 4.x+
- ▶ JAVA 1.6+
- ▶ Maven 2.x
- ▶ Atlassian Plugin SDK
- ▶ An IDE of your choice. The examples in the book use Eclipse and SQL Developer.

Some of the recipes are too simple to use the fully-fledged plugin development process, and you will see this highlighted as you read through the book!

Who this book is for

If you are a JIRA developer or project manager who wants to fully exploit the exciting capabilities of JIRA, then this is the perfect book for you.

Conventions

In this book, you will find a number of styles of text that distinguish between different kinds of information. Here are some examples of these styles, and an explanation of their meaning.

Code words in text are shown as follows: "The fields oldvalue and newvalue are populated using the method getChangelogValue."

A block of code is set as follows:

```
<!-- entity to represent a single change to an issue. Always part of a
change group -->
    <entity entity-name="ChangeItem" table-name="changeitem" package-
    name="">
        <field name="id" type="numeric"/>
        <field name="group" col-name="groupid" type="numeric"/>
        <!--relations and indexes -->
    </entity>
```

When we wish to draw your attention to a particular part of a code block, the relevant lines or items are set in bold:

```
<!-- entity to represent a single change to an issue. Always part of a
change group -->
    <entity entity-name="ChangeItem" table-name="changeitem" package-
    name="">
        <field name="oldvalue" type="extremely-long"/>
        <!-- a string representation of the new value (i.e.
        "Documentation" instead of "4" for a component which might be
         deleted) -->
        <!--relations and indexes -->
    </entity>
```

Any command line input or output is written as follows:

```
maven war:webapp
```

New terms and **important words** are shown in bold. Words that you see on the screen, in menus or dialog boxes for example, appear in the text like this: "You must have noticed the new **View Issue** page."

Warnings or important notes appear in a box like this.

Tips and tricks appear like this.

Reader feedback

Feedback from our readers is always welcome. Let us know what you think about this book—what you liked or may have disliked. Reader feedback is important for us to develop titles that you really get the most out of.

To send us general feedback, simply send an e-mail to feedback@packtpub.com, and mention the book title via the subject of your message.

If there is a book that you need and would like to see us publish, please send us a note in the **SUGGEST A TITLE** form on www.packtpub.com or e-mail suggest@packtpub.com.

If there is a topic that you have expertise in and you are interested in either writing or contributing to a book, see our author guide on www.packtpub.com/authors.

Customer support

Now that you are the proud owner of a Packt book, we have a number of things to help you to get the most from your purchase.

Downloading the example code for this book

You can download the example code files for all Packt books you have purchased from your account at http://www.PacktPub.com. If you purchased this book elsewhere, you can visit http://www.PacktPub.com/support and register to have the files e-mailed directly to you.

Errata

Although we have taken every care to ensure the accuracy of our content, mistakes do happen. If you find a mistake in one of our books—maybe a mistake in the text or the code—we would be grateful if you would report this to us. By doing so, you can save other readers from frustration and help us improve subsequent versions of this book. If you find any errata, please report them by visiting http://www.packtpub.com/support, selecting your book, clicking on the **errata submission form** link, and entering the details of your errata. Once your errata are verified, your submission will be accepted and the errata will be uploaded on our website, or added to any list of existing errata, under the Errata section of that title. Any existing errata can be viewed by selecting your title from http://www.packtpub.com/support.

Piracy

Piracy of copyright material on the Internet is an ongoing problem across all media. At Packt, we take the protection of our copyright and licenses very seriously. If you come across any illegal copies of our works, in any form, on the Internet, please provide us with the location address or website name immediately so that we can pursue a remedy.

Please contact us at copyright@packtpub.com with a link to the suspected pirated material.

We appreciate your help in protecting our authors, and our ability to bring you valuable content.

Questions

You can contact us at questions@packtpub.com if you are having a problem with any aspect of the book, and we will do our best to address it.

1

Plugin Development Process

In this chapter, we will cover:

- ▶ Setting up the development environment
- ▶ Creating a Skeleton plugin
- ▶ Deploying a JIRA plugin
- ▶ Testing and debugging

Introduction

Atlassian JIRA, as we all know, is primarily an **Issue Tracking** and **Project Tracking System**. What many people do not know, though, is the power of its numerous customization capabilities, using which we can turn it into a different system altogether! Maybe a helpdesk system, a user story management system, an online approval process, and a lot more. This is in addition to the issue tracking and project tracking capabilities for which JIRA, arguably, is the best player in the market.

So what are these customizations? How can we convert the JIRA we know into a product we want? Or maybe just add extra functionalities that are specific to our organization?

The answer to these questions probably can be summarized in a single word—**plugins**. JIRA has given the power to its users to write plugins and customize the functionality in a way they find suitable.

But is that the only way? Definitely not! JIRA itself provides a lot of customization options through its user interface, and in more demanding cases, using property files like **jira-application.properties**. In some cases, you will also find yourself modifying some of the JIRA core files to tweak functionality or to work around a problem. We will see more of that in the chapters to come but the best entry point to JIRA customizations are plugins. And that is where we start our cookbook, before we move on to the in-depth details.

What is a JIRA plugin?

So, what is a JIRA plugin? JIRA itself is a web application written in Java. But that doesn't mean you need to know JAVA to write a plugin, though in most cases you will need to. You might end up writing a simple descriptor file to add few links here and there. If that makes the non-Java developer in you happy, watch out for the different plugin modules JIRA supports.

A JIRA plugin is a JAR file that has a mandatory plugin **descriptor** and some optional Java classes and velocity templates. The velocity templates are used to render the HTML pages associated with your plugin, but in some cases, you might also want to introduce JSPs to make use of some pre-existing templates in JIRA. JSPs, as opposed to velocity templates, cannot be embedded in the plugin, but instead they should be dropped into the appropriate folders in the JIRA web application.

The plugin descriptor, the only mandatory part of a plugin, is an XML file which must be named `atlassian-plugin.xml`. This file is located at the root of the plugin. The `atlassian-plugin.xml` file defines the various modules in a plugin. The different types of available plugin modules include reports, custom field types, and so on, and these are discussed in detail in the next chapter.

The plugin development process

The process of developing a JIRA plugin can be of varying complexity depending on the functionality we are trying to achieve. The plugin development process essentially is a four step process:

1. Develop the plugin.
2. Deploy it into our local JIRA.
3. Test the plugin functionality.
4. Make changes and re-deploy the plugin, if required.

Each of these is explained in detail through the various recipes in this book!

JIRA, on start-up, identifies all the plugins that are deployed in the current installation. You can deploy multiple plugins, but there are some things you need to keep an eye on!

The `atlassian-plugin.xml` file has a plugin **key** which should be unique across all the plugins. It is much similar to a Java package. Each module in the plugin also has a key that is unique within the plugin. The plugin key combined with the module key, separated by a colon, forms the complete key of a plugin module.

Following is a sample `atlassian-plugin.xml` file without any plugin modules in it:

```
<!-- the unique plugin key -->
<atlassian-plugin key="com.jtricks.demo" name="Demo Plugin" plugins-
version="2">
    <!-- Plugin Info -->
    <plugin-info>
        <description>This is a Demo Description</description>
        <version>1.0</version>
        <!-- optional  vendor details -->
        <vendor name="J-Tricks" url="http://www.j-tricks.com"/>
    </plugin-info>
    . . . 1 or more plugin modules . . .
</atlassian-plugin>
```

The plugin, as you can see, has details such as description, version, vendor-details, and so on.

When a plugin is loaded, all the unique modules in it are also loaded. The plugin classes override the system classes and so if there is an action that has the same **alias** name as that of a JIRA action, it is the plugin action class that will be loaded. We will see more about extending actions in the coming chapters.

Suppose you have a report module in your plugin, it will look as follows:

```
<report key="demo-report" name="My Demo Report" ....>
...
</report>
```

The plugin key, in this case, will be `com.jtricks.demo` and the module key will be `com.jtricks.demo:demo-report`.

Hang on, before you start writing your little plugin for a much wanted feature, have a look at the Atlassian plugin exchange to see if someone else has already done the dirty work for you!

Atlassian plugin exchange

Atlassian plugin exchange is a one stop shop where you can find the entire list of commercial and open source plugins people around the world have written. See `https://plugins.atlassian.com/search/by/jira` for more details.

Troubleshooting

A common scenario that people encounter while deploying their plugin is when the plugin fails to load even though everything looks fine. Make sure your plugin's key is unique and is not duplicated in one of yours or another third-party's plugin!

The same applies to individual plugin modules.

Setting up the development environment

Now that we know what a plugin is, let 's aim at writing one! The first step in writing a JIRA plugin is to set up your environment, if you haven't done that already. In this recipe, we will see how to set up a local environment.

To make plugin development easier, Atlassian provides the **Atlassian Plugin Software Development Kit** (**SDK**). It comes along with Maven and a pre-configured `settings.xml` to make things easier.

Atlassian Plugin SDK can be used to develop plugins for other Atlassian products, including Confluence, Crowd, and so on, but we are concentrating only on JIRA.

Getting ready

The following are the pre-requisites for running the Atlassian plugin SDK:

- ▶ The default port for the SDK: 2990 should be available. This is important because different ports are reserved for different Atlassian products.
- ▶ JDK Java version 1.5 - 6 must be installed.
- ▶ Make sure `JAVA_HOME` is set properly and the command `java -version` outputs the correct Java version details.
- ▶ And of course, JIRA 4.x+ should be installed in your development environment.

> Make sure you use a context path for your JIRA because there are known issues with the SDK not working when the context path is empty. See `https://studio.atlassian.com/browse/AMPS-122` for more details.

How to do it...

1. Once we have Java installed and the port ready, we can download the latest version of Atlassian Plugin SDK from `https://maven.atlassian.com/content/repositories/atlassian-public/com/atlassian/amps/atlassian-plugin-sdk/`.

2. Unzip the version into a directory of your choice. Let's call this directory `SDK_HOME` going forward.

3. Add the SDK's bin directory into the environment `PATH` variable.

4. Create a new environment variable `M2_HOME` pointing to the Apache-Maven directory in your SDK Home.

5. A lot of commonly used dependencies are already available in the repository folder embedded in the SDK. To use this, edit the `settings.xml` under `M2_HOME/conf/` and modify the `localRepository` attribute to point to the embedded repository folder. By default, it will use the `USER_HOME/.m2/repository`.

6. Install the IDE of your choice. Atlassian recommends Eclipse, IntelliJ IDEA, or NetBeans, as they all support Maven.

7. Ready, Set, Go...

How it works...

With these steps executed properly, we have a development environment for JIRA plugins.

The next step is to create a Skeleton plugin, import it into your IDE, and start writing some code! Creating the Skeleton plugin, deploying it, and so on, is explained in detail in the following recipes.

There's more...

Even though the aforementioned steps will work in most cases, we will come across scenarios where the setting up of the development environment is not that straightforward. For example, there are extra settings needed for Maven if the machine is behind a firewall. You might even have a local Maven version already installed. In this section, we will see some useful tips on similar cases.

Proxy settings for Maven

If you are behind a firewall, make sure you configure the proxy in the Maven `settings.xml` file. The proxy can be configured as follows:

```xml
<settings>
  .
  <proxies>
   <proxy>
      <active>true</active>
      <protocol>http</protocol>
      <host>proxy.demo.com</host>
      <port>8080</port>
      <username>demouser</username>
      <password>demopassword</password>
      <nonProxyHosts>localhost|*.demosite.com</nonProxyHosts>
    </proxy>
  </proxies>
  .
</settings>
```

Find out more about that and other aspects of Maven at `http://maven.apache.org/index.html`.

Using local Maven

If you are a developer, in many cases you will have Maven already installed in your local machine. In that case, point `M2_HOME` to your local Maven and update the respective `settings.xml` with the repository details in the default `settings.xml` that ships with Atlassian plugin SDK.

Configuring IDEs to use SDK

If you are using IntelliJ IDEA, it is an easy job because IDEA integrated Maven out-of-the-box. Just load the project by selecting the `pom.xml`!

If you are using Eclipse, make sure you have M2Eclipse installed. This is because Eclipse integrates Maven through the Sonatype M2Eclipse plugin. You can find more details on configuring this at `http://confluence.atlassian.com/display/DEVNET/Configuring+Eclipse+to+use+the+SDK`.

Troubleshooting

If you see Maven download errors like *Could not resolve artifact*, make sure you verify the following:

- ► Entry in Maven `settings.xml` is correct. That is, it points to the correct repositories
- ► Proxy configuration is done if required
- ► Antivirus in the local machine is disabled if none of the above works! Seriously, it makes a difference.

See also

- ► *Creating a skeleton plugin*

Creating a skeleton plugin

In this recipe, we will look at creating a skeleton plugin. We will use the Atlassian Plugin SDK to create the skeleton!

Getting ready

Make sure you have the Atlassian Plugin SDK installed and a version of JIRA 4.x running on your local machine.

How to do it...

1. Open a command window and go to the folder where you want to create the plugin.

 Make sure you use a directory without any spaces because there are known issues with the SDK not working in directories with spaces in it. See `https://studio.atlassian.com/browse/AMPS-126` for details.

2. Type `atlas-create-jira-plugin` and press *Enter*.

3. Enter the `groupID` when prompted. GroupID would normally be coming from your organization name and mostly resembles the Java package. Of course, you can enter a different package name as we move forward if you want to keep it separate. GroupID will be used to identify your plugin along with `artifactId`.

   For example: `com.jtricks.demo`.

4. Enter the `artifactId`—the identifier for this artifact. Do not use spaces here.

   For example: `demoplugin`.

5. `Version`—the default version is `1.0-SNAPSHOT`. Enter a new version if you want to change it or press *Enter* to keep the default.

   For example: `1.0`

6. `Package`—press *Enter* if the package value is same as the `groupID`. If not, enter the new value here and press *Enter*.

   For example, `com.jtricks.mypackage`

7. Confirm the selection when prompted. If you want to change any of the entered values, type `N` and press *Enter*.

8. Wait for the `BUILD SUCCESSFUL` message. You might see a few warnings which can be ignored.

How it works...

A skeleton plugin is nothing but a set of directories and sub directories along with a `pom.xml` (Maven Project Object Model) file and some sample Java and XML files in the appropriate folders.

Here is a snapshot of how the project will look like in Eclipse. It also shows the design view of the default `atlassian-plugin.xml` file:

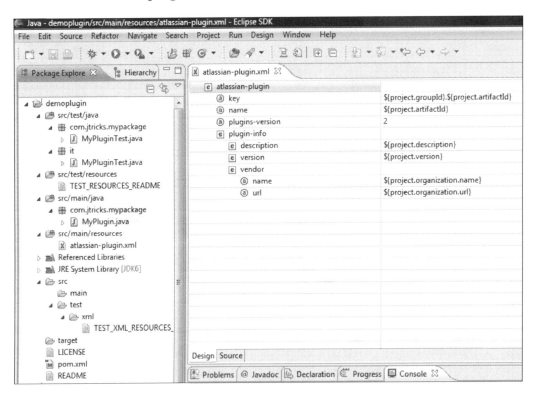

As you can see, there is a `pom.xml` at the root level and a `src` folder. A sample `LICENSE` file and a `README` file are also created for you at the root level.

Under the `src` folder, you will find out two folders, `main` and `test`, with identical folder structure. All your main Java code goes under the `main` folder. Any JUnit tests you write will go into the same location under the `test` folder. There is an additional folder, `it`, under the test folder where all the integration tests will go!

You will find the plugin descriptor under `src/main/resources` with sample values already populated in it. The values in the preceding screenshot are populated from the `pom.xml`. In our case, the plugin key will be populated as `com.jtricks.demo:demoplugin` when the plugin is built.

There are two more folders under the `src/test`. `src/test/resources`, which will hold any resources required for unit tests or integration tests, and the `src/test/xml` folder can hold the XML data from any other JIRA instance. If the XML is supplied, the SDK will use it to configure the JIRA instance before running the integration tests.

So, that is our plugin Skeleton. All that is pending is some useful Java code and proper module types in the `atlassian-plugin.xml` file!

> Remember, the first Maven run is going to take some time as it downloads all the dependencies into your local repository. A coffee break might not be enough!! If you have a choice, plan your meals. ;)

There's more...

Sometimes, for the geeks, it is much easier to run a single command to create a project without bothering about the step-by-step creation. In this section, we will quickly see how to do it. We will also have a look at how to create an Eclipse project if you opt out of installing m2eclipse.

One step to your skeleton plugin

You can ignore the interactive mode by passing the parameters like `groupID`, `artifactId`, and so on, as arguments to the `atlas-create-jira-plugin` command.

```
atlas-create-jira-plugin -g my_groupID -a my_artefactId -v my_version -p my_package --non-interactive
```

In this example, for the values we saw previously, the single line command will be:

```
atlas-create-jira-plugin -g com.jtricks.demo -a demoplugin -v 1.0 -p com.jtricks.mypackage --non-interactive
```

You can pick and choose the parameters and provide the rest in an interactive mode as well!

Creating an Eclipse project

If you are not using m2eclipse, just run the following command from the folder where you have the `pom.xml` file:

```
atlas-mvn eclipse:eclipse
```

This will generate the plugin project for Eclipse and you can then import this project into the IDE.

Type `atlas-mvn eclipse:clean eclipse:eclipse` if you want to clean the old project and create again!

With IDEA or m2eclipse, just opening a file will do. That is, you can just import the project using the option **File | Import | Existing Maven Projects**, and select the relevant project.

See also

▶ *Deploying a plugin*

▶ *Making changes and re-deploying a plugin*

Deploying a plugin

In this recipe, we will see how to deploy a plugin into JIRA. We will see both the automated deployment using Atlassian Plugin SDK and the manual deployment.

Getting ready

Make sure you have the development environment set up, as we discussed earlier. Also the skeleton plugin should now have the plugin logic implemented in it.

How to do it...

Installing a JIRA plugin using Atlassian Plugin SDK is a cake walk. Here is how it is done:

1. Open a command window and go to your plugin's root folder, that is, the folder where your `pom.xml` resides.

2. Type `atlas-run` and press *Enter*. It is possible to pass more options as argument to this command for which the details can be found at: `http://confluence.atlassian.com/display/DEVNET/atlas-run`.

3. You will see a lot of things happening as Maven downloads all the dependent libraries into your local repository. As usual, it is going to take lot of time when you run it for the first time.

4. If you are on Windows, and if you see a security alert popping up, click on **Unblock** to allow incoming network connections.

5. When the installation is completed, you will see the following message:

   `[WARNING] [talledLocalContainer] INFO: Server startup in 123558 ms`

   `[INFO] [talledLocalContainer] Tomcat 6.x started on port [2990]`

   `[INFO] jira started successfully and available at http:// localhost:2990/jira`

   `[INFO] Type CTRL-C to exit`

6. Open `http://localhost:2990/jira` in your browser.

7. Login using the username as **admin** and password as **admin**.

8. Test your plugin! You can always go to the **Administration | Plugin** menu to confirm that the plugin is deployed properly.

If you already have a local JIRA installed or if you want to manually install your plugin for some reason, all you need to do is to package the plugin JAR and copy it across to the `JIRA_Home/plugins/installed-plugins` directory.

You can package the plugin using the following command:

```
atlas-mvn clean package
```

Use `atlas-mvn clean install` if you also want to install the package plugin into your local repository.

How it works...

There is only one single command that does the whole thing: `atlas-run`. When you execute this command, it does the following:

1. Builds your plugin JAR file

2. Downloads the latest/specified version of JIRA to your local machine if it is the first time you're running the command.

3. Creates a virtual JIRA installation under your plugin/target folder.

4. Copies the JAR file into the `/target/jira/home/plugins/installed-plugins` directory

5. Starts JIRA in the Tomcat container.

Now, if you look at your target folder, you will see a lot of new folders which were created for the virtual JIRA installation! The two main folders are the `container` folder, which has the Tomcat container setup, and the `jira` folder, which has the JIRA WAR along with the JIRA home setup!

You will find the database (`HSQLDB`), indexes, backups, and attachments under `/target/jira/home`. And you will see your `jira-webapp` at `/target/container/tomcat6x/cargo-jira-home/webapps/jira`.

If you have any JSPs that need to be put under the webapp, you will have to copy it to the appropriate folder under the aforementioned path!

There's more...

There's more to this.

Using a specific version of JIRA

As mentioned earlier, `atlas-run` deploys the latest version of JIRA. But what if you want to deploy the plugin into an earlier version of JIRA and test it?

There are two ways to do it:

1. Mention the JIRA version as an argument to `atlas-run`; make sure you run `atlas-clean`, if you already have the latest version deployed:

   ❑ Run `atlas-clean` (if required).

   ❑ Run `atlas-run -v 4.1.2` or `atlas-run -version 4.1.2` if you are developing for JIRA version 4.1.2. Replace the version number with a version of your choice.

2. Permanently change the JIRA version in your plugin `pom.xml`:

   ❑ Go to your `pom.xml`.

   ❑ Modify the `jira.version` property value to the desired version.

   ❑ Modify the `jira.data.version` to a matching version.

This is how it will look for JIRA 4.1.2:

```
<properties>
    <jira.version>4.1.2</jira.version>
    <jira.data.version>4.1</jira.data.version>
</properties>
```

Reusing the configurations in each run

Suppose you added some data on to virtual JIRA, how do you retain it when you clean start-up JIRA next time?

This is where a new SDK command comes to our rescue.

After the `atlas-run` is finished, that is, after you pressed *Ctrl + C*, execute the following command:

```
atlas-create-home-zip
```

This will generate a file named `generated-test-resources.zip` under the target folder. Copy this file to the `/src/test/resources` folder or any other known locations. Now modify the `pom.xml` to add the following entry under configurations in the `maven-jira-plugin`:

```
<productDataPath>${basedir}/src/test/resources/generated-test-
resources.zip</productDataPath>
```

Modify the path accordingly. This will reuse the configurations the next time you run `atlas-run`.

Troubleshooting

▶ Missing JAR file exception? Make sure the local-repository attribute in the `settings.xml` file points to the embedded Maven repository that comes with the SDK. If the problem still persists, manually download the missing JAR files and use `atlas-mvn install` to install them in to the local repository.

  Watch out for the proxy settings or antivirus settings that can potentially block the download in some cases!

▶ BeanCreationException? Make sure your plugin is of version 2. Check your `atlassian-plugin.xml` to see if the following entry is there or not. If not, add the entry:

```
<atlassian-plugin key="${project.groupId}.${project.artifactId}"
name="${project.artifactId}" plugins-version="2">
```

Run `atlas-clean` followed by `atlas-run` after you do that.

Making changes and re-deploying a plugin

Now that we have deployed the test plugin, it is time to add some proper logic, re-deploy the plugin, and test it. Making the changes and re-deploying a plugin is pretty easy. In this recipe, we will quickly look at how to do this.

How to do it...

You can make changes to the plugin and re-deploy it while the JIRA application is still running. Here is how we do it:

1. Keep the JIRA application running in the window where we ran `atlas-run`.

2. Open a new command window and go to the root plugin folder where your `pom.xml` resides.

3. Run `atlas-cli`.

4. Wait for the command—Waiting for messages.

5. Run pi. Pi stands for "plugin install" and this will compile your changes, package the plugin JAR, and install it into the installed-plugins folder.

Now, there is one thing you need to keep an eye on! Not all the plugin modules can be redeployed like this prior to JIRA 4.4. The following is a list of the plugin modules that can be reloaded with pi in JIRA 4.0.x:

- ▶ ComponentImport
- ▶ Gadget
- ▶ ModuleType
- ▶ Resource
- ▶ REST
- ▶ ServletContextListener
- ▶ ServletContextParameter
- ▶ ServletFilter
- ▶ Servlet
- ▶ WebItem
- ▶ WebResource
- ▶ WebSection

If your plugin module is not there in the preceding list or if the changes doesn't seem to be reflected, press *Ctrl + C* in the command window running atlas-run and re-run the atlas-run command. That will re-deploy the plugin and restart JIRA.

Post JIRA 4.1, SDK supports reloading of more modules, but whether it works or not depends on what the module does internally.

JIRA 4.4+ supports reloading of all the plugin modules.

Debugging in Eclipse

It is also possible to run the plugin in debug mode and point your IDE's remote debugger to it.

Following are the steps to do this in Eclipse:

1. Use atlas-debug instead of atlas-run.

2. Once the virtual JIRA is up and running with tour plugin deployed in it, go to **Run | Debug Configurations** in Eclipse.

3. Create a new Remote Java Application.

4. Give a name, keep the defaults, and give the port number as 5005. This is the default debug port on which the virtual JIRA runs.

5. Happy Debugging!

See also

▶ *Setting up the development environment*

▶ *Creating a skeleton plugin*

Testing and debugging

In the world of **Test Driven Development** (**TDD**), writing tests is a part and parcel of the development process. I don't want to bore you with why testing is important! Let us just say, all these holds true for JIRA plugin development as well.

In this recipe, we will see the various commands for running unit tests and integration tests in JIRA plugins.

Getting ready

Make sure you have the plugin development environment set up and the skeleton plugin created!

You might have noticed that there are two sample test files, one each for unit tests and integration tests, created under the `src/test/java/your_package/` and `src/test/java/it` folders.

Once you have it ready, it is time to write some tests and run those tests to make sure things work as expected!

How to do it...

The first step is to write some tests! We recommend you to use some powerful testing frameworks like JUnit in collaboration with mocking frameworks like **PowerMock** or **Mockito**. Make sure you have the valid dependencies added on to your `pom.xml`.

Let us now make a huge assumption that you have written a few tests!

Following is the command to run your unit tests from the command line:

```
atlas-unit-test
```

The normal Maven command `atlas-mvn clean test` also does the same thing. If you are running the integration tests, the command to use is:

```
atlas-integration-test
```

Or the Maven command: `atlas-mvn clean integration-test`.

Once we are on to the stage of running tests, we will see it failing at times. There comes the need for debugging. Checkout the `*.txt` and `*.xml` files created under `target/surefire-reports/` which has all the required information on the various tests that are executed.

Now, if you want to skip the tests at the various stages, use `-skip-tests`. For example, `atlas-unit-test --skip-tests` will skip the unit tests.

You can also use the Maven options directly to skip the unit/integrations tests or both together.

▶ `-Dmaven.test.skip=true`: skips both unit and integration tests

▶ `-Dmaven.test.unit.skip=true`: skips unit tests

▶ `-Dmaven.test.it.skip=true`: skips integration tests

How it works...

The `atlas-unit-test` command merely runs the related Maven command: `atlas-mvn clean test` in the backend to execute the various unit tests. It also generates the outputs into the `surefire-reports` directory for reference or debugging.

The `atlas-integration-test` does a bit more. It runs the integration tests in a virtual JIRA environment. It will start up a new JIRA instance running inside a Tomcat container, set up the instance with some default data including a temporary license that lasts for three hours, and execute your tests!

How does JIRA differentiate between the unit tests and integration tests? This is where the folder structure plays an important role. Anything under the `src/test/java/it/` folder will be treated as integration tests and everything else will be treated as unit tests!

There's more...

There is more to it.

Using custom data for Integration/Functional Tests

While `atlas-integration-test` makes our life easier by setting up a JIRA instance with some default data in it, we might need some custom data as well to successfully run a few functional tests.

We can do this in a couple of steps:

1. Export the data from a pre-configured JIRA instance into XML.

2. Put it under the `src/test/xml/` directory.

3. Provide this path as the value for the `jira.xml.data.location` property in the `localtest.properties` under `src/main/resources`.

The XML resource will then be imported to JIRA before the tests are executed.

Testing against different version of JIRA/Tomcat

Just like the `atlas-run` command, you can use the `-v` option to test your plugin against a different version of JIRA. As before, make sure you do an `atlas-clean` before running the tests if you had tested it against another version before.

You can also use the `-c` option to test it against a different version of the Tomcat container.

For example, `atlas-clean && atlas-integration-test -v 3.0.1 -c tomcat5x` will test your plugin against JIRA version 3.0.1 using Tomcat container 5.

See also

▶ *Setting up the development environment*

▶ *Deploying a plugin*

2
Understanding Plugin Framework

In this chapter, we will see more details on the JIRA Architecture and the plugin framework. We will also see the following recipes:

- ▶ Converting plugins from v1 to v2
- ▶ Adding resources into plugins
- ▶ Adding web resources to the plugin
- ▶ Building JIRA from source
- ▶ Adding new webwork actions to JIRA
- ▶ Extending a webwork action in JIRA

Introduction

As we saw in the previous chapter, the JIRA plugin development process is probably an easier task than we expected it to be. With the help of Atlassian Plugin SDK, developers can spend more time worrying about the plugin logic than on the troublesome deployment activities. And yes, after all, it is the plugin logic that is going to make an impact!

This chapter details how the various components fit into JIRA's architecture and how JIRA exposes the various pluggable points. We will also see an overview of the JIRA's system plugins to find out how JIRA uses the plugin architecture to its own benefit, followed by some useful recipes!

JIRA Architecture

We will quickly see how the various components within JIRA fit in to form the JIRA we know. It is best described in a diagram and Atlassian has a neat one along with a detailed explanation at `http://confluence.atlassian.com/display/JIRA/JIRA+Architectural+Overview`. We will re-draw the diagram a little bit to explain it in a brief but useful way.

Third-party components

Before we dig deeper into the JIRA Architecture, it is probably useful to understand a few key components and familiarize yourself with them. JIRA's major third-party dependencies are outlined next.

 It is not mandatory to know all about these frameworks, but it will be very helpful during plugin development if you have an understanding of these.

Webwork

Webwork is nothing but a Java web application development framework. The following is a quick overview of Webworks as you find it in the OpenSymphony documentation:

> *"It is built specifically with developer productivity and code simplicity in mind, providing robust support for building reusable UI templates, such as form controls, UI themes, internationalization, dynamic form parameter mapping to JavaBeans, robust client- and server-side validation, and much more."*

Read more about Webwork1 at the archived link: `http://web.archive.org/web/20080328114803/http://www.opensymphony.com/webwork_old/src/docs/manual/`.

Note that JIRA uses Webwork1 and not 2. In this book, all instances of webwork refer to the webwork1 version. JIRA itself refers to the technology as webwork, but you will notice that the files, plugin modules, and so on, use webwork1 in it just to emphasize the version.

Seraph

Seraph is Atlassian's opensource web authentication framework. It provides a simple, extensible authentication system that JIRA uses for all authentication purposes.

Read more about Seraph at `http://docs.atlassian.com/atlassian-seraph/latest/`.

OSUser

OSUser is OpenSymphony's user and group management framework. It is designed to provide a simple-to-use API for user-management. JIRA uses OSUserframework in versions prior to JIRA 4.3.

Read more about it at `http://www.opensymphony.com/osuser/`.

JIRA 4.3+ uses Crowd as its new User API for which the details can be found at `http://docs.atlassian.com/atlassian-crowd/current/com/atlassian/crowd/embedded/api/CrowdService.html`.

PropertySet

PropertySet is again another open source framework from OpenSymphony that helps you to store a set of properties against any 'entity' with a unique ID. The properties will be key/value pairs and can only be associated with a single entity at a time.

Read about all that and more at `http://www.opensymphony.com/propertyset/`.

OSWorkflow

OSWorkflow is yet another open source framework from the OpenSymphony group. It is an extremely flexible workflow implementation that is capable of driving complex conditions, validators, post functions, and so on, along with many other features.

Read more about OSWorkflow at `http://www.opensymphony.com/osworkflow/`.

OfBiz Entity Engine

OfBiz stands for **Open For Business** and the **OfBiz Entity Engine** is a set of tools and patterns used to model and manage entity-specific data.

As per the definition from the standard Entity-Relation modeling concepts of Relational Database Management Systems, *an Entity is a piece of data defined by a set of fields and a set of relations to other entities.*

Read more about the Entity Modeling and concepts at `http://ofbiz.apache.org/docs/entity.html`.

Apache Lucene

The following is a simple definition of **Apache Lucene** that you can find in its documentation:

> *"Apache Lucene(TM) is a high-performance, full-featured text search engine library written entirely in Java. It is a technology suitable for nearly any application that requires full-text search, especially cross-platform."*

More about Lucene and its potential can be found at `http://lucene.apache.org/java/docs/index.html`.

Atlassian Gadget JavaScript Framework

JIRA4 introduces a powerful gadget framework. Atlassian has gone **OpenSocial** with gadgets and in order to help developers in creating gadgets, Atlassian has introduced **Gadgets Javascript Framework** that encapsulates a lot of common requirements and functionalities used between gadgets.

More about gadget development can be read at `http://confluence.atlassian.com/display/GADGETDEV/Using+the+Atlassian+Gadgets+JavaScript+Framework`.

Quartz

Quartz is an open source job scheduling service. It can be used to create jobs that can be scheduled within any JAVA EE and SE applications. The tasks are defined as standard Java components and scheduler includes many enterprise-class features, such as JTA transactions and clustering.

Read more at `http://www.quartz-scheduler.org/`.

Architecture explained...

It is best to learn the intricacies of system architecture with the help of a diagram. For the benefit of a brief but meaningful explanation on the JIRA Architecture, let us have a quick look (or a long stare, whichever you are comfortable!) at the following diagram:

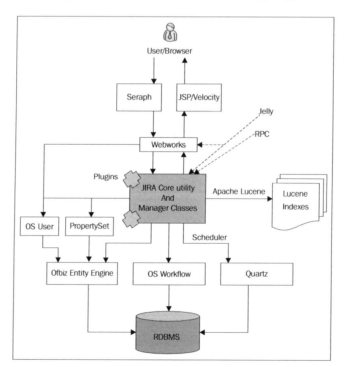

JIRA is a web application built using the MVC Architecture. It is fully written in JAVA and is deployed as a WAR file into a JAVA Servlet Container such as Tomcat.

The majority of the JIRA core functionality revolves around the **JIRA Utility and Manager Classes** which thus becomes the heart of JIRA. But it also interacts with a lot of third-party components, which we saw earlier, to deliver powerful functionalities like Workflows, Permissions, User Management, Searching, and so on.

As with any other web application, let us start with the incoming requests. Users interact with JIRA using web browsers. But there are other ways to interact with JIRA like using the **Jelly scripts** or by making remote calls using **REST/SOAP/XML-RPC**.

Authentication and user management

The user authentication, whichever way the request comes, is done in JIRA using Seraph, Atlassian's open source web authentication framework. Seraph is implemented as a servlet filter and it intercepts each and every incoming request and associates them with a specific user. It supports various authentication mechanisms like HTTP Basic Authentication, form-based authentication, and so on, and even looking up already stored credentials in a user session when implemented with SSO (Single sign on).

However, Seraph doesn't do any user management itself. It delegates this to the OSUser framework. One additional thing that Seraph does in JIRA is to intercept URLs starting with `/admin/` and allow users only if they have the 'Global Admin' permission.

Coming back to authentication and other user management functions, it is OSUser that does the work for JIRA in versions prior to 4.3. It does the following activities:

- ▶ User management—Creates/Updates/Deletes users and stores the details in JIRA database. Stores user preferences.
- ▶ Group management—Creates/Updates/Deletes groups and stores the details in JIRA database. Manages group memberships.
- ▶ Authentication—Password matching.

From JIRA 4.3, user management in JIRA is done using Crowd. **Crowd** is a single sign-on and identity management system from Atlassian which is now embedded in JIRA 4.3+. Plugin developers can now use **CrowdService** to manage users and groups, for which more information can be found at `http://docs.atlassian.com/atlassian-crowd/current/com/atlassian/crowd/embedded/api/CrowdService.html`.

Property management

JIRA lets you add key/value pairs as properties on any available 'entity' like User, Group, Project, Issue, and so on. It uses OpenSymphony's PropertySet to do this. Three major cases where PropertySet is used internally in JIRA are as follows:

- ▶ To store user preferences by the OSUser framework like e-mail, full name, and so on
- ▶ To store application properties
- ▶ To store chosen preferences of Portlets/Gadgets on user dashboards

We can also use the PropertySet in our plugins to store custom data as key/value pairs.

In earlier versions of JIRA, PropertySet was the only technology used to store plugin information and other data-related to plugins. But JIRA now supports a new technology called **ActiveObjects** which can be used to store plugin data. It is explained in detail in the coming chapters.

Presentation

The presentation layer in JIRA is built using **JSPs** and **Velocity** templates. The web requests, coming on to JIRA, are processed by OpenSymphony's Webwork1 framework. The requests are handled by webwork actions which internally use the JIRA Service layer. The service classes expose the core Utility and Manager classes that perform the tasks behind the scenes!

Database

JIRA talks to its database using the **Ofbiz Entity Engine** module. Its database schema is defined in the `entitmodel.xml` residing at `WEB-INF/classes/entitydefs`. The DB connectivity configuration goes in to `entityengine.xml` under `WEB-INF/classes`.

JIRA supports a wide variety of database products for which more details can be found at `http://confluence.atlassian.com/display/JIRA/Connecting+JIRA+to+a+Database`.

Workflows

Workflows are one of the most important features in JIRA. It provides us with a highly configurable workflow engine, which uses OpenSymphony's OSWorkflow behind the scenes. It lets us customize the workflows by adding new steps and transitions and for each transition we can add conditions, validators, or post functions. We can even write plugins to add more of these, in addition to the ones that ship with JIRA. We will see all that in detail in the coming chapters.

Searching

JIRA uses Apache Lucene to perform indexing in JIRA. Whenever an issue is changed in JIRA, it performs a partial re-indexing to update the related indexes. JIRA also lets us do a full re-index at any time manually from the Administration screen.

Searching in JIRA is done using these indexes which are stored in the local drive. We can even store search queries as filters whose results gets updated as the indexes changes.

Scheduled jobs

JIRA uses the Quartz API to schedule jobs within JIRA. The jobs, including the subscriptions to the filters and the custom ones we add, are stored in the JIRA database, and are executed by the Quartz job scheduling service.

JIRA's built-in scheduled job details can be found at `scheduler-config.xml`.

It is possible to schedule new events in JIRA using the SAL services implementation. As Atlassian puts it:

> *"The Shared Access Layer, or SAL inshort, provides a consistent, cohesive API to common plugin tasks, regardless of the Atlassian application into which your plugin is deployed."*

More information on scheduling events in JIRA using SAL can be found at `https://developer.atlassian.com/display/DOCS/Plugin+Tutorial+-+Scheduling+Events+via+SAL`.

Plugins

Last, but not the least, plugins fit into the JIRA Architecture to provide extra functionalities or to alter some of the existing ones. The plugins mostly use the same JIRA core utility classes and manager classes as webwork actions do, but in some cases also add/contribute to the list.

There are different pluggable points in JIRA which we will see in detail in this chapter.

This, I hope, gives you a brief introduction to the JIRA architecture and the major components used in it. We will see most of these in detail in the coming chapters and how to customize them by writing plugins. Off you go!

Types of plugin modules

Let us briefly see the different types of plugin modules supported in JIRA 4.x. All these modules are various extension points, using which we can not only add new functionalities in to JIRA, but also extend some of the existing functionalities.

Let us group them based on functionality instead of seeing them all together!

Reporting

Module type	Description
Portlet	Adds new portlets to the user's dashboard. It is deprecated in JIRA 4.x, but is still supported. Usage of Gadgets is recommended.
Gadget	Adds new Gadgets into the user's dashboard. These gadgets can also be accessed from other applications.
Report	Adds new reports into JIRA.

Workflows

Module type	Description
workflow-condition	Adds new workflow conditions to the JIRA workflow. It can then be used to limit the workflow actions to users, based on pre-defined conditions.
workflow-validator	Adds new workflow validations to the JIRA workflow. Validations can be used to prevent certain workflow actions when the criteria are not met.
workflow-function	Adds new workflow post functions to the JIRA workflow. These can be used to perform custom actions after a workflow action is executed

Custom fields

Module type	Description
customfield-type	Adds new custom field types to JIRA. We can customize the look-and-feel of the fields in addition to custom logic. See also `customfield-searcher`.

Searching

Module Type	Description
customfield-searcher	Adds new field searchers on to JIRA. The searcher needs to be mapped with the relevant custom fields.
jqlfunction	Adds new JQL Functions to be used with JIRA's advanced searching.
search-request-view	Adds a new view in the Issue Navigator. They can be used to show the search results in different ways.

Links and tabs

Module Type	Description
issue-operation	Adds new Issue Operations in the **View** issue screen. This module is unavailable from JIRA 4.1.x. Web Items (see *web-item* module) are used from 4.1.x instead of issue-operation module.
web-section	Adds new sections in application menus. Each section can contain one or more links under it.
web-item	Adds new links that will appear at a defined section. The section here can be the new ones we added or the existing JIRA web sections.
project-tabpanel	Adds new tabs to the Browse **Project** screen. We can define what has to appear in the tab.
component-tabpanel	Adds new tabs to the Browse **Component** screen. As above, we can define what to appear in the tab.
version-tabpanel	Adds new tabs to the Browse **Version** screen. Same as above.
issue-tabpanel	Adds new tabs to the **View Issue** screen. Similar to other tabs, here also we can define what appears in the tab.
web-panel	It is newly introduced in JIRA 4.4. Defines panels or sections that can be inserted into an HTML page.

Remote invocation

Module type	Description
rest	Creates new REST APIs for JIRA to expose more services and data entities.
rpc-soap	Publishes new SOAP end-points for JIRA. It is deployed as a new SOAP service and exposes a new WSDL with the operations we have published in the plugin.
rpc-xmlrpc	Same as above. Exposes XML-RPC endpoints, instead of SOAP, within JIRA.

Actions and components

Module type	Description
webwork	Adds new webwork actions along with views into JIRA which can add new functionality or override existing ones.
component	Adds components to JIRA's component system. These are then available for use in other plugins and can be injected into them.
component-import	Imports components shared by other plugins.

Other plugin modules

Module type	Description
resource	Adds downloadable resources into the plugins. A resource is a non-JAVA file such as JavaScript, CSS, image files, and so on.
web-resource	Similar to the above, adds downloadable resources into the plugins. But these are added to the top of the page with the cache-related headers set to never expire. We can also specify the resources to be used only in specific contexts. Multiple resource modules will appear under a web-resource module.
servlet	Deploys a JAVA servlet onto JIRA.
servlet-context-listener	Deploys a JAVA Servlet Context Listener.
servlet-context-param	Sets parameters in the Servlet context shared by the plugin's servlets, filters, and listeners.
servlet-filter	Deploys a JAVA servlet filter onto JIRA. The order and position in the application's filter chain can be specified.
user-format	Adds custom behaviors for user details. Used to enhance the user profile.
keyboard-shortcut	Available only from 4.1.x. Defines new keyboard shortcuts for JIRA. You can also override the existing shortcuts from JIRA 4.2.x!
module-type	Dynamically adds new plugin module types to the plugin framework. The new module can be used by other plugins.

What goes into atlassian-plugin.xml?

Let's look deeper into the plugin descriptor named `atlassian-plugin.xml`.

Following is how the plugin descriptor will look like when the skeleton plugin is created:

```
<atlassian-plugin key="${project.groupId}.${project.artifactId}"
name="${project.artifactId}" plugins-version="2">
  <plugin-info>
    <description>${project.description}</description>
    <version>${project.version}</version>
    <vendor name="${project.organization.name}"url="${project.
organization.url}" />
  </plugin-info>
</atlassian-plugin>
```

We need to add more details into it depending on the type of plugin we are going to develop. The plugin descriptor can be divided into three parts:

1. **atlassian-plugin** element: This forms the root of the descriptor. The following attributes populates the `atlassian-plugin` element:

   ❑ **key**: This is probably the most important part. It should be a unique key across the JIRA instance and will be used to refer the different modules in the plugin, just like we use the packages in a Java application.
   If you see `${project.groupId}.${project.artifactId}` as the plugin key, it picks up the values from your `pom.xml` file. When the plugin is built, the key will be `YOUR_GROUP_ID.YOUR_ARTIFACT_ID`.

   ❑ **name**: Give an appropriate name for your plugin. This will appear in the plugin menu under administration.

   ❑ **plugins-version**: This is different from the version attribute. `plugins-version` defines whether the plugin is version 1 or 2. `plugins-version="2"` defines the plugin as a version 2 plugin. Remove the entire attribute to make it a version 1 plugin.

   ❑ **state**: This is an optional element to define the plugin as disabled, by default. Add `state="disabled"` under the `atlassian-plugin` element.

2. **plugin-info** element : This section contains information about a plugin. It not only provides information that is displayed to administrators but also, optionally, provides bundle instructions to the OSGI network:

   ❑ **description**: A simple description about your plugin.

   ❑ **version**: The actual version of you plugin which will be displayed under the plugin menu along with the Name and Description.

   ❑ **application-version**: Here you can define the minimum and maximum version of the JIRA application that is supported by your plugin.
   `<application-version min="4.0.2" max="4.1"/>` will be supported from 4.0.2 to 4.1.
   But remember, this is only for information's sake. The plugin might still work fine in JIRA 4.2!

   ❑ **vendor**: Here you can provide details about the plugin vendor. It supports two attributes: **name** and **url**, which can be populated with the organization's Name and URL respectively.
   Similar to plugin key, you can populate this from the `pom.xml`file,as you would have noticed in the skeleton descriptor.

   ❑ **param**: This element can be used to define name/value attributes for the plugin. You can pass as many attributes as you want.
   For example, `<paramname="configure.url">/secure/JTricksConfigAction.jspa</param>` defines the configuration URL for our demo plugin.

❑ **bundle-instructions**: Here we define the OSGI bundle instructions which will be used by the Maven Bundle plugin while generating the OSGI bundle. More about this can be read under aQutebndtool: `http://www.aqute.biz/Code/Bnd`. Following are the two elements in a snapshot:

> ▶ **Export-Package**: This element defines the package in this plugin that can be exposed to other plugins. All other packages will remain private.

> ▶ **Import-Package**: This element defines the packages that are outside this plugin but that are exported in other plugins.

3. **Plugin Modules**: This is the section where the actual plugin modules, which we saw a bit earlier and will see in detail later in this book, will appear.

Hopefully, you now have your plugin descriptor ready with all the necessary attributes!

Working with the Plugins1 and Plugins2 versions

Let us also quickly see how to deal with the Plugins1 and Plugins2 versions.

Before we go on to the details, it is essential to understand the importance of both the versions. Post 4.x, JIRA used to support only Plugins1 version. So why do we need Plugins2 version?

The key motive behind version 2 plugins is to keep the plugins as a bundle isolated from the other plugins and the JIRA core classes. It makes use of the OSGI platform (`http://www.osgi.org`) to achieve this. While it keeps the plugins isolated, it also gives you a way to define dependencies between plugins leaving it to the plugin developer's convenience. It even lets you import or export selected packages within the plugin giving increased flexibility.

The fact that the version2 plugins are deployed as OSGI bundles also means that the plugins are dynamic in nature. They may be installed, started, updated, stopped, and uninstalled at any time during the running of the framework.

It is the developer's choice to go for the Plugins1 version or the Plugins2 version, depending on the nature of the plugin.

Let us see the key differences at various stages of plugin development for both the versions.

Development

	Plugins1	Plugins2
Version	No `plugins-version` element in `atlassian-plugin.xml`.	Include the `plugins-version` element in the `atlassian-plugin.xml` as follows: `<atlassian-plugin key="${project.groupId}.${project.artifactId}" name="${project.artifactId}" plugins-version="2">`
External Dependencies	Include the dependent libraries with the **provided** scope in your `pom.xml` file if the jars are added into `WEB-INF/lib` or **compile** scope if the jars should be embedded into the plugin.	Dependent libraries must be included in the plugin as the plugin cannot make use of resources under `WEB-INF/lib`. This can be done in two ways. ▶ Provide the scope in the `pom.xml` file as compile. In this case, the jars will be picked up by the Plugin SDK and added into the `META-INF/lib` folder of the plugin. ▶ Manually add the dependent jar files into the `META-INF/lib` directory inside the plugin. You can also make your plugin dependent on other bundles. See *Managing Complex Dependencies* in this table.
Dependency Injection	Done by Pico Container in JIRA. All registered components can be injected directly.	Done by the plugin framework. Not all JIRA's core components are available for injection in the constructor. Use the `component-import` module to access some of the dependencies that are not directly accessible within the plugin framework. Use it also to import public components declared in other plugins.
Declaring new Components	Use the component module to register new components. Once done, it is available to all the plugins.	Use the component module to register components. To make it available to other plugins, set the public attribute to 'true'. It is 'false' by default, making it available only to the plugin in which it is declared.

	Plugins1	**Plugins2**
Managing Complex dependencies	All the classes in version1 plugins are available to all other plugins and JIRA core classes.	Version2 plugins allows us to optionally import/export selected packages using **bundle-instructions** in the plugin descriptor or alternatively by the Import-Packge/Export-Packge options while building the bundle.
		The **Bundle Dependency System** hence allows you to define complex dependencies between plugins, eliminating the class path contradictions and upgradation of plugins.

Installation

Plugins1	**Plugins2**
Plugin must be on the application classpath.	Plugin must *not* be on the application classpath. It is loaded using the plugin framework.
Hence deploy it under the `WEB-INF/lib` folder.	Hence the plugin is deployed under `${jira-home}/plugins/installed-plugins/`.
	`Jira-home` is declared in the `jira-application.properties` file under `WEB-INF/classes`.

Right, we now know how the two plugin versions work. Maybe it is time to see the plugins that JIRA comes with!

JIRA System plugins

In this section, we will see a brief overview of the JIRA System plugins.

A lot of JIRA's functionality is written in the form of plugins. It not only showcases what we can achieve using plugins, but also helps us, as developers, to understand how the various pieces fit together.

If it is the `atlassian-plugin.xml` file that describes the plugin functionalities, JIRA maintains the information in `*.xml` files placed under `WEB-INF/classes`. You will also find the related classes in the exploded folders under `WEB-INF/classes`.

Let us have a quick look at the various system plugin XMLs that can be found in `WEB-INF/classes` and the functionality they support:

System plugin XML	Functionality
`system-contentlinkresolvers-plugin.xml`	**System Content Link Resolvers**—Resolves parsed content links into Link objects. ▶ Attachment Link Resolver ▶ Anchor Link Resolver ▶ JIRA Issue Link Resolver ▶ User Profile Link Resolver
`system-customfieldtypes-plugin.xml`	**JIRA System custom fields**—All the out-of-the-box custom fields in JIRA and the searcher associations. Examples: ▶ Text Field ▶ Text Area ▶ .... ▶ User Picker ▶ Select
`system-footer-plugin.xml`	This plugin renders the content of the footer in JIRA.
`system-issueoperations-plugin.xml`	**System Issue Operations**—Renders the issue operations using web-items grouped using web-sections. Examples: ▶ Edit issue ▶ Assign Issue ▶ .... ▶ Log Work
`system-issuetabpanels-plugin.xml`	**System Issue Tab Panels**—Renders the various tabs on the **View Issue** page: ▶ All Tab Panel ▶ Comment Tab Panel ▶ Work Log Tab Panel ▶ Change history Tab Panel ▶ CVS Tab Panel

System plugin XML	Functionality
`system-issueviews-plugin.xml`	Renders the **single issue view** and the various **search request views**. ▶ Single Issue Views : XML, Word, Printable ▶ Search Views : XML, RSS, RSS (Comments), Printable, Word, Full Content, Excel (All fields), Excel (Current fields), Charts
`system-jql-function-plugin.xml`	Built-in **JQL Functions**.
`system-keyboard-shortcuts-plugin.xml`	Built-in **Keyboard Shortcuts**.
`system-macros-plugin.xml`	JIRA's base **System Macros**.
`system-portlets-plugin.xml`	Built-in **portlets**.
`system-project-plugin.xml`	**System Project Panels**—Renders the Browse Project, Browse Version, and Browse Component panels.
`system-projectroleactors-plugin.xml`	**System Project Role Actors**—built-in project role actors (User Role Actor and Group Role Actor) and the associated webwork actions.
`system-renderercomponentfactories-plugin.xml`	**Renderer Component Factories Plugin**—instantiates Renderer Components using the plugin system. Macro Renderer, Link Renderer, URL Renderer, and so on.
`system-renderers-plugin.xml`	Built-in **System Renderers**: ▶ Wiki Style Renderer ▶ Default Text Renderer
`system-reports-plugin.xml`	Built-in **System Reports**.
`system-top-navigation-plugin.xml`	Renders the content of the **top navigation bar** in JIRA. Has a collection of web-items and web-sections.
`system-user-format-plugin.xml`	Renders a user in JIRA differently at different places.
`system-user-profile-panels.xml`	Renders the panels on the **User Profile** page.
`system-webresources-plugin.xml`	**System Web Resources**—Includes static resources like JavaScript files, style sheets, and so on.
`system-webwork1-plugin.xml`	**System webwork Plugin**—Can be used to add custom webwork actions, which can also be done using plugins.
`system-workflow-plugin.xml`	System workflow **conditions**, **functions**, and **validators.**

In addition to use these files as a starting point for JIRA plugin development, we might sometimes end up modifying these files to override the way JIRA works.

Care must be taken to upgrade the changes during the time of a JIRA upgrade.

So that was a pretty lengthy introduction to the JIRA Architecture! Let us quickly move on to the recipes in this chapter. Time to code!!

Converting plugins from v1 to v2

If you are moving to JIRA 4.x from JIRA 3.13.x or earlier versions, one of the important differences is the introduction of v2 plugins. While designing the upgrade to JIRA 4.x, it makes perfect sense to sometimes migrate the plugins from v1 to v2, although it is not a mandatory step. In this recipe, we will see how to convert a version1 plugin to a version2 plugin.

Getting ready

There are a couple of questions we need to ask before the plugin is converted:

▶ **Are all the packages used by the plugin available to OSGi plugins?** This is very important because JIRA doesn't expose all the packages to OSGi plugins.

The list of packages exported and made available to the plugins2 version can be found in the `com.atlassian.jira.plugin.DefaultPackageScannerConfiguration` class.

▶ **Are all the components used by the plugin available to OSGi plugins?** Similar to the previous question, we need to make sure the components are also exposed to the OSGi plugins.

Unfortunately, there is no definite list provided by Atlassian for JIRA. To check if the components are available, use dependency injection. The plugin will fail in the start-up if the component is not available.

How to do it...

The actual conversion process of v1 plugins to v2 is easier than you think if the packages and the components that you have used in the plugin are available to the OSGi plugins. Here are the steps for conversion.

1. Add the `plugins-version="2"` attribute in `atlassian-plugin.xml`. This is probably the only mandatory step in the conversion process. You will be amazed to see that many of the plugins will work as it is! Once added, the plugin descriptor looks like the following:

   ```
   <atlassian-plugin key="${project.groupId}.${project.artifactId}"
   name="Demo Plugin" plugins-version="2">
   . . . . . . . . . . . . . . . . . . .
   </atlassian-plugin>
   ```

2. Modify the source code, if required. This includes migration to the new API if you are moving to a new JIRA version with API changes, working out the changes if some of the packages/components not exported to OSGi are used in the v1 plugin, and so on.

3. Customize the package imports and exports by defining them in the bundle manifest. You can do this by using the Bundle Instructions we saw while explaining the `atlassian-plugin.xml` earlier in this chapter or simply by adding the appropriate entries into the manifest file in your jar.

   This is an optional step which you need to do only if you want to import packages from another plugin/bundle or you want to export some of your packages to make it available to other plugins.

4. Expose your custom plugin components to other plugins using the `component` module. You must set the public attribute to true in the component registered in your `atlassian-plugin.xml` file. That is, `public="true"`

   You must import the components specifically if you want to use the components declared publicly in other plugins. Use the `component-import` module to do this.

   ```
   <component-import key="democomponent" interface="com.jtricks.
   DemoComponent" />
   ```

5. You can also optionally add advanced spring configurations by adding **Spring Dynamic Modules (SpringDM)** configuration files (of the format `*.xml`) under the `META-INF/spring/` directory. These files will then be loaded by the Spring DM Loader. The details are outside the scope of this book.

How it works...

The v2 plugin JAR file created with the Atlassian descriptor containing the required modules, goes through the following journey:

1. The plugin is loaded at JIRA start-up and JIRA identifies the new jar.

2. `DirectoryLoader` checks whether the new plugin is version2 or version1.

3. If version2, it checks for the OSGI manifest entries which you can enter in the `MANIFEST.MF` file. If found, the plugin is installed as an OSGI bundle and started.

4. If the OSGI manifest entries are not present, JIRA uses the BND tool (`http://www.aqute.biz/Code/Bnd`) to generate the manifest entries and insert them into the `MANIFEST.MF` file.

5. It then checks for the presence of an explicit `atlassian-plugin-spring.xml`. If the file is present, the plugin is then deployed as an OSGI bundle, as in step 2.

6. If `atlassian-plugin-spring.xml` file is absent, it then scans the `atlassian-plugin.xml` file and converts the registered components and others into OSGI references or OSGI services and creates an `atlassian-plugin-spring.xml` file.

7. Once the `atlassian-plugin-spring.xml` file is created, the plugin is deployed as an OSGI bundle and installed into the PluginManager.

JIRA thus gives us the flexibility to define our own custom OSGI manifest entries and references or let JIRA do the dirty work by defining them appropriately in the plugin descriptor.

See also

▶ *Deploying your plugin* in *Chapter 1, Plugin Development Process*

▶ *Creating a skeleton plugin* in *Chapter 1*

Adding resources into plugins

It is often required to add static resources like JavaScript files, CSS files, and so on in our plugins. To enable JIRA to serve these additional static files, they should be defined as downloadable resources.

Getting ready

A resource can be of different types. It is normally defined as a non-Java file that the plugin requires to operate.

Examples of resources that you will come across during JIRA plugin development include, but are not restricted to, the following:

▶ Velocity (`*.vm`) files required to render a view

▶ JavaScript files

▶ CSS files

▶ Property files for localization

How to do it...

To include a resource, add the resource module to the `atlassian-plugin.xml` file. The resource module can be added as part of the entire plugin or can be included within another module, restricting it just for that module.

The following are the attributes and elements available for the resource module and their uses:

Name	Description
name	Name of the resource. This is used by the plugin or module to locate a resource. You can even define a directory as a resource by adding a trailing /.
namePattern	Pattern to use when loading a directory resource.

Name	Description
type	Type of the resource.
	Examples:
	▶ download for resources like CSS, JavaScript, Images, and so on
	▶ velocity for velocity files
location	Location of the resource within the plugin jar. The full path to the file without a leading slash is required. When using, namePattern or pointing to directory resource, a trailing / is required.
property (key/value)	Used to add properties as key/value pairs to the resource. Added as a child tag to resources.
	Example: <property key="content-type" value="text/css"/>
param (name/value)	Used to add name/value pairs. Added as a child tag to resources.
	Example: <param name="content-type" value="image/gif"/>

All you have to do is to add the resource tag to the atlassian-plugin.xml file, either at the plugin level or at a module level. The resource will then be available for use.

The resource definition for an image will look as follows:

```
<resource type="download" name="myimage.gif" location="includes/
images/ myimage.gif">
  <param name="content-type" value="image/gif"/>
</resource>
```

A CSS file might looks as follows:

```
<resource type="download" name="demostyle.css" location="com/jtricks/
demostyle.css"/>
```

Once the resource is defined in the plugin descriptor, you can use it anywhere in the plugin. Following is how you refer to the resource.

Let us consider that you have a directory referenced as follows:

```
<resource type="download" name="images/"location="includes/images/"/>
```

A file demoimage.gif can be a reference in your velocity template as follows:

```
$requestContext.baseUrl/download/resources/${your_plugin_
key}:${module_key}/images/ demoimage.gif
```

A sample piece of code used in your plugin module looks as follows:

```
<img id="demo-image" src="$requestContext.baseUrl/download/resources/
com.jtricks.demo:demomodule/images/ demoimage.gif"/>
```

Where `com.jtricks.demo` is the plugin key and `demomodule` is the module key.

Adding web resources into plugins

The web resources plugin module, like the resource module we just saw, allows defining downloadable resources. The difference is that the web resources are added at the top of the page in the header with the cache-related headers set to never expire.

An additional advantage of using web resources module is that we can specify the resources to be included in specific contexts within the application.

How to do it...

The root element for the web resource plugin module is **web-resource**. It supports the following attributes:

Name	Description
Key	The only mandatory attribute. This should be unique within the plugin.
Disabled	Indicates whether the plugin module should be disabled by default or not.
i18n-name-key	The localization key for the human-readable name of the plugin module.
Name	Human-readable name of the web resource.

The following are the key elements supported.

Name	Description
description	Description of the module.
resource	All the resources to be added as web resources. See *Adding resources into plugins*.
dependency	Used to define dependency on the other web-resource modules. The dependency should be defined as `pluginKey:web-resourceModuleKey`. Example: `<dependency>com.jtricks.demoplugin:demoResource</dependency>`
context	Define the context where the web resource is available.

We can define the web-resource module by populating the attributes and elements appropriately.

An example would look as follows:

```
<atlassian-plugin  name="Demo Plugin" key="com.jtricks.demoplugin"
plugins-version="2">
  <plugin-info>
    <description>Demo Plugin for web-resources</description>
    <vendor name="J Tricks"url="http://www.j-tricks.com"/>
    <version>1.0</version>
  </plugin-info>

  <web-resource key="demoresource" name="Demo">
    <resource type="download" name="demoscript.js" location="includes/
      js/demoscript.js" />
    <resource type="download" name=" demoscript1.js"
      location="includes/js/demoscript1.js" />
  </web-resource>
</atlassian-plugin>
```

How it works...

When a webresource is defined, it is available for you in the plugin just like your downloadable plugin resources. As mentioned earlier, the resources are added to the top of the page in the header section.

In your action class or servlet, you can access these resources with the help of **WebResourceManager.** Inject the manager class into your constructor and you can then use it to define the resource as follows:

```
webResourceManager.requireResource("com.jtricks.demoplugin:
demoresource");
```

The argument should be `pluginKey:web-resourceModuleKey`.

By default, all the resources under the web-resource module are served in batch mode, that is, in a single request. This reduces the number of HTTP requests from the web browser.

There's more...

Before we wind up this recipe, it is probably a good idea to identify the available contexts for web resources and also to see how we can turn off the batch mode while loading resources.

Web resource contexts

Following are the available web resource contexts:

- ▶ `atl.general`: Everywhere except administration screens
- ▶ `atl.admin`: Administration screens
- ▶ `atl.userprofile`:User profile screens

You can have multiple contexts added like this:

```
<web-resource key="demoresource" name="Demo">
    <resource type="download" name="demoscript.js" location="includes
/js/ demoscript.js" />
    <context>atl.general</context>
    <context>atl.admin</context>
</web-resource>
```

Turning off batchmode

As mentioned earlier, the resources are loaded in one batch to reduce the number of HTTP requests from the browser. But if you want to switch off the batch mode for some reason, it can be achieved in two ways.

1. You can switch of batch mode `system-wide` by adding a property `plugin.` `webresource.batching.off=true` into `jira-application.properties`.

2. It can be turned off by individual resources by adding a `param` element as follows:

```
<resource type="download"  name="demoscript.js"
location="includes/js/ demoscript.js">
        <param name="batch" value="false"/>
</resource>
```

See also

- ▶ *Adding resources into plugins*

Building JIRA from source

One of the best things about JIRA, if you have a valid license, is that you get to see the source code. To see it, modify it, break it... err modify it because you have the license to do it!

Getting ready

Following are some of the pre-requisites prior to building JIRA from the source.

- ▶ A valid JIRA license to get access to the source code.

- ▶ An environment with JDK 1.5 or higher for JIRA 4.2 and lower versions. JDK 1.6 or higher for JIRA 4.3+.

- ▶ You will need both Maven1 and Maven2 if you are building versions prior to JIRA 4.3. Download Maven version 1.0.x and 2.1.x from `http://maven.apache.org`. JIRA 4.3+ needs only Maven 2.1.0.

> You need both Maven1 and Maven2 for versions prior to JIRA 4.3 because Maven1 is required to build the JIRA source and Maven2 is required to build plugins for JIRA. JIRA has bundled plugins thatneed to be built along with JIRA and so Maven2 is also a must.
>
> Maven 2.1.0+ is required for the plugin development process.

How to do it...

Let us see the steps to build JIRA WAR from the source for versions prior to JIRA 4.3:

1. Configure **Maven 1.0.x**.

   - ❑ Extract the Maven 1.0.x version downloaded earlier to a directory, which we will now refer to as `MAVEN_INSTALL_DIR`.

   - ❑ Download an Atlassian patched version of Ant jar from `http://confluence.atlassian.com/download/attachments/185729661/ant-optional-1.5.3-1.jar?version=1&modificationDate=1276644963420` and copy it to `MAVEN_INSTALL_DIR/maven-1.0/lib`.

   - ❑ Set the `MAVEN_HOME` environment variable, which will be `MAVEN_INSTALL_DIR/maven-1.0`.

   - ❑ Add Maven's bin directory to the path variable.

2. Configure **Maven 2.1.x**. If you have already setup your development environment using Atlassian Plugin SDK, you can skip this test as it comes along with a bundled Maven 2.x.

   - ❑ Install Maven 2.1.x, as per the instructions at `http://maven.apache.org/download.html`.

   - ❑ Configure the `settings.xml` by following the example `settings.xml` provided by Atlassian at `http://confluence.atlassian.com/display/DEVNET/Example+settings.xml`.

3. Download the JIRA source ZIP file from `http://www.atlassian.com/software/jira/JIRASourceDownloads.jspa`.

4. Extract the JIRA source to a directory which we call `JIRA_DIR`.

5. Go to the `jira` subdirectory, that is, `JIRA_DIR/jira`.

6. Run the following command to create an open WAR:

   `maven war:webapp`

   If you want to create a closed WAR, execute the following:

   `maven war:war`

7. See `http://maven.apache.org/maven-1.x/plugins/war/goals.html` for more Maven WAR goals.

8. Confirm that the WAR is created properly.

The following are the steps to create the WAR on JIRA 4.3 and higher versions.

1. Configure Maven 2.1.0.

2. Download and install the required third-party libraries, as these libraries are not available in the public Maven repositories:

   ❑ Download the correct version of the jar files, as mentioned below:

activation	javax.activation:activation	1.0.2
jms	javax.jms:jms	1.1
jmxri	com.sun.jmx:jmxri	1.2.1
jmxtools	com.sun.jdmk:jmxtools	1.2.1
jndi	jndi:jndi	1.2.1
jta	Jta:jta	1.0.1B
mail	javax.mail:mail	1.3.2

   ❑ Install them to the local Maven repository using the Maven install command:

   ```
   mvninstall:install-file -DgroupId=javax.activation
   -DartifactId=activation -Dversion=1.0.2 -Dpackaging=jar
   -Dfile=activation-1.0.2.jar
   mvninstall:install-file -DgroupId=javax.jms -DartifactId=jms
   -Dversion=1.1 -Dpackaging=jar -Dfile=jms-1.1.jar
   mvninstall:install-file -DgroupId=com.sun.jmx
   -DartifactId=jmxri -Dversion=1.2.1 -Dpackaging=jar
   -Dfile=jmxri.jar
   mvninstall:install-file -DgroupId=com.sun.jdmk
   -DartifactId=jmxtools -Dversion=1.2.1 -Dpackaging=jar
   -Dfile=jmxtools.jar
   ```

```
mvninstall:install-file -DgroupId=jndi -DartifactId=jndi
-Dversion=1.2.1 -Dpackaging=jar -Dfile=jndi.jar
mvninstall:install-file -DgroupId=jta -DartifactId=jta
-Dversion=1.0.1 -Dpackaging=jar -Dfile=jta-1_0_1B-classes.
jar
mvninstall:install-file -DgroupId=javax.mail
-DartifactId=mail -Dversion=1.3.2 -Dpackaging=jar
-Dfile=mail.jar
```

3. Extract the JIRA source archive to a local directory, which we call `JIRA_DIR`.

4. Navigate to the extracted sub directory with the name `atlassian-jira-X.Y-source` where X.Y is the version.

5. Run `build.bat` if on Windows, or `build.sh` if on Linux or Mac.

6. Confirm that the WAR file is created properly under `JIRA_DEV/jira-project/jira-distribution/jira-webapp-dist/target` subdirectory.

How it works...

As you have seen, the process is pretty straightforward and the actual build is done by Maven, the magician.

JIRA ships with the `project.xml` or `pom.xml` if in 4.3+, called the Project Object Model, which is used by Maven to build the WAR file.

You will be able to find the JIRA dependencies inside the `project.xml` / `pom.xml`. Maven will first build the dependencies and then build the JIRA WAR file using them.

The only key thing here is to setup Maven correctly. There are a couple of issues normally observed while building JIRA WAR, both related to Maven. Maybe it is worth touching upon them before we move ahead.

▶   Error while downloading dependencies due to the *java.net.ConnectException: Connection timed out: connect* exception.

    If you encounter this, make sure that the Maven proxy settings are configured properly. If already configured and still you are getting the error, try disabling your antivirus!

▶   *Failed to resolve artifact* error. Building JIRA 4.0 fails to download javax jms jar. In such cases, download the jar manually and install them into the local repository using `mvn install`.

    ```
    mvninstall:install-file -Dfile=<path-to-file> -DgroupId=<group-
    id> -DartifactId=<artifact-id> -Dversion=<version>
    -Dpackaging=<packaging>
    ```

    In 4.3+, refer to step 2 in the recipe where the relevant `mvn install` commands are given.

Once the WAR file is created, deploy it into a supported application server, and enjoy the power of JIRA!

> **Downloading the example code for this book**
>
> You can download the example code files for all Packt books you have purchased from your account at `http://www.PacktPub.com`. If you purchased this book elsewhere, you can visit `http://www.PacktPub.com/support` and register to have the files e-mailed directly to you.

There's more...

Along with the JIRA source, we have access to the source code of some of the JIRA dependencies from Atlassian. You might want to build them separately if you ever want to modify their behavior.

Building JIRA dependencies

Similar to JIRA, the dependent projects also use Maven. But it uses Maven1 in some cases and Maven2 in some others.

You can determine whether the dependency uses Maven1 or Maven2 by checking its Project Object Model by looking in the root directory. If the file is named `project.xml`, it uses Maven1 and if the file is named `pom.xml`, it uses Maven2.Simple, right?

Use the following command to generate the jar file for a dependency if it uses Maven1.

```
maven jar
```

For dependencies with Maven2, use:

```
mvn package
```

See also

▶ *Setting up the development environment* in *Chapter 1*

Adding new webwork actions to JIRA

Most of the time plugin developers will find themselves writing new actions in JIRA to introduce new functionality. Usually these actions are invoked from new web-item links configured at different places in the UI. It could also be from customized JSPs or other parts of the JIRA framework.

New actions can be added to JIRA with the help of the webwork plugin module.

Getting ready

Before we start, it probably makes sense to have a look at the webwork plugin module. Following are the key attributes supported:

Name	Description
Key	A unique key within the plugin. It will be used as the identifier for the plugin.
Class	This will be `java.lang.Object` as the real logic will reside in the action, Class.
i18n-name-key	The localization key for the human-readable name of the plugin module.
Name	Human-readable name of the webwork action.

The following are the key elements supported:

Name	Description
description	Description of the webwork module.
actions	This is where we specify the webwork1 actions.
	A webwork module must contain atleast one action element. It can have any number of actions.

For each webwork1 action, we should have the following attributes populated:

Name	Description
name	Fully qualified name of the action class. The class must extend `com.atlassian.jira.action.JiraActionSupport`.
alias	An alias name for the action class. JIRA will use this name to invoke the action.

The following element is supported for the webwork1 action:

Name	Description
view	Delegates the user to the appropriate view, based on the output of the action. This element has an attribute: name that maps to the return value of the action class.

Now that you have seen the attributes and elements supported, we can have a look at a sample webwork module before proceeding to create one!

```
<webwork1 key="demoaction" name="JTricks Demo Action" class="java.
lang.Object">
  <actions>
    <action name="com.jtricks.DemoAction" alias="DemoAction">
      <view name="input">/templates/input.vm</view>
      <view name="success ">/templates/joy.vm</view>
      <view name="error">/templates/tears.vm</view>
    </action>
  </actions>
</webwork1>
```

How to do it...

Let us now aim at creating a sample webwork action. For the example, we can create an action that takes a user input, prints it out in the console, and displays it on the output page after modifying the input.

Following are the steps to perform:

1. Add the new webwork action module into your `atlassian-plugin.xml`. Let us say, we add the same aforementioned snippet.

2. Create the action class `DemoAction` under the package `com.jtricks`. The class must extend `com.atlassian.jira.action.JiraActionSupport`.

3. Identify the parameters that you need to receive from the user. Create private variables for them with the name exactly similar to that of the related HTML tag.

   In our example, we need to take a user input. Let us say, it is the name of the user. The HTML code in the input view (in our case, `/templates/input.vm`) will be as follows:

   ```
   Name:   <input type="text" name="userName">
   ```

   So, we need to create a String variable of the name `userName` in our action class.

4. Create setter methods for the variables that are used to get values from the input view.

   In our example, we retrieve the `userName` from the input view and process it in the action class. So we need to create a setter method for that which will look like this.

   ```
   public void setUserName(String userName) {
     this.userName = userName;
   }
   ```

5. Identify the parameter that needs to be printed in the output page. In our case, we will print `modifiedName` in the output page.

6. Create getter methods for the parameters to be printed. Velocity or JSPs will invoke the getter methods to retrieve the value from the `Action` class. For our example, we have a getter method for `modifiedName`, which looks as follows:

```
public String getModifiedName() {
    return modifiedName;
}
```

7. Override the methods of interest. This is where the actual logic will fit it. It is entirely up to the plugin developer to determine which methods to be overridden. It totally depends on the logic of the plugin.

   The three main methods of interest are the following. But you can completely omit these methods and write your own commands and related methods:

   ❑ `doValidation`: This is the method where the input validation happens. Plugin developers can override this method and add our own bits of custom validations.

   ❑ `doExecute`: This is where the action execution happens. When the input form is submitted, the `doExecute` method is called if there are no validation errors. All the business logic is done here and the appropriate 'view' name is returned, based on the execution result.

   In our example, we use this method to modify the input String:

   ```
   this.modifiedName = "Hi,"+userName;
   return "success";
   ```

   ❑ `doDefault`: This method is invoked when the 'default' command is used. In our example, `DemoAction!default.jspa` will invoke the `doDefault` method.

   In our example, we use this method to redirect the user to the input page:

   ```
   return "input";
   ```

8. Create the Velocity template for the input view. The 'input' view, in our example, uses the template: `/templates/input.vm`. Add the HTML code of the input text within a form whose action invokes `DemoAction`:

```
<h2>My Input Form</h2><br><br>
<form method="POST" action="/secure/DemoAction.jspa">
     Name:   <input type="text" name="userName"><br>
             <input type="submit">
</form>
```

9. Create the success view to print the `modifiedName` in `/templates/joy.vm`: The output: `$modifiedName`.

10. Create the error view in `/templates/error.vm`: `Oh No, Error!`

11. Package the plugin and deploy it.

12. Point your browser to `${jira_base_url}/secure/DemoAction!default.jspa`. Enter some name and submit the form to see it in action!

 The example given here is just for the sake of understanding how the webwork action works.

How it works...

It is probably worth utilizing this section to see how the flow works in our example. Let us see it happening as a step-by-step process.

1. When `${jira_base_url}/secure/DemoAction!default.jspa` is invoked, the plugin framework looks for the action `DemoAction` registered in the `atlassian-plugin.xml` file and identifies the command and view associated with it.

2. Here the `default` command is invoked and so the `doDefault` method in the action class is executed.

3. `doDefault` method returns the view name as `input`.

4. The input view is resolved as `input.vm`, which presents the form to the user.

5. On the form, webwork populates the `userName` value in the action class using the setter method.

   In the execution flow, first the `doValidation` method is invoked. If no error is there, which is the case in our example, it invokes the `doExecute` method.

   If there is any error in `doValidation`, the execution stops and the input view is shown. You can print the error messages appropriately on the input view, if there are any. See webwork1 documentation for details.

6. The input String, `userName`, is then modified and assigned to `modifiedName` in the action class (the `doExecute` method) and `success` is returned.

7. The success view is resolved as `joy.vm` where the `modifiedName` is printed. `$modifiedName` will invoke the `getModifiedName()` method to print the modified name.

   If error is returned, the view is resolved as error.vm and the appropriate error message is shown!

Like this, we can write complex actions in JIRA that can be used to customize a lot of aspects of JIRA.

There's more...

It is also possible to add custom commands to the webwork actions, in addition to the `doExecute` and `doDefault` methods. This enables the developer to invoke the action using user-friendly commands, say `ExampleAction!hello.jspa`.

Adding new commands to the action

The following is a short example of how to add custom commands in the webwork action module.

The `atlassian-plugin.xml` file should be modified to include the new command under the action:

```
<action name="com.jtricks.DemoAction" alias="DemoAction">
    <view name="input">/templates/input.vm</view>
    <view name=" success ">/templates/joy.vm</view>
    <view name="error">/templates/tears.vm</view>
    <command name="hello" alias="DemoHello">
        <view name="success">/templates/hello.vm</view>
        <view name="error">/templates/tears.vm</view>
    </command>
</action>
```

In this case, we need to create a method `doHello()` in the action class.

You can invoke the method by calling `DemoAction!hello.jspa`, in which case the method will be executed and the returning "success" message will take the user `to /templates/joy.vm`.

You can have separate views for the command which can be invoked by calling the associated alias name, `DemoHello.jspa`. In this case, returning "success" will take the user to `/templates/hello.vm`.

See also

▶ *Deploying your plugin* in *Chapter 1*

Extending a webwork action in JIRA

There are so many user stories for this one! How do you override some of the JIRA built-in actions? How do you do some additional stuff in the JIRA built-in action? (Like doing some crazy things immediately after creation before the page returns to the user, or doing some innovative validations on some of those actions)

Extending the existing JIRA action is an answer to all these questions. Let us see in detail how to do that.

How to do it...

Extending a JIRA action is done with the help of the webwork plugin module. Most of it is very similar to writing new webwork actions.

Let us take the case of the **create issue** action. What should we do if we need to extend the create action? Say, to do some additional validation and to do some extra things after the actual creation is done?

The following are the steps, in a nutshell:

1. Identify the action to be overridden by looking up the `actions.xml` under WEB-INF/classes in your JIRA installation directory.

   In our case, `CreateIssueDetails` is the action class that does the creation of the issue:

   ```
   <action name="issue.CreateIssueDetails"
   alias="CreateIssueDetails">
       <view name="error">/secure/views/createissue-details.jsp</view>
       <view name="input">/secure/views/createissue-details.jsp</view>
   </action>
   ```

   This snippet defines the action class and the related views thatare using JSP files.

2. Determine whether we need to override the action or just modify the JSP files. In our example, let us do some extra validation.

3. Add the webwork plugin module in the `atlassian-plugin.xml`:

   ```
   <webwork1 key="jtricks-create-issue-details" name="JTricks Create
   Issue Details">
     <actions>
       <action name="com.jtricks.MyCreateIssueDetails"
   alias="CreateIssueDetails">
           <view name="error">/secure/views/createissue-details.jsp</
   view>
           <view name="input">/secure/views/createissue-details.jsp</
   view>
       </action>
     </actions>
   </webwork1>
   ```

4. Note the change in action class name. We can also change the JSP files if that is needed. But most importantly, the `alias` name should be exactly the same as the action alias name in `actions.xml`. In this case, the `alias` name is `CreateIssueDetails`

5. Create the action class `com.jtricks.MyCreateIssueDetails`

6. We can do the full action class implementation in `MyCreateIssueDetails`. But in most cases, you might just need to override some methods of the existing action class, as in our example. If so, just extend the original action class like this:

```
public class MyCreateIssueDetails extends CreateIssueDetails{
```

7. Add the appropriate constructor to carry out dependency injection and to call the super class constructor. Eclipse, or the IDE you use, will usually prompt this. If you need any other manager classes to add your extra logic, inject them as well in the constructor.

8. Override the methods you want. In our example, we need to do extra validation. Let us see how to add a validation to check if the current user is the assignee or not!

```
@Override
protected void doValidation() {
    //Our custom validation here
    String assignee = getSingleValueFromParameters("assignee");
    if (assignee == null || !assignee.equals(getRemoteUser().
getName())){
addErrorMessage("Assignee is not the current user, got U!");
    }
super.doValidation();
}
```

9. Here we check if the current user is the assignee or not, and add an error message if not.

10. Package the plugin and deploy it.

11. Create an issue with and without the assignee as yourself and see how JIRA behaves!

How it works...

The key aspect of extending an existing action is to use the same `alias` name in your webwork plugin module. JIRA registers all the actions in `actions.xml` and overwrites them with the actions in plugins, if the same alias name is found.

In this case, JIRA registers the class `com.jtricks.MyCreateIssueDetails` for the `CreateIssueDetails` action instead of the original `issue.CreateIssueDetails` class.

See also

▶ *Adding new webwork actions to JIRA*

▶ *Deploying your plugin* in Chapter 1

3
Working with Custom Fields

In this chapter, we will cover:

- ▶ Writing a simple custom field
- ▶ Custom field searchers
- ▶ Dealing with custom fields on an issue
- ▶ Programming custom field options
- ▶ Overriding validation of custom fields
- ▶ Customizing change log value
- ▶ Migrating from one custom field type to another
- ▶ Making custom fields sortable
- ▶ Displaying custom fields on subtask columns on parent issue
- ▶ User and date fields from 4.1.x
- ▶ Adding custom fields to notification mails
- ▶ Adding help text for a custom field
- ▶ Removing the 'none' option from a select field
- ▶ Making the custom field project importable
- ▶ Changing the size of a text area custom field

Introduction

For an issue tracking application, the more details you can provide about an issue, the better. JIRA helps by giving us some standard issue fields that are most likely to be used while creating an issue. But what if we need to capture additional information such as the name of the reporter's dad or something else that is worth capturing, perhaps the SLA or the estimated costs? For this, we can make use of custom fields.

With JIRA comes a group of pre-defined custom field types. It includes types like Number Field, User Picker, and so on, which are most likely to be used by JIRA users. But as you become a power user of JIRA, you might come across the need for a customized field type. That is where people start writing custom field plugins to create new field types or custom searchers.

We will use this chapter to learn more about custom fields.

Writing a simple custom field

In this recipe, we will see how to write a new custom field type. Once created, we can create a number of custom fields of this type on our JIRA instance that can then be used to capture information on the issues.

New Custom field types are created with the help of the `customfield-type` module. The following are the key attributes and elements supported.

Attributes:

Name	Description
key	This should be unique within the plugin.
class	Must implement the `com.atlassian.jira.issue.customfields.CustomFieldType` interface.
i18n-name-key	The localization key for the human-readable name of the plugin module.
Name	Human-readable name of the web resource.

Elements:

Name	Description
Description	Description of the custom field type.
resource type="velocity"	Velocity templates for the custom field views.

Getting ready

Before we start, create a skeleton plugin. Next, create an eclipse project using the skeleton plugin, and we are good to go!

How to do it...

In this recipe, let us look at an example custom field type to ease understanding. Let us consider the creation of a `Read Only` custom field that stores the name of the user who edited the issue the last time. It is simple in functionality and enough to explain the basic concepts.

The following are the major steps to do:

1. Modify the `atlassian-plugin.xml` file to include the `customfield-type` module. Make sure the appropriate class name and views are added.

   For our example, the modified `atlassian-plugin.xml` will look as follows:

   ```
   <customfield-type key="readonly-user" name="Read Only User CF"
   class="com.jtricks.ReadOnlyUserCF">
      <description>Read Only User CF Description</description>
      <resource type="velocity" name="view" location="templates/com/
   jtricks/view-readonly-user.vm" />
      <resource type="velocity" name="column-view"
   location="templates/com/jtricks/view-readonly-user.vm" />
      <resource type="velocity" name="xml" location="templates/com/
   jtricks/view-readonly-user.vm" />
      <resource type="velocity" name="edit" location="templates/com/
   jtricks/edit-readonly-user.vm" />
   </customfield-type>
   ```

2. Make sure the key is unique inside the plugin.

3. Implement the class. As mentioned in the introduction, the class must implement the `com.atlassian.jira.issue.customfields.CustomFieldType` interface. Now if you do this, make sure you implement all the methods in the interface.

>
> An easier way is to override some of the existing custom field implementations, if there are any similar to the type you are developing. In such cases, you will need to only override certain methods or maybe just modify the velocity templates!
>
> The details on existing implementations can be found at the Javadocs for the `CustomFieldType` interface. `NumberCFType`, `DateCFType`, `UserCFType`, and so on, are some useful examples.

In our example, the class is `com.jtricks.ReadOnlyUserCF`. Now, our field type is nothing but a text field in essence and so it makes sense to override the already existing `TextCFType`.

Following is how the class will look:

```
public class ReadOnlyUserCF extends TextCFType{
    private final JiraAuthenticationContext authContext;
    public ReadOnlyUserCF(CustomFieldValuePersister
      customFieldValuePersister,
      StringConverter stringConverter,  GenericConfigManager
      genericConfigManager,
      JiraAuthenticationContext authContext) {
        super(customFieldValuePersister, stringConverter,
        genericConfigManager);
        this.authContext = authContext;
    }
    // Overridden methods here
}
```

As you can see, the class extends the `TextCFType` class. We perform a 'constructor injection' to call the super class constructor. All you need to do is add the required component as an argument in the public constructor of the class and Spring will inject an instance of that component at runtime. Here, `JiraAuthenticationContext` is injected as we use it in our class. As you can see, `authContext` is an argument that is injected and is assigned to a class variable with the same name for using it later in the various methods.

4. Implement/Override the methods of interest. As mentioned earlier, implement all the required methods, if you are implementing the interface directly.

    In our case, we extend the `TextCFType`, and so we need to only override the selected methods.

    The only method that we override here is the `getVelocityParameters` method where we populate the velocity params with additional values. In this case, we add the current user's name. We will later use this params in the velocity context to generate the views. The same method is used in creating the different views in different scenarios, that is, create, edit, and so on. The following is the code snippet:

```
@Override
public Map getVelocityParameters(Issue issue, CustomField
    field, FieldLayoutItem fieldLayoutItem){
    Map params = super.getVelocityParameters(issue, field,
    fieldLayoutItem);
    params.put("currentUser", authContext.getUser().getName());
    return params;
}
```

Note: Use the `authContext.getLoggedInUser` method if using JIRA 4.3+.

5. Create the templates defined in the `atlassian-plugin.xml` file. The templates could be written in a way you want the fields to appear in different scenarios.

   If you take a closer look, we have defined four velocity resources but using only two velocity template files, as the `view-readonly-user.vm` is shared across 'view', 'column-view', and 'xml' resources. In this example, we only need to show the `readonly` field in all the three mentioned cases, and so the template will look as follows:

   ```
   #if ($value)  $value  #end
   ```

   This code uses velocity syntax, the details of which can be found at `http://velocity.apache.org/engine/devel/developer-guide.html`. Here we display the existing custom field value of the issue.

6. The edit template should be a `readonly textfield` with `id` as the custom field's ID, as JIRA uses this to store values back into the database when the issue is edited. The template looks as follows:

   ```
   <input type="text" name="$customField.id" value="$currentUser"
   id="$customField.id"  class="textfield" readonly="readonly" />
   ```

   Here we use the field `currentUser`, as we added into the velocity context in step 4. The value of the text field is `$currentUser`. Also note that the ID is `$customfield.id` and the `readonly` attribute is present to make it read only.

7. Package the plugin and deploy it!

Remember, more complex logic and beautifications can go into the class and velocity templates. As they say, the sky is the limit!

How it works...

Once the plugin is installed, it is available under **Administration | Issue Fields | Custom Fields**.

Create a new custom field of the type we just created and map it into the appropriate issue types and projects. Also add the fields to the appropriate screens. Once done, the field will be available on the issue at the appropriate places.

More details on adding a custom field can be found at `http://confluence.atlassian.com/display/JIRA/Adding+a+Custom+Field`.

In our example, whenever an issue is edited, the name of the user who edited it is stored in the custom field.

There's more...

You might have noticed that we added only one parameter in the velocity context, that is, `currentUser`, but we have used `$value` in the view template. Where does this variable `value` come from?

JIRA already populates the custom field velocity contexts with some existing variables in addition to the new ones we add. `value` is just one among them and the full list can be found at `http://confluence.atlassian.com/display/JIRADEV/Custom+field+Velocity+context+unwrapped`.

You may notice that `authContext` is already available in the velocity context and so we could have implemented this example by getting the current user in the velocity template itself instead of injecting the `JiraAuthenticationContext` in the constructor of the class and getting the `currentUser` variable from it in the class. But we have done that just for the purpose of explaining the example.

See also

- ► *Creating a skeleton plugin* in *Chapter 1, Plugin Development Process*
- ► *Deploying your plugin* in *Chapter 1*

Custom field searchers

Writing the custom field type is one thing, but making it available to one of JIRA's most powerful functionalities, that is, Search, is another! When you create the custom field, you can associate the searcher to be used along with it.

In most cases, you wouldn't need a custom searcher. Instead, you can use the built-in custom field searchers in JIRA itself. The list includes, but is not restricted to, Text Field Searcher, Date Searcher, Number Searcher, User Searcher, and so on.

The first step, of course, is to determine what the kind of Searcher your new field needs. For example, a Select field can easily be searched with Text Searcher or an Exact Text Searcher! A User Picker field can be searched with a User Searcher or a Text Searcher. You might even want to extend one of these Searchers to add some extra functionality, like some special conditions or hacks you want to introduce! Yeah, you know what I mean!

Here is how JIRA has defined the Text Searcher for its system custom fields:

```
<customfield-searcher key="textsearcher" name="Free Text Searcher"
        i18n-name-key="admin.customfield.searcher.textsearcher.name"
        class="com.atlassian.jira.issue.customfields.searchers.
TextSearcher">
```

```
        <description key="admin.customfield.searcher.textsearcher.
desc">Search for values using a free text search.</description>

        <resource type="velocity" name="search" location="templates/
plugins/fields/edit-searcher/search-basictext.vm"/>
        <resource type="velocity" name="view" location="templates/
plugins/fields/view-searcher/view-searcher-basictext.vm"/>
        <valid-customfield-type package="com.atlassian.jira.plugin.
system.customfieldtypes" key="textfield"/>
        <valid-customfield-type package="com.atlassian.jira.plugin.
system.customfieldtypes" key="textarea"/>
        <valid-customfield-type package="com.atlassian.jira.plugin.
system.customfieldtypes" key="readonlyfield"/>
</customfield-searcher>
```

As you can see, it makes use of the `customfield-searcher` module. The custom fields that should be searchable using this **Free Text Searcher** should be added under the `valid-customfield-type` tag.

The following are the key attributes and elements supported by the `customfield-searcher` module.

Attributes:

Name	Description
key	This should be unique within the plugin
class	Must implement the `com.atlassian.jira.issue.customfields.CustomFieldSearcher` interface
i18n-name-key	The localization key for the human-readable name of the plugin module
name	Human-readable name of the web resource

Elements:

Name	Description
description	Description of the custom field searcher module
resource type="velocity"	Velocity templates for the custom field searcher views
valid-customfield-type	Defines the custom field types this searcher can apply to. It has two attributes: `package` – the key of the atlassian plugin where the custom field resides and `key` – the module key for the custom field type.

Let us see in detail how to define a searcher for the custom field we wrote in the previous recipe.

Getting ready

Make sure you have created the `Read Only User` custom field (`com.jtricks.ReadOnlyUserCF`) using the previous recipe.

How to do it...

As usual, we will do it as a step-by-step procedure:

1. Add the `customfield-searcher` module into the `atlassian-plugin.xml` file.

   In our example, the field is a read-only text field that holds the username, and so it makes sense to use the existing `TextSearcher` instead of writing a new Searcher class. The module will look as follows:

   ```
   <customfield-searcher key="readonly-user-searcher" name="Read Only
   User Searcher"  class="com.atlassian.jira.issue.customfields.
   searchers.TextSearcher">
     <description key="admin.customfield.searcher.textsearcher.
   desc">Search for Read Only User using a free text search.</
   description>
     <resource type="velocity" name="search" location="templates/
   plugins/fields/edit-searcher/search-basictext.vm"/>
     <resource type="velocity" name="view" location="templates/
   plugins/fields/view-searcher/view-searcher-basictext.vm"/>
     <valid-customfield-type package="com.jtricks" key="readonly-
   user"/>
   </customfield-searcher>
   ```

   Here we use `com.atlassian.jira.issue.customfields.searchers.TextSearcher` that implements the `com.atlassian.jira.issue.customfields.CustomFieldSearcher` interface. If we need to write custom searchers, the appropriate class should appear here.

   We also need to define the velocity templates for `edit` and `view` scenarios.

2. Implement the custom field searcher class. In this case, we can skip this step, as we are going with the already implemented class `TextSearcher`.

   Even if we are implementing a custom searcher, it might be wise to extend an already existing searcher class and override only the methods of interest to avoid implementing everything from scratch. Having said that, it is entirely up to the developer to give a brand new implementation.

   The only mandatory thing to note is that the searcher class must implement the `com.atlassian.jira.issue.customfields.CustomFieldSearcher` interface.

3. Write the velocity templates. For a custom field searcher, there are two views. `Edit` and `view`, both of which will appear on the issue navigator.

   The `edit` template is used when the filters are created / edited. The `view` template is used when the filter is viewed or the search results are viewed by clicking on **View and Hide** ('Search' from JIRA 4.3) on the issue navigator.

   In our example, we have used the in-built JIRA templates, but it is perfectly fine to give a custom implementation of these templates.

4. Make sure the `valid-customfield-type` tags are correctly entered.

   There is a basic, but very common, error you might make here. The `package` attribute here refers to the atlassian-plugin key where the custom field resides and not the Java package where the Searcher class resides! Just to make it clear, the atlassian plugin key is the key in the first line of your `atlassian-plugin.xml`, which is `com.jtricks` in our case:

   ```
   <atlassian-plugin key="com.jtricks" name="J-Tricks Customfields
   Plugin"  plugins-version="2">
   ```

   This package (plugin key) along with the custom field key (`readonly-user` in this case) will point to the right custom field. This would also mean that you can have the same `readonly-user` in another plugin with a different plugin key!

5. Package the plugin and deploy it.

How it works...

Once the custom field type is associated with a searcher using the `customfield-searcher` module, you will see it appear in the searcher drop-down when a custom field of that type is created.

For any existing custom fields, the searcher can be defined or modified using the edit operation. Once the searcher is changed, a re-indexing must be done for the changes to be effective.

We can define more than one custom field using the `valid-customfield-type` element for a single searcher.

Similarly, the same custom field type can be defined under more than one searcher. This will be useful when two different custom fields of the same type can potentially use two different searchers. For example, text fields can use `TextSearcher` or `ExactTextSearcher`.

Once the searcher is defined against the custom field, you can see it appearing in the issue navigator **when the correct context is selected**. The last part is extremely important because the field will be available to search only when the context chosen is correct. For example, if field X is available only on bugs, it won't appear on the issue navigator when the issue types selected has both bugs and new features. Refresh the search menu after the correct context is selected to see your field. This is applicable only for **simple** searching.

There's more...

With the introduction of v2 plugins, courtesy of OSGI bundles, referring to the built-in JIRA searcher classes directly in the `atlassian-plugin.xml` file will fail sometimes because it can't resolve all the dependencies (the notorious **Unsatisfied dependency** errors!). This is because some of the classes are not available for dependency injection in the version 2 plugins, as they were in version 1 plugins.

But there is an easy hack to do it. Just create a dummy custom Searcher class with the constructor that does the dependency injection for you:

```
public class MySearcher extends SomeJiraSearcher {
    public MySearcher(PluginComponent ioc) {
        super(ioc, ComponentManager.getInstanceOfType(anotherType));
    }
}
```

If that doesn't work, add the field to the `system-customfield-types.xml` file under `WEB-INF/classes` along with the JIRA system custom fields, that is, one more `valid-customfield-type` entry into the relevant `customfield-searcher` element. If you do this, remember to apply this workaround when JIRA is upgraded!

Dealing with custom fields on an issue

In this recipe, we will see how to work with custom fields on an issue. It covers reading a custom field value from an issue and then updating the custom field value on the issue, with and without notifications.

Getting ready

Identify the places where the custom fields needs to be manipulated, be it on a listener, workflow element, or somewhere else in our plugins.

How to do it...

We will see how to access the value of a custom field and modify the value as we go along.

The following are the steps to read the custom field value from an `Issue` object.

1. Create an instance of the `CustomFieldManager` class. This is the manager class that does most of the operations on custom fields. There are two ways to retrieve a manager class:

    ❑ Inject the manager class in the constructor of your plugin class implementation.

❑ Retrieve the `CustomFieldManager` directly from the `ComponentManager` class. It can be done as follows:

```
CustomFieldManager customFieldManager = ComponentManager.
getInstance().getCustomFieldManager();
```

2. Retrieve the `customField` object using the `customfield` name or the ID:

```
CustomField customField = customFieldManager.
getCustomFieldObject(new Long(10000));
```

OR

```
CustomField customField = customFieldManager.getCustomFieldObjectB
yName(demoFieldName);
```

3. Once the custom field object is available, its value for an issue can be retrieved as follows:

```
Object value = customField.getValue(Issue)
```

OR

```
Object value = issue.getCustomFieldValue(customField);
```

The latter works fine in all scenarios, whereas the former seems to fail in cases like workflow validators and post functions.

4. Cast the value object to the appropriate class. For example, String for a text field, `List<String>` for a multi select field, `Double` for a number field, and so on.

If you want to update the custom field values back on to the issue, continue with the following steps.

1. Create a modified value object with the old value and the new value:

```
ModifiedValue modifiedValue = new ModifiedValue(value,
newValueObject);
```

2. Obtain the `FieldLayoutItem` associated with the custom field for this issue

```
FieldLayoutManager fieldLayoutManager = ComponentManager.
getInstance().getFieldLayoutManager();
FieldLayoutItem fieldLayoutItem = fieldLayoutManager.
getFieldLayout(issue).getFieldLayoutItem(customField);
```

3. Update the custom field value for the issue using the `fieldLayoutItem`, `modfiedValue` and a default change holder:

```
customField.updateValue(fieldLayoutItem, issue, modifiedValue, new
DefaultIssueChangeHolder());
```

The advantage of doing this, or the disadvantage depending on your perception, is that the custom field value change will not trigger a notification. If you want to trigger notifications, please follows these steps to update the issue instead of previous steps.

1. Modify the custom field value for the issue:

```
issue.setCustomFieldValue(customField, value);
```

2. Create the action parameters Map using `issueObject`, `remoteUser` details, and so on:

```
Map actionParams = EasyMap.build("issue", getIssue(),
"issueObject", getIssueObject(), "remoteUser", ComponentManager.
getInstance().getJiraAuthenticationContext().getUser());
```

3. Execute the `ISSUE_UPDATE` operation:

```
ActionResult aResult = CoreFactory.getActionDispatcher().
execute(ActionNames.ISSUE_UPDATE, actionParams);
```

This will throw an issue update event and all the handlers will be able to pick it up.

An alternate, and probably simpler, way to update the custom fields is to use the type of the field, as shown next:

```
customField.getCustomFieldType().updateValue(customField, issue,
newValue);
```

How it works...

The following are the things taking place at the backend when the custom field value is changed using one of the aforementioned methods.

- ▶ The Value is updated in the database
- ▶ A change record is created and change history is updated with the latest changes
- ▶ Indexes are updated to hold the new values
- ▶ An *Issue Updated* event is fired if `ActionDispatcher` is used to update the field, which in turn fires notifications and listeners

See also

- ▶ *Working with custom fields and SOAP* in Chapter 9, *Remote Access to JIRA*

Programming custom field options

We have seen how to create a custom field type, search for it, and read/update its value from/ on an issue. But one important aspect of multi-valued custom fields and one that we haven't seen yet is custom field options.

On a multi-valued custom field, the administrator can configure the allowed set of values, also called `options`. Once the options are configured, users can only select values within that set of options and there is a validation done to ensure that this is the case.

So, how do we programmatically read those options or add a new option to the custom field so that it can be later set on an issue? Let us have a look at that in this recipe.

Getting ready

Create a multi-valued custom field, say X, in your JIRA instance. Add a few options onto the field X.

How to do it...

To deal with custom field options, Atlassian has written a manager class named `OptionsManager`.

Following are the steps to get the options configured for a custom field:

1. Get an instance of the `OptionsManager` class. Similar to any other manager class, this can be done in two ways.

    ❏ Inject the manager class in the constructor

    ❏ Directly get an instance from the `ComponentManager` class as shown:

    ```
    optionsManager = ComponentManager.getOSGiComponentInstanceOf
    Type(OptionsManager.class);
    ```

2. Retrieve the field configuration schemes for the custom field.

    There could be more than one field configuration scheme for a custom field, each with its own set of projects, issue types, and so on, defined in different contexts. We need to identify the field configuration scheme of interest to us:

    ```
    List<FieldConfigScheme> schemes = fieldConfigSchemeManager.getConf
    igSchemesForField(customField);
    ```

3. Retrieve the field configuration from the scheme:

    ```
    FieldConfig config = fieldConfigScheme.getOneAndOnlyConfig();
    ```

4. Once the field configuration is available, we can use it to retrieve the options on the custom field for that field configuration. The options could be different for different contexts and that is the reason why we retrieve the `config` first and use it to get the options:

```
Options options = this.optionsManager.getOptions(config);
List<Option> existingOptions = options.getRootOptions();
```

`option.getValue()` will give the name of the option while iterating on the preceding list.

`option.getChildOptions()` will retrieve the child options in the case of a cascading select or any other multilevel select

If you need to add new options to the list, it is again `OptionsManager` who comes to the rescue. We do it as follows:

1. Create the new option:

```
Option option = this.optionsManager.createOption(fieldConfig,
null, sequence, value);
```

The first parameter is `fieldConfig` that we saw earlier. The second parameter is the `parent option ID`, used in case of a multi-level custom field like cascading select. It will be `null` for single-level custom fields. The third parameter is `sequence`, which determines the order in which the options will appear. The fourth parameter is the actual `value` to be added as an option.

2. Add the new `option` to the list of options and update!

```
this.optionsManager.updateOptions(modifiedOptions);
```

3. Deleting and updating options are also possible like this, but we shouldn't forget to handle existing issues with those option values.

4. `OptionsManager` exposes a lot of other useful methods to handle custom field options, which can be found in the Javadocs.

See also

▶ *Writing a simple custom field*

Overriding validation of custom fields

We have seen how to write a custom field and set its options programmatically. We also discussed how the value set on a multi-valued custom field is validated against its set of pre-configured options. If the value doesn't belong to it, the validation fails and the issue can't be created or updated.

But what if we have a scenario where we need to suppress this validation? What if we need to add values to an issue which doesn't come from its pre-configured options? Normally, you would add this to the options programmatically, as we've seen before but what if we don't want to do this due to some reason? This is when you can suppress the validation in your custom field.

Getting ready

Create your custom field, as we have seen in the first recipe of this chapter.

How to do it...

All you need to do here is to suppress the validation happening in the original parent custom field if you are extending an existing custom field type like `MultiSelectCFType`. The following is the method you should override:

```
@Override
public void validateFromParams(CustomFieldParams arg0, ErrorCollection
arg1, FieldConfig arg2) {
  // Suppress any validation here
}
```

You can add any additional validation in this method as well!

If you are writing a custom field type from scratch, you will be implementing the `CustomFieldType` interface. You will then need to implement the above method and can do the same thing.

And if you are interested and have access to the JIRA source code, go and have a look at how the validation is done in some existing custom field types!

See also

▶ *Writing a simple custom field*

Customizing the change log value

One scenario we might come across when writing certain custom field types is to manipulate the way we display the change log. For a normal Version Picker custom field, the change log is displayed as follows.

Jobin Kuruvilla made changes - 16/Jan/11 10:14 AM

| Test Version | Test2 [10010] | Test1 [10000] |

Here **Test Version** is the field name. The first value you see, `Test2 [10010]`, is the old value and the second value, `Test1 [10000]`, is the new value.

Getting ready

Write your custom field type, as described in the first recipe of this chapter.

How to do it...

As you have seen in the preceding screen, the change log value for both old value and new value are displayed in the following format:

```
change log string [change log id]
```

Both the string value and ID value are stored in the `ChangeItem` table. But before storing the value in the database, this value is generated from the individual custom fields. That is where we need to intercept to manipulate the way change log is written.

There are two methods, one for `change log string` and another for `change log id`, which need to be modified. Following are the method definitions in the interface:

```
public String getChangelogValue(CustomField field, Object value);
public String getChangelogString(CustomField field, Object value);
```

All you need to do is implement these methods or override them if you are extending an existing custom field type to put your custom implementation.

If you don't want the string to appear in the change history, just return `null` in the `getChangelogString` method. Note that if `null` is returned in the `getChangelogValue` method, the change log isn't created!

Let us consider a simple example where the change history string is truncated when the length of a string is more than 100 characters. In this case, the `getChangelogValue` returns an empty string and `getChangelogString` returns the truncated string. The overridden methods are as shown next:

```
@Override
public String getChangelogValue(CustomField field, Object value) {
  return "";
}

@Override
public String getChangelogString(CustomField field, Object value) {
  String val = (String) value;
  if (val != null && val.length() > 100){
    val = val.substring(0, 100) + "....";
  }
  return val;
}
```

How it works...

Whenever a value is changed for a custom field, it updates the value in the `CustomFieldValue` table. In addition, it also stores the changes on the issue by making a change log entry.

For every set of changes happening on an issue at a single update, a record is created under the `ChangeGroup` table. It stores the name of the user who made the change (author), the time when the change was made (created), and the issue ID (issue).

For every change group, there will be one or more change items stored in the `ChangeItem` table. It is in this table that the old and new values for fields are stored. For both old and new value, there are two columns in the table – one for the string representation and another for the ID. The following is the entity definition for the `ChangeItem` table:

```
<!-- entity to represent a single change to an issue. Always part of a
change group -->
    <entity entity-name="ChangeItem" table-name="changeitem" package-
name="">
        <field name="id" type="numeric"/>
        <field name="group" col-name="groupid" type="numeric"/>

        <!-- whether this is a built in field ('jira') or a custom
field ('custom') - basically used to avoid naming scope problems -->
        <!-- also used for keeping record of the bug_id of a bug from
Bugzilla Import-->
        <!-- and for keeping record of ids in issue move-->
        <field name="fieldtype" type="long-varchar"/>
        <field name="field" type="long-varchar"/>

        <field name="oldvalue" type="extremely-long"/>
        <!-- a string representation of the new value (i.e.
"Documentation" instead of "4" for a component which might be deleted)
-->
        <field name="oldstring" type="extremely-long"/>

        <field name="newvalue" type="extremely-long"/>
        <!-- a string representation of the new value -->
        <field name="newstring" type="extremely-long"/>
        <prim-key field="id"/>
        <!—relations and indexes -->
    </entity>
```

The fields `oldvalue` and `newvalue` are populated using the method `getChangelogValue`. Similarly, the fields `oldstring` and `newstring` are populated using `getChangelogString`.

These fields are the ones used while displaying the change history.

Migrating from one custom field type to another

Have you been using JIRA for more than a year or are you a power user of JIRA? That is, have you performed huge customizations, created numerous plugins, used lot of use cases, and so on? Then it is very likely that you have come across this scenario. You want to move the values from an old custom field to a new field.

JIRA doesn't have a standard way of doing this. But you can achieve this to an extent by modifying the JIRA database. Even with SQL, there are some restrictions for doing this.

The first and foremost thing to check is that both the fields are compatible. You can't move the values from a text field to a number field without extra checks and validations. If there is a value `1234a` stored in one of the issues, it can't be stored as a number field as it is not a valid number. The same applies to all the field types.

Let us see the migration of compatible types and discuss a few other scenarios in this recipe.

How to do it...

Let us assume you have two text fields `Field A` and `Field B`. We need to migrate the values on every issue from `Field A` to `Field B`. Following are the steps that should be executed:

1. Shut down the JIRA instance.
2. Take a backup of the database. We can revert to this backup if anything goes wrong.
3. Connect to your database:
4. Execute the following SQL query:

    ```
    Update customfieldvalue set customfield = (select id from
    customfield where cfname='Field B')  where customfield = (select
    id from customfield where cfname='Field A')
    ```

    The query assumes that the custom field names are unique. If you have more than one custom field with the same name, use the IDs instead.

5. Commit the changes.
6. Disconnect from the database.
7. Start JIRA.
8. Re-index JIRA by going to **Administration | System | Indexing**.

That should do it! Verify your changes both on the issue and in the filters.

All the SQL statements and database references are based on Oracle 10g. Please modify it to suit your database.

How it works...

All that we did here was change the custom field ID in the `customfieldvalue` table. The other steps are standard steps for executing any SQL in JIRA.

Remember, if you have two custom fields with the same `name`, make sure you use the correct `id` instead of finding it using the `name` in SQL.

Now, this will work fine if both the fields are of the same type. But what if you want to move the values from one type to another? This may not always be possible because some of the values in the `customfieldvalue` table may not be compatible with other custom field types.

Let us consider migrating a normal text field to a text area custom field. The value in the text area custom field is stored as a `CLOB` in the `textvalue` column in the database. But the value in a normal text field is stored as VARCHAR 2(255) in the `stringvalue` column. So, when you convert, we need to update the custom field ID, read the VARACHAR2(255) value from the `stringvalue` column and store it in the `textvalue` column as a `CLOB`. And set the no longer used `stringvalue` to `null` in order to free space in the database.

In this example, if you are trying the reverse order, that is, migrating from text area to text field, you should take into consideration the length of the text, and remove the extra text, as the text field can hold only up to 255 characters.

You can find the data type for the various custom fields by looking at the `getDatabaseType` method. For a `TextField`, the method looks as follows:

```
protected PersistenceFieldType getDatabaseType()
{
    return PersistenceFieldType.TYPE_LIMITED_TEXT;
}
```

Other available field types are `TYPE_UNLIMITED_TEXT` (for example, text area), `TYPE_DATE` (Date custom field), and `TYPE_DECIMAL` (for example, number field).

There's more...

Sometimes we just need to change the type of a custom field instead of creating a new one and then migrating the values across. Let us quickly see how to do it.

Changing the type of a custom field

In this case, the table that needs to be updated is the `CustomField` table. All we need to do is to update the `customfieldtypekey`. Just set the new custom field type key which will be `{YOUR_ATLASSIAN_PLUGIN_KEY}:{MODULE_KEY}`.

For a text field, the key is `com.atlassian.jira.plugin.system.customfieldtypes:textfield`.

For incompatible types, we need to consider all aforementioned cases and update the `CustomFieldValue` table accordingly.

See also

▶ *Retrieving custom field details from database*

Making custom fields sortable

We have seen the creation of new custom fields, writing new searchers for them, and so on. Another important feature with the fields, be it custom fields or the standard JIRA fields, is to use them for sorting. But simply writing a new custom field type won't enable sorting on that field.

In this recipe, we will see how to enable sorting on custom fields.

Getting ready

Create the new custom field type that we need to enable searching for.

How to do it...

This is easy to do. There are only two simple steps that you need to do to make sure the custom field is a sortable field:

1. Implement the `SortableCustomField` interface. A new custom field type will look like the following:

   ```
   public class DemoCFType extends AbstractCustomFieldType implements
   SortableCustomField
   ```

   If you are extending an existing custom field type like `TextCFType`, it already implements the interface.

2. Implement the `compare` method. Following is an example:

```
public int compare(Object customFieldObjectValue1, Object
customFieldObjectValue2, FieldConfig fieldConfig)
{
    return new DemoComparator().compare(customFieldObjectValue1,
customFieldObjectValue2);
}
```

`DemoComparator` here is a custom comparator that we can write to implement the sorting logic.

Just invoke `SortableCustomField.compare()` if a custom comparator is not needed.

How it works...

Once the custom field implements the `SortableCustomField` interface, we can click on its header on the issue navigator, and see it getting sorted based on the logic we implemented.

There's more...

`BestNameComparator`, `FullNameComparator`, `LocaleComparator`, `GenericValueComparator`, and so on, are some reusable comparators that ships with JIRA. There is no definite list, but you will find quite a lot of them in the JIRA source, if you have access.

See also

- ▶ *Writing a simple custom field*
- ▶ *Making the custom field project importable*

Displaying custom fields on subtask columns

This is one of the easiest things that you can do! But it adds a lot of value at times. We are talking about adding extra columns for subtasks on the parent issue page.

We know how to add extra fields, don't we? Let us see how to do it and especially how to add custom fields.

How to do it...

In short, you need to modify the `jira.table.cols.subtasks` property in the `jira-application.properties`. Following are the steps to do it. We add a custom field in the example shown here.

1. Stop JIRA.

2. Navigate to the `WEB-INF/classes` folder and modify the `jira.table.cols.subtasks` property in the `jira-application.properties` file:

   ```
   jira.table.cols.subtasks = issuetype, status, assignee,
   customfield_10140, progress
   ```

3. Add the extra fields you want to add along with the existing fields like status, assignee, and so on. For a custom field to be added in the columns, add `customfield_xxxxxx` where xxxxx is the unique numeric ID of the custom field. You can find this unique ID from the database or from the URL when you hover over any of the operations on the custom field (for example, Edit).

4. Start JIRA.

From JIRA 4.4, this property is available under **Administration | General Configuration | Advanced**. There is no need to modify the property file and restart JIRA.

How it works...

JIRA renders the subtask columns on the view issue page by looking at the preceding property. While adding the standard subtask fields are useful, adding custom fields can be extremely helpful sometimes.

In our example, we have added `customfield_10140`, where `10140` is the numeric ID for the custom field. It stores the URL associated with the task, as shown:

Looks useful, doesn't it?

User and date fields from 4.1.x

If you have upgraded from a pre 4.1 to a post 4.1 version, you must have noticed the new **View Issue** page. People have different opinions on the new UI usability, but one thing that gets everyone's vote is how the date and user fields are arranged in the UI. You will see a section of its own for the user and date fields, as shown in the next screenshot:

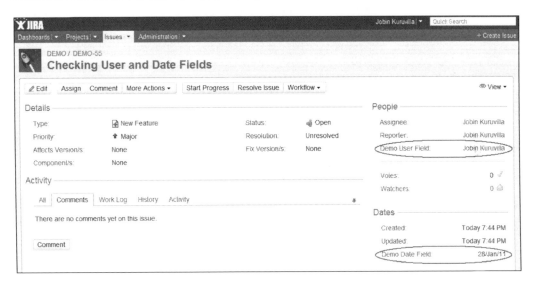

So how do our fields appear in that section?

How to do it...

When you write your new date fields or user fields, all you need to do to make it appear in the correct sections is to implement the right interface!

For a user field, the new custom field type class should implement the following interface:

```
com.atlassian.jira.issue.fields.UserField
```

For a date field, implement:

```
com.atlassian.jira.issue.fields.DateField
```

If you are extending the existing date fields or user fields, they already implement the interface, and hence they will appear automatically in there!

What if you do not want your field in the special date/user sections? Simply ignore these interfaces. The fields will appear just like normal custom fields and will then appear in the order specified under field configurations.

How it works...

This is quite simple. JIRA looks out for classes implementing the `UserField`/`DateField` interfaces and displays them in the respective sections. On the standard custom field section, it doesn't show these fields.

Ever wondered where this check is done in the JIRA source code? The view is rendered in the `ViewIssue` class, but the actual check is done in the `util` class: `com.atlassian.jira.issue.fields.util.FieldPredicates`.

See also

▶ *Writing a simple custom field*

Adding custom fields to notification mails

One of the main features of JIRA is its capability to send notifications – to selected people on selected events! It is often a requirement from JIRA users to customize these notifications, mainly to add more content in the form of custom fields.

If you understand velocity templates, adding custom fields to notification mails is a cakewalk, as we would see in this recipe.

Getting ready

You should know the custom field ID that you need to add into the template. The `id` can be found in the URL that you see when you hover over the 'Edit' operation on the custom field in the administration page.

How to do it...

Let us have a look at adding a custom field, X, into a notification mail when an issue is updated. The following are the steps:

1. Identify the template that needs to be updated. For each event in JIRA, you can find the template associated with it in the `email-template-id-mappings.xml` residing under the `WEB-INF/classes` folder.

   In this case, the event is `Issue Updated`, and the matching template is `issueupdated.vm`.

   Once the template is identified, the files are present under `WEB-INF/classes/templates/email/text/` and `WEB-INF/classes/templates/email/html/`.

2. Modify the template to include the custom field name and value wherever required.

The name of the custom field can be retrieved as follows:

```
$customFieldManager.getCustomFieldObject("customfield_10010").
getName()
```

The actual value can be retrieved as follows:

```
$issue.getCustomFieldValue($customFieldManager.getCustomFieldObjec
t("customfield_10010")))
```

In both the cases, `10010` is the numeric ID of the `customfield` that we discussed before.

How it works...

The e-mail notifications are rendered using velocity templates. JIRA already has a lot of objects in the velocity context including `customFieldManager` and `issue` objects that we have just used. The full list of objects available in the velocity context for e-mail templates can be found in the Atlassian documentation at `http://confluence.atlassian.com/display/JIRADEV/Velocity+Context+for+Email+Templates`.

In this case, we use the `customFieldManager` object to retrieve information about the custom field and then we use the `issue` object to retrieve its value from the issue.

Adding help text for a custom field

As our JIRA instance grows, demanding more and more information from the users through the custom fields, it becomes a norm to let the users know what we expect from them. Apart from a bunch of tutorials that we can prepare for them, it makes sense to give them some help right there on the screen, next to the field.

Let us see the various options on how to do it.

Getting ready

Make sure you have the custom field, for which the help needs to be displayed and configured properly.

How to do it...

There are various ways to provide help. Let us see the most widely accepted ways:

1. Link to a help page.

   This is just common sense. Just link to a documentation about the field, hosted somewhere. We can do this easily by adding few hyperlinks in the description of the custom field. We just need to reuse some of the JIRA styles to make sure the help appears consistent across the system.

   The hyperlinks again can be added in two ways. They are as follows:

   a. Open the help document in a new window

      Here we just link to an external page, which opens in a new window.

      ```
      My Demo Field <a class="localHelp" href="http://www.j-
      tricks.com" title="Get My Help" target="_blank"><img src="/
      jira/images/icons/help_blue.gif"</a>
      ```

      `My Demo Field` here is the custom field name. As you can see, we use the image that ships along with JIRA for the consistency we discussed before. One thing we need to note here is the URL of the image – `/jira/images/icons/help_blue.gif`. In this case, we assume that `/jira` is the context path for this instance. If there is no context path, just use `/images/icons/help_blue.gif` or replace `/jira` using the context path of your instance!

      Also notice the CSS class `localHelp`, which is again used for consistency across help texts. Modify the help URL and title as per your needs.

   b. Open the help document as a popup

      Here we open the help document as a popup instead of opening a new window. The focus is passed to the new window.

      ```
      My Demo Field <a class="localHelp" href="http://www.j-
      tricks.com" onclick="var child = window.open('http://www.
      google.com', 'myHelp', 'width=600, height=500, resizable,
      scrollbars=yes'); child.focus(); return false;"><img src="/
      jira/images/icons/help_blue.gif" title="Get My Help "></a>
      ```

      Again, the image and CSS files remain the same. Here we can specify the width, height, and so on, of the pop-up window as shown in the preceding code. Everything else remains the same!

2. Provide inline help.

   This is suitable if the help isn't big enough to be put in documentation, but at the same time you don't want them to appear along with the description of the field! In this case, we go for a little JavaScript trick where we hide the help text under an HTML `DIV` and toggle the visibility as the user clicks on the help image.

Put the following under the field description after modifying the relevant text. Here, `My Demo Field` is the actual field description and `Inline help for my demo field!` is the extra help we added:

```
My Demo Field
<a class="localHelp" href="#"  onclick=" AJS.$('#mdfFieldHelp').
toggle();"><img src="/jira/images/icons/help_blue.gif"></a>
<div id="mdfFieldHelp" style="display:none">
Inline help for my demo field!
</div>
```

Short and sweet, right?

How it works...

JIRA, thankfully, allows HTML rendering on its description field. We have just used the HTML capabilities to provide some help for the field. It gives us lot of options and the aforementioned ones are just pointers on how to exploit it.

Removing the 'none' option from a select field

If you are a JIRA plugin developer, you must have come across this feature request before. Some people just don't like the 'none' option in the select fields for various reasons. One reason, obviously, is to force the users to select a valid value.

How to do it...

`Select Field` is a system custom field that uses velocity templates to render the view and edit screens. In order to remove the `none` option, we need to modify the edit template.

For any system custom field, you can find the associated classes and their velocity templates from the file `system-customfieldtypes-plugin.xml` residing under the `WEB-INF/classes` folder.

In our case, we can find the following snippet related to `select-field`:

```
<customfield-type key="select" name="Select List"
        i18n-name-key="admin.customfield.type.select.name"
        class="com.atlassian.jira.issue.customfields.impl.
SelectCFType">
        <description key="admin.customfield.type.select.desc">A single
select list with a configurable list of options.</description>
        <resource type="velocity" name="view" location="templates/
plugins/fields/view/view-rawtext.vm"/>
```

```
        <resource type="velocity" name="edit" location="templates/
plugins/fields/edit/edit-select.vm"/>
        <resource type="velocity" name="xml" location="templates/
plugins/fields/xml/xml-basictext.vm"/>
    </customfield-type>
```

As evident from the preceding snippet, the edit template for the select field is `templates/plugins/fields/edit/edit-select.vm`. That is the file we need to modify.

All we need to do now is to navigate to the file and remove the following lines:

```
#if (!$fieldLayoutItem || $fieldLayoutItem.required == false)
    <option value="-1">$i18n.getText("common.words.none")</option>
    #else
    <option value="">$i18n.getText("common.words.none")</option>
    #end
```

The remaining code in the template *must not* be deleted.

Restart JIRA to make the change effective.

> The same approach can be used to remove the none option from other fields like 'radio buttons', 'multi select', 'cascading select', and so on. The actual code to remove will differ, but the approach is the same.

There's more...

There's more to it...

Reloading velocity changes without restart (auto reloading)

You can configure JIRA to reload the changes to velocity templates without a restart. To do this, you need to make two changes to the `velocity.properties` file under `WEB-INF/classes`:

1. Set the `class.resource.loader.cache` property to `false`. It is true, by default.
2. Uncomment the `velocimacro.library.autoreload=true` property. This can be done by removing the # at the beginning of the line.

Restart JIRA and then the changes to the velocity templates will be reloaded without another restart!

See also

▶ *Changing the size of a text area custom field*

Making the custom field project importable

As of JIRA 3.13, individual projects can be imported from an existing JIRA backup file. More information on this can be found at `http://confluence.atlassian.com/display/JIRA/Restoring+a+Project+from+Backup`.

While importing projects, JIRA lets you copy all the issue data across, but only if it is asked to do so! Let us see how we can make the custom fields' project importable, or in simple words, inform JIRA that our fields are okay to be imported!

How to do it...

All we need to do to tag our custom field project as importable is to implement the following interface: `com.atlassian.jira.imports.project.customfield.ProjectImportableCustomField`.

You will have to then implement the following method:

```
ProjectCustomFieldImporter getProjectImporter();
```

There are already existing implementations for the `ProjectCustomFieldImporter` class like the `SelectCustomFieldImporter` class, which we can reuse. It is in this class that we check whether the value getting imported is a valid value or not.

For example, in the case of a `select` field, we need to make sure that the value being imported is a valid option configured in the custom field on the target system. It is entirely up to the users to implement the various rules at this stage.

See the Javadocs at: `http://docs.atlassian.com/jira/latest/com/atlassian/jira/imports/project/customfield/ProjectCustomFieldImporter.html` for more details on doing custom `ProjectCustomFieldImporter` implementations.

See also

▶ *Making custom fields sortable*

Changing the size of a text area custom field

As we have discussed before, JIRA ships with some pre-defined custom field types. One such commonly used type is the Text Area field.

The Text Area field has a pre-defined width and height which is not customizable. It is often a requirement from the JIRA users to increase the size of the field either globally or for a particular custom field.

We will have a look at how to achieve this in the recipe.

How to do it...

Just like any other custom fields, the Text Area field is also rendered using velocity templates. From the `system-customfieldtypes-plugin.xml` file, we can find out that the location of the edit template is `templates/plugins/fields/edit/edit-textarea.vm`.

```
<customfield-type key="textarea" name="Free Text Field (unlimited
text)"
    .........................................
    <resource type="velocity" name="edit" location="templates/plugins/
    fields/edit/edit-textarea.vm"/>
    .............................
</customfield-type>
```

If we need to increase the size, we need to modify the template to increase the `rows` or `cols` property, as per the requirement.

If we need to increase the width (number of columns) to 50 and height (number of rows) to 8, the `cols` and `rows` properties need to be updated to 50 and 8, respectively. The template will then look like the following code:

```
#controlHeader ($action $customField.id $customField.name
$fieldLayoutItem.required $displayParameters.noHeader)

#if ($!customField.isRenderable() && $rendererDescriptor)

  ## setup some additional parameters
  $!rendererParams.put("rows", "8")
  $!rendererParams.put("cols", "50")
  $!rendererParams.put("wrap", "virtual")

  ## let the renderer display the edit component
  $rendererDescriptor.getEditVM($!value, $!issue.key,
$!fieldLayoutItem.rendererType, $!customField.id, $!customField.name,
$rendererParams, false)
```

```
#else
  <textarea name="$customField.id"
            id="$customField.id"
            class="textfield"
            rows="8" cols="50" wrap="virtual"
  >$textutils.htmlEncode($!value)</textarea>
#end

#controlFooter ($action $fieldLayoutItem.fieldDescription
$displayParameters.noHeader)
```

If this needs to be done only for a selected `customfield`, just add a condition at the beginning of the template to handle the custom field separately. The template will then look like the following lines of code:

```
#controlHeader ($action $customField.id $customField.name
$fieldLayoutItem.required $displayParameters.noHeader)

#if ($!customField.id=="customfield_10010")
   ## Modify rows and cols only for this custom field
   $!rendererParams.put("rows", "8")
   $!rendererParams.put("cols", "50")
   $!rendererParams.put("wrap", "virtual")

   ## let the renderer display the edit component
   $rendererDescriptor.getEditVM($!value, $!issue.key,
$!fieldLayoutItem.rendererType, $!customField.id, $!customField.name,
$rendererParams, false)

#elseif ($!customField.isRenderable() && $rendererDescriptor)
 // reminder of the above snippet here
.......................................................

#controlFooter ($action $fieldLayoutItem.fieldDescription
$displayParameters.noHeader)
```

Hopefully, that gives you an idea about increasing the size of the Text Area custom field.

As usual, JIRA should be restarted to make this change effective, unless *velocity autoloading* is enabled, as we discussed in the previous recipe.

See also

 ▶   *Removing the 'none' option from a select field*

4
Programming Workflows

In this chapter, we will cover:

- ▶ Writing a workflow condition
- ▶ Writing a workflow validator
- ▶ Writing a workflow post function
- ▶ Editing an active workflow
- ▶ Making issue editable/non-editable based on workflow status
- ▶ Including/excluding resolutions for specific transitions
- ▶ Permissions based on workflow status
- ▶ Internationalization in workflow transitions
- ▶ Getting available workflow actions programmatically
- ▶ Programmatically progressing on workflows
- ▶ Getting workflow history from database
- ▶ Re-ordering workflow actions in JIRA
- ▶ Creating common transitions in workflows
- ▶ Jelly escalation

Introduction

Workflows are one standout feature which help users to transform JIRA into a user-friendly system. It helps users to define a lifecycle for the issues, depending on the issue type, the purpose for which they are using JIRA, and so on. As the Atlassian documentation says at `http://confluence.atlassian.com/display/JIRA/Configuring+Workflow`:

> *A JIRA workflow is the set of steps and transitions an issue goes through during its lifecycle. Workflows typically represent business processes.*

JIRA uses Opensymphony's OSWorkflow which is highly configurable, and more importantly pluggable, to cater for the various requirements. JIRA uses three different plugin modules to add extra functionalities into its workflow, which we will see in detail through this chapter.

To make things easier, JIRA ships with a default workflow. We can't modify the default workflow, but can copy it into a new workflow and amend it to suit our needs. Before we go into the development aspect of a workflow, it makes sense to understand the various components of a workflow.

The two most important components of a JIRA workflow are **Step** and **Transition**. At any point of time, an **Issue** will be in a step. Each step in the workflow is linked to a workflow Status (`http://confluence.atlassian.com/display/JIRA/Defining+%27Status%27+F ield+Values`) and it is this status that you will see on the issue at every stage. A transition, on the other hand, is a link between two steps. It allows the user to move an issue from one step to another (which essentially moves the issue from one status to another).

Few key points to remember or understand about a workflow:

- ▶ An issue can exist in only one step at any point in time
- ▶ A status can be mapped to only one step in the workflow
- ▶ A transition is always one-way. So if you need to go back to the previous step, you need a different transition
- ▶ A transition can optionally specify a screen to be presented to the user with the right fields on it

OSWorkflow, and hence JIRA, provides us with the option of adding various elements into a workflow transition which can be summarized as follows:

- ▶ **Conditions**: A set of conditions that need to be satisfied before the user can actually see the workflow action (transition) on the issue
- ▶ **Validators**: A set of validators which can be used to validate the user input before moving to the destination step
- ▶ **Post Functions**: A set of actions which will be performed after the issue is successfully moved to the destination step

These three elements give us the flexibility of handling the various use cases when an issue is moved from one status to another. JIRA ships with a few built-in conditions, validators, and post functions. There are plugins out there which also provide a wide variety of useful workflow elements. And if you still don't find the one you are looking for, JIRA lets us write them as plugins. We will see how to do it in the various recipes in this chapter.

Hopefully, that gives you a fair idea about the various workflow elements. A lot more on JIRA workflows can be found in the JIRA documentation at `http://confluence.atlassian.com/display/JIRA/Configuring+Workflow`,

Writing a workflow condition

What are workflow conditions? They determine whether a workflow action is available or not. Considering the importance of a workflow in installations and how there is a need to restrict the actions either to a set of people, roles, and so on, or based on some criteria (for example, the field is not empty!), writing workflow conditions is inevitable.

Workflow conditions are created with the help of the `workflow-condition` module. The following are the key attributes and elements supported. See `http://confluence.atlassian.com/display/JIRADEV/Workflow+Plugin+Modules#WorkflowPluginModules-Conditions` for more details.

Attributes:

Name	Description
key	This should be unique within the plugin.
class	Class to provide contexts for rendered velocity templates. Must implement the `com.atlassian.jira.plugin.workflow.WorkflowPluginConditionFactory` interface.
i18n-name-key	The localization key for the human-readable name of the plugin module.
name	Human-readable name of the workflow condition.

Elements:

Name	Description
description	Description of the workflow condition.
condition-class	Class to determine whether the user can see the workflow transition. Must implement `com.opensymphony.workflow.Condition`. Recommended to extend the `com.atlassian.jira.workflow.condition.AbstractJiraCondition` class.
resource type="velocity"	Velocity templates for the workflow condition views.

Getting ready

As usual, create a skeleton plugin. Create an eclipse project using the skeleton plugin and we are good to go!

How to do it...

In this recipe, let's assume we are going to develop a workflow condition that limits a transition only to the users belonging to a specific project role. The following are the steps to write our condition:

1. Define the inputs needed to configure the workflow condition.

   We need to implement the `WorkflowPluginFactory` interface, which mainly exists to provide velocity parameters to the templates. It will be used to extract the input parameters that are used in defining the condition. To make it clear, the inputs here are not the inputs while performing the workflow action, but the inputs in defining the condition.

   The condition factory class, `RoleConditionFactory` in this case, extends the `AbstractWorkflowPluginFactory`, which implements the `WorkflowPluginFactory` interface. There are three abstract methods that we should implement, that is, `getVelocityParamsForInput`, `getVelocityParamsForEdit`, and `getVelocityParamsForView`. All of them, as the name suggests, are used for populating the velocity parameters for the different scenarios.

   In our example, we need to limit the workflow action to a certain project role, and so we need to select the project role while defining the condition. The three methods will be implemented as follows:

```
private static final String ROLE_NAME = "role";
private static final String ROLES = "roles";
............ .
@Override
protected void getVelocityParamsForEdit(Map<String, Object>
velocityParams, AbstractDescriptor descriptor) {
    velocityParams.put(ROLE, getRole(descriptor));
    velocityParams.put(ROLES, getProjectRoles());
}

  @Override
  protected void getVelocityParamsForInput(Map<String, Object>
velocityParams) {
    velocityParams.put(ROLES, getProjectRoles());
  }
```

```
@Override
protected void getVelocityParamsForView(Map<String, Object>
velocityParams, AbstractDescriptor descriptor) {
   velocityParams.put(ROLE, getRole(descriptor));
}
```

Let's look at the methods in detail:

- ❑ getVelocityParamsForInput: This method defines the velocity parameters for input scenario, that is, when the user initially configures the workflow. In our example, we need to display all the project roles so that the user can select one to define the condition. The method getProjectRoles merely returns all the project roles and the collection of roles is then put into the velocity parameters with the key ROLES.

- ❑ getVelocityParamsForView: This method defines the velocity parameters for the view scenario, that is, how the user sees the condition after it is configured. In our example, we have defined a role and so we should display it to the user after retrieving it back from the workflow descriptor. If you have noticed, the descriptor, which is an instance of AbstractDescriptor, is available as an argument in the method. All we need is to extract the role from the descriptor, which can be done as follows:

```
private ProjectRole getRole(AbstractDescriptor descriptor){
    if (!(descriptor instanceof ConditionDescriptor)) {
        throw new IllegalArgumentException("Descriptor must be
a ConditionDescriptor.");
    }

    ConditionDescriptor functionDescriptor =
(ConditionDescriptor) descriptor;

    String role = (String) functionDescriptor.getArgs().
get(ROLE);
    if (role!=null && role.trim().length()>0)
      return getProjectRole(role);
    else
      return null;
}
```

  Just check if the descriptor is a condition descriptor or not, and then extract the role as shown in the preceding snippet.

- ❑ getVelocityParamsForEdit: This method defines the velocity parameters for the edit scenario, that is, when the user modifies the existing condition. Here we need both the options and the selected value. Hence, we put both the project roles collection and the selected role on to the velocity parameters.

2. The second step is to define the velocity templates for each of the three aforementioned scenarios: **input**, **view**, and **edit**. We can use the same template here for input and edit with a simple check to keep the old role selected for the edit scenario. Let us look at the templates:

❑ edit-roleCondition.vm: Displays all project roles and highlights the already-selected one in the edit mode. In the input mode, the same template is reused, but the selected role will be null and hence a null check is done:

```
<tr bgcolor="#ffffff">
    <td align="right" valign="top" bgcolor="#fffff0">
        <span class="label">Project Role:</span>
    </td>
    <td bgcolor="#ffffff" nowrap>
        <select name="role" id="role">
        #foreach ($field in $roles)
          <option value="${field.id}"
            #if ($role && (${field.id}==${role.id}))
                SELECTED
            #end
            >$field.name</option>
        #end
        </select>
        <br><font size="1">Select the role in which the user
should be present!</font>
        </td>
</tr>
```

❑ view-roleCondition.vm: Displays the selected role:

```
#if ($role)
   User should have ${role.name} Role!
#else
   Role Not Defined
#end
```

3. The third step is to write the actual condition. The condition class should extend the AbstractJiraCondition class. Here we need to implement the passesCondition method. In our case, we retrieve the project from the issue, check if the user has the appropriate project role, and return true if the user does:

```
public boolean passesCondition(Map transientVars, Map args,
PropertySet ps) throws WorkflowException {
    Issue issue = getIssue(transientVars);
    User user = getCaller(transientVars, args);
```

```
project project = issue.getProjectObject();
String role = (String)args.get(ROLE);
Long roleId = new Long(role);

return projectRoleManager.isUserInProjectRole(user,
projectRoleManager.getProjectRole(roleId), project);
}
```

The issue on which the condition is checked can be retrieved using the `getIssue` method implemented in the `AbstractJiraCondition` class. Similarly, the user can be retrieved using the `getCaller` method. In the preceding method, `projectRoleManager` is injected in the constructor, as we have seen before.

4. We can see that the `ROLE` key is used to retrieve the project role ID from the `args` parameter in the `passesCondition` method. In order for the `ROLE` key to be available in the `args` map, we need to override the `getDescriptorParams` method in the condition factory class, `RoleConditionFactory` in this case. The `getDescriptorParams` method returns a map of sanitized parameters, which will be passed into workflow plugin instances from the values in an array form submitted by velocity, given a set of `name:value` parameters from the plugin configuration page (that is, the 'input-parameters' velocity template). In our case, the method is overridden as follows:

```
public Map<String, String> getDescriptorParams(Map<String, Object>
conditionParams) {
    if (conditionParams != null && conditionParams.
containsKey(ROLE))
        {
            return EasyMap.build(ROLE, extractSingleParam(conditio
nParams, ROLE));
        }
        // Create a 'hard coded' parameter
        return EasyMap.build();
    }
```

The method here builds a map of the `key:value` pair, where key is ROLE and the value is the role value entered in the input configuration page. The `extractSingleParam` method is implemented in the `AbstractWorkflowPluginFactory` class. The `extractMultipleParams` method can be used if there is more than one parameter to be extracted!

5. All that is left now is to populate the `atlassian-plugin.xml` file with the aforementioned components. We use the `workflow-condition` module and it looks like the following block of code:

```
<workflow-condition key="role-condition" name="Role Based
Condition"  class="com.jtricks.RoleConditionFactory">
    <description>Role Based Workflow Condition</description>
```

```
<condition-class>com.jtricks.RoleCondition</condition-class>
    <resource type="velocity" name="view"  location="templates/
com/jtricks/view-roleCondition.vm"/>
    <resource type="velocity" name="input-parameters"
location="templates/com/jtricks/edit-roleCondition.vm"/>
    <resource type="velocity" name="edit-parameters"
location="templates/com/jtricks/edit-roleCondition.vm"/>
</workflow-condition>
```

6. Package the plugin and deploy it!

How it works...

After the plugin is deployed, we need to modify the workflow to include the condition. The following screenshot is how the condition looks when it is added initially. This, as you now know, is rendered using the input template:

After the condition is added (that is, after selecting the **Developers** role), the view is rendered using the view template and looks as shown in the following screenshot:

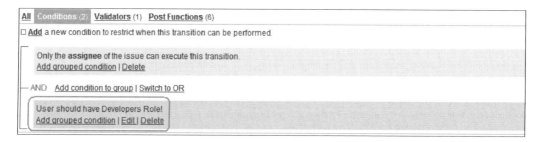

If you try to edit it, the screen will be rendered using the edit template, as shown in the following screenshot:

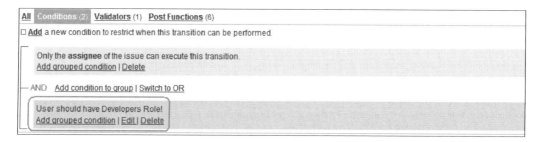

Note that the **Developers** role is already selected.

After the workflow is configured, when the user goes to an issue, he/she will be presented with the transition only if he/she is a member of the project role where the issue belongs. It is while viewing the issue that the `passesCondition` method in the `condition` class is executed.

See also

▶ *Creating a skeleton plugin* in *Chapter 1, Plugin Development Process*

▶ *Deploying your plugin* in *Chapter 1*

Writing a workflow validator

Workflow validators are specific validators that check whether some pre-defined constraints are satisfied or not while progressing on a workflow. The constraints are configured in the workflow and the user will get an error if some of them are not satisfied. A typical example would be to check if a particular field is present or not before the issue is moved to a different status.

Workflow validators are created with the help of the `workflow- validator` module. The following are the key attributes and elements supported.

Attributes:

Name	Description
key	This should be unique within the plugin.
class	Class to provide contexts for rendered velocity templates. Must implement the `com.atlassian.jira.plugin.workflow.WorkflowPluginValidatorFactory` interface.
i18n-name-key	The localization key for the human-readable name of the plugin module.
name	Human-readable name of the workflow validator.

Elements:

Name	Description
description	Description of the workflow validator.
validator-class	Class which does the validation. Must implement `com.opensymphony.workflow.Validator`.
resource type="velocity"	Velocity templates for the workflow validator views.

See `http://confluence.atlassian.com/display/` `JIRADEV/Workflow+Plugin+Modules#WorkflowPluginM` `odules-Validators` for more details.

Getting ready

As usual, create a skeleton plugin. Create an eclipse project using the skeleton plugin and we are good to go!

How to do it...

Let us consider writing a validator that checks whether a particular field has a value entered on the issue or not! We can do this using the following steps:

1. Define the inputs needed to configure the workflow validator:

   We need to implement the `WorkflowPluginValidatorFactory` interface, which mainly exists to provide velocity parameters to the templates. It will be used to extract the input parameters that are used in defining the validator. To make it clear, the inputs here are not the input while performing the workflow action, but the inputs in defining the validator.

   The validator factory class, `FieldValidatorFactory` in this case, extends the `AbstractWorkflowPluginFactory` interface and implements the `WorkflowPluginValidatorFactory` interface. Just like conditions, there are three abstract methods that we should implement. They are `getVelocityParamsForInput`, `getVelocityParamsForEdit`, and `getVelocityParamsForView`. All of them, as the names suggest, are used for populating the velocity parameters in different scenarios.

   In our example, we have a single input field, which is the name of a custom field. The three methods will be implemented as follows:

   ```
   @Override
   protected void getVelocityParamsForEdit(Map velocityParams,
   AbstractDescriptor descriptor) {
     velocityParams.put(FIELD_NAME, getFieldName(descriptor));
     velocityParams.put(FIELDS, getCFFields());
   }

   @Override
   protected void getVelocityParamsForInput(Map velocityParams) {
       velocityParams.put(FIELDS, getCFFields());
   }
   ```

```
@Override
protected void getVelocityParamsForView(Map velocityParams,
AbstractDescriptor descriptor) {
    velocityParams.put(FIELD_NAME, getFieldName(descriptor));
}
```

You may have noticed that the methods look quite similar to the ones in a workflow condition, except for the business logic! Let us look at the methods in detail:

- ❏ `getVelocityParamsForInput`: This method defines the velocity parameters for input scenario, that is, when the user initially configures the workflow. In our example, we need to display all the custom fields, so that the user can select one to use in the validator. The method `getCFFields` returns all the custom fields and the collection of fields is then put into the velocity parameters with the key fields.

- ❏ `getVelocityParamsForView`: This method defines the velocity parameters for the view scenario, that is, how the user sees the validator after it is configured. In our example, we have defined a field and so we should display it to the user after retrieving it back from the workflow descriptor. You may have noticed that the descriptor, which is an instance of `AbstractDescriptor`, is available as an argument in the method. All we need is to extract the field name from the descriptor, which can be done as follows:

```
private String getFieldName(AbstractDescriptor descriptor){
    if (!(descriptor instanceof ValidatorDescriptor)) {
      throw new IllegalArgumentException('Descriptor must be a
ValidatorDescriptor.');
    }

  ValidatorDescriptor validatorDescriptor =
(ValidatorDescriptor) descriptor;

  String field = (String) validatorDescriptor.getArgs().
get(FIELD_NAME);
    if (field != null && field.trim().length() > 0)
      return field;
    else
      return NOT_DEFINED;
}
```

Just check if the descriptor is a validator descriptor or not and then extract the field as shown in the preceding snippet.

❑ `getVelocityParamsForEdit`: This method defines the velocity parameters for the edit scenario, that is, when the user modifies the existing validator. Here we need both the options and the selected value. Hence we put both the custom fields' collection and the field name onto the velocity parameters.

2. The second step is to define the velocity templates for each of the three aforementioned scenarios, namely, input, view, and edit. We can use the same template here for input and edit with a simple checking to keep the old field selected for the edit scenario. Let us look at the template:

❑ `edit-fieldValidator.vm`: Displays all custom fields and highlights the already selected one in edit mode. In input mode, the field variable will be null, and so nothing is pre-selected:

```
<tr bgcolor="#ffffff">
  <td align="right" valign="top" bgcolor="#fffff0">
    <span class="label">Custom Fields :</span>
  </td>
  <td bgcolor="#ffffff" nowrap>
    <select name="field" id="field">
    #foreach ($cf in $fields)
      <option value="$cf.name"
        #if ($cf.name.equals($field)) SELECTED #end
      >$cf.name</option>
    #end
    </select>
    <br><font size="1">Select the Custom Field to be
validated for NULL</font>
  </td>
</tr>
```

❑ `view-fieldValidator.vm`: Displays the selected field:

```
#if ($field)
  Field '$field' is Required!
#end
```

3. The third step is to write the actual validator. The validator class should implement the `Validator` interface. All we need here is to implement the `validate` method. In our example, we retrieve the custom field value from the issue and throw an `InvalidInputException` if the value is null (empty):

```
public void validate(Map transientVars, Map args, PropertySet ps)
throws InvalidInputException, WorkflowException {
    Issue issue = (Issue) transientVars.get("issue");
```

```
String field = (String) args.get(FIELD_NAME);

CustomField customField = customFieldManager.getCustomFieldObj
ectByName(field);

if (customField!=null){
  //Check if the custom field value is NULL
  if (issue.getCustomFieldValue(customField) == null){
    throw new InvalidInputException("The field:"+field+" is
        required!"); }
}
}
```

The issue on which the validation is done can be retrieved from the `transientVars` map. `customFieldManager` is injected in the constructor as usual.

4. All that is left now is to populate the `atlassian-plugin.xml` file with these components. We use the `workflow-validator` module, and it looks like the following block of code:

```
<workflow-validator key="field-validator" name="Field Validator"
class="com.jtricks.FieldValidatorFactory">
    <description>Field Not Empty Workflow Validator</description>

    <validator-class>com.jtricks.FieldValidator</validator-class>

    <resource type="velocity" name="view" location="templates/com/
jtricks/view-fieldValidator.vm"/>
    <resource type="velocity" name="input-parameters"
location="templates/com/jtricks/edit-fieldValidator.vm"/>
    <resource type="velocity" name="edit-parameters"
location="templates/com/jtricks/edit-fieldValidator.vm"/>
</workflow-validator>
```

5. Package the plugin and deploy it!

Note that we have stored the role name instead of the ID in the workflow, unlike what we did in the workflow condition. However, it is safe to use the ID because administrators can rename the roles, which would then need changes in the workflows.

How it works...

After the plugin is deployed, we need to modify the workflow to include the validator. The following screenshot is how the validator looks when it is added initially. This, as you now know, is rendered using the input template:

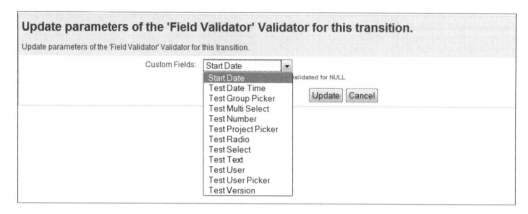

After the validator is added (after selecting the **Test Number** field), it is rendered using the view template and looks as follows:

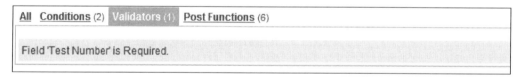

If you try to edit it, the screen will be rendered using the edit template, as shown in the following screenshot:

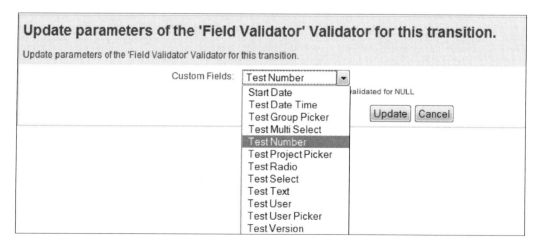

Note that the **Test Number** field is already selected.

After the workflow is configured, when the user goes to an issue and tries to progress it, the validator will check if the **Test Number** field has a value or not. It is at this point that the `validate` method in the `FieldValidator` class is executed.

If the value is missing, you will see an error, as shown in the following screenshot:

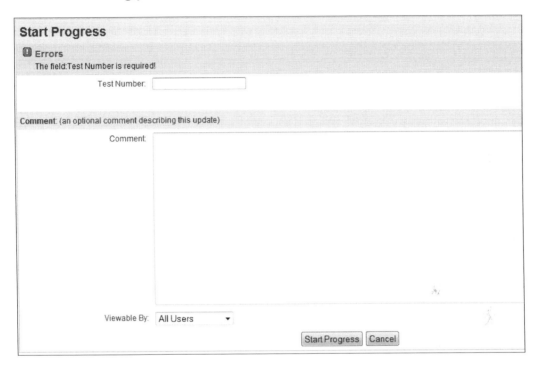

See also

▶ *Creating a skeleton plugin* in *Chapter 1*

▶ *Deploying your plugin* in *Chapter 1*

Writing a workflow post function

Let us now look at workflow post functions. Workflow post functions are very effective and heavily used. They allow you to do a lot of things when you progress on the workflow on an issue. A lot of customizations and workarounds take this route!

Workflow post functions are created with the help of the `workflow-function` module. The following are the key attributes and elements supported.

Attributes:

Name	Description
key	This should be unique within the plugin.
Class	Class to provide contexts for rendered velocity templates. Must implement the `com.atlassian.jira.plugin.workflow.WorkflowNoInputPluginFactory` interface if the function doesn't need input, or `com.atlassian.jira.plugin.workflow.WorkflowPluginFunctionFactory` if it needs input.
i18n-name-key	The localization key for the human-readable name of the plugin module.
name	Human-readable name of the workflow function.

Elements:

Name	Description
description	Description of the workflow function.
function-class	Class which does the validation. Must implement `com.opensymphony.workflow.FunctionProvider`. Recommended to extend `com.atlassian.jira.workflow.function.issue.AbstractJiraFunctionProvider`, as it already implements many useful methods.
resource type="velocity"	Velocity templates for the workflow function views.

There are three other elements that can be used with a post function. They are explained as follows:

- ► orderable – (true/false) Specifies if this function can be re-ordered within the list of functions associated with a transition. The position within the list determines when the function actually executes.

- ► unique – (true/false) Specifies if this function is unique, that is, if it is possible to add multiple instances of this post function on a single transition.

- ► deletable – (true/false) Specifies if this function can be removed from a transition.

See `http://confluence.atlassian.com/display/JIRADEV/Workflow+Plugin+Modules#WorkflowPluginModules-Functions` for more details.

Getting ready

As usual, create a skeleton plugin. Create an eclipse project using the skeleton plugin and we are good to go!

How to do it...

Assume we have a user custom field and we want to set the current user or a specified user name on to the custom field when a particular transition happens. A typical use case for this will be to store the name of the user who last resolved an issue. The following are the steps to write a generic post function that sets the current username or a username provided by the user on a user custom field:

1. Define the inputs needed to configure the workflow post function:

   As opposed to workflow conditions and validators, there are two interfaces available for a workflow post function factory class. If there are no inputs needed to configure the function, the factory class must implement `WorkflowNoInputPluginFactory`. An example will be to set the current user's name as the custom field value instead of the user configured name. If inputs are needed to configure the post function, the factory class must implement `WorkflowPluginFunctionFactory`. In our example, we take the username as the input.

   Both the interfaces mainly exist to provide velocity parameters to the templates. They will be used to extract the input parameters that are used in defining the functions. To make it clear, the inputs here are not the input while performing the workflow action, but the inputs in defining the post function.

   The function factory class, `SetUserCFFunctionFactory` in this case, extends the `AbstractWorkflowPluginFactory` and implements the `WorkflowPluginFunctionFactory` interface. Just like conditions, there are three abstract methods that we should implement, namely, `getVelocityParamsForInput`, `getVelocityParamsForEdit`, and `getVelocityParamsForView`. All of them, as the names suggest, are used for populating the velocity parameters for the different scenarios:

```
@Override
protected void getVelocityParamsForEdit(Map velocityParams,
AbstractDescriptor descriptor) {
    velocityParams.put(USER_NAME, getUserName(descriptor));
}

@Override
protected void getVelocityParamsForInput(Map velocityParams) {
    velocityParams.put(USER_NAME, CURRENT_USER); }
```

```
@Override
protected void getVelocityParamsForView(Map velocityParams,
AbstractDescriptor descriptor) {
    velocityParams.put(USER_NAME, getUserName(descriptor));
}
```

You may have noticed that the methods look very similar to the ones in workflow conditions or validators, except for the business logic! Let us look at the methods in detail:

❑ `getVelocityParamsForInput` : This method defines the velocity parameters for input scenario, that is, when the user initially configures the workflow. In our example, we need to use a text field that captures the username to be added on the issue.

❑ `getVelocityParamsForView`: This method defines the velocity parameters for the view scenario, that is, how the user sees the post function after it is configured. In our example, we have defined a field, and so we should display it to the user after retrieving it from the workflow descriptor. You may have noticed that the descriptor, which is an instance of `AbstractDescriptor`, is available as an argument in the method. All we need is to extract the username from the descriptor, which can be done as follows:

```
private String getUserName(AbstractDescriptor descriptor){
    if (!(descriptor instanceof FunctionDescriptor)) {
        throw new IllegalArgumentException("Descriptor must be
a FunctionDescriptor.");
    }

    FunctionDescriptor functionDescriptor =
(FunctionDescriptor) descriptor;

    String user = (String) functionDescriptor.getArgs().
get(USER_NAME);
    if (user!=null && user.trim().length()>0)
        return user;
    else
        return CURRENT_USER;
}
```

Just check if the descriptor is a validator descriptor or not, and then extract the field as shown in the preceding snippet.

❑ `getVelocityParamsForEdit`: This method defines the velocity parameters for the edit scenario, that is, when the user modifies the existing validator. Here we need both the options and the selected value. Hence, we put both the custom fields' collection and the field name on to the velocity parameters.

2. The second step is to define the velocity templates for each of the three scenarios: input, view, and edit. We can use the same template here for input and edit with a simple checking to keep the old field selected for the edit scenario. Let us look at the templates:

   ❑ `edit-userCFFunction.vm`: Displays all custom fields and highlights the already selected one in the edit mode:

   ```
   <tr bgcolor="#ffffff">
     <td align="right" valign="top" bgcolor="#fffff0">
       <span class="label">User Name :</span>
     </td>
     <td bgcolor="#ffffff" nowrap>
       <input type="text" name="user" value="$user"/>
     <br><font size="1"> Enter the userName to be set on the Test
     User CustomField </font>
     </td>
   </tr>
   ```

   ❑ `view-userCFFunction.vm` .displays the selected field:

   ```
   #if ($user)
       The 'Test User' CF will be set with value : $user!
   #end
   ```

3. The third step is to write the actual function. The function class must extend the `AbstractJiraFunctionProvider` interface. All we need here is to implement the `execute` method. In our example, we retrieve the username from the issue and set it on the `Test User` custom field:

```
public void execute(Map transientVars, Map args, PropertySet ps)
throws WorkflowException {
    MutableIssue issue = getIssue(transientVars);
    User user = null;

    if (args.get("user") != null) {
        String userName = (String) args.get("user");
        if (userName.equals("Current User")){
            // Set the current user here!
            user = authContext.getUser();
        } else {
            user = userUtil.getUser(userName);
        }
    } else {
        // Set the current user here!
        user = authContext.getUser();
    }
    // Now set the user value to the custom field
    CustomField userField = customFieldManager.getCustomFieldObjec
tByName("Test User");
    if (userField != null) {
```

```
      try {
        setUserValue(issue, user, userField);
      } catch (FieldLayoutStorageException e) {
        System.out.println("Error while setting the user Field");
      }
    }
  }
```

Like a validator, the issue on which the post function is executed can be retrieved using the `transientVars` map. The user can be retrieved from the `args` map.

Here the `setUserValue` method simply sets the username on the passed custom field, as shown in the following block of code:

```
private void setUserValue(MutableIssue issue, User user,
CustomField userField) throws FieldLayoutStorageException {
    issue.setCustomFieldValue(userField, user);
    Map modifiedFields = issue.getModifiedFields();
    FieldLayoutItem fieldLayoutItem = ComponentManager.
getInstance().getFieldLayoutManager().getFieldLayout(issue).
getFieldLayoutItem(userField);
    DefaultIssueChangeHolder issueChangeHolder = new
DefaultIssueChangeHolder();
    final ModifiedValue modifiedValue = (ModifiedValue)
modifiedFields.get(userField.getId());    userField.
updateValue(fieldLayoutItem, issue, modifiedValue,
issueChangeHolder);
}
```

4. All that is left now is to populate the `atlassian-plugin.xml` file with these components. We use the `workflow-condition` module and it looks like the following block of code:

```
<workflow-function key="set-usercf" name="Set User CF Post
Function" class="com.jtricks.SetUserCFFunctionFactory">
    <description>Set Defined User or Current User</description>
    <function-class>com.jtricks.SetUserCFFunction</function-class>
    <orderable>true</orderable>
    <unique>false</unique>
    <deletable>true</deletable>

    <resource type="velocity" name="view" location="templates/com/
jtricks/view-userCFFunction.vm"/>
    <resource type="velocity" name="input-parameters"
location="templates/com/jtricks/edit-userCFFunction.vm"/>
    <resource type="velocity" name="edit-parameters"
location="templates/com/jtricks/edit-userCFFunction.vm"/>

</workflow-function>
```

5. Package the plugin and deploy it!

How it works...

After the plugin is deployed, we need to modify the workflow to include the function. The following is where the function appears along with the built-in ones:

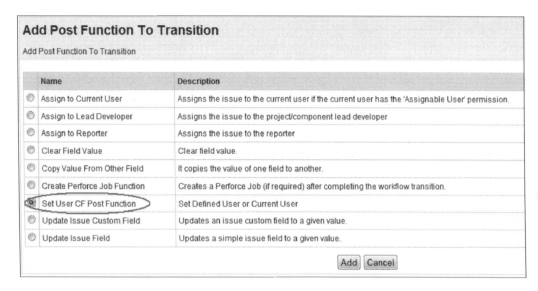

Clicking on our post function takes us to the configuration page, shown next. This, as you now know, is rendered using the input template:

After the function is added (after entering in the **UserName** field), it looks as follows:

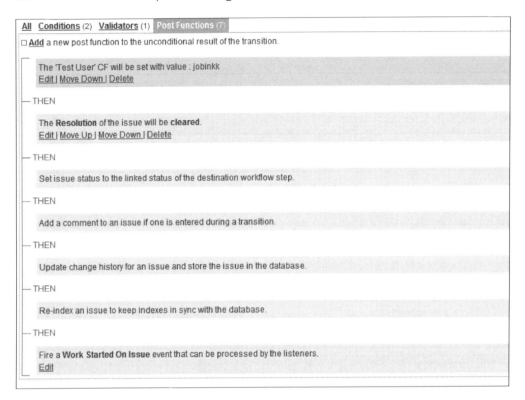

If you try to edit, the screen will be rendered using the edit template, as shown in the following screenshot:

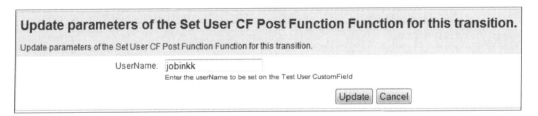

Note that the **UserName** field is already populated.

After the workflow is configured, when the user executes the workflow action, the **Test User** custom field is set with the value **jobinkk**.

See also

▶ Creating a skeleton plugin in Chapter 1

▶ Deploying your plugin in Chapter 1

Editing an active workflow

We have seen how the workflow plays an important role in configuring our JIRA and how we can write plugins to add more workflow conditions, validators, and post functions. Once these plugins are added, we need to modify the workflow to include the newly created components at the appropriate transitions.

Modifying an inactive workflow or creating a new workflow is pretty easy. You can add the conditions/validators/post functions when you create the transition or just click on the transition to modify them. But to edit an active workflow, there are a few more steps involved which we will see in this recipe.

A workflow is active when it is being used in an active workflow scheme that is tied to a project. You can check whether a workflow is active by navigating to **Administration | Global Settings | Workflows**.

How to do it...

The following are the steps to edit an active workflow:

1. Login as a JIRA Administrator.
2. Navigate to **Administration | Global Settings | Workflows**.
3. Click on the **Create a draft workflow** link on the workflow you want to edit. The link can be found under the **Operations** column.
4. Click on the *step* or *transition* that you want to modify.
5. Make the changes. The changes won't be effective until the workflow is published.
6. After all the changes are made, click on the **publish this draft** link at the top of the page if you are still viewing the modified workflow. You can also click on **Publish** under the **Operations** column while viewing all the workflows.
7. Make a copy of the old workflow, when prompted, if you need a backup, and click on **Publish**.

How it works...

After making changes on the draft and clicking on **Publish**, the new workflow will be active. However, there are some limitations to this procedure, which are detailed as follows:

- ▶ You can't delete an existing workflow step
- ▶ You can't edit the status associated with an existing step
- ▶ If an existing step has no outgoing transitions, you can't add any new outgoing transitions
- ▶ You can't change the step IDs for any existing steps

If you want to overcome these limitations, you need to copy the workflow, modify the copy, and make it active by migrating the projects on to the new workflow.

After the new workflow is active, any transitions on the issue will be based on the new workflow.

There's more...

If you want to modify an active workflow, thus overcoming some of the limitations aforementioned but don't want to go through the pain of migrating all the projects involved, you might want to look at modifying it directly in the JIRA database.

Note that we should be careful about the workflow changes when we do this. For example, if there are issues in a status that is removed in the modified workflow, those issues will be stuck at the removed status. The same can happen for the removed steps.

Modifying workflows in JIRA database

The following are the steps to modify the workflows in the database:

1. Export the workflow that needs to be modified into XML. You can do it using the XML link under the **Operations** column of a workflow.
2. Modify the XML to include your changes (or alternatively, make changes in a copy of the JIRA workflow and export that as XML).
3. Stop the JIRA instance.
4. Connect to your JIRA database.
5. Take a backup of the existing database. We can revert to this backup if anything goes wrong.

6. Update the `JIRAWORKFLOWS` table to modify the `descriptor` column with the new XML file for the appropriate workflow. When the workflow XML is huge, it might be useful to rely on database-specific methods to update the table. For example, we can use Oracle XML database utilities (`http://download.oracle.com/docs/cd/B12037_01/appdev.101/b10790/xdb01int.htm`), if JIRA is connected to the Oracle database.

7. Commit the changes and disconnect from the database.

8. Start the JIRA instance.

9. Re-index JIRA.

Making an issue editable/non-editable based on workflow status

We know that the edit permission on an issue is controlled through the **Edit Issue Permission**. This is used within the permissions schemes tied to a project and it blocks/allows editing of the issue, irrespective of which status it is in! But many a times the need arises to block an issue being edited at a specific status. An example would be to prevent editing on a closed issue.

We will have a quick look at how to achieve this using workflow properties.

How to do it...

We can make an issue editable or non-editable using the `jira.issue.editable` workflow property. The following is the step-by-step procedure:

1. Login as a JIRA Administrator.

2. Navigate to **Administration | Global Settings | Workflows**.

3. Create a draft of the workflow, if it is active. Navigate to the *step* which needs to be modified.

4. Click on the **View step's properties** link.

5. Enter **jira.issue.editable** into the **Property Key** field.

6. Enter **false** in the **Property Value** field, if you want to prevent editing on the issue after this transition is performed. Use **true** as the value, if you want to make it as editable.

7. Go back and publish the workflow if it was active. If not, associate the workflow with the appropriate schemes.

Note that the property is added on a workflow *step* and not a *transition*.

How it works...

When an issue is viewed, the edit operation is available only if you have the edit permission and the workflow manager passes the issue as editable. The workflow manager retrieves the list of properties added onto the issue's current status (that is, the step linked to the status) and checks the value of the `jira.issue.editable` property to see if it set to `false` or not before passing the issue as editable.

The properties against an issue workflow step are retrieved as follows:

```
JiraWorkflow workflow = workflowManager.getWorkflow(issue);
StepDescriptor currentStep = workflow.getLinkedStep(ManagerFactory.
getConstantsManager().getStatus(status));
Map properties = currentStep.getMetaAttributes();
```

The `jira.issue.editable` property value is retrieved as `properties.get(JiraWorkflow.JIRA_META_ATTRIBUTE_EDIT_ALLOWED)`, where `JiraWorkflow.JIRA_META_ATTRIBUTE_EDIT_ALLOWED = "jira.issue.editable"`.

The same approach can be used to retrieve any other property added on a workflow step.

See also

▶ *Permissions based on workflow status*

Including/excluding resolutions for specific transitions

If you haven't noticed already, resolutions in JIRA are global. If you have a resolution **Resolved**, it appears whenever the resolution field is added on a transition screen. This might not make sense in some cases. For example, it doesn't make sense to add the resolution **Resolved** when you are rejecting an issue.

Let us see how we can pick and choose resolutions based on workflow transitions.

How to do it...

We can include/exclude specific resolutions on workflow transitions using the `jira.field.resolution.include` and `jira.field.resolution.exclude` properties. The following is the step-by-step procedure:

1. Login as a JIRA Administrator
2. Navigate to **Administration | Global Settings | Workflows**.

3. Create a draft of the workflow, if it is active. Navigate to the transition which needs to be modified.

4. Click on the **View properties of this transition** link.

5. Enter **jira.field.resolution.include** or **jira.field.resolution.exclude** into the **Property Key** field, depending on whether you want to include or exclude a specific resolution.

6. Enter the comma-separated list of resolution IDs that you want to include/exclude, under the **Property Value** field. The resolution ID can be obtained by navigating to **Administration | Issue Settings | Resolutions**, and hovering over the **Edit** link:

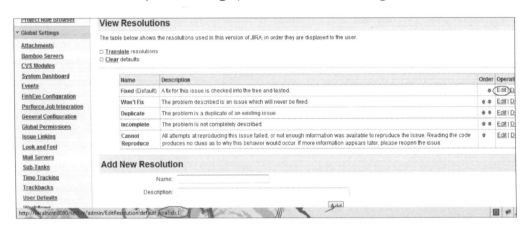

You can also find the resolution ID by querying the `resolutions` table in the database.

7. Click on **Add**.

8. Go back and publish the workflow if it was active. If not, associate the workflow with the appropriate schemes.

Note that the property is added on a workflow *transition* and not a *step*.

How it works...

When the `jira.field.resolution.exclude` property is added, all the resolutions whose IDs are entered as a comma-separated values under the `Property Value` field are excluded from the screen during that transition.

On the other hand, if `jira.field.resolution.include` is added, only the resolutions whose IDs are entered as a comma-separated values under the `Property Value` field are shown in the screen.

Permissions based on workflow status

We have seen how to restrict editing on an issue based on the workflow status. JIRA gives us an even bigger set of options to restrict many of these operations (such as edit, comment, and so on) on the issue or its subtasks, depending on the issue status.

Let us see this in detail.

How to do it...

This is done in a similar way to making an issue editable/non-editable. Here, also, we add a property on the concerned workflow step. The following are the steps:

1. Log in as a JIRA Administrator

2. Navigate to **Administration | Global Settings | Workflows**.

3. Create a draft of the workflow, if it is active. Navigate to the step which needs to be modified.

4. Click on the **View step's properties** link.

5. Enter the permission property into the **Property Key** field. The property is of the form – `jira.permission.[subtasks.]{permission}.{type}[.suffix]` where:

   ❑ `subtasks` – This is optional. If included, the permission is applied on the issue's subtasks. If not, the permission is applied on the actual issue.

   ❑ `permission` – A short name specified in the `Permissions` (http://docs.atlassian.com/software/jira/docs/api/latest/com/atlassian/jira/security/Permissions.html) class.

   The following are the permitted values, as of JIRA 4.2: `admin, use, sysadmin, project, browse, create, edit, scheduleissue, assign, assignable, attach, resolve, close, comment, delete, work, worklogdeleteall, worklogdeleteown, worklogeditall, worklogeditown, link, sharefilters, groupsubscriptions, move, setsecurity, pickusers, viewversioncontrol, modifyreporter, viewvotersandwatchers, managewatcherlist, bulkchange, commenteditall, commenteditown, commentdeleteall, commentdeleteown, attachdeleteall, attachdeleteown.`

   ❑ `type` – Type of permission granted/denied. The values can be `group, user, assignee, reporter, lead, userCF, projectrole.`

   ❑ `suffix` – An optional suffix to make the property unique when you have the same type added more than once! `jira.permission.edit.group.1, jira.permission.edit.group.2,` and so on. This is because of the OSWorkflow restriction that the property value should be unique.

6. Enter the appropriate value in the **Property Value** field. If the type is group, enter a group. If it is a user, enter a username, and so on.

It might be useful to give a few examples here:

- ❏ `jira.permission.comment.group=some-group`
- ❏ `jira.permission.comment=denied`
- ❏ `jira.permission.edit.group.1=some-group-one`
- ❏ `jira.permission.edit.group.2=some-group-two`
- ❏ `jira.permission.modifyreporter.user=username`
- ❏ `jira.permission.delete.projectrole=10000`
- ❏ `jira.permission.subtasks.delete.projectrole=10000`

You can even use the value as 'denied' when the type is not used. For example, `jira.permission.comment=denied` means the comment feature is disabled at this state.

7. Go back and publish the workflow, if it was active. If not, associate the workflow with the appropriate schemes.

How it works...

When a particular permission property is tied to a workflow status, JIRA looks at it and enforces it. It is to be noted that workflow permissions can only restrict permissions set in the permission scheme, not grant permissions.

For example, if you have the edit permission restricted to `jira-administrators` in the permission scheme, adding `jira.permission.edit.group=jira-users` wouldn't grant the permission to `jira-users`.

But instead, if you had both of these groups with the edit permission, only `jira-users` will be allowed to edit, as defined in the workflow permission.

See also

▸ *Making an issue editable/non-editable based on workflow status*

Internationalization in workflow transitions

If your JIRA instance is used by people around the world speaking different languages, it is likely that you use internationalization to convert JIRA into their own language. But things like the workflow action name, button name, and so on are configured in the workflows and not as i18n properties. And therefore, they are limited to a single language.

This is where workflow properties come to our rescue, again!

How to do it...

We can modify the workflow action submit button name or the action name using the properties `jira.i18n.submit` or `jira.i18n.title` respectively. The following are the steps:

1. Open the jar file `atlassian-jira/WEB-INF/lib/language_<language code>_<country code>.jar`. From JIRA 4.3, the jar filename is of the form `jira-lang-<language code>_<country code>-<jira version>.jar`.

2. Edit the file `\com\atlassian\jira\web\action\ JiraWebActionSupport_<language code>_<country code>.properties` inside the jar. You can use a utility such as 7zip to edit the file inside the jar. Alternatively, you can extract the jar, modify the file, and archive it again!

3. Add your i18n property and its value: `my.submit.button=My Submit Button in English`.

4. Update the file and restart JIRA to pick up the new property.

5. Log in as a JIRA Administrator.

6. Navigate to **Administration | Global Settings | Workflows**.

7. Create a draft of the workflow, if it is active. Navigate to the transition which needs to be modified.

8. Click on the **View properties of this transition** link.

9. Enter **jira.i18n.submit** or **jira.i18n.title** into the **Property Key** field, depending on whether you want to modify submit button name or action name. Let us consider the example of the Submit button

10. Enter i18n key that we used in the property file, under the **Property Value** field. In our example, the key is **my.submit.button**.

11. Click on **Add**.

12. Go back and publish the workflow, if it was active. If not, associate the workflow with the appropriate schemes.

How it works...

Once the workflow is published, JIRA will populate the submit button name from the i18n property file the next time the transition happens. In our example, the transition screen will look like the following screenshot:

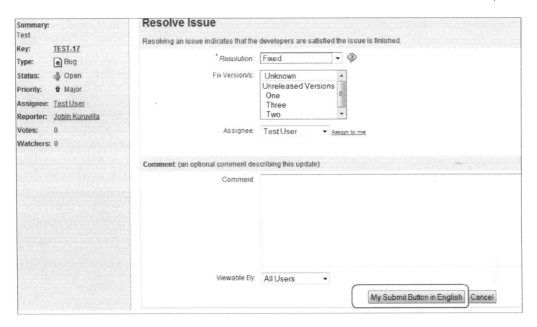

As you can see, the button name is changed to **My Submit Button in English**. All you need to do now is modify the other language jars to include the proper translations!

See also

▶ *Internationalization in v2 plugins*

Obtaining available workflow actions programmatically

Often in our programs, we may come across the need to retrieve the current workflow actions, available on the issue. Let us have a look at how to do this using the JIRA API.

How to do it...

Follow these steps:

1. Retrieve the JIRA workflow object associated with the issue:

   ```
   JiraWorkflow workFlow = componentManager.getWorkflowManager().
   getWorkflow(issue);
   ```

   Here, issue is the current issue, which is an instance of com.atlassian.jira.
   issue.Issue class.

2. Get the issue status and use it to retrieve the current workflow step linked to the issue:

```
GenericValue status = issue.getStatusObject().getGenericValue();
com.opensymphony.workflow.loader.StepDescriptor currentStep =
workFlow.getLinkedStep(status);
```

3. Retrieve the set of available actions from the current step:

```
List<ActionDescriptor> actions = currentStep.getActions();
```

Here, `actions` is a list of `com.opensymphony.workflow.loader.ActionDescriptor`.

4. Iterate on the `ActionDescriptors` and get the details for each action, depending on the requirement! The name of the available action can be printed as follows:

```
for (ActionDescriptor action : actions) {
    System.out.println("Action: "+action.getName())
}
```

How it works...

WorkflowManager is used to perform a lot of operations related to workflows such as creating/updating/deleting a workflow, copying it, creating a draft, and so on. Here we use it to retrieve the workflow object, based on the issue selected. Please check the API (`http://docs.atlassian.com/jira/latest/com/atlassian/jira/workflow/WorkflowManager.html`) for a full list of available operations using `WorkflowManager`.

Once we retrieve the JIRA workflow, we get the current step using the status. As you have seen before in this chapter, a workflow *status* is linked to one and only one workflow *step*. Once we get the *step*, we can get a load of information from it, including the available actions from that *step*.

Jolly good?

There's more...

There's more to it...

Getting the Action IDs, given name

The same method can be used to retrieve the action ID, given an action name. Remember, it is the action ID that we use while programmatically progressing on the workflows.

Once the action name is available, you can easily retrieve the action ID by iterating on the list of actions, as shown in the following lines of code:

```
private int getActionIdForTransition(List<ActionDescriptor> actions,
String actionName) {
   for (ActionDescriptor action : actions) {
      if (action.getName().equals(actionName)) {
              return action.getId();
         }
   }
   return -1; // Handle invalid action
}
```

Programmatically progressing on workflows

Another operation that we perform normally on workflows is to programmatically transit the issues through its workflows. Let us have a look at how to do this using the JIRA API.

How to do it...

Since JIRA 4.1, transitioning issues is done using the `IssueService` (http://docs. atlassian.com/jira/latest/com/atlassian/jira/bc/issue/IssueService. html). Here's is how you do it:

1. Get the `IssueService` object either by injecting it in the constructor or as follows:

   ```
   IssueService issueService = ComponentManager.getInstance().
   getIssueService();
   ```

2. Find out the action ID for the action to be executed. You can either get it by looking at the workflows (the number within brackets alongside the transition name), if you know it is not going to change or retrieve it using the action name (refer to the previous recipe).

3. Populate the `IssueInputParameters` if you want to modify anything on the issue such as assignee, reporter, resolution, and so on! It represents an issue builder and is used to provide parameters that can be used to update the issue during the transition:

   ```
   IssueInputParameters issueInputParameters = new
   IssueInputParametersImpl();
   issueInputParameters.setAssigneeId("someotherguy");
   issueInputParameters.setResolutionId("10000");
   ```

4. A full list of supported fields can be found at `http://docs.atlassian.com/jira/latest/com/atlassian/jira/issue/IssueInputParameters.html`.

5. Validate the transition:

```
TransitionValidationResult transitionValidationResult
= issueService.validateTransition(user, 12345L, 10000L,
issueInputParameters);
```

- ❏ `User` – The current user or the user who will be performing the transition
- ❏ `12345L` – The issue ID
- ❏ `10000L` – The action ID
- ❏ `issueInputParameters` – The parameters we populated in the previous step

6. If `transitionValidationResult` is valid, invoke the transition operation. Handle it if it is not valid. Make sure you use the same user.

```
if (transitionValidationResult.isValid()){
        IssueResult transitionResult = issueService.
transition(user, transitionValidationResult);
        if (!transitionResult.isValid()){
            // Do something
        }
}
```

We need to do a final check on the result as well to see if it is valid!

7. That will transit the issue to the appropriate state.

Prior to `IssueService`, the transition was done using `WorkflowTransitionUtil` (`http://docs.atlassian.com/jira/latest/com/atlassian/jira/workflow/WorkflowTransitionUtil.html`). It is still supported, but `IssueService` is recommended.

The following is how the transitioning is done using `WorkflowTransitionUtil`:

Get the `WorkflowTransitionUtil` object:

```
WorkflowTransitionUtil workflowTransitionUtil =
(WorkflowTransitionUtil) JiraUtils .loadComponent(WorkflowTransiti
onUtilImpl.class);
```

Create a map of parameters that need to be updated on the issue:

```
Map paramMap = EasyMap.build();
paramMap.put(IssueFieldConstants.RESOLUTION, "10000");  paramMap.
put(IssueFieldConstants.COMMENT, comment);
```

Populate the `workflowTransitionUtil` with the details:

```
workflowTransitionUtil.setParams(paramMap);  workflowTransitionUtil.
setIssue(12345L);  workflowTransitionUtil.setUsername(user);
workflowTransitionUtil.setAction(10000L);
```

Validate the transition:

```
ErrorCollection c1 = workflowTransitionUtil.validate();
```

If there is no error, progress with the workflow. Handle the errors, if any:

```
ErrorCollection c2 = workflowTransitionUtil.progress();
```

And we should have the issue in its new status! Check the error collection to handle errors, if any.

How it works...

Once the action ID is correct and the parameters are validated properly, `IssueService` or `WorkflowTransitionUtil` will do the background work of transitioning the issues.

Obtaining workflow history from the database

JIRA captures changes on an issue in its "change history". It is pretty easy to find them by going to the change history tab on the view issue page.

But often, we would like to find out specific details about the various workflow statuses that an issue has gone through in its lifecycle. Going through the change history and identifying the status changes is a painful task when there are tens of hundreds of changes on an issue. People normally write plugins to get around this or go directly to the database.

Even when it is achieved using plugins, the background logic is to look at the tables in the database. In this recipe, we will look at the tables involved and writing the SQL query to extract workflow changes for a given issue.

Getting ready

Make sure you have an SQL client installed and configured that will help you to connect to the JIRA database.

How to do it...

Follow these steps:

1. Connect to the JIRA database.

2. Find out the `id` of the issue for which you want to extract the workflow changes. If you don't have the ID in hand, you can get it from the database using the issue key as follows:

```
select id from jiraissue where pkey = "JIRA-123"
```

Where `JIRA-123` is the issue key.

3. Extract all the change groups created for the issue. Every set of changes made on an issue during a single operation (for example, edit, workflow transition, and so on) are grouped in to a single `changegroup` by JIRA. It is on the `changegroup` record that JIRA stores the associated `issueid` and the `created` date (date when the change was made):

```
select id from changegroup where issueid = '10010'
```

Where `10010` is the `issue id`, the ID we extracted in the previous step.

While extracting the change groups, we can even mention the created date if you want to see only changes on a specific date! Use the author field to restrict this to changes made by a user.

4. Extract `status` changes for the group/groups selected:

```
select oldstring, newstring from changeitem where fieldtype =
"jira" and field = "status" and groupid in ( 10000, 10010 )
```

Here the `groupid` 10000, 10010, and so on are IDs extracted in the previous step. Here, `oldstring` is the original value on the issue and `newstring` is the updated value.

Include `oldvalue` and `newvalue`, if you want to get the status IDs as well.

You can write it in a single query, as shown next, or modify it to include more details. But hopefully, this gives you a starting point!

```
select oldstring, newstring from changeitem where fieldtype = "jira"
and field = "status" and groupid in ( select id from changegroup where
issueid = '10010');
```

Another example to extract the details along with the created date is to use inner join as follows:

```
select ci.oldstring, ci.newstring, cg.created from changeitem ci inner
join changegroup cg on ci.groupid = cg.id where ci.fieldtype = "jira" and
ci.field = "status" and cg.issueid = '10010';
```

Over to you DBAs now!

How it works...

As mentioned, the changes at any single operation on an issue are stored as a `changegroup` record in the JIRA database. The main three columns `issueid`, `author`, and `created` are all parts of this table.

The actual changes are stored in the `changeitem` table with its foreign key `groupid` pointing to the `changegroup` record.

In our case, we are looking specifically at the workflow statuses, and hence we query for records that have the `fieldtype` value of `jira` and `field` of `status`.

The output of the query (that uses an inner join) is as follows:

```
mysql> select ci.oldstring, ci.newstring, cg.created from changeitem ci inner jo
in changegroup cg on ci.groupid = cg.id where ci.fieldtype = "jira" and ci.field
= "status" and cg.issueid = '10000';
+-------------+-------------+---------------------+
| oldstring   | newstring   | created             |
+-------------+-------------+---------------------+
| Open        | In Progress | 2010-03-23 08:44:39 |
| In Progress | Open        | 2010-03-23 08:52:52 |
| Open        | Resolved    | 2010-03-23 08:55:08 |
| Resolved    | Reopened    | 2010-03-25 20:00:37 |
| Reopened    | In Progress | 2010-03-25 20:00:45 |
| In Progress | Open        | 2010-04-30 20:21:27 |
| Open        | In Progress | 2010-04-30 20:21:34 |
+-------------+-------------+---------------------+
7 rows in set (0.00 sec)
```

See also

▶ *Retrieving workflow details from a table*

Re-ordering workflow actions in JIRA

On a JIRA workflow, the available actions that appear in the **View Issue** page are normally ordered in the sequence those transitions were created. This works fine most of the time, but in some cases, we will want to change the order in which it appears on the issue screen!

To achieve this logical ordering of workflow actions on the **View Issue** page, JIRA provides us with a workflow property named `opsbar-sequence`. Let us see how we modify the ordering using this property instead of tampering with the workflow.

How to do it...

Follow these steps:

1. Log in as a JIRA Administrator

2. Navigate to **Administration** | **Global Settings** | **Workflows**.

3. Create a draft of the workflow, if it is active. Navigate to the transition which needs to be modified.

4. Click on the **View properties of this transition** link.

5. Enter **opsbar-sequence** into the **Property Key** field.

6. Enter the **sequence** value under the **Property Value** field. This value should be relative to the values entered in the other transitions.

7. Click on **Add**.

8. Go back and publish the workflow, if it was active. If not, associate the workflow with the appropriate schemes.

Note that the property is added on a workflow *transition* and not a *step*.

How it works...

Let us consider the following example where the **Reject this** workflow action appears first:

Normally, people would want to see this as the last option because it is most likely the least used operation.

As there are four operations here, we can order them as shown in the following table with the sequence values against them:

Workflow action	Sequence
Start Progress	10
Resolve Issue	20
Close Issue	30
Reject this	40

Note that the sequence numbers can even be 1, 2, 3, and 4. There are no restrictions on how and where the numbers should start. It is advised to keep 10, 20, and so on so that we can insert new transitions in between, if required in future.

After we modify the workflow using the property and the aforementioned sequence numbers, as we saw in the previous section, the actions are ordered as follows:

Remember, the order of the workflow actions is changed only in the **View Issue** page and not in the **View Workflow Steps** page, where you modify the workflow steps.

Creating common transitions in workflows

Configuring workflows can be a painful thing. Especially when there are similar transitions used in 10 different places and those get changed every now and then. The change might be the simplest thing possible, such as editing just the name of the transition, but we end up modifying it in 10 places.

This is where OSWorkflow's common actions come to our rescue. A little bit on the theory can be read at http://www.opensymphony.com/osworkflow/3.3%20Common%20and%20 Global%20Actions.html.

JIRA already makes use of common actions in its default workflow. We can't modify the default workflow, but if we make a copy of it and rename the **Resolve** transition to **New Resolve**, it appears as shown in the following screenshot:

Step Name (id)	Linked Status	Transitions (id)	Operations
Open (1)	Open	*Start Progress* (4) >> In Progress *New Resolve* (5) >> Resolved *Close Issue* (2) >> Closed	Add Transition | Delete Transitions | Edit | View Properties
In Progress (3)	In Progress	*Stop Progress* (301) >> Open *New Resolve* (5) >> Resolved *Close Issue* (2) >> Closed	Add Transition | Delete Transitions | Edit | View Properties
Resolved (4)	Resolved	*Close Issue* (701) >> Closed *Reopen Issue* (3) >> Reopened	Add Transition | Delete Transitions | Edit | View Properties
Reopened (5)	Reopened	*New Resolve* (5) >> Resolved *Close Issue* (2) >> Closed *Start Progress* (4) >> In Progress	Add Transition | Delete Transitions | Edit | View Properties
Closed (6)	Closed	*Reopen Issue* (3) >> Reopened	Add Transition | Delete Transitions | Edit | View Properties

Note that the transition is renamed at all the three places where it appears!

In this recipe, let us look at adding a new common transition.

How to do it...

There are two ways of adding common transitions.

1. Copy the JIRA default workflow and modify it to suit our needs.
2. Create workflow using XML.

The first one is useful only if our workflow needs are limited, that is, only if we can live by modifying the existing transitions.

If we need to configure a bigger workflow with new common transitions, we need to take the XML route. Let us see the steps:

1. To make things easier, export the existing workflow that needs to be modified into an XML. You can do this using the XML link on the view workflows page. You could create a workflow XML from scratch, but that needs lot of effort and knowledge of OSWorkflow. In this case, we export the standard JIRA workflow.

2. Identify the `common-actions` section in the workflow XML. It comes in the starting immediately after `initial-actions`.

3. Add our new `common-action`. There are a few things that we need to notice here. The action ID should be a unique ID within the XML. You will find examples of all this in the standard workflow XML or you can read more about them in the OSWorkflow documentation.

   The following is how a simple action looks:

```xml
<action id="6" name="Start Again">
  <meta name="jira.description">Testing Common Actions</meta>
  <results>
    <unconditional-result old-status="Finished" status="Open"
step="1">
        <post-functions>
          <function type="class">
            <arg name="class.name">com.atlassian.jira.workflow.
function.issue.UpdateIssueStatusFunction</arg>
          </function>
          <function type="class">
            <arg name="class.name">com.atlassian.jira.workflow.
function.misc.CreateCommentFunction</arg>
          </function>
          <function type="class">
            <arg name="class.name">com.atlassian.jira.workflow.
function.issue.GenerateChangeHistoryFunction</arg>
          </function>
          <function type="class">
            <arg name="class.name">com.atlassian.jira.workflow.
function.issue.IssueReindexFunction</arg>
          </function>
          <function type="class">
            <arg name="class.name">com.atlassian.jira.workflow.
function.event.FireIssueEventFunction</arg>
            <arg name="eventTypeId">13</arg>
          </function>
        </post-functions>
    </unconditional-result>
  </results>
</action>
```

4. Make sure you modify the name, description, status, step, eventTypeId, and the post functions. Here we used `Finished` as the `old-status` as it is used in the other common actions in the JIRA standard workflow. You can also add new meta attributes, conditions, validators, and so on, but it probably is a good idea to start simple and modify everything else in the JIRA UI once it is imported to JIRA.

5. Include the common action in the other steps, wherever required:

```
<step id="1" name="Open">
  <meta name="jira.status.id">1</meta>
  <actions>
    <common-action id=".." />
    ..................
    <common-action id="6" />
    <action id=" .....
    ....................
    </action>
  </actions>
</step>
```

Note that the ID here should be the action ID of the `common-action` we added in the previous steps. Also, the `common-actions` should appear before the `action` elements in the *step* in order to comply with the OSWorkflow syntax.

6. Import the modified XML as a workflow to JIRA. You can do this using the **Import a Workflow from XML** link. Check out `http://confluence.atlassian.com/display/JIRA/Configuring+Workflow#ConfiguringWorkflow-UsingXMLtocreateaworkflow` for details.

7. The workflow is now ready to use.

How it works...

JIRA workflows are fundamentally using OpenSymphony's OSWorkflow, as we saw in *Chapter 2, Understanding Plugin Framework*. OSWorkflow gives us the flexibility to add common actions by modifying the workflow XML. We have used this feature by modifying the existing workflow XML and importing it back in to JIRA.

The following screenshot is how the updated workflow looks:

Step Name (id)	Linked Status	Transitions (id)	Operations
Open (1)	🗂 Open	*Start Progress* (4) >> In Progress *New Resolve* (5) >> Resolved *Close Issue* (2) >> Closed *Start Again* (6) >> Open	Add Transition | Delete Transitions | Edit | View Properties
In Progress (3)	🗂 In Progress	*Stop Progress* (301) >> Open *New Resolve* (5) >> Resolved *Close Issue* (2) >> Closed *Start Again* (6) >> Open	Add Transition | Delete Transitions | Edit | View Properties
Resolved (4)	👍 Resolved	*Close Issue* (701) >> Closed *Reopen Issue* (3) >> Reopened *Start Again* (6) >> Open	Add Transition | Delete Transitions | Edit | View Properties
Reopened (5)	👍 Reopened	*New Resolve* (5) >> Resolved *Close Issue* (2) >> Closed *Start Progress* (4) >> In Progress *Start Again* (6) >> Open	Add Transition | Delete Transitions | Edit | View Properties
Closed (6)	🔒 Closed	*ReOpen* (711) >> Open *Reopen Issue* (3) >> Reopened	Add Transition | Delete Transitions | Edit | View Properties

Note that the new transition **Start Again** is added to all the steps other than the last one. Suppose we want to modify the name to **Start Again & Again**, it can be done just by editing one of these transitions. The modified workflow looks as follows:

Step Name (id)	Linked Status	Transitions (id)	Operations
Open (1)	🗂 Open	*Start Progress* (4) >> In Progress *New Resolve* (5) >> Resolved *Close Issue* (2) >> Closed *Start Again & Again* (6) >> Open	Add Transition | Delete Transitions | Edit | View Properties
In Progress (3)	🗂 In Progress	*Stop Progress* (301) >> Open *New Resolve* (5) >> Resolved *Close Issue* (2) >> Closed *Start Again & Again* (6) >> Open	Add Transition | Delete Transitions | Edit | View Properties
Resolved (4)	👍 Resolved	*Close Issue* (701) >> Closed *Reopen Issue* (3) >> Reopened *Start Again & Again* (6) >> Open	Add Transition | Delete Transitions | Edit | View Properties
Reopened (5)	👍 Reopened	*New Resolve* (5) >> Resolved *Close Issue* (2) >> Closed *Start Progress* (4) >> In Progress *Start Again & Again* (6) >> Open	Add Transition | Delete Transitions | Edit | View Properties
Closed (6)	🔒 Closed	*ReOpen* (711) >> Open *Reopen Issue* (3) >> Reopened	Add Transition | Delete Transitions | Edit | View Properties

We can similarly modify any attributes on the transition, and it will be reflected in all the places where the transition is used.

Jelly escalation

Before winding up this chapter, let us have a quick look at how we can use one of the useful features of JIRA to escalate inactive issues by transitioning them to a pre-defined workflow status.

Jelly Service is a built-in service in JIRA using which we can run useful Jelly scripts at regular intervals. Atlassian explains in its documentation at `http://confluence.atlassian.com/display/JIRA/Jelly+Escalation` about running a Jelly script to move issues that were not updated in the last seven days to an inactive status.

Let us have a look at this recipe at how to modify the script and transition issues in to different workflow statuses.

Getting ready

Make sure Jelly is turned on in your JIRA instance. It is disabled by default due to security concerns. You can turn it ON by setting the `jira.jelly.on` property to `true`.

You can set the property by adding `-Djira.jelly.on=true` into the `JAVA_OPTS` variable. Adding this variable depends on the server and operating system.

For example, the property can be set on the Tomcat server in Windows by adding it into `setenv.bat` under the `/bin` folder.

How to do it...

The following are the steps to close issues that have been inactive for the last 15 days:

1. Create a filter that displays issues that are not updated for the last 15 days. You can do this by executing the following JQL query:

   ```
   updated <= -15d
   ```

   Save the filter with some name and make a note of the filter ID.

Favourite Filters

Filters are issue searches that have been saved for re-use. This page shows you all your favourite filters.

Name	Issues	Author	Shared With	Subscriptions	Operations
⭐ Stories Reported by Me	11	Jobin Kuruvilla (jobinkk)	👤 Private filter	None - Subscribe	Edit | Delete | Columns
⭐ Updated before 15 days	29	Jobin Kuruvilla (jobinkk)	👤 Private filter	None - Subscribe	Edit | Delete | Columns

2. You can find the filter ID by hovering over the **Edit** link, as shown. The URL will be like `http://localhost:8080/secure/EditFilter!default.jspa?atl_token=084b891405e500819d6443d8378ed37a5bbe4c72&filterId=10010&returnUrl=ManageFilters.jspa` where `filterId` is 10010.

Modify the Jelly script provided by Atlassian in order to include the new filter ID, workflow step name, username, and password. Also modify the comment accordingly.

Here is the modified script:

```
<JiraJelly xmlns:jira="jelly:com.atlassian.jira.jelly.enterprise.
JiraTagLib" xmlns:core="jelly:core" xmlns:log="jelly:log" >
<jira:Login username="jobinkk" password="[password here]">
<log:warn>Running Inactivate issues service</log:warn>
    <!-- Properties for the script -->
    <core:set var="comment">Closing out this issue since it has
been inactive for 15 days!</core:set>
    <core:set var="workflowStep" value="Close Issue" />
    <core:set var="workflowUser" value="jobinkk" />
    <core:set var="filter15Days" value="10010" />

    <!-- Run the SearchRequestFilter -->
    <jira:RunSearchRequest filterid="${filter15Days}" var="issues"
/>

    <core:forEach var="issue" items="${issues}">
    <log:warn>Inactivating issue ${issue.key}</log:warn>

    <jira:TransitionWorkflow key="${issue.key}"
user="${workflowUser}" workflowAction="${workflowStep}"
comment="${comment}"/>   </core:forEach>
</jira:Login>
</JiraJelly>
```

3. Save the script and put it under some location in the server where JIRA is running.

4. Go to **Administration | System | Services in JIRA**.

5. Add the escalation service:

   ❏ **Name**: Escalation Task

   ❏ **Class**: Click on **Built-in services** and select **Run Jelly Script**. The class will be selected as `com.atlassian.jira.jelly.service.JellyService`

   ❏ **Delay**: Select a suitable delay, in minutes.

   ❏ Click on **Add Service**

6. On the **Add Service** page, enter the following details:

- ❑ **Input File**: Path to the script file we saved in the server
- ❑ **Output File**: Path to an output log file.
- ❑ **Delay**: Modify if required.

The script will now run the configured delay.

How it works...

JIRA has its own API for the **Jelly Scripting**. As you can see from the script, following are the steps executed:

1. The script runs the search request on the filter we saved in the first step using the `RunSearchRequest` method. It then stores the retrieved results in variable issues.

2. Script then iterates on the issues and transitions each of them in the workflow using the `TransitionWorkflow` method. It makes use of the key from the issue, the workflow user we configured, and the workflow action. It also adds the comment we entered in the script.

   Note that the workflow action should be available on the issue from its current status. If it is not, the transition will not work. For example, Close workflow action will throw an error if attempted on an issue that is already Closed.

We can modify the script to transition the issue to any workflow status based on any filter criteria.

A lot of other useful things about Jelly Scripting can be found at `http://confluence.atlassian.com/display/JIRA/Jelly+Tags`.

5
Gadgets and Reporting in JIRA

In this chapter, we will cover:

- ▶ Writing a JIRA report
- ▶ Reports in Excel format
- ▶ Data validation in JIRA reports
- ▶ Restricting access to reports
- ▶ Object configurable parameters for reports
- ▶ Creating a pie chart in JIRA
- ▶ Writing JIRA 4 gadgets
- ▶ Invoking REST services from gadgets
- ▶ Configuring user preferences in gadgets
- ▶ Accessing gadgets outside of JIRA

Introduction

Reporting support in an application like JIRA is inevitable! With so much data spanning across different projects, issues, and lot of project planning done on it, we need more and more reports with customized data according to our needs.

There are two different kinds of reporting available in JIRA:

1. Gadgets that can be added into a user's dashboard – From 4.x, the JIRA dashboard was revamped to include gadgets, replacing the legacy portlets. These gadgets are mini applications built using HTML and JavaScript that can run on any OpenSocial gadget container. They communicate with JIRA using REST APIs and retrieve the required information before rendering the display for the user appropriately.

    As the JIRA dashboard is now an OpenSocial gadget container, we can even add third-party gadgets onto it provided they meet the gadget specifications. Similarly, JIRA gadgets can be added on to other containers like iGoogle, Gmail, and so on, but not all features of JIRA gadgets are supported by other gadget containers.

2. Normal JIRA reports – JIRA also provides an option to create reports that show statistics for particular people, projects, versions, or other fields within issues. These reports can be found under 'Browse Project', and can be used to generate simple tabular reports, charts, and so on, and can then be exported to Excel if supported.

    JIRA provides a number of built-in reports, the details of which can be found at `http://confluence.atlassian.com/display/JIRA/Generating+Reports`.

In addition to the Gadgets and Reports that JIRA provides, there are a lot of them available in the Atlassian plugin exchange. But still, we will end up writing some that are customized specifically for our organization and that is where JIRA's plugin architecture helps us by providing two plugin modules, one for reports and one for gadgets.

In this chapter, we will see more details on writing JIRA reports and gadgets, converting legacy portlets into gadgets, and so on.

In addition to that, we will also have a quick look at the **JIRA Query Language** (**JQL**), which provides advanced searching capabilities within the issue navigator. JQL helps us to generate a lot of the reports in issue navigator and export them into convenient views like Excel, Word, and so on.

Writing a JIRA report

As we just mentioned, a JIRA report can display statistical information based on all elements within JIRA – for example, issues, projects, users, issue types, and so on. They can have HTML results and optionally Excel results.

To add new reports in JIRA, you can use the **Report Plugin Module**. The following are the key attributes and elements supported:

Attributes:

Name	Description
key	This should be unique within the plugin.
class	Class to provide contexts for rendered velocity templates. Must implement the com.atlassian.jira.plugin.report. Report interface. Recommended to extend the com.atlassian. jira.plugin.report.impl.AbstractReport class.
i18n-name-key	The localization key for the human-readable name of the plugin module.
name	Human-readable name of the report. Appears in the plugins page. Default is the plugin key.

Elements:

Name	Description
description	Description of the report.
label	User visible name of the report.
resource type="velocity"	Velocity templates for the report views.
resource type="18n"	JAVA properties file for the i18n localization
properties	Reports configurable parameters that used to accept user inputs.

Getting ready

Create a skeleton plugin using the Atlassian plugin SDK.

How to do it...

Let us consider creating a very simple report with little business logic in it. The example we choose here is to display the key and summary of all *issues* in a selected *project*. The only input for the report will be the *project name*, which can be selected from a drop-down list.

The following is the step-by-step procedure to create this report:

1. Add the report plugin module in the plugin descriptor.

   In this first step, we will look at populating the entire plugin module in the `atlassian-plugin.xml` file.

   a. Include the report module:

   ```
   <report key="allissues-report" name="All Issues Report"
   class="com.jtricks.AllIssuesReport">
     <description key="report.allissues.description">This
   report shows details of all isses a specific project. </
   description>
       <!-- the label of this report, which the user will use to
   select it -->        <label key="report.allissues.label" />
   </report>
   ```

   As usual, the plugin module should have a unique key. The other most important attribute here is the class. `AllIssuesReport`, in this case, is the class that populates the context for the velocity templates used in the report display. It holds the business logic to retrieve the report results based on the criteria entered by the user.

   b. Include the `i18n` property resource that can be used for internationalization within the report. The keys entered, such as `report.allissues.label`, will be mapped to a key within the property file:

   ```
   <!-- this is a .properties file containing the i18n keys for
   this report -->
   <resource type="i18n" name="i18n" location="com.jtricks.
   allissues.AllIssuesReport" />
   ```

   Here, the `AllIssuesReport.properties` file will be present in the `com.jtricks.allissues` package under the resources folder in your plugin. All the keys that you used should be present in the properties file with the appropriate values.

   c. Include the velocity template resources within the report module:

   ```
   <!-- the 'view' template is used to render the HTML result
   -->
   <resource type="velocity" name="view" location="templates/
   allissues/allissues-report.vm" />
   ```

   Here we have defined the velocity templates that will be used to render the HTML and the Excel views for the report.

   d. Define the user-driven properties:

   ```
   <!-- the properties of this report which the user must
   select before running it -->
    <properties>
     <property>
   ```

```
    <key>projectId</key>
    <name>Project</name>
    <description>report.allissues.project.description</
description>
    <!-- valid types are string, text, long, select, date
etc-->
    <type>select</type>
    <!-- the values generator is a class which will
generate values for this select list -->
    <values class="com.jtricks.ProjectValuesGenerator"/>
  </property>
</properties>
```

This is a list of properties that will be rendered appropriately on the report input page. In our example, we need to select a project from a select list before generating the report. For this, we have defined a project property here for which the type is `select`. JIRA will automatically render this as a select list by taking the key/value pair from the `ProjectValuesGenerator` class. We will see more details on the types supported in the coming recipes.

Now we have the plugin descriptor filled in with the details required for the report plugin module. The entire module now looks as follows:

```
<report key="allissues-report" name="All Issues Report"
class="com.jtricks.AllIssuesReport">
  <description key="report.allissues.description">This report
shows details of all isses a specific project. </description>
  <label key="report.allissues.label" />
  <resource type="velocity" name="view" location="templates/
allissues/allissues-report.vm" />
  <resource type="i18n" name="i18n" location="com.jtricks.
allissues.AllIssuesReport" />
  <properties>
    <property>
      <key>projectId</key>
      <name>Project</name>
      <description>report.allissues.project.description</
description>
      <type>select</type>
      <values class="com.jtricks.ProjectValuesGenerator"/>
    </property>
  </properties>
</report>
```

2. Create the `i18n` resource properties file. As mentioned, it will be created in the `com.jtricks.allissues` package under the resources folder. The name of the file will be `AllIssuesReport.properties`. We have used three properties so far, which will be populated with the appropriate values:

```
report.allissues.description=Displays all Issues from a project
report.allissues.label=All Issues report
report.allissues.project.description=Project to be used as the
basis of the report
```

    You can create `AllIssuesReport.proprties_{language}_{countrycode}` to support other locales.

3. Create the **Value Generator** class. This is the class that is used to generate the values to be used for rendering the user properties on the report input page. In our example, we have used the `ProjectValuesGenerator` class.

    The class that generates the values should implement the `ValuesGenerator` interface. It should then implement the `getValues()` method to return a key/value map. The value will be used for display, and the key will be returned as the property value which will be used in the report class.

    In the `ProjectValuesGenerator` class, we use the project ID and the name as the key/value pair.

```
public class ProjectValuesGenerator implements ValuesGenerator{
   public Map<String, String> getValues(Map userParams) {
      Map<String, String> projectMap = new HashMap<String,
String>();
      List<Project> allProjects = ComponentManager.getInstance().
getProjectManager().getProjectObjects();
      for (Project project : allProjects) {
         projectMap.put(project.getId().toString(), project.
getName());
      }
      return projectMap;
   }
}
```

4. Create the report class. This is where the actual business logic lies.

    The report class, `AllIssuesReport` in this case, should extend the `AbstractReport` class. It can just implement the `Report` interface, but `AbstractReport` has some already implemented methods, and hence is recommended.

    The only mandatory method we need to implement here is the `generateReportHtml` method. We need to populate a map here that can be used to render the velocity views. In our example, we populate the map with variable issues, which is a list of issue objects in the selected project.

The selected project can be retrieved using the key value entered in the property in the `atlassian-plugin.xml` file:

```
final String projectid = (String) reqParams.get("projectId");
final Long pid = new Long(projectid);
```

We now use this `pid` to retrieve the list of issues using the method `getIssuesFromProject`:

```
List<Issue> getIssuesFromProject(Long pid) throws
SearchException {
    JqlQueryBuilder builder = JqlQueryBuilder.newBuilder();
    builder.where().project(pid);
    Query query = builder.buildQuery();
    SearchResults results = ComponentManager.getInstance().
getSearchService().search(ComponentManager.getInstance().
getJiraAuthenticationContext().getUser(), query, PagerFilter.
getUnlimitedFilter());
    return results.getIssues();
}
```

Now all we need to do here is populate the map with this and return the rendered view as follows:

```
final Map<String, Object> velocityParams = new HashMap<String,
Object>();
velocityParams.put("issues", getIssuesFromProject(pid));
return descriptor.getHtml("view", velocityParams);
```

You can populate any useful variable like this, and it can then be used in the velocity templates to render the view.

The class now looks as follows:

```
public class AllIssuesReport extends AbstractReport {

    public String generateReportHtml(ProjectActionSupport action,
Map reqParams) throws Exception {
        return descriptor.getHtml("view", getVelocityParams(action,
reqParams));
    }

private Map<String, Object> getVelocityParams(ProjectActionSupport
action, Map reqParams) throws SearchException {
        final String projectid = (String) reqParams.get("projectId");
        final Long pid = new Long(projectid);

        final Map<String, Object> velocityParams = new HashMap<String,
Object>();
        velocityParams.put("report", this);
        velocityParams.put("action", action);
        velocityParams.put("issues", getIssuesFromProject(pid));
```

```
        return velocityParams;
    }

    List<Issue> getIssuesFromProject(Long pid) throws
SearchException {
        JqlQueryBuilder builder = JqlQueryBuilder.newBuilder();
        builder.where().project(pid);
        Query query = builder.buildQuery();
        SearchResults results =    ComponentManager.getInstance().
getSearchService().search(ComponentManager.getInstance().
getJiraAuthenticationContext().getUser(), query, PagerFilter.
getUnlimitedFilter());
        return results.getIssues();
    }
}
```

5. Create the velocity template. In our case, we are using `templates/allissues/` `allissues-report.vm`. We will use the issues variable we populated in the report class, iterate on it, and display the issue key and summary:

```
<table id="allissues-report-table" border="0" cellpadding="3"
cellspacing="1" width="100%">
    <tr class="rowNormal">
    <th>Key</th>
    <th>Summary</th>
  </tr>
    #foreach ($issue in $issues)
      <tr class="rowNormal">
      <td>$issue.key</td>
        <td>$issue.summary</td>
    </tr>
    #end
</table>
```

6. With that, our report is ready. Package the plugin and deploy it. We will see more on creating Excel reports, validation within reports, and so on in the coming recipes.

How it works...

The whole logic of how it works can be outlined as follows:

▶ The input view of reports is generated by the object configurable properties, a set of pre-defined properties used to populate input parameters in JIRA. In our example, we used the `select` property. We will see more of this in detail later in this chapter.

▶ The report class gets the properties, uses them to retrieve the details required in the report, and populates the velocity context with the details.

▶ Velocity templates use the details in its context to render the report.

After the plugin is deployed, you can see the report among other JIRA reports in the **Browse Project** section, as shown in the following screenshot:

After clicking on the report, the input screen is displayed, which is constructed using the properties entered in the plugin descriptor, **Project** drop-down in our case:

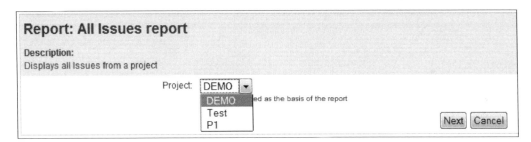

Clicking on **Next**, the report will be generated using the Report class and will be rendered using the velocity template as follows:

Report: All Issues report

Description:
Displays all Issues from a project

Key	Summary
TEST-18	Test
TEST-17	Test
TEST-16	Test3

See also

▶ *Creating a skeleton plugin* in *Chapter 1, Plugin Development Process*

▶ Deploying your plugin in *Chapter 1*

Reports in Excel format

In the previous recipe, we saw how to write a simple report. We will now see how to modify the report plugin to include Excel reports.

Getting ready

Create the report plugin, as mentioned in the previous recipe.

How to do it...

The following are the steps to include the provision of exporting the report to Excel.

1. Add the velocity resource type for the Excel view in the plugin descriptor if not added already:

```
<resource type="velocity" name="excel" location="templates/
allissues/allissues-report-excel.vm" />
```

2. Override the `isExcelViewSupported` method in the report class to return true. In our case, we add this in the `AllIssuesReport.java`:

```
@Override
public boolean isExcelViewSupported() {
  return true;
}
```

This method returns false by default, as it is implemented that way in the `AbstractReport` class.

3. Override the `generateReportExcel` method returning the Excel view. This is very similar to the `generateReportHtml` we implemented in the previous recipe. The only difference is the view returned. The method looks as follows:

```
@Override
public String generateReportExcel(ProjectActionSupport action, Map
reqParams) throws Exception {
  return descriptor.getHtml("excel", getVelocityParams(action,
reqParams));
}
```

Here the `getVelocityParams` method is exactly the same as what is used in the `generateReportHtml` method in the previous recipe. It retrieves the list of issues and populates the map of velocity parameters with the variable name issues.

4. Create the Excel velocity template. The template is created using HTML tags and velocity syntax, just like the other templates. In our example, it will be `allissues-report-excel.vm` under the folder `templates/allissues/` under resources. This is where the view can be customized for Excel.

   In our example, all we have is a list of issues with its summary and key. Hence, we can even use the same template for Excel. It appears as follows:

```
<table id="allissues-report-table" border="0" cellpadding="3"
cellspacing="1" width="100%">
    <tr class="rowNormal">
     <th>Key</th>
     <th>Summary</th>
    </tr>
    #foreach ($issue in $issues)
      <tr class="rowNormal">
       <td>$issue.key</td>
       <td>$issue.summary</td>
      </tr>
    #end
</table>
```

5. Package the plugin and deploy it.

How it works...

Once the Excel view is added into the reports, a link **Excel View** will appear on the right-hand top side of the generated reports, as shown in the next screenshot:

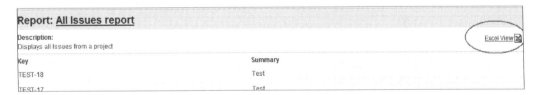

On clicking the link, the `generateReportExcel` method is executed, which in turn will generate the report and render the Excel view using the appropriate template that is defined in the plugin descriptor.

There's more...

You may have noticed that when you click on the **Excel View** link, the excel report that opens is of the name `ConfigureReport!excelView.jspa`, and we need to rename that to `.xls` to make it Excel-friendly.

To do it automatically, we need to set the **content-disposition** parameter in the response header, as shown:

```
final StringBuilder contentDispositionValue = new
StringBuilderStringBuffer(50);
    contentDispositionValue.append("attachment;filename=\"");
    contentDispositionValue.append(getDescriptor().getName()).
append(".xls\";");
final HttpServletResponse response = ActionContext.getResponse();
    response.addHeader("content-disposition", contentDispositionValue.
toString());
```

This snippet is added in the `generateReportExcel` method before returning the excel view using the descriptor. The report will now open as a `.xls` file and can then be opened in Excel without any renaming.

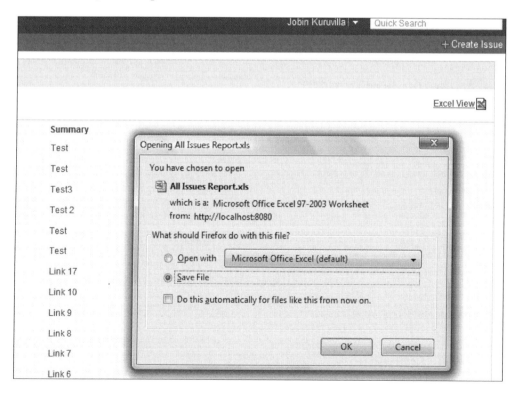

Please refer to `http://support.microsoft.com/kb/260519` and `http://jira.atlassian.com/browse/JRA-8484` for some details on this.

See also

▶ *Writing a JIRA report*

Data validation in JIRA reports

Whenever we take user inputs, it is always a good idea to validate them to make sure the input is in the format that is expected. The same applies to reports also. JIRA reports, as we have seen in the previous recipes, accept user inputs based on which the reports are generated. In the example we used, a project is selected and the details of issues in the selected project are displayed.

In the previous example, the likelihood of a wrong project being selected is low as the project is selected from a valid list of available projects. But still, the final URL that generates the report can be tampered with to include a wrong project ID, and so it is best to do the validation no matter how the input is taken.

Getting ready

Create the report plugin, as explained in the first recipe.

How to do it...

All we need here is to override the validate method to include our custom validations. The following are the steps:

1. Override the `validate` method in the report class we created in the previous recipe.

2. Extract the input parameters from the request parameters, which is an argument to the `validate` method:

    ```
    final String projectid = (String) reqParams.get("projectId");
    ```

    reqParams here is an argument of the `validate` method:

    ```
    public void validate(ProjectActionSupport action, Map reqParams)
    ```

3. Check the validity of the input parameter. In our example, the input parameter is the `projectId`. We can check if it is valid by verifying if a project exists with the given ID. The following condition returns true if it is an invalid project ID:

```
if (ComponentManager.getInstance().getProjectManager().
getProjectObj(pid) == null)
```

4. If the parameter is invalid, add an error to the action with the appropriate error message:

```
action.addError("projectId", "Invalid project Selected");
```

Here we pass the field name to the `addError` method so that the error message appears on top of the field.

You can use internationalization here as well to include appropriate error messages.

5. Add similar validation for all the interested parameters. The following is how the method looks like in our example:

```
@Override
public void validate(ProjectActionSupport action, Map reqParams) {
    // Do your validation here if you have any!
    final String projectid = (String) reqParams.get("projectId");
    final Long pid = new Long(projectid);

    if (ComponentManager.getInstance().getProjectManager().
getProjectObj(pid) == null) {
        action.addError("projectId", "No project with id:"+projectId+"
exists!");
    }
    super.validate(action, reqParams);
}
```

6. Package the plugin and deploy it!

How it works...

Just before the report is generated, the `validate` method is executed. If there is any error, the user is taken back to the input screen with the error highlighted as follows:

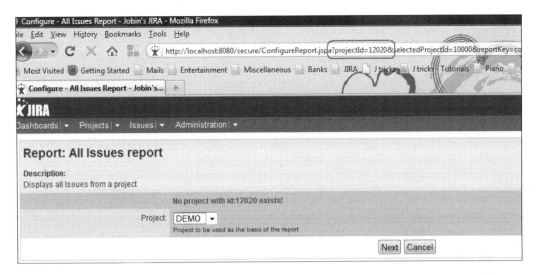

This example shows an error when the report URL is tampered with to include an invalid project with ID 12020.

See also

▶ *Writing a JIRA report*

Restricting access to reports

It is possible to restrict access to JIRA reports based on pre-defined criteria, such as making the report visible only to a certain group of people, or showing the report only in certain projects, and so on. Let us quickly have a look at how to code permissions for a JIRA report.

Getting ready

Create the report plugin, as explained in the first recipe.

How to do it...

All we need to do here is to implement the `showReport` method on the report. Let us assume we want to restrict the report only to JIRA Administrators. The following are the steps:

1. Override the `showReport` method in the report class we created in the previous recipes.

2. Implement the logic to return `true` only if the condition is satisfied. In our example, the report should be visible only to JIRA Administrators, and hence we should return `true` only if the current user is a JIRA Administrator:

```
@Override
public boolean showReport() {
  User user = ComponentManager.getInstance().
getJiraAuthenticationContext().getUser();
  return ComponentManager.getInstance().getUserUtil().
getAdministrators().contains(user);
}
```

Note that the method `getJiraAdministrators` should be used from JIRA v 4.3.

3. Package the plugin and deploy it.

How it works...

If the user is an Administrator, he/she will see the report link under the Browse projects area. If not, the report link won't be visible. We can include similar conditions and evaluate them in the `showReport` method before returning true:

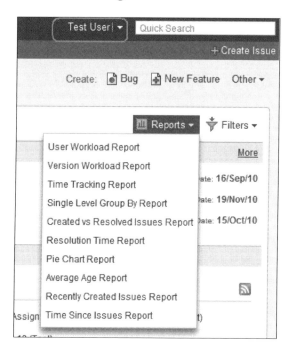

The user **Test User**, highlighted in the preceding screenshot, is not a JIRA Administrator and therefore, not able to see the **All Issues** report.

See also

▶ *Writing a JIRA report*

Object configurable parameters for reports

We have seen how to write JIRA reports and we also had a brief look at how JIRA lets us configure the input parameters. The example we have chosen in the previous recipe, on creating JIRA reports, explained the usage of the `select` type. In this recipe, we will see the various property types supported and some examples on how to configure them.

There are a number of property types supported in JIRA. The full list supported by your JIRA version can be found in the `com.atlassian.configurable.ObjectConfigurationTypes` class. For JIRA 4.2.*, the following are the types supported for reports:

Type	Input HTML type
string	Text Box
long	Text Box
hidden	NA. Hidden to the user.
date	Text Box with Calendar popup
user	Text Box with User Picker
text	Text Area
select	Select List
multiselect	Multi select List
checkbox	Check Box
filterpicker	Filter Picker
filterprojectpicker	Filter or Project Picker
cascadingselect	Cascading Select List. Dependant on a parent Select List.

How to do it...

Let us quickly see each property and how it is used:

string: The `string` property is used to create a Text Box. The Java data type is String. All you need here is to add the `property` tag with the type as `string`:

```
<property>
  <key>testString</key>
  <name>Test String</name>
  <description>Example String property</description>
  <type>string</type>
  <default>test val</default>
</property>
```

Each of the property types, including the `string` property, can have a default value populated using the `default` tag, as shown.

long: The `long` property is used to create a Text Box. The Java data type is again String:

```
<property>
  <key>testLong</key>
  <name>Test Long</name>
  <description>Example Long property</description>
  <type>long</type>
</property>
```

select: The select property is used to create a Select List. The Java data type is String. We have seen an example of this in the previous recipe. There are two ways you can populate the values of a select property:

1. **Using a Value Generator class**: The class should implement the `ValuesGenerator` interface and return a map of key/value pairs. The *key* will be the value returned to the report class, whereas the *value* is the display value to the user. Let us use the same example in the previous recipe here:

```
<property>
  <key>projectId</key>
  <name>Project</name>
  <description>report.allissues.project.description</description>
  <type>select</type>
  <values class="com.jtricks.ProjectValuesGenerator"/>
</property>
```

`ProjectValuesGenerator` implements the `getValues()` method as follows:

```
public class ProjectValuesGenerator implements ValuesGenerator{
  public Map<String, String> getValues(Map userParams) {
    Map<String, String> projectMap = new HashMap<String,
String>();
```

```
    List<Project> allProjects = ComponentManager.getInstance().
getProjectManager().getProjectObjects();
    for (Project project : allProjects) {
        projectMap.put(project.getId().toString(), project.
getName());
    }
    return projectMap;
  }
}
```

2. **Using pre-defined key/value pairs in the property**: The following is an example:

```
<property>
    <key>testSelect</key>
    <name>Test Select</name>
    <description>Example Select Property</description>
    <type>select</type>
    <values>
      <value>
          <key>key1</key>
          <value>Key 1</value>
      </value>
      <value>
          <key>key2</key>
          <value>Key 2</value>
      </value>
      <value>
          <key>key3</key>
          <value>Key 3</value>
      </value>
    <values>
</property>
```

multiselect: The `multiselect` property is used to create a Multi Select List. It is the same as the select property. The only difference is that the type name is multiselect. Here the Java type will be a String if only one value is selected, and it will be an array of Strings (`String[]`) if more than one value is selected!

hidden: The `hidden` property is used to pass a Hidden Value. The Java data type is String:

```
<property>
  <key>testHidden</key>
  <name>Test Hidden</name>
  <description>Example Hidden property</description>
  <type>hidden</type>
  <default>test hidden val</default>
</property>
```

We need to provide a value using the `default` tag as the user won't be seeing the field to enter a value.

date: The `date` property is used to create a Date Picker. The Java data type is String. We should then parse it to the `Date` object in the report:

```
<property>
  <key>testDate</key>
  <name>Test Date</name>
  <description>Example Date property</description>
  <type>date</type>
</property>
```

user: The `user` property is used to create a User Picker. The Java data type is String and it will be the username:

```
<property>
  <key>testUser</key>
  <name>Test User</name>
  <description>Example User property</description>
  <type>user</type>
</property>
```

text: The `text` property is used to create a Text Area. The Java data type is String:

```
<property>
  <key>testText</key>
  <name>Test Text Area</name>
  <description>Example Text property</description>
  <type>text</type>
</property>
```

checkbox: The `checkbox` property is used to create a Checkbox. The Java data type is String and the value will be `true` if selected. If the checkbox is unchecked, the value will be `null`:

```
<property>
  <key>testCheckbox</key>
  <name>Test Check Box</name>
  <description>Example Checkbox property</description>
  <type>checkbox</type>
</property>
```

filterpicker: The `filterpicker` property is used to create a Filter Picker. The Java data type is String and it will hold the ID of the selected filter:

```
<property>
  <key>testFilterPicker</key>
  <name>Test Filter Picker</name>
```

```
      <description>Example Filter Picker property</description>
      <type>filterpicker</type>
    </property>
```

filterprojectpicker: Used to create a Filter or Project Picker. The Java data type is String, and it will be the ID preceded by filter (if a filter is selected) and project (if a project is selected):

```
      <property>
        <key>testFilterProjectPicker</key>
        <name>Test Filter or Project Picker</name>
        <description>Example Filter or Project Picker property</
          description>
        <type>filterprojectpicker</type>
      </property>
```

cascadingselect: Used to create a Cascading Select, based on another select box:

```
      <property>
        <key>testCascadingSelect</key>
        <name>Test Cascading Select</name>
        <description>Example Cascading Select</description>
        <type>cascadingselect</type>
        <values class="com.jtricks.CascadingValuesGenerator"/>
        <cascade-from>testSelect</cascade-from>
      </property>
```

Here the cascading select `testCascadingSelect` depends on the select property named `testSelect`. We have seen the `testSelect` property with the key/value pairs. The next important thing is the values generator class. As with the other value generator classes, this one also generates a map of key/value pairs.

Here the key in the key/value pair should be the value that will be returned to the user. The value should be an instance of a `ValueClassHolder` class, which is a static class. The `ValueClassHolder` class will look like the following:

```
  private static class ValueClassHolder {
    private String value;
    private String className;

    public ValueClassHolder(String value, String className) {
      this.value = value;
      this.className = className;
    }
    public String getValue() {
      return value;
    }
```

```
    public String getClassName() {
      return className;
    }

    public String toString() {
      return value;
    }
  }
```

The `value` in the `ValueClassHolder` will be the display value of the cascading select options to the user. The `className` attribute will be the `key` of the parent select option.

In our example, the parent select property is `testSelect`. It has three keys – `key1`, `key2`, and `key3`. The `getValues()` method will, therefore, look as follows:

```
    public Map getValues(Map arg0) {
      Map allValues = new LinkedHashMap();

      allValues.put("One1", new ValueClassHolder("First Val1", "key1"));
      allValues.put("Two1", new ValueClassHolder("Second Val1",
  "key1"));
      allValues.put("Three1", new ValueClassHolder("Third Val1",
  "key1"));
      allValues.put("One2", new ValueClassHolder("First Val2", "key2"));
      allValues.put("Two2", new ValueClassHolder("Second Val2",
  "key2"));
      allValues.put("One3", new ValueClassHolder("First Val3", "key3"));

      return allValues;
    }
```

If you take a single line, for example, `allValues.put("One1", new ValueClassHolder("First Val1", "key1"))`, it will have the key/value pair `One1/ First Val1` when the select list has the key `key1` selected!

After selecting the appropriate values, they can be retrieved in the report class, as shown in the following lines of code:

```
      final String testString = (String) reqParams.get("testString");
      final String testLong = (String) reqParams.get("testLong");
      final String testHidden = (String) reqParams.get("testHidden");
      final String testDate = (String) reqParams.get("testDate");
      final String testUser = (String) reqParams.get("testUser");
      final String testText = (String) reqParams.get("testText");
      final String[] testMultiSelect = (String[]) reqParams.
  get("testMultiSelect");
```

```
    final String testCheckBox = (String) reqParams.
get("testCheckBox");
    final String testFilterPicker = (String) reqParams.
get("testFilterPicker");
    final String testFilterProjectPicker = (String) reqParams.
get("testFilterProjectPicker");
    final String testSelect = (String) reqParams.get("testSelect");
    final String testCascadingSelect = (String) reqParams.
get("testCascadingSelect");
```

Special mention should be given to the `filterprojectpicker`. The value will be
`filter-10000` if a filter with the ID 10000 is selected. The value will be `project-10000` if
a project with ID 10000 is selected.

How it works...

When the report input screen is presented to the user, the properties mentioned in the plugin
descriptor are converted into the appropriate HTML elements, as discussed. We can then
retrieve their values in the report class and process them to generate the report.

The following two screenshots show how these properties appear on the input screen:

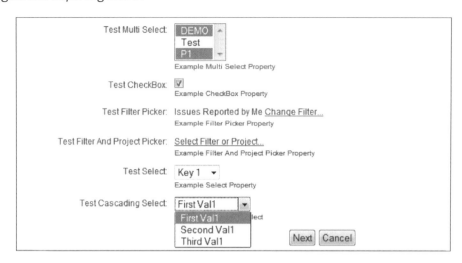

If you print the extracted values into the console in the report class, it will appear as follows:

```
Object Configurable Properties Demo
**************************************
Test String:test default
Test Long:50
Test Hidden:test hidden val
Test Date:18/Mar/11
Test User:jobinkk
Test Text:Test Long Description!!!
Test Multi Select:[10000, 10020]
Test Checkbox:true
Test Filter Picker:10000
Test Filter Project Picker:project-10000
Test Select:key2
Test Cascading Select:Two2
**************************************
```

Hopefully, that gives you a fair idea of how to use Object Configurable Parameters in JIRA reports.

See also

▶ *Writing a JIRA report*

Creating a pie chart in JIRA

As we have already seen in the previous recipes, JIRA ships with a bunch of built-in reports. It also lets us write our own reports using the report plugin module. One of the reports that attract a lot of users in JIRA is the Pie Chart. While the existing JIRA pie reports are really good at what it is meant for, sometimes the need arises to write our own pie charts.

Writing a pie chart in JIRA is easy because JIRA already supports `JFreeChart` and has utility classes which do most of the work in creating these charts. In this recipe, we will see how to write a simple pie chart with the help of Atlassian Utility classes.

Getting ready...

Create a skeleton plugin using Atlassian Plugin SDK.

How to do it...

Let us try to create a very simple pie chart without any business logic. To keep things simple and to concentrate on the pie chart, let us go for a report without any input parameters and with just the HTML view. The following are the steps to accomplish this:

1. Add the report plugin module in the plugin descriptor:

```
<report key="pie-chart" name="Pie Chart" class="com.jtricks.
PieChart">
  <description>Sample Pie Chart</description>
  <label>Eaxmple Pie Chart</label>
  <resource type="velocity" name="view" location="templates/pie/
pie-chart.vm" />
</report>
```

All it has is a class and a velocity template for the HTML view.

2. Create the report class. As usual, it should implement the `AbstractReport` class. All we do here is to populate the velocity templates with parameters from the pie chart we create using a custom `PieChartGenerator` class.

Here is how the `generateReportHtml` looks:

```
public String generateReportHtml(ProjectActionSupport action, Map
reqParams) throws Exception {
  final Map<String, Object> params = new HashMap<String,
Object>();
  params.put("report", this);
  params.put("action", action);
  params.put("user", authenticationContext.getUser());

  final Chart chart = new JTricksPieChartGenerator().generateChart
(authenticationContext.getUser(),REPORT_IMAGE_WIDTH, REPORT_IMAGE_
HEIGHT);

  params.putAll(chart.getParameters());

  return descriptor.getHtml("view", params);
}
```

The `Chart` class is an Atlassian class of the type `com.atlassian.jira.charts.Chart`. The business logic of creating the chart is done inside a custom utility class, `JTricksPieChartGenerator`, which we will see next.

3. Create the `JTricksPieChartGenerator` utility class, which generates the pie chart.

   This is where the business logic of creating the chart is done, and therefore, we will see them in detail:

   ❑ Create the `DefaultPieDataset`, which will be the data set for the pie chart. This is a `JFreeChart` class for which the Java Docs can be found at `http://www.jfree.org/jfreechart/api/javadoc/org/jfree/data/general/DefaultPieDataset.html`.

   ```
   DefaultPieDataset dataset = new DefaultPieDataset();
   ```

   ❑ Populate the values in `dataset`:

   ```
   dataset.setValue("One", 10L);
   dataset.setValue("Two", 15L);
   ```

   In the example, we just populated two key/value pairs with a *name* and a *number value*. This is the data, using which the pie chart is generated. When we generate custom charts, we should replace this with the appropriate data that we are interested in.

   ❑ Get an `i18nBean`. This is required in the Atlassian utility class:

   ```
   final I18nBean i18nBean = new I18nBean(remoteUser);
   ```

   ❑ Create the chart:

   ```
   final ChartHelper helper = new PieChartGenerator(dataset,
   i18nBean).generateChart();
   helper.generate(width, height);
   ```

   Here we use the `com.atlassian.jira.charts.jfreechart.PieChartGenerator` class to generate the chart using the dataset we just created and the `i18nBean`. Make sure you invoke the generate method, as shown in the preceding snippet.

   ❑ Populate a map with all the required parameters from the generated `ChartHelper` and return a `Chart` object, as shown next:

   ```
   params.put("chart", helper.getLocation());
   params.put("chartDataset", dataset);
   params.put("imagemap", helper.getImageMap());
   params.put("imagemapName", helper.getImageMapName());

   return new Chart(helper.getLocation(), helper.getImageMap(),
   helper.getImageMapName(), params);
   ```

You can add all parameters available, but we are limiting it to the absolute minimum. `params.putAll(chart.getParameters())` in the report class will then populate the velocity context with all these parameters.

❏ The `generateChart` method will now look as follows:

```
public Chart generateChart(User remoteUser, int width, int
  height) {
try {
  final Map<String, Object> params = new HashMap<String,
    Object>();
  // Create Dataset
  DefaultPieDataset dataset = new DefaultPieDataset();

  dataset.setValue("One", 10L);
  dataset.setValue("Two", 15L);

  final I18nBean i18nBean = new I18nBean(remoteUser);

  final ChartHelper helper = new PieChartGenerator(dataset,
    i18nBean).generateChart();
  helper.generate(width, height);

  params.put("chart", helper.getLocation());
  params.put("chartDataset", dataset);
  params.put("imagemap", helper.getImageMap());
  params.put("imagemapName", helper.getImageMapName());
  return new Chart(helper.getLocation(), helper.
    getImageMap(), helper.getImageMapName(), params);

  } catch (Exception e) {
  e.printStackTrace();
  throw new RuntimeException("Error generating chart", e);
  }
}
```

4. Create the velocity template for the HTML view using the context we populated in the report class. In our example, the template is `templates/pie/pie-chart.vm`. It looks like the following block of code:

```
Sample Chart: <br><br>
<table width="100%" class="report">
  <tr>
    <td>
      #if ($chart)
          #if ($imagemap)
            $imagemap
          #end
```

```
        <p class="report-chart">
            <img src='$baseurl/charts?filename=$chart' border='0'
#if ($imagemap) usemap="\#$imagemapName" #end/>
            </p>
        #end
      </td>
    </tr>
</table>
```

Here we display the chart we created. The chart is available at the URL $baseurl/ charts?filename=$chart, where $chart is the location generated by the helper class. We populated this earlier in the context.

5. Package the plugin, deploy it, and test it!

How it works...

In short, the bit we need to do here is to create the DefaultPieDataset and everything else is done by JIRA for you. The generateChart method may take more arguments depending on the complexity of the reports we are going to create. For example: startDate, endDate, and so on. The data set will then be created using these arguments instead of our hardcoded values!

In our example, the chart appears as follows:

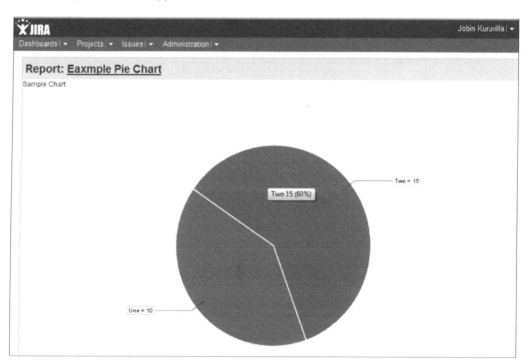

There's more...

Have a look at the other helper classes under the `com.atlassian.jira.`
`charts.jfreechart` package, for example, `StackedBarChartGenerator`,
`HistogramChartGenerator`, `CreatedVsResolvedChartGenerator`, and
so on, for other types of charts!

See also

▶ *Writing a JIRA report*

Writing JIRA 4 gadgets

Gadgets are a big leap in JIRA's reporting features! The fact that JIRA is now an OpenSocial
container lets its user add useful gadgets (both JIRA's own and third-party) into its dashboard.
At the same time, gadgets written for JIRA can be added in other containers like iGoogle,
Gmail, and so on!

In this recipe, we will have a look at writing a very simple gadget, one that says 'Hello from
JTricks'. By keeping the content simple, it will let us concentrate more on writing the gadget!

Before we start writing the gadget, it is probably worth understanding the key components of
a JIRA gadget:

1. Gadget XML is the most important part of a JIRA Gadget. It holds the specification of
   the gadget and includes the following:

   ❑ **Gadget Characteristics**. It includes title, description, author's name, and so
      on

   ❑ **Screenshot and a thumbnail image**. Please note that the screenshot is
      not used within Atlassian containers such as JIRA or Confluence. We can
      optionally add it if we want them to be used in other OpenSocial containers

   ❑ **Required features** that the gadget container must provide for the gadget

   ❑ **User preferences** which will be configured by the gadget users

   ❑ The **Gadget content** created using HTML and JavaScript

2. A screenshot and thumbnail image will be used during preview and while selecting
   the gadget from the container.

3. An `i18n` property file used for internationalization in the gadget

4. Optional CSS and JavaScript file used to render the display in the **Content** section of
   the gadget

We will see each of them in the recipe.

Getting ready

Create a skeleton plugin using Atlassian Plugin SDK.

How to do it...

The following are the steps to write our first gadget, one that shows the greetings from JTricks!

1. Modify the plugin descriptor with the gadget module and the resources required for our gadget:

   ❑ Add the `Gadget` module in the plugin descriptor:

   ```
   <gadget key="hello-gadget" name="Hello Gadget"
   location="hello-gadget.xml">
      <description>Hello Gadget! </description>
   </gadget>
   ```

   As you can see, this has a unique `key` and points to the `location` of the gadget XML! You can have as many gadget definitions as you want in your `atlassian-plugin.xml` file, but in our example, we stick with the preceding one.

   ❑ Include the thumbnail and screenshot images and downloadable resources in the plugin descriptor. We have seen details of this in the previous chapter and more can be learned at `http://confluence.atlassian.com/display/JIRADEV/Downloadable+Plugin+Resources`. In our example, the resources are added on to the plugin descriptor as:

   ```
   <resource type="download" name="screenshot.png" location="/
   images/screenshot.png"/>
   <resource type="download" name="thumbnail.png" location="/
   images/thumbnail.png"/>
   ```

   The location is relative to the `src/main/resources` folder in the plugin. As mentioned before, the screenshot is optional.

2. Add the `i18n` properties file that will be used in the gadget also as a downloadable resource:

   ```
   <resource type="download" name="i18n/messages.xml" location="i18n/
   messages.xml">
      <param name="content-type" value="text/xml; charset=UTF-8"/>
   </resource>
   ```

The `atlassian-plugin.xml` will now look like this:

```xml
<atlassian-plugin key="com.jtricks.gadgets" name="Gadgets Plugin"
plugins-version="2">
    <plugin-info>
      <description>Gadgets Example</description>
      <version>2.0</version>
      <vendor name="JTricks" url="http://www.j-tricks.com/" />
    </plugin-info>
    <gadget key="hello-gadget" name="Hello Gadget"
location="hello-gadget.xml">
        <description>Hello Gadget!</description>
    </gadget>

    <resource type="download" name="screenshot.png" location="/
images/screenshot.png"/>
    <resource type="download" name="thumbnail.png" location="/
images/thumbnail.png"/>

    <resource type="download" name="i18n/messages.xml"
location="i18n/messages.xml">
        <param name="content-type" value="text/xml; charset=UTF-8"/>
    </resource>
  </atlassian-plugin>
```

3. Add the screenshot and thumbnail images under the `src/main/resources/images` folder. The thumbnail image should be of the size 120 x 60 pixels.

4. Add the `i18n` properties file under the `src/main/resources/i18n` folder. The name of the filer we defined in `messages.xml`.

This file is an XML file wrapped within the `messagebundle` tag. Each property in the file is entered as an XML tag, as shown next:

```xml
<msg name="gadget.title">Hello Gadget</msg>
```

The `msg` tag has a `name` attribute, which is the property, and the corresponding Value is enclosed in the `msg` tag. We use three properties in our example and the entire file in our example looks like the following:

```xml
<messagebundle>
  <msg name="gadget.title">Hello Gadget</msg>
  <msg name="gadget.title.url">http://www.j-tricks.com</msg>
  <msg name="gadget.description">Example Gadget from J-Tricks</
msg>
</messagebundle>
```

5. Write the Gadget XML.

    The Gadget XML has a Module element at the root of the XML. It has mainly three elements underneath – `ModulePrefs`, `UserPref`, and `Content`. We will write of each of them in this example. The entire set of attributes and elements and other details of the gadget specification can be read at `http://confluence.atlassian.com/display/GADGETDEV/Creating+your+Gadget+XML+Specification`.

    ❑   Write the `ModulePrefs` element. This element holds the information about the gadget. It also has two child elements – `Require` and `Optional`, that are used to define the required or optional features for the gadget.

    The following is how the `ModulePrefs` element looks in our example after it is populated with all the attributes:

    ```
    <ModulePrefs title="__MSG_gadget.title__"
                 title_url="__MSG_gadget.title.url__"
                 description="__MSG_gadget.description__"
                 author="Jobin Kuruvilla"
                 author_email=jobinkk@gmail.com
                 screenshot='#staticResourceUrl("com.jtricks.
    gadgets:hello-gadget", "screenshot.png")'
                 thumbnail='#staticResourceUrl("com.jtricks.
    gadgets:hello-gadget", "thumbnail.png")' height="150"  >
    </ModulePrefs>
    ```

    As you can see, it holds information like `title`, `title URL` (to which the gadget title will link to), `description`, `author` name and `email`, `height` of the gadget, and URLs to screenshot and thumbnail images.

    Anything that starts with `__MSG_` and ends with `__` is a property that is referred from the `i18n` properties file.

    The `height` of the gadget is optional and 200, by default. The images are referenced using `#staticResourceUrl` where the first argument is the fully qualified gadget module key which is of the form `${atlassian-plugin-key}:${module-key}`. In our example, the plugin key is `com.jtricks.gadgets` and the module key is `hello-gadget`.

    ❑   Add the optional gadget directory feature inside `ModulePrefs`. This is currently supported only in JIRA:

    ```
    <Optional feature="gadget-directory">
      <Param name="categories">
        Other
      </Param>
    </Optional>
    ```

    In the example, we add the category as `Other`!

    Other values supported for category are: `JIRA`, `Confluence`, `FishEye`, `Crucible`, `Crowd`, `Clover`, `Bamboo`, `Admin`, `Charts`, and `External Content`.

You can add the gadget to more than one category by adding the categories within the `Param` element, each in a new line.

❑ Include `Required` features if there are any under the XML tag `require`. A full list of supported features can be found at `http://confluence.atlassian.com/display/GADGETDEV/Including+Features+into+your+Gadget`.

❑ Add the `Locale` element to point to the `i18n` properties file:

```
<Locale messages="__ATLASSIAN_BASE_URL__/download/resources/
com.jtricks.gadgets/i18n/messages.xml"/>
```

Here the property `__ATLASSIAN_BASE_URL__` will be automatically substituted with JIRA's configured base URL when the gadget is rendered. The path to the property file here is `__ATLASSIAN_BASE_URL__/download/resources/com.jtricks.gadgets`, where `com.jtricks.gadgets` is the Atlassian plugin key. The path to the XML file `/i18n/messages.xml` is what is defined in the resource module earlier.

❑ Add User Preferences if required, using the `UserPref` element. We will omit the same in this example as the 'Hello Gadget' doesn't take any inputs from the user.

❑ Add the `Content` for the gadget. This is where the gadget is rendered using HTML and JavaScript. In our example, we just need to provide the static text 'Hello From JTricks' and it is fairly easy.

The entire content is wrapped within the `<![CDATA[` and `]]>`, so that they won't be treated as XML tags. The following is how it looks in our example:

```
<Content type="html" view="profile">
  <![CDATA[ Hello From JTricks ]]>
</Content>
```

Our gadget's XML is now ready and looks like the following block of code:

```
<?xml version="1.0" encoding="UTF-8" ?>
<Module>
  <ModulePrefs title="__MSG_gadget.title__"
               title_url="__MSG_gadget.title.url__"
               description="__MSG_gadget.description__"
               author="Jobin Kuruvilla"
               author_email=jobinkk@gmail.com
               screenshot='#staticResourceUrl("com.jtricks.
gadgets:hello-gadget", "screenshot.png")'
               thumbnail='#staticResourceUrl("com.jtricks.
gadgets:hello-gadget", "thumbnail.png")' height="150" >
    <Optional feature="gadget-directory">
      <Param name="categories">
        Other
      </Param>
    </Optional>
```

```
       <Locale messages="__ATLASSIAN_BASE_URL__/download/resources/
com.jtricks.gadgets/i18n/messages.xml"/>
       </ModulePrefs>
       <Content type="html" view="profile">
        <![CDATA[ Hello From JTricks ]]>
       </Content>
</Module>
```

6. Package the plugin, deploy it, and test it.

How it works...

Once the plugin is deployed, we need to add the gadget in the JIRA dashboard. The following is how it appears in the **Add Gadget** screen. Note the thumbnail is the one we have in the plugin and also note that it appears in the **Other** section:

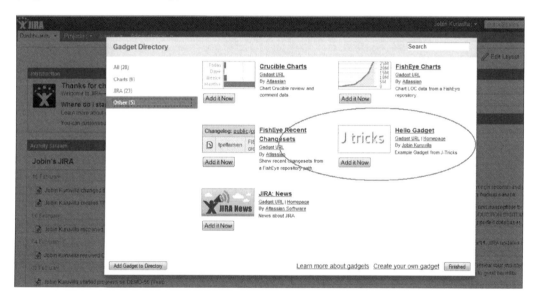

Once it is added, it appears as follows in the **Dashboards** section:

There's more...

We can modify the look-and-feel of the gadgets by adding more HTML or gadget preferences! For example, `<font color="red">Hello From JTricks</font>` will make it appear in red.

We can adjust the size of the gadget using the dynamic-height feature. We should add the following under the `ModulePrefs` element:

```
<Require feature="dynamic-height"/>
```

We should then invoke `gadgets.window.adjustHeight();` whenever the content is reloaded. For example, we can do it in a window onload event, as shown next:

```
<script type="text/javascript" charset="utf-8">
  function resize()
  {
    gadgets.window.adjustHeight();
  }
  window.onload=resize;
</script>
```

The `gadget xml` file, in this case, will look like this:

```
<?xml version="1.0" encoding="UTF-8" ?>
<Module>
    <ModulePrefs title="__MSG_gadget.title__"
                 title_url="__MSG_gadget.title.url__"
                 description="__MSG_gadget.description__"
                 author="Jobin Kuruvilla"
                 author_email="jobinkk@gmail.com"
                 screenshot='#staticResourceUrl("com.jtricks.
gadgets:hello-gadget", "screenshot.png")'
                 thumbnail='#staticResourceUrl("com.jtricks.
gadgets:hello-gadget", "thumbnail.png")'
        height="150">
        <Optional feature="gadget-directory">
            <Param name="categories">
             Other
            </Param>
        </Optional>
    <Require feature="dynamic-height"/>
    <Locale messages="__ATLASSIAN_BASE_URL__/download/resources/com.
jtricks.gadgets/i18n/messages.xml"/>
    </ModulePrefs>
    <Content type="html" view="profile">
```

```
        <![CDATA[
<script type="text/javascript" charset="utf-8">
    function resize()
    {
  gadgets.window.adjustHeight();
    }
window.onload=resize;
</script>
Hello From JTricks
        ]]>
    </Content>
</Module>
```

The gadget should now appear as follows:

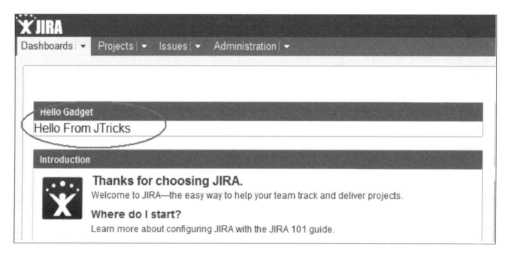

Note that the size is adjusted to just fit the text!

Invoking REST services from gadgets

In the previous recipe, we saw how to write a gadget with static content. In this recipe, we will have a look at creating a gadget with dynamic content or the data that is coming from the JIRA server.

JIRA uses REST services to communicate between the gadgets and the server. We will see how to write REST services in the coming chapters. In this recipe, we will use an existing REST service.

Getting ready

Create the **Hello Gadget**, as described in the previous recipe.

How to do it...

Let us consider a simple modification to the existing **Hello Gadget** to understand the basics of invoking REST services from gadgets. We will try to greet the current user by retrieving the user details from the server instead of displaying the static text: **Hello From JTricks**.

JIRA ships with some inbuilt REST methods, one of which is to retrieve the details of the current user. The method can be reached in the URL: `/rest/gadget/1.0/currentUser`. We will use this method to retrieve the current user's full name and then display it in the gadget greeting. If the user's name is **Jobin Kuruvilla**, the gadget will display the message as **Hello, Jobin Kuruvilla**.

As we are only changing the content of the gadget, the only modification is required in the gadget XML, which is `hello-gadget.xml` in our example. Only the `Content` element needs to be modified, which will now invoke the REST service and render the content.

The following are the steps:

1. Include the common Atlassian gadget resources:

    ```
    #requireResource("com.atlassian.jira.gadgets:common")
    #includeResources()
    ```

    `#requireResource` will bring in the JIRA gadget JavaScript framework into the gadget's context. `#includeResources` will write out the HTML tags for the resource in place. Check out `http://confluence.atlassian.com/display/ GADGETDEV/Using+Web+Resources+in+your+Gadget` for more details.

2. Construct a gadget object as follows:

    ```
    var gadget = AJS.Gadget
    ```

    The gadget object has four top-level options:

    - ❏ `baseUrl`: An option to pass the base URL. It is a mandatory option, and we use `__ATLASSIAN_BASE_URL__` here which will be rendered as JIRA's base URL.

    - ❏ `useOauth`: An optional parameter. Used to configure the type of authentication which must be a URL. `/rest/gadget/1.0/currentUser` is commonly used.

    - ❏ `config`: Another optional parameter. Only used if there are any configuration options for the gadget.

    - ❏ `view`: Used to define the gadget's view.

In our example, we don't use authentication or any configuration options. We will just go with the `baseUrl` and `view` options. The following is how the Gadget is created using JavaScript:

```
<script type="text/javascript">
   (function () {
         var gadget = AJS.Gadget({
            baseUrl: "__ATLASSIAN_BASE_URL__",
            view: {
            ...
         }
         });
   })();
</script>
```

3. Populate the gadget view.

   The `view` object has the following properties:

   ❑ `enableReload`: Optional. Used to reload the gadget at regular intervals.

   ❑ `onResizeReload`: Optional. Used to reload the gadget when the browser is resized.

   ❑ `onResizeAdjustHeight`: Optional and used along with the `dynamic-height` feature. This will adjust the gadget height when the browser is resized.

   ❑ `template`: Created the actual view.

   ❑ `args`: An array of objects or function that returns an array of objects. It has two attributes. `Key` –used to access the data from within the template and `ajaxOptions` – set of request options used to connect to the server and retrieve data.

   In our example, we will use the `template` and `args` properties to render the view. First, let us see `args` because we use the data retrieved here in the `template`. `args` will look like the following:

```
args: [{
   key: "user",
   ajaxOptions: function() {
      return {
         url: "/rest/gadget/1.0/currentUser"
      };
   }
}]
```

As you can see, we invoke the `/rest/gadget/1.0/currentUser` method and use the key `user` to refer the data we retrieved while rendering the view. `ajaxOptions` uses the jQuery Ajax Options, details of which can be found at `http://api.jquery.com/jQuery.ajax#options`.

The key `user` will now hold the user details from the REST method, as follows:

```
{"username":"jobinkk","fullName":"Jobin
Kuruvilla","email":"jobinkk@gmail.com"}
```

The `template` function will now use this `args` object (defined earlier) and its `key`, `user` to render the view as follows:

```
template: function(args) {
  var gadget = this;

  var userDetails = AJS.$("<h1/>").text("Hello, "+args.
user["fullName"]);
  gadget.getView().html(userDetails);
}
```

Here, `args.user["fullName"]` will retrieve the user's `fullName` from the REST output. Username or e-mail can be retrieved in a similar fashion.

`AJS.$` will construct the view as `<h1>Hello, Jobin Kuruvilla</h1>`, where `Jobin Kuruvilla` is the `fullName` retrieved.

The entire `Content` section will look as shown in the following lines of code:

```
<Content type="html" view="profile">
    <![CDATA[
          #requireResource("com.atlassian.jira.
gadgets:common")
        #includeResources()

        <script type="text/javascript">
    (function () {
        var gadget = AJS.Gadget({
            baseUrl: "__ATLASSIAN_BASE_URL__",
            view: {
            template: function(args) {
             var gadget = this;
             var userDetails = AJS.$("<h1/>").text("Hello,
"+args.user["fullName"]);
            gadget.getView().html(userDetails);
            },
            args: [{
            key: "user",
```

```
                    ajaxOptions: function() {
                      return {
                        url: "/rest/gadget/1.0/currentUser"
                      };
                  }
                }]
              }
            });
          })();
            </script>
            ]]>
          </Content>
```

4. Package the gadget and deploy it.

How it works...

After the modification to the gadget XML, the gadget will now display the method as follows:

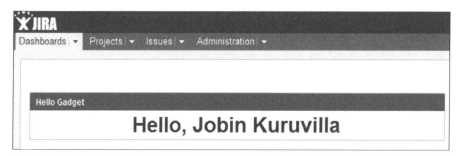

See also

▶ *Writing JIRA 4 gadgets*

Configuring user preferences in gadgets

In the previous two recipes, we saw how to create gadgets from static content and dynamic content. In this recipe, we will go one step further and display the gadget content, based on user input.

The user will configure the gadget during its creation, or modify it later and the gadget content will vary depending on the configuration parameters.

Getting ready...

Create the **Hello Gadget**, populated with dynamic content, as described in the previous recipe.

How to do it...

In this recipe, we will let the user choose whether to display the name in the greeting message or not. There will be a property on the gadget named `displayName`. If it is set to `true`, the gadget will display the username and the greeting message will be **Hello, Jobin Kuruvilla**. If the `displayName` is set to false, the greeting message will be **Hello!**

The following are the steps to configure user preferences:

1. Include the `setprefs` and the `views` features under the `ModulePrefs` element:

   ```
   <Require feature="setprefs" />
   <Require feature="views" />
   ```

   `setprefs` is required to persist user preferences, whereas `views` determines whether the current user can edit the preferences or not.

2. Include the gadget, the `common` locale, under `ModulePrefs`, along with our custom `Locale` element:

   ```
   #supportedLocales("gadget.common")
   ```

   This is required to get the gadget configuration language properly.

3. Include the required `UserPref` elements. This element defines the various user preferences. The element supports the following fields:

   - ❏ `name`: Required. Name of the user preferences. The value of this can then be accessed using `gadget.getPref("name")`.
   - ❏ `display_name`: Display name of the field. By default, it will be the same as the name.
   - ❏ `urlparam`: Optional string to pass as the parameter name for content `type="url"`.
   - ❏ `datatype`: Data type of the field. Valid options include: `string`, `bool`, `enum`, `hidden`, or `list`. Default is string.
   - ❏ `required`: Marks the field as required. Default is false.
   - ❏ `default_value`: Sets a default value.

   In our example, we add the `displayName` property as follows:

   ```
   <UserPref name="displayName" datatype="hidden" default_
   value="true"/>
   ```

The field is marked as `hidden` so that it won't appear in the OpenSocial gadget configuration form!

4. Modify the creation of `AJS.Gadget` to include the `config` property. `config` is normally of the form:

```
...
config: {
    descriptor: function(){...},
    args: {Function, Array}
},
...
```

Here, `descriptor` is a function that returns a new Configuration Descriptor. `args` is an array of objects or a function that returns one similar to `view`.

In our example, we define a function to return a descriptor with the configuration details of the `displayName` property. It looks like the following:

```
config: {
  descriptor: function (args) {
    var gadget = this;
    return   {
      fields: [
        {
          userpref: "displayName",
          label: gadget.getMsg("property.label"),
          description:gadget.getMsg("property.description"),
          type: "select",
          selected: gadget.getPref("displayName"),
          options:[
            {
              label:"Yes",
              value:"true"
            },
            {
              label:"No",
              value:"false"
            }
          ]
        }
      ]
    };
  }
}
```

Here, there is only one field: `displayName`. It is of the type `select` and has a `label` and `description`, both populated from the `i18n` property file using the `gadget.getMsg` method. The `Selected` attribute is populated with the current value – `gadget.getPref("displayName")`. `Options` are given as an array, as shown in the preceding snippet.

More details on the various other field types and their properties can be found at `http://confluence.atlassian.com/display/GADGETDEV/Field+Definitions`.

5. Add the new `i18n` properties to the message bundle:

```
<msg name="property.label">Display Name?</msg>
<msg name="property.description">Example Property from J-Tricks</msg>
```

6. Include the `UserPref - isConfigured`:

```
<UserPref name="isConfigured" datatype="hidden" default_value="false"/>
```

The user preferences are set every time the gadget loads, and we use this property which is specially designed to prevent this.

When this property is used, `AJS.gadget.fields.nowConfigured()` should be added as an additional field under the `config descriptor`.

7. Modify the view to display usernames based on the configured property.

The `template` function is modified as follows:

```
if (gadget.getPref("displayName") == "true")
   var userDetails = AJS.$("<h1/>").text("Hello, "+args.
user["fullName"]);
} else {
   var userDetails = AJS.$("<h1/>").text("Hello!");
 }
```

As you can see, the configured property is retrieved using `gadget.getPref("displayName")`. If it is `true`, the username is used.

The entire `Content` section now looks like the following lines of code:

```
<Content type="html" view="profile">
<![CDATA[#requireResource("com.atlassian.jira.gadgets:common")
#includeResources()
<script type="text/javascript">
        (function () {
var gadget = AJS.Gadget({
        baseUrl: "__ATLASSIAN_BASE_URL__",
        config: {
descriptor: function (args) {
var gadget = this;
return {
fields: [
{
```

```
userpref: "displayName",
label: gadget.getMsg("property.label"),
description:gadget.getMsg("property.description"),
type: "select",
selected: gadget.getPref("displayName"),
options:[
                        {
label:"Yes",
value:"true"
                },
                        {
label:"No",
value:"false"

                        }
                    ]
},
AJS.gadget.fields.nowConfigured()
                    ]
};
}
        },
            view: {
template: function(args) {
var gadget = this;
if (gadget.getPref("displayName") == "true")
                {
varuserDetails = AJS.$("<h1/>").text("Hello, "+args.
user["fullName"]);
                } else {
varuserDetails = AJS.$("<h1/>").text("Hello!");
                }
gadget.getView().html(userDetails);
},
args: [{
key: "user",
ajaxOptions: function() {
return {
url: "/rest/gadget/1.0/currentUser"
                    };
                }
            }]
        }
        });
        })();
</script>
]]>
</Content>
```

8. Package the gadget and deploy it.

How it works...

Once the user configurable properties are added, the gadget on its creation will ask the user to configure the `displayName` property, as shown next. The default value will be `true` (label :Yes) as we configured it.

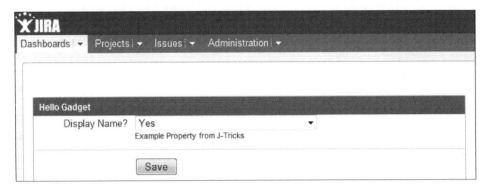

When **Yes** is selected, it appears as:

If you click on the gadget options now, you can see the **Edit** option, as shown in the following screenshot:

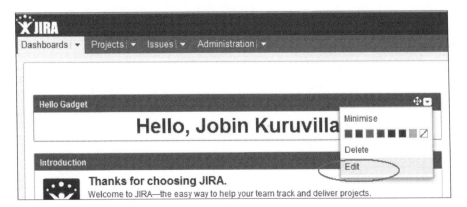

The following screenshot appears while clicking on **Edit**:

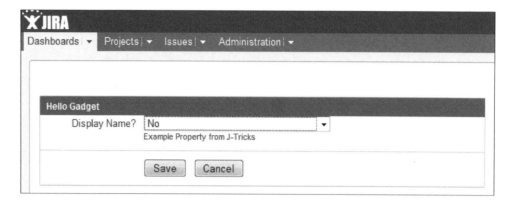

On selecting **No**, the message is displayed without the username, as shown in the following screenshot:

There's more...

One of the most popular user preferences in JIRA gadgets, and therefore, worth a special mention, is its ability to auto refresh itself at a configured interval. JIRA has a pre-defined feature that helps us to do it.

There are only a couple of things you need do to implement this feature:

1. Add the `refresh` UserPref:

   ```
   <UserPref name="refresh" datatype="hidden" default_value="false"/>
   ```

2. Include the `enableReload: true` property in the `view`:

   ```
   view: {
     enableReload: true,
       template: function(args) {
       ...
   ```

```
    },
    args: [{
        ...
    }]
}
```

You will now see an extra **Refresh** action on the gadget properties, as shown in the next screenshot:

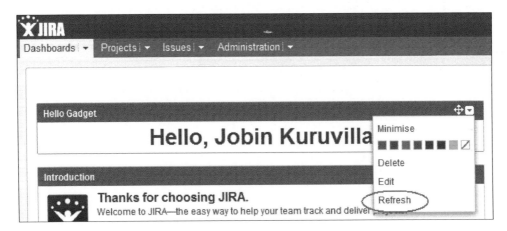

This can be used to refresh the gadget at any time.

On clicking on **Edit**, the automatic refresh interval can be selected, as shown in the following screenshot:

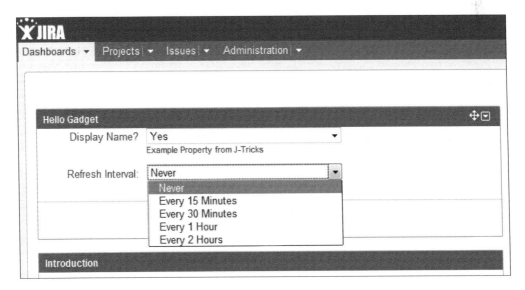

See also

▶ *Writing JIRA 4 gadgets*

▶ Invoking REST services from gadgets

Accessing gadgets outside of JIRA

We have seen how to write a gadget and add it onto the JIRA Dashboard. But have we made use of all the advantages of an OpenSocial gadget? How about adding them onto other OpenSocial containers such as Gmail or iGoogle?

In this recipe, we will see how to add a gadget in to Gmail. The process is pretty much similar for other containers as well.

How to do it...

The following is a quick step-by-step procedure to add a gadget to Gmail:

1. Identify the Gadget URL for the gadget that we are going to add. We can find this URL from the JIRA gadgets directory, as shown in the next screenshot. In the example, we choose to add the **Favourite Filters** gadget:

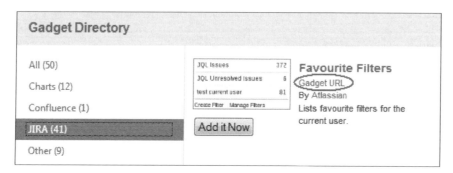

2. Go to **Gmail | Settings | Gadgets**. Enter the URL, as shown in the next screenshot:

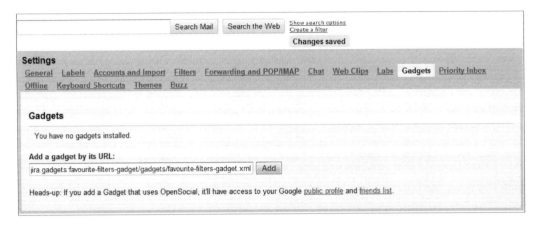

Note that this is the only process that will be different for different containers. We need to enter this URL in the appropriate place for each different container.

3. Once added, the gadget will appear in the settings as shown in the following screenshot:

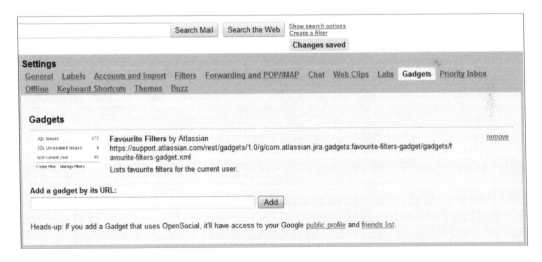

4. The gadget should now be available under the list of gadgets you have in your Gmail sidebars. Save the configurations. In our example, we need to choose whether to display the count of issues or not and the refresh interval.

    Refer to the next screenshot to see how it appears in Gmail.

5. The gadget now shows no results because we haven't connected to JIRA with a proper username/password. Edit the gadget settings and you will see an option, **Login & Approve**, which allows you to log in to your JIRA instance and approve the retrieval of data to be displayed in Gmail:

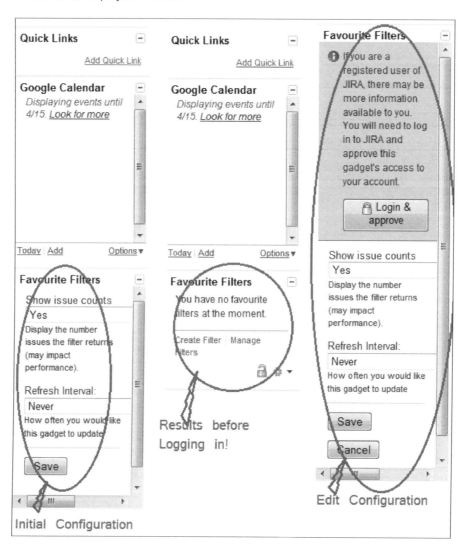

6. **Approve Access**, as shown in the following screenshot. The gadget should now show the results:

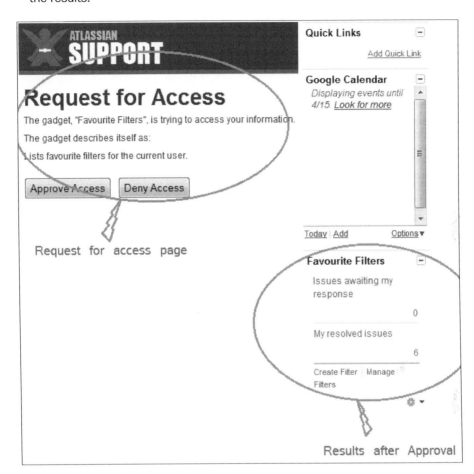

How it works...

The way it works is identical to that of its behavior in JIRA Dashboards. The gadget will communicate with JIRA using the REST APIs and the data is rendered using the HTML and JavaScript code under the `view` section in the gadget XML's `Content` element.

See also

▶ *Writing JIRA 4 gadgets*

▶ *Invoking REST services from gadgets*

6
The Power of JIRA Searching

In this chapter, we will cover:

- ▶ Writing a JQL function
- ▶ Sanitizing JQL functions
- ▶ Adding a search request view
- ▶ Smart querying using quick search
- ▶ Searching in plugins
- ▶ Parsing a JQL query in plugins
- ▶ Linking directly to search queries
- ▶ Index and de-index programmatically
- ▶ Managing filters programmatically

Introduction

JIRA is known for its search capabilities. It allows us to extend them in a way that impresses its users! In this chapter, we will look at customizing the various searching aspects of JIRA such as JQL, searching in plugins, managing filters, and so on.

Before we start, it would make sense to look at one of the major enhancements in JIRA 4, that is, **JQL – JIRA Query Language**. JQL brings to the table advanced searching capabilities, using which the users can search for issues in their JIRA instance and then exploit all the capabilities of issue navigator.

In addition to the previous searching capabilities, now called **Simple Searching**, JQL or the **Advanced Searching** introduces support for logical operations, including AND, OR, NOT, NULL, and EMPTY. It also introduces a set of JQL functions, which can be used effectively to search based on predefined criteria.

JQL is a structured query language that lets us find issues using a simple SQL-like syntax. It is simple because of its auto-complete features and maintains a query history to navigate easily to the recent searches. As Atlassian puts it:

> *"JQL allows you to use standard boolean operators and wild cards to perform complex searches, including fuzzy, proximity, and empty field searches. It even supports extensible functions, allowing you to define custom expressions like "CurrentUser" or "LastSprint" for dynamic searches."*

A query in *Advanced Search* consists of a **field**, followed by an **operator**, followed by a **value** or **function**. To find out all issues in a project, we can use:

```
project = "TEST"
```

`project` is the field, `=` is the operator, and `TEST` is the value.

Similarly, we can find all issues assigned to the current user using:

```
assignee = currentUser()
```

`assignee` is the field, `=` is the operator, and `currentUser()` is a JQL function.

At this point of time, JQL doesn't support comparison of two fields or two functions in a single query. But we can use logical operators and keywords to introduce more control as follows:

```
project = "TEST" AND assignee = currentUser()
```

This query will display issues that are in the project `TEST` and that have the current user as the `assignee`. A more detailed explanation on Advanced Searching, along with the full reference to the Keywords, Operators, Fields, and Functions used can be found at `http://confluence.atlassian.com/display/JIRA/Advanced+Searching`.

Writing a JQL function

As we have seen, a **JQL function** allows us to define custom expressions or searchers. JIRA has a set of built-in JQL functions, the details of which can be found at `http://confluence.atlassian.com/display/JIRA/Advanced+Searching#AdvancedSearching-FunctionsReference`. In this recipe, we will look at writing a new JQL function.

JQL functions provide a way for values within a JQL query to be calculated at runtime. It takes optional arguments and produces results based on the arguments at runtime.

In our example, let us consider creating a function `projects()`, which can take a list of project keys and return all issues in the supplied projects. For example,

```
project in projects("TEST", "DEMO")
```

It will be equivalent to:

```
project in ("TEST","DEMO") and also to project = "TEST" OR project = "DEMO"
```

We are introducing this new function just for the sake of this recipe.

Getting ready

Create a skeleton plugin using the Atlassian plugin SDK.

How to do it...

JIRA uses the **JQL Function Module** to add new JQL functions to the Advanced Search. The following is the step-by-step process for our example:

1. Modify the plugin descriptor to include the JQL function module:

    ```xml
    <jql-function key="jql-projects" name="Projects Function"
    class="com.jtricks.ProjectsFunction">
      <!--The name of the function-->
      <fname>projects</fname>

      <!--Whether this function returns a list or a single value-->
      <list>true</list>
    </jql-function>
    ```

    As with any other plugin modules, a JQL function module also has a unique **key**. The other major attribute of the function module is the function **class**. In this example, `ProjectsFunction` is the function class. The root element, `jql-function`, has two other elements—fname and `list`:

    - ❑ `fname` holds the JQL function name that is visible to the user. This will be used in the JQL query.

    - ❑ `list` indicates whether the function returns a list or not. In our example, we return a list of projects, and hence we use the value `true` to indicate that it is a list. A list can be used along with operators IN and NOT IN, whereas a scalar can be used with operators =, !=, <, >, <=, >=, IS, and IS NOT.

2. Implement the function class:

The class name here is the name used in the module description, `ProjectsFunction` in this case. The class should extend the `AbstractJqlFunction` class. We now need to implement the major methods detailed next:

❑ `getDataType` – This method defines the return type of the function. In our example, we take a list of project keys and return valid projects, and hence we will implement the method to return the `PROJECT` datatype as follows:

```
public JiraDataType getDataType() {
  return JiraDataTypes.PROJECT;
}
```

Check out the `JiraDataTypes` class to see other supported data types.

❑ `getMinimumNumberOfExpectedArguments` – It returns the smallest number of arguments that the function may accept. The auto-population of the method in the issue navigator takes this into consideration and puts sufficient double quotes within brackets when the function is selected.

For example, in our case, we need at least one project key in the function name and hence we `return 1` as follows:

```
public int getMinimumNumberOfExpectedArguments() {
  return 1;
}
```

The pre-populated function will then look like `projects("")`.

❑ `validate` – This method is used to do validation of the arguments we have passed. In our example, we need to check if the method has at least one argument or not and make sure all the arguments passed are valid project keys. The validate method looks like the following:

```
public MessageSet validate(User searcher, FunctionOperand
operand, TerminalClauseterminalClause) {
  List<String> projectKeys = operand.getArgs();
  MessageSet messages = new MessageSetImpl();
  if (projectKeys.isEmpty()) {
    messages.addErrorMessage("Atleast one project key
needed");
  } else {
    for (String projectKey : projectKeys) {
      if (projectManager.getProjectObjByKey(projectKey) ==
null){
        messages.addErrorMessage("Invalid Project Key:" +
projectKey);
      }
    }
  }
  return messages;
}
```

Here we instantiate a new `MessageSet` and add error messages to it, if the validation fails. We must always return a `MessageSet`, even if it is empty. Returning `null` is not permitted. We can also add warning messages which doesn't prevent the JQL execution, but warns the user about something.

The most important argument in the `validate` method is `FunctionOperand`, as it holds the arguments of the function which can be retrieved as `operand. getArgs()`. The other argument `terminalClause` is JIRA's representation of the JQL condition we are validating for. We can extract the name, operator, and function from the argument using `terminalClause.getName`, `terminalClause. getOperator`, and `terminalClause.getOperand` respectively.

The `AbstractJqlFunction` has a validation method in it to check the number of arguments. So if we know the expected number of arguments (which is not the case in our example as we can have any number of projects passed in the example), we can validate it using:

```
MessageSet messages = validateNumberOfArgs(operand, 1);
```

This code adds an error if the number of arguments is not 1.

- ❑ `getValues` – This is the method that takes the arguments and returns the date type as a list or scalar depending on the function. In our example, the `getValues` method returns a list of literals that has the project ID.

  The method is implemented as follows in our example:

  ```
  public List<QueryLiteral> getValues(QueryCreationContext
  context, FunctionOperand operand,
  TerminalClauseterminalClause) {
     notNull("queryCreationContext", context);
     List<QueryLiteral> literals = new
  LinkedList<QueryLiteral>();
     List<String> projectKeys = operand.getArgs();
     for (String projectKey : projectKeys) {
        Project project = projectManager.
  getProjectObjByKey(projectKey);
        if (project != null) {
           literals.add(new QueryLiteral(operand, project.
  getId())));
        }
     }
     return literals;
  }
  ```

  `notnull()` is a predefined method from the `Asserions` class that checks whether the query creation context is null or not and throws an error if null. This is not mandatory and can be handled in some other way if needed.

The arguments `operand` and `terminalClause` are the same as what we have seen in the validate method. The `QueryCreationContext` argument holds the context in which the query is executed. `QueryCreationContext.getUser` will retrieve the user who executed the query, and the `QueryCreationContext.isSecurityOverriden` method indicates whether or not this function should actually perform security checks.

The function should always return a list of `QueryLiteral` objects. Even when the function returns a scalar instead of list, it should return a list of `QueryLiteral`, which can be created like the following:

```
Collections.singletonList(new QueryLiteral(operand, some_value))
```

A `QueryLiteral` represents either a `String`, `Long`, or `EMPTY` value. These three represent JQL's distinguishable types. Construct it with no value and it will represent EMPTY, construct it with a String and it represents a String, or construct it with a Long and it represents a Long.

In our example, we use the project ID (LONG) which is unique across projects. For projects, we can even use the key (STRING) or name (STRING), as they are also unique. However, it may not work with fields such as Fix For Version as you might find two Fix Versions with the same name. It is recommended to return the ID wherever possible to avoid such unambiguous search results.

To summarize, we find out the project objects using the project keys supplied by the user and return a list of `QueryLiterals`, created using the project IDs.

3. Package the plugin and deploy it.

How it works...

Once the plugin is deployed, we can go to the Issue Navigator and open the advanced search to start using our brand new function! When you start typing **project in p**, JIRA auto-populates the available options including our new function, as shown:

Issue Navigator

Query: ✓ line: 1 character: 13   Query syntax ⓘ

project in p|

P1 (PONE)

projects("")   Turn off auto-complete

Once the function with appropriate arguments is added, the search is executed and results are shown as follows:

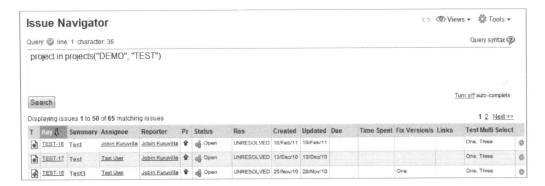

When an invalid project key is given as the argument, our `validate` method populates the error message, as shown in the following screenshot:

See also

▶ _Creating a skeleton plugin_ in _Chapter 1, Plugin Development Process_

▶ _Deploying your plugin_

Sanitizing JQL functions

If you don't want to make your JQL function violate the strict security aspects of your JIRA instance, sanitizing the JQL functions is a must! So, what does this actually mean?

Imagine a filter created by you to find out issues in a pre-defined set of projects. What will happen if you share the filter with a friend of yours who is not supposed to see the project or know that the project existed? The person with whom you shared it won't be able to modify the issues in the protected project due to JIRA's permission schemes but he/she will surely see the name of the project in the JQL query that is used in the filter!

This is where sanitizing of the JQL function will help. In essence, we just modify the JQL query to protect the arguments in line with the permission schemes. Let us see an example of doing that by sanitizing the JQL function we created in the previous recipe.

Getting ready

Develop the JQL function, as explained in the previous recipe.

How to do it...

In our JQL function, we use the project keys as the arguments. To explain the Function Sanitization, we will look to replace the keys with project IDs whenever the user doesn't have the permission to browse a project. The following is the step-by-step process showing you how to do it:

1. Modify the JQL function class to implement the `ClauseSanitisingJqlFunction` interface:

```
public class ProjectsFunction extends AbstractJqlFunction
implements ClauseSanitisingJqlFunction{
```

2. Implement the `sanitiseOperand` method:

```
@NotNull FunctionOperand santiseOperand(User searcher, @
NotNullFunctionOperand operand);
```

Here we read all the existing arguments of the JQL function, from the `FunctionOperand` argument, and modify it to include project IDs instead of keys, wherever the user doesn't have Browse permissions:

```
public FunctionOperand sanitiseOperand(User user, FunctionOperand
functionOperand) {
  final List<String> pKeys = functionOperand.getArgs();
  boolean argChanged = false;
  final List<String> newArgs = new ArrayList<String>(pKeys.
size());
  for (final String pKey : pKeys) {
    Project project = projectManager.getProjectObjByKey(pKey);
    if (project != null && !permissionManager.
hasPermission(Permissions.BROWSE, project, user)) {
      newArgs.add(project.getId().toString());
      argChanged = true;
    } else {
      newArgs.add(pKey);
    }
  }

  if (argChanged) {
```

```
            return new FunctionOperand(functionOperand.getName(),
         newArgs);
            } else {
            return functionOperand;
            }
         }
```

3. Package and deploy the modified plugin.

How it works...

Once the plugin is deployed, if a user doesn't have the permission to browse a project, he/she will see the project ID instead of the key that was originally entered when the filter was created. Following is a sample screenshot of how the query will look in that case. In this case, I just removed myself from the Browse permission of the TEST project, and you can see that the query is modified to replace the key TEST with its unique ID, which doesn't reveal much information!

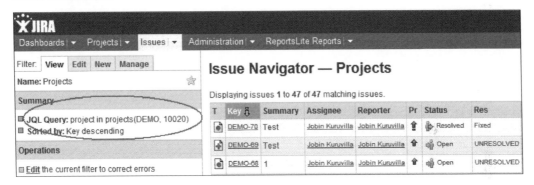

What if you try to edit the filter now? Our validation will now kick in as it is not able to find a project with the ID, as shown next! Nice, eh?

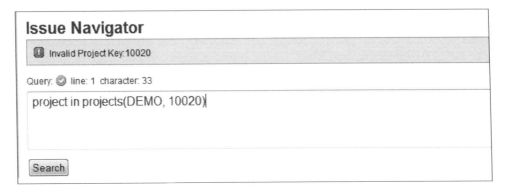

This is only an example, and we can sanitize the query in a similar way in every other case.

See also

▶ *Writing a JQL function*

Adding a search request view

One of the customizable features in JIRA is its **Issue Navigator**. It lets us search based on numerous criteria, choose the fields that need to be shown, in a way we want to see them!

The normal or the default view in the issue navigator is the tabular view to display the issues and the fields we have chosen by configuring the issue navigator. JIRA also gives us a few other options to see the search results in different formats, to export them into Excel, Word, or XML, and so on with the help of the pre-defined search request views.

In this recipe, we will see how we can add more search views in to JIRA that enables us to see the search results in a format we like. To achieve this we need to use the **Search Request View Plugin** module.

Getting ready

Create a plugin skeleton using Atlassian Plugin SDK.

How to do it...

As mentioned before, we use the Search Request View Plugin module to create custom search views. In our example, let us create a simple HTML view that just displays the issue key and summary.

The following is the step-by-step process:

1. Define the plugin descriptor with the search request view module:

```
<search-request-view key="simple-searchrequest-html" name="Simple
HTML View" class="com.jtricks.SimpleSearchRequestHTMLView" st
ate='enabled'                          fileExtension="html"
contentType="text/html">
  <resource type="velocity" name="header" location="templates/
searchrequest-html-header.vm"/>
  <resource type="velocity" name="body" location="templates/
searchrequest-html-body.vm"/>
  <resource type="velocity" name="footer" location="templates/
searchrequest-html-footer.vm"/>

  <order>200</order>
</search-request-view>
```

As usual, the module has a unique key. Following are the other attributes:

❑ `name`: The name that will appear in the Issue Navigator for the View

❑ `class`: The search request view class. This is where we populate the velocity contexts with the necessary information

❑ `contentType`: The `contentType` of the file that is generated. `text/html`, `text/xml`, `application/rss+xml`, `application/vnd.ms-word`, `application/vnd.ms-excel`, and so on

❑ `fileExtension`: The extension of the file generated. `html`, `xml`, `xml`, `doc`, `xls`, and so on

❑ `state`: Enabled or disabled. Determines whether the module is enabled at startup

The Search-Request-View element also has few child elements to define the velocity templates required for the various views and to determine the `order` in which the views will appear. Modules with lower `order` values are shown first. JIRA uses an order of 10 for the built-in views. A lower value will put the new view above the built-in views and a higher value will put the new view at the bottom.

2. Implement the Search Request View class.

The Search Request View class must implement the `SearchRequestView` interface. To make things easier, we can extend the `AbstractSearchRequestView` class that already implements this interface. When we do that, we have one method, `writeSearchResults`, to be implemented!

This method takes a writer argument using which we can generate the output using the various template views we define. For example:

```
writer.write(descriptor.getHtml("header", headerParams));
```

It will identify the velocity template with the view named as `header` and will use the variables on the map – `headerParams` to render the template. We can similarly define as many templates as we want and write them to create the view that we need.

In our example, we have three views defined – header, body, and footer. These views can be named in any way we want, but the same names that we define in the `atlassian-plugin.xml` should be used in the Search Request View class.

In our class implementation, we use the three views to generate the simple HTML view. We use the header and footer views in the beginning and end and will use the body view to generate the issue view for each individual issue in search results. The following is how we do it:

❑ Generate a map with the default velocity context parameters:

```
final Map defaultParams = JiraVelocityUtils.getDefaultVeloci
tyParams(authenticationContext);
```

❑ Populate the map with the variables that we need in the context to render the header template and write the header. In our example, let us keep the header fairly simple and just use the filter name and the current user:

```
final Map headerParams = new HashMap(defaultParams);
headerParams.put("filtername", searchRequest.getName());
headerParams.put("user", authenticationContext.getUser());
writer.write(descriptor.getHtml("header", headerParams));
```

❑ Now we need to write the search results. We should iterate over each issue in the search results and write it to the writer using the format we defined. To ensure that this doesn't result in huge memory consumption, only one issue should be loaded into memory at a time. This can be guaranteed by using a **Hitcollector**. This collector is responsible for writing out each issue as it is encountered in the search results. It will be called for each search result by the underlying Lucene search code:

```
final Searcher searcher = searchProviderFactory.getSearcher(
SearchProviderFactory.ISSUE_INDEX);
final Map issueParams = new HashMap(defaultParams);
final DocumentHitCollectorhitCollector = new IssueWriterHitC
ollector(searcher, writer, issueFactory){
  protected void writeIssue(Issue issue, Writer writer)
throws IOException{
    //put the current issue into the velocity context and
render the //single issue view
    issueParams.put("issue", issue  writer.write(descriptor.
getHtml("body", issueParams));
  }
};
searchProvider.searchAndSort(searchRequest.getQuery(), user,
hitCollector, searchRequestParams.getPagerFilter());
```

All we do here is define the `HitCollector` and invoke the `searchAndSort` method, which will then use the `HitCollector` to generate the view for each issue. Here we can add more variables if we need them in the view.

❑ We can now write the footer before we finish. Let us again put the user just for educational purpose:

```
writer.write(descriptor.getHtml("footer", EasyMap.
build("user", user)));
```

Here we created a simple map just to show that we need only the variables we use in the view.

The method will now look as follows:

```
@Override
public void writeSearchResults(final SearchRequestsearchRequest,
final SearchRequestParams searchRequestParams, final Writer
```

```
writer) throws SearchException{
  final Map defaultParams = JiraVelocityUtils.getDefaultVelocityPa
rams(authenticationContext);
  final Map headerParams = newHashMap(defaultParams);
headerParams.put("filtername", searchRequest.getName());
headerParams.put("user", authenticationContext.getUser());
  try{
    //Header
    writer.write(descriptor.getHtml("header", headerParams));

    //Body
    final Searcher searcher =searchProviderFactory.getSearcher(Sea
rchProviderFactory.ISSUE_INDEX);
    final Map issueParams = new HashMap(defaultParams);
    final DocumentHitCollector hitCollector = new IssueWriterHitCo
llector(searcher, writer, issueFactory) {
      protected void writeIssue(Issue issue, Writer writer) throws
IOException{
        //put the current issue into the velocity context and
render the single issue view
        issueParams.put("issue", issue);      writer.
write(descriptor.getHtml("body", issueParams));
      }
    };
    searchProvider.searchAndSort(searchRequest.getQuery(),
authenticationContext.getUser(),hitCollector, searchRequestParams.
getPagerFilter());

    //Footer
    writer.write(descriptor.getHtml("footer", EasyMap.
build("user", authenticationContext.getUser())));
  }catch (IOException e){
    throw new RuntimeException(e);
  }catch (SearchException e){
    throw new RuntimeException(e);
  }
}
```

3. Write the velocity templates. As we saw, we are using three views:

    ❏ **Header** – The velocity template is `templates/searchrequest-html-header.vm`. The following is how it looks:

    ```
    Hello $user.fullName , have a look at the search
    results!<br><br>
    #set($displayName = 'Anonymous')
    #if($filtername)
      #set($displayName = $textutils.htmlEncode($filtername))
    #end
    <b>Filter</b> : $displayName<br><br>
    <table>
    ```

We just greet the user and display the filter name here. It also has a `<table>` tag which is used at the beginning of the issue table. The table will be closed in the footer.

❏ **Body** – The velocity template is `templates/searchrequest-html-body.vm`. The following is how it looks:

```
<tr>
  <td><font color="green">$!issue.key</font></td>
  <td>$!issue.summary</td>
</tr>
```

Whatever appears here is common to all the issues. Here we create a table row for each issue and display the key and summary appropriately.

❏ **Footer** – The velocity template is `templates/searchrequest-html-footer.vm`. The following code shows how it looks:

```
</table>
<br><br>...And that's all we have got now , $user.fullName !
```

We just close the table and wind up with a message!

4. Package the plugin and deploy it.

How it works...

Once the plugin is deployed, we will find a new view in the issue navigator named **Simple HTML View**:

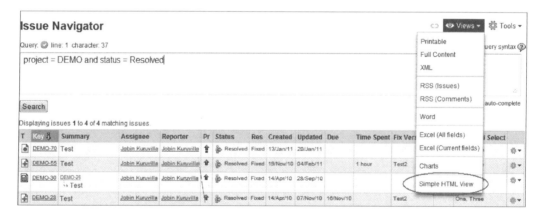

On selecting the view, the current search results will appear as follows:

> Hello Jobin Kuruvilla , Have a look at the search results!
>
> **Filter** : Anonymous
>
> DEMO-70 Test
> DEMO-55 Test
> DEMO-30 Test
> DEMO-28 Test
>
>
> ...And that's all we have got now , Jobin Kuruvilla !

If the results belong to a filter, it will display the filter name instead of Anonymous:

> Hello Jobin Kuruvilla , Have a look at the search results!
>
> **Filter** : All Resolved Issues in DEMO Project
>
> DEMO-70 Test
> DEMO-55 Test
> DEMO-30 Test
> DEMO-28 Test
>
>
> ...And that's all we have got now , Jobin Kuruvilla !

It is now left to our creativity to make it more beautiful or use an entirely different content type instead of HTML. An example of how an XML view is generated can be found in the JIRA documentation at `https://developer.atlassian.com/display/JIRADEV/Search+Request+View+Plugin+Module`.

See also

▶ *Creating a skeleton plugin* in Chapter 1, *Plugin Development Process*

▶ *Deploying your plugin*

Smart querying using quick search

The name says it all! JIRA allows smart querying using its Quick Search functionality and it enables the users to find critical information with ease. There is a pre-defined set of search keywords that JIRA recognizes and we can use them to search smart and fast!

In this recipe, we will look at how we can do smart querying on some of the JIRA fields.

How to do it...

Before we start, the **Quick Search** box is located at the right-hand top corner of JIRA, as shown:

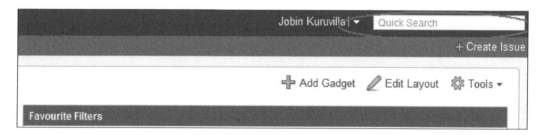

The following is how we can search on some of the fields as of JIRA 4.4. Don't forget to check how many of them are supported in your version of JIRA!

▶ **Issue key**: If you already know the issue key that you want to see, it doesn't get any better! Just type the issue key in the **Quick Search** box and JIRA will take you to the view issue page.

And there's more! If you are browsing a project or viewing an issue and if you want to see another issue for which the key is known, all you need to type is the number in the unique key (just the numerical part). There isn't even a need to type in the full key.

For example, **TEST-123** will take you to that issue directly. Typing **125** will then take you to **TEST-125**!

▶ **Project**: If you type in the project key, the quick search will show you all the issues in that particular project. The project name can also be used as long as there are no spaces in it.

For example, **TEST** will return all issues in the project TEST or a project with the key **TEST**. 'TEST Project' will not display issues in the project with the name 'Test Project', as the quick search interprets it as two different keywords.

▶ **Assignee**: The keyword **my** can be used to find all issues assigned to me.

▶ **Reporter**: The keyword **r:** is followed by **me**, or the *reporter name* can find all issues reported by me or the user respectively For example, **r:none** is also supported and it returns issues without any reporter.

r:me will retrieve all issues reported by me, whereas **r:admin** will retrieve all issues reported by the user – admin.

▶ **Date fields**: Quick Search can be done based on the three major date fields on the issue – **created**, **updated**, and **due date**. The keywords used are **created**, **updated**, and **due** respectively. The keyword should be followed by **:** and the date range without any spaces.

The date range can use one of the following keywords – **today, tomorrow, yesterday**, or a single date range (for example,. '-5d') or two date ranges (for example,. '-2w,1w'). The date ranges cannot have spaces in them. Valid date/time abbreviations are: 'w' (week), 'd' (day), 'h' (hour), and 'm' (minute). For example:

- ❑ **created:today** will retrieve all issues created on the date.
- ❑ **updated:-5d** will retrieve all issues updated in the last five days.
- ❑ **due:-2w,1w** will retrieve all issues due in the last two weeks and in the next week.

You can also use the keyword **overdue** to retrieve all issues that are overdue (has a past due date).

▶ **Priority**: The quick search can be done using the priority values **blocker, critical, major, minor**, and **trivial**. Just typing the value will retrieve all the issues that have the given priority value.

For example, all issues with the priority **major** can be retrieved by searching with **major**.

▶ **IssueType**: Issue type names can be used in the Quick search as long as it doesn't have any spaces in it. Even plurals will work.

For example, typing **bug** or **bugs** will retrieve all the issues with the issue type of bug.

▶ **Versions**: Quick Search can find issues with known Affected Versions or Fix for versions using the keywords **v:** or **ff:** followed by the value without any space. There shouldn't be any spaces between **v:** and the version name. It can also use wild card search. The search will also find all issues with version values that contain the string you specify, followed immediately by a space. For example:

❑ **v:2.0** will find issues in versions – 2.0, 2.0 one, 2.0 beta, and so on. But it wouldn't find issues in version 2.0.1

❑ **v:2.*** will find issues in versions – 2.0, 2.0 one, 2.0.1, 2.2, and so on.

The same applies to fixes for versions. The prefix only changes to ff:

▶ **Components**: Quick search can find issues with component names using the prefix **c:** followed by the component name. It will retrieve all issues where the component has the value somewhere in its name, not necessarily starting with it.

For example, **c:jql** will find all issues in components that have the word 'jql' in it. It will work for the components jql, jql performance, advanced jql, and so on.

There's more...

Quick Search can also be used to search for any word within the issue(s) you are looking for, provided the word is in the summary, description, or comments of the issue. It is called **Smart Search**.

If you think you want to use any of these keywords without using Smart search, the query can be run without smart search when the results are displayed.

Smart Querying can have multiple keywords combined to narrow down the search. It can even be combined with Free Text Search.

For example, **my open bugs** will retrieve all bugs that are opened and assigned to me. It is equivalent to the JQL:

```
issuetype = Bug AND assignee = currentUser() AND status = Open
```

my open bugs jql will retrieve all bugs that are opened and assigned to me and has the word 'jql' in its summary, description, or comments. It is equivalent to:

```
(summary ~ jql OR description ~ jql OR comment ~ jql) AND issuetype =
Bug AND assignee = currentUser() AND status = Open
```

my open bugs jql performance is equivalent to:

```
(summary ~ "jql performance" OR description ~ "jql performance"
OR comment ~ "jql performance") AND issuetype = Bug AND assignee =
currentUser() AND status = Open.
```

More on advanced searching or JQL can be found at `http://confluence.atlassian.com/display/JIRA/Advanced+Searching`.

Searching in plugins

With the invention of JQL, JIRA Search APIs have changed drastically from 3.x versions. Searching in plugins is now done using APIs supporting JQL. In this recipe, we will see how to search for issues within our plugins using those APIs.

How to do it...

For the sake of concentrating on the search APIs, we will look at writing a simple method, `getIssues()`, that returns a list of issue objects based on some search criteria.

The essence of searching is to build a `Query` object using `JqlQueryBuilder`. A `Query` object will have a `where` clause and an `order by` clause, which are built using the `JqlClauseBuilder`. We can also incorporate conditions in between clauses using `ConditionBuilders`.

For now, let us assume we want to find all the issues in a particular project (project ID: 10000, Key: DEMO) and assigned to the current user within our plugin. The JQL equivalent for this is:

```
project = "DEMO" and assignee = currentUser()
```

The following are the steps to do this programmatically:

1. Create a JqlQueryBuilder (`http://docs.atlassian.com/software/jira/docs/api/latest/com/atlassian/jira/jql/builder/JqlQueryBuilder.html`) object.

    `JqlQueryBuilder` is used to build the query that is used to perform issue searching. The following is how a `JqlQueryObject` is created:

    ```
    JqlQueryBuilder builder = JqlQueryBuilder.newBuilder();
    ```

2. Create a `where` clause that returns a JqlClauseBuilder (`http://docs.atlassian.com/software/jira/docs/api/latest/com/atlassian/jira/jql/builder/JqlClauseBuilder.html`). A query is constructed with one or more JQL clauses with different conditions added in between.

    `builder.where()` returns a `JqlClauseBuilder` object for our `QueryBuilder` on which we can then add multiple clauses.

3. Add the project clause to search for a project with its ID as argument. The project clause will return a `ConditionBuilder`:

    ```
    builder.where().project(10000L)
    ```

4. Add the `assignee` clause using the `AND` condition on the `ConditionBuilder`:

```
builder.where().project(10000L).and().assigneeIsCurrentUser();
```

We can have numerous clauses added like this using the different conditions. Let us see some examples in the 'There's More...' section.

5. Add ordering, if you have any, using the `Order By` clause. We can sort based on assignee as follows:

```
builder.orderBy().assignee(SortOrder.ASC);
```

`SortOrder.DESC` can be used for descending orders.

6. Build the `Query` (`com.atlassian.query.Query`) object:

```
Query query = builder.buildQuery();
```

The `Query` object is immutable; once it is created it cannot be changed. The `JqlQueryBuilder` represents the mutable version of a `Query` object. We can create a Query from an already existing Query by calling `JqlQueryBuilder.newBuilder(existingQuery)`.

7. Get an instance of the `SearchService`. It could be injected in the constructor of your plugin using dependency injection or can be retrieved from the `ComponentManager` class as follows:

```
SearchService searchService = ComponentManager.getInstance().
getSearchService();
```

8. Search using the query to retrieve the SearchResults (`http://docs.atlassian.com/jira/latest/com/atlassian/jira/issue/search/SearchResults.html`):

```
SearchResults results = searchService.search(user, query,
PagerFilter.getUnlimitedFilter());
```

Here we used `PagerFilter.getUnlimitedFilter()` to retrieve all the results. It is possible to limit the results to a particular range, say from 20 to 80 results, using the method `PagerFilter.newPageAlignedFilter(index, max)`. This will be useful when Pagination is done, such as in the case of issue navigator.

9. Retrieve the issues from the search results:

```
List<Issue> issues = results.getIssues();
```

The entire method will look as follows:

```
private List<Issue>getIssues(User user) {
    JqlQueryBuilder builder = JqlQueryBuilder.newBuilder();
    builder.where().project(10000L).and().assigneeIsCurrentUser();
    builder.orderBy().assignee(SortOrder.ASC);
```

```
Query query = builder.buildQuery();
    SearchService searchService = ComponentManager.getInstance().
getSearchService();
    SearchResults results = searchService.search(user, query,
PagerFilter.getUnlimitedFilter());
    returnresults.getIssues();
}
```

Hopefully, that is a good starting point from which to write more complex queries!

<h2>There's more...</h2>

As promised earlier, let us look at writing complex queries with a couple of examples.

- ▶ We can extend the aforementioned search to include multiple projects, assignees, and a custom field. The JQL representation of the query will be:

  ```
  project in ("TEST", "DEMO") and assignee in ("jobinkk", "admin")
  and "Customer Name" = "Jobin"
  ```

  The where clause is written as:

  ```
  builder.where().project("TEST", "DEMO").and().assignee().
  in("jobinkk", "admin").and().customField(10000L).eq("Jobin");
  ```

  10000L is the ID of the custom field Customer Name.

- ▶ We can group the conditions using sub() and endsub() to write even more complex queries:

  ```
  project in ("TEST", "DEMO") and (assignee is EMPTY or reporter is
  EMPTY)
  ```

  It can be written as:

  ```
  builder.where().project("TEST", "DEMO").and().sub().
  assigneeIsEmpty().or().reporterIsEmpty().endsub();
  ```

Similarly, we can write more complex queries.

<h2>See also</h2>

- ▶ *Writing a JQL funcion*

Parsing a JQL query in plugins

In the previous recipe, we saw how to build a Query to search within JIRA. In this recipe, we will see searching again, but without building a Query using the APIs. We will use the JQL Query as it is written in the Issue Navigator in advanced mode and search using the same.

How to do it...

Suppose we know the query that we want to execute. Let us assume it is the same we saw in the previous recipe: `project = "DEMO" and assignee = currentUser()`.

The following is how we do it:

1. Parse the JQL query:

    ```
    String jqlQuery = "project = \"DEMO\" and assignee =
    currentUser()";
    SearchService.ParseResult parseResult = searchService.
    parseQuery(user, jqlQuery);
    ```

2. Check if the parsed result is valid or not:

    ```
    if (parseResult.isValid()){
       // Carry On
    } else {
       // Log the error and exit!
    }
    ```

3. If the result is valid, get the `Query` object from the `ParseResult`:

    ```
    Query query = parseResult.getQuery()
    ```

4. Search for the issues and retrieve the `SearchResults`, as we have seen in the previous recipe:

    ```
    SearchResults results = searchService.search(user, query,
    PagerFilter.getUnlimitedFilter());
    ```

5. Retrieve the list of issues from the search results:

    ```
    List<Issue> issues = results.getIssues();
    ```

How it works...

Here the `parseQuery` operation in `SearchService` converts the `String` JQL query in to the `Query` object we normally construct using `JqlQueryBuilder`. The actual parse operation is done by `JqlQueryParser` behind the scenes.

See also

▶ *Searching in plugins*

Linking directly to search queries

Haven't you wondered how we can link to a query from a template or JSP from a custom page or plugin page? In this recipe, we will see how we can create a link programmatically and otherwise to use in various places.

How to do it...

Let us first look at creating a search link programmatically. Perform the following steps:

1. Create the `Query` object using `JqlQueryBuilder`, as we have seen in the previous recipe.

2. Get an instance of the `SearchService`. It could be injected in the constructor of your plugin using dependency injection or can be retrieved from the `ComponentManager` class as follows:

   ```
   SearchService searchService = ComponentManager.getInstance().
   getSearchService();
   ```

3. Retrieve the query string from the `Query` object using `SearchService`, as shown:

   ```
   String queryString = searchService.getQueryString(user, query);
   ```

4. Construct the link using the context path. In JSPs, you can do it as shown next:

   ```
   <a href="<%= request.getContextPath() %>/secure/IssueNavigator.
   jspa?reset=true<ww:property value="/queryString" />&amp;mode=hide"
   title="">Show in Navigator</a>
   ```

   Here, `getQueryString()` in the `Action` class returns the preceding `queryString`.

   And in velocity templates:

   ```
   <a href="$requestContext.baseUrl/secure/IssueNavigator.jspa?reset=
   true$queryString&amp;mode=hide" title="">Show in Navigator</a>
   ```

   Here, `$queryString` is the preceding `queryString` in context!

   The `mode` parameter can have the values `hide` or `show` depending on whether you want to open the issue navigator in view or edit mode!

How it works...

The `getQueryString` method in `SearchService` returns the `queryString` in a manner in which it can be used in a URL. It starts with `&jqlQuery=`, followed by the actual query as a web URL:

```
reset=true<ww:property value="/queryString" />&amp;mode=hide will be
then reset=true&amp;jqlQuery=someQuery&amp;mode=hide
```

There's more...

Linking to a Quick Search is also pretty easy and useful. We can even store such searches in our browser favorites. All we need to do is find out the URL by replacing `%s` in JIRA's URL as follows:

```
http://<Context_Path>/secure/QuickSearch.jspa?searchString=%s
```

For example, if your JIRA instance is `http://localhost:8080/` and you want to Quick Search for all the issues where you are the assignee, the relevant quick search string will be: **my open**.

And the URL will then be:

```
http://localhost:8080/secure/QuickSearch.jspa?searchString=my+open
```

Please note that the spaces in Quick Search are replaced by + while substituting `%s`.

Other examples:

▶ `http://localhost:8080/secure/QuickSearch.jspa?searchString=my+open+critical` retrieves all open critical issues assigned to you

▶ `http://localhost:8080/secure/QuickSearch.jspa?searchString=created:-1w+my` retrieves all the issues assigned to you, created in the past week

Index and de-index programmatically

As we have seen in the JIRA architecture explained in *Chapter 2, Understanding Plugin Framework*, searching in JIRA is based on Apache Lucene. The Lucene indexes are stored in the File System and are used as the basis for the search queries executed in JIRA. Whenever an issue is updated, more records are created or existing records are updated for that particular issue in the filesystem.

It is possible to programmatically index selected or all issues or de-index an issue. Also, we can switch OFF or ON indexing selectively in our plugins if needed. In this recipe, we will see both of these.

How to do it...

Most of the indexing operations can be done with the help of `IssueIndexManager`. An instance of `IssueIndexManager` can be created either by injecting in the constructor or as follows:

```
IssueIndexManager indexManager = ComponentManager.getInstance().
getIndexManager();
```

The following are the important operations supported by `IssueIndexManager`:

- ▶ `reIndexAll()` – Indexes all the issues in JIRA. A good method if you want a custom admin operation to do indexing as well!

- ▶ `reIndex(GenericValue issue)` or `reIndex(Issue issue)` – To selectively index an issue by passing the `Issue` object or its `GenericValue`.

- ▶ `deIndex(GenericValue issue)` – Method to de-index an issue. Once this is done, the issue won't appear in the search results.

  Be aware that when the issue is later updated or a comment is added on the issue, JIRA automatically indexes again. So don't rely on calling this just once to permanently hide your issue from searches. To do so, the `IssueIndexer` should be overridden so that it won't index the issue again.

- ▶ `reIndexIssues(final Collection<GenericValue> issues)` or `reIndexIssueObjects(final Collection<? extends Issue>issueObjects)` – Indexes a Collection of issues.

Checkout the Java Docs at `http://docs.atlassian.com/software/jira/docs/api/latest/com/atlassian/jira/issue/index/IssueIndexManager.html` for more available methods on the `IssueIndexManager`.

If we want to make sure that indexing is turned ON when we make a major update on an issue, we can do the following:

```
// Store the current state of indexing
boolean wasIndexing = ImportUtils.isIndexIssues();
// Set indexing to true
ImportUtils.setIndexIssues(true);
// Update the issue or issues
.................
// Reset indexing
ImportUtils.setIndexIssues(wasIndexing);
```

Here we use `ImportUtils` to save the current indexing state and turn it ON. After the update to issue(s) is done, indexing is turned back to whatever it was!

See also

▶ *Searching in plugins*

Managing filters programmatically

Be it a beginner in JIRA or a pro, one of the features used often is creating and managing filters. The fact that we can save the searches, share them, and subscribe to it adds a lot of value to JIRA. So, how do we programmatically create and manage filters?

In this recipe, we will learn how to manage filters programmatically.

How to do it...

We will see the various aspects of managing the filters one-by-one:

Creating a filter

Most of the operations on managing filters are done using `SearchRequestService`. For creating a filter, following are the steps:

1. Create the Query to be saved as filter. The Query can be created using `JqlQueryBuilder`, as we have seen in the previous recipes.

2. Create a `SearchRequest` object from the Query

    ```
    SearchRequest searchRequest = new SearchRequest(query);
    ```

3. Create a JIRA Service Context. If you are in an action class, you can get the service context by calling `getJiraServiceContext()` and if not, an instance can be created as:

    ```
    JiraServiceContext ctx = new JiraServiceContextImpl(user);
    ```

    Where user is the user for which the filter should be created.

4. Get an instance of `SearchRequestService`. It can be either injected in the constructor or as follows:

    ```
    SearchRequestService searchRequestService = ComponentManager.
    getInstance().getSearchRequestService();
    ```

5. Create the filter:

    ```
    final SearchRequest newSearchRequest = searchRequestService.
    createFilter(ctx, searchRequest, favourite);
    ```

    Where `favourite` is a boolean which can be set to true, if you want the filter to be made a favorite.

Updating a filter

Updating a filter is much similar to creating a filter. Once the `SearchRequest` is updated and context is created, we need to invoke the following method to update and persist in the database the filter with the new search parameters, that is, the new query:

```
SearchRequest updatedSearchRequest = searchRequestService.updateSearch
Parameters(JiraServiceContextserviceCtx, SearchRequest request);
```

To update the attributes such as name, description, and so on, one of the following methods is invoked, depending on whether we want to make the filter favorite or not:

```
SearchRequest updatedFilter = searchRequestService.updateFilter(JiraSe
rviceContextserviceCtx, SearchRequest request);
```

Alternatively, we can use:

```
SearchRequest updatedFilter = searchRequestService.updateFilter(JiraSe
rviceContextserviceCtx, SearchRequest request, booleanisFavourite);
```

Deleting a filter

JIRA takes the filter ID as the input for deleting a filter. Before we actually delete the filter, we need to validate the deletion as follows:

```
searchRequestService.validateForDelete(ctx, filterId);
```

If there are any errors, it will be added into the Action's error collection. We can then check for the errors and delete the filter, if there are no errors.

```
if(!ctx.getErrorCollection().hasAnyErrors())){
  searchRequestService.deleteFilter(ctx, filterId);
}
```

We can also delete all the filters of a user using:

```
deleteAllFiltersForUser(JiraServiceContextserviceCtx, User user);
```

Retrieving filters

The `SearchRequestService` also has few methods to retrieve favorite filters, filters owned by a user, non-private filters, and so on. Key methods are listed as follows:

```
Collection<SearchRequest>getFavouriteFilters(User user);
Collection<SearchRequest>getOwnedFilters(User user);
Collection<SearchRequest>getNonPrivateFilters(User user);
Collection<SearchRequest>getFiltersFavouritedByOthers(User user);
```

The method names are self explanatory.

Sharing a filter

In order to share a filter, we need to retrieve the relevant filter and set the permissions on it using:

```
searchRequest.setPermissions(permissions);
```

Where permissions is a set of `SharePermission` objects. The `SharePermission` objects can be created from a JSONArray using the `SharePermissionUtils utility` class. The JSONObject can have three keys – `Type`, `Param1`, and `Param2`.

The `Type` can have the following values: `global`, `group`, or `project`.

- ▶ When `Type` is `global`, `Param1` and `Param2` are not required.
- ▶ When it is `group`, `Param1` is populated with the `groupname`.
- ▶ When it is `project`, `Param1` is the ID of the project and `Param2` is the ID of the project role

Example of JSON arrays is as follows:

```
[{"type":"global"}]
```

```
[{"type":"group","param1":"jira-administrators"},{"type":"project","param1":"10000","param2":"10010"}]
```

See also

- ▶ *Searching in plugins*

Subscribing to a filter

We have seen various methods of managing filters. While filters are a great way to save searches and access them quickly at a later point of time, filter subscriptions are even better! The subscriptions help us to see the issues of interest at regular intervals without even logging in to JIRA.

How do we subscribe to a filter programmatically? In this recipe, we will focus on subscribing to a filter in our plugins.

How to do it...

For the subscription of filters, JIRA provides a manager class implementing the `FilterSubscriptionService` interface. This class provides the important methods needed for managing filter subscriptions.

There are three important parameters for Filter Subscriptions:

1. **Cron Expression**: This is the most important part of a subscription. It tells us when the subscription has to run, or in other words, it defines the schedule of a subscription.

   Cron expressions consist of the following fields separated by spaces.

Field	Allowed Values	Allowed Special Characters
Second	0-59	, - * /
Minute	0-59	, - * /
Hour	0-23	, - * /
Day-of-Month	1-31	, - * / ? L W C
Month	1-12 Or JAN-DEC	, - * /
Day-of-week	1-7 Or SUN-SAT	, - * / ? L C #
Year (Optional)	1970-2099	, - * /

   The special characters denote the following:

Special Character	Usage
,	List of values. For example, 'MON,WED,FRI' means 'every Monday, Wednesday, and Friday'.
-	Range of Values. For example, 'MON-WED' means 'every Monday, Tuesday, Wednesday'.
*	All possible values. For example, * in the Hour field means 'every hour of the day'.
/	Increments to the give value. For example, 1/3 in Hour field means ' every 3 hours during the day, starting from 1.00 AM'.
?	No particular value. This is useful when you need to specify a value for only one of the two fields, Day-of-month or Day-of-week, but not the other.
L	Last possible value. It has different meanings based on the context. For example:

   - ▶ L in Day-of-week means 'Last day of every week'
   - ▶ 7L means 'last Saturday of the month'
   - ▶ L in Day-of-month means 'last day of the month'
   - ▶ LW means 'last weekday of the month'

Special Character	Usage
W	Weekday (MON-FRI) nearest to the given day of the month.
	For example, 1W means 'nearest working day to the 1st of the month' – useful when you want to get the first working day of the month!
	It cannot be used with a range of days.
#	N'th occurance of a given day of the week.
	For example, MON#3 means '3rd Monday of the month'

We need to create a valid Cron expression based on the subscription we want to set up. The following are some examples based on these rules:

❑ 0 7 30 * * ? – 7:30 AM Every Day

❑ 0 0/15 15 * * ? – Every 15 minutes starting at 3.00PM ending at 3:59 PM

You can find more examples in the Atlassian documentation for filter subscriptions at `http://confluence.atlassian.com/display/JIRA/Receiving+Search+R esults+via+Email`.

2. **Group Name**: This is the group that we want to subscribe the filter. If the value is null, it will be considered as a personal subscription and the user in the context will be used.

3. **Email On Empty**: It is a boolean value which is `true` if you want the subscription to send an e-mail, even when it has no results.

Now let us see the steps to subscribe to a known filter:

1. Get an instance of the `FilterSubscriptionService`. You can either inject the class in the constructor or get it using the `ComponentManger` class as follows:

```
FilterSubscriptionService filterSubscriptionService =
ComponentManager.getInstance().getComponentInstanceOfType(FilterSu
bscriptionService.class)
```

2. Define the cron expression based on the aforementioned rules:

```
String cronExpression = "0 0/15 * * * ? *"; // Denotes every 15
minutes
```

3. Define the group name. Use `null` if it is a personal subscription:

```
String groupName = "jira-administrators";
```

4. Create a JIRA Service Context. If you are in an action class, you can get the service context by calling `getJiraServiceContext()`, and if not, an instance can be created as:

```
JiraServiceContext ctx = new JiraServiceContextImpl(user);
```

Where `user` is the user for whom the filter is subscribed, in case it is a personal subscription.

5. Define whether an e-mail should be sent, even when the number of results is zero or not:

```
booleane mailOnEmpty = true;
```

6. Validate the cron expression:

```
filterSubscriptionService.validateCronExpression(ctx,
cronExpression);
```

If there are any errors, the Error Collection in `JiraServiceContext` will be populated with an error message.

7. If there are no errors, use the `FilterSubscriptionService` class to store the subscription:

```
if (!ctx.getErrorCollection().hasAnyErrors()){
    filterSubscriptionService.storeSubscription(ctx, filterId,
groupName, cronExpression, emailOnEmpty);
}
```

Here `filterId` is the ID of the filter we want to subscribe to and can be obtained as `searchRequest.getId()`!

The subscription should now be saved and the mails will be sent based on the schedule defined by the cron expression.

We can also update an existing subscription using `FilterSubscriptionService` using the following method:

```
filterSubscriptionService.updateSubscription(ctx, subId, groupName,
cronExpression, emailOnEmpty);
```

Where `subId` is the existing subscription ID!

How it works...

Each subscription we create is stored as **Quartz** scheduled jobs in the system, which runs based on the cron expression we have defined while storing the subscription.

There's more...

If you want to use a Web Form, like the one used in JIRA, to create filter subscriptions and you don't want to write the cron expression, you can create a `CronEditorBean` using the parameters from the Web Form.

The various attributes supported in the form can be found from the `CronEditorBean` class. The Java Docs can be found at `http://docs.atlassian.com/software/jira/docs/api/latest/com/atlassian/jira/web/component/cron/CronEditorBean.html`.

Once the `CronEditorBean` is created, it can be parsed into a cron expression as follows:

```
String cronExpression = new CronExpressionGenerator().getCronExpressio
nFromInput(cronEditorBean);
```

See also

▶ *Searching in plugins*

7
Programming Issues

In this chapter, we will cover:

- ▶ Creating an issue from your plugin
- ▶ Creating subtasks on an issue
- ▶ Updating an issue
- ▶ Deleting an issue
- ▶ Adding new issue operations
- ▶ Conditions on issue operations
- ▶ Working with attachments
- ▶ Time tracking and worklog management
- ▶ Working with comments on issues
- ▶ Programming Change Logs
- ▶ Programming Issue Links
- ▶ Validations on issue linking
- ▶ Discarding fields while cloning!
- ▶ JavaScript tricks on issue fields

Introduction

We have so far seen how to develop custom fields, workflows, Reports & Gadgets, JQL functions, and other pluggable things associated with them. In this chapter, we will learn about programming "issues", that is, creating, editing, or deleting issues, creating new issue operations, and managing the various other operations available on issues via JIRA APIs etc.

Creating an issue from a plugin

In this recipe, we will see how to create an issue from a plugin programmatically. Prior to version 4.1, JIRA used `IssueManager` to create an issue. From JIRA 4.1, there is this `IssueService` class that drives the issue operations. Since `IssueService` is recommended over `IssueManager`, we will use it in our recipes to create an issue.

How to do it...

The main advantage of `IssueService` over the `IssueManager` class is that it takes care of the validation and error handling. The following are the steps to create an issue using the `IssueService`:

1. Create an instance of the `IssueService` class. You can either inject it in the constructor or get it from the `ComponentManager`, as shown:

   ```
   IssueService issueService = ComponentManager.getInstance().
   getIssueService();
   ```

2. Create the issue input parameters. In this step, we will set all the values that are required to create the issue using the `IssueInputParameters` class.

   a. Create an instance of the `IssueInputParameters` class.

   ```
   IssueInputParameters issueInputParameters = new
   IssueInputParametersImpl();
   ```

   b. Populate the `IssueInputParameters` with the values required to create the issue as shown in the next few lines of code:

   ```
   issueInputParameters.setProjectId(10100L).
   setIssueTypeId("8").setSummary("Test Summary").
   setReporterId("jobinkk").setAssigneeId("jobinkk").
   setDescription("Test Description").setStatusId("10010").
   setPriorityId("2").setFixVersionIds(10000L, 12121L);
   ```

   c. Make sure all the required values like project, issue type, summary, and other mandatory values required when the issue is created using the user interface is set on the `IssueInputParameters`.

   d. Here, we have used test values, but make sure to replace them with appropriate values. For example, the project, issue type ID, priority ID, Fix version IDs, reporter, and assignee should have appropriate values.

3. Validate the input parameters using `IssueService`.

   ```
   CreateValidationResult createValidationResult = issueService.
   validateCreate(user, issueInputParameters);
   ```

Here, the `user` is the one creating the issue. The validation is done based on the user permissions and the `createValidationResult` variable will have errors if the validation fails due to permission issues or due to invalid input parameters!

4. If the `createValidationResult` is valid, create the issue using `IssueService`.

```
if (createValidationResult.isValid()) {
  IssueResult createResult = issueService.create(user,
createValidationResult);
}
```

Here, we use the `createValidationResult` object to create the issue, as it already has the processed input parameters. If the result is not valid, handle the errors as shown in the following code:

```
if (!createValidationResult.isValid()) {
  Collection<String> errorMessages = createValidationResult.
getErrorCollection().getErrorMessages();
  for (String errorMessage : errorMessages) {
    System.out.println(errorMessage);
  }
  Map<String, String> errors = createValidationResult.
getErrorCollection().getErrors();
  Set<String> errorKeys = errors.keySet();
  for (String errorKey : errorKeys) {
    System.out.println(errors.get(errorKey));
  }
}
```

Here, we just print the error to the console if the result is invalid. The `errorMessages` will have all non-field-specific errors like permission issue-related errors, and so on, but any field-specific errors, like input validation errors, will appear in the `errors` map where the key will be the field name. We should handle both the error types as appropriate.

5. After the creation of an issue, check if the `createResult` is valid or not. If not, handle it appropriately. The `createResult` object will have errors only if there is a severe problem with JIRA (for example, one can't communicate with the DB, the workflow has changed since you invoked validate, and so on).

```
if (!createResult.isValid()) {
  Collection<String> errorMessages = createResult.
getErrorCollection().getErrorMessages();
  for (String errorMessage : errorMessages) {
    System.out.println(errorMessage);
  }
}
```

Here again, we just print the error to the console.

6. If `createResult` is valid, then the issue is created successfully and you can retrieve it as:

```
MutableIssue issue = createResult.getIssue();
```

How it works...

By using `IssueService`, JIRA now validates the inputs we give using the rules we have set up in JIRA via the user interfaces, such as the mandatory fields, permission checks, individual field validations, and so on. Behind the scenes, it still uses the `IssueManager` class.

There's more...

As mentioned before, prior to JIRA 4.1, we need to use the `IssueManager` class to create the issues. It can still be used in JIRA 4.1+, but this is not recommended as it overrides all the validations. Here is how we do it, if it is required.

Using IssueManager to create the issue

Follow these steps:

1. Initialize an issue object using the `IssueFactory` class:

    ```
    MutableIssue issue = ComponentManager.getInstance().
    getIssueFactory().getIssue();
    ```

2. Set all the fields required on the issue object:

    ```
    issue.setProjectId(10100L);
    issue.setIssueTypeId("8");
    issue.setAssigneeId("jobinkk");
    ```

3. Create the issue using `IssueManager`:

    ```
    GenericValue createdIssue = ComponentManager.getInstance().
    getIssueManager().createIssue(user, issue);
    ```

4. Handle `CreateException` to capture any errors.

Creating subtasks on an issue

In this recipe, we will see how to create a subtask on an existing issue programmatically.

How to do it...

There are two steps in creating a subtask:

1. Create an issue object. A subtask is nothing but an issue object in the backend. The only difference is that it has a parent issue associated with it. So, when we create a subtask issue object, we will have to define the parent issue in addition to what we normally do while creating a normal issue.

2. Link the newly created subtask issue to the parent issue.

Let's see the steps in more detail:

1. Create the subtask issue object similar to how we created the issue in the previous recipe. Here, the `IssueInputParameters` is constructed (after changing the methods like `setIssueTypeId()` appropriately).

   For this issue, we will use the `validateSubTaskCreate` method instead of `validateCreate`, which takes an extra parameter `parentId`.

   ```
   CreateValidationResult createValidationResult = issueService.
   validateSubTaskCreate(user, parent.getId(), issueInputParameters);
   ```

   Here, parent is the issue object on which we are creating the subtask.

2. Create an issue after checking for errors, as we have seen before.

   ```
   if (createValidationResult.isValid()) {
      IssueResult createResult = issueService.create(user,
   createValidationResult);
      }
   ```

3. Create a link between the newly created subtask issue and the parent issue:

   a. Get an instance of `SubTaskManager`. You can either inject it in the constructor or get it from `ComponentManager`.

   ```
   SubTaskManager subTaskManager = ComponentManager.
   getInstance().getSubTaskManager();
   ```

   b. Create the subtask link.

   ```
   subTaskManager.createSubTaskIssueLink(parent,
   createResult.getIssue(), user);
   ```

4. The subtask should now be created with a link back to the original parent issue.

See also

▶ *Creating an Issue from your plugin*

Updating an issue

In this recipe, let's look at editing an existing issue.

How to do it...

Let's assume that we have an existing issue object. We will just modify the `Summary` to a new summary. Following are the steps to do the same:

1. Create the `IssueInputParameters` object with the input fields that need to be modified:

   ```
   IssueInputParameters issueInputParameters = new
   IssueInputParametersImpl();
   issueInputParameters.setSummary("Modified Summary");
   ```

   In JIRA 4.1.x version, there is a bug, because of which we need to populate `IssueInputParameters` with all the current fields on the issue along with the modified field to make sure the existing values are not lost in an update. However, it is resolved in JIRA 4.2+ and hence the previous code is enough to modify the summary alone.

   Still, if you do not want to retain the existing values and just want the summary on the issue to be updated, you can set the `retainExistingValuesWhenParameterNotProvided` flag as shown:

   ```
   issueInputParameters.setRetainExistingValuesWhenParameterNotPro
   vided(false);
   ```

2. Validate the input parameters using `IssueService`:

   ```
   UpdateValidationResult updateValidationResult = issueService.
   validateUpdate(user, issue.getId(), issueInputParameters);
   ```

   Here, the issue is the existing issue object.

3. If `updateValidationResult` is valid, update the issue:

   ```
   if (updateValidationResult.isValid()) {
       IssueResult updateResult = issueService.update(user,
   updateValidationResult);
   }
   ```

   If it is not valid, handle the errors as we did while creating the issue.

4. Validate the `updateResult` and handle the error if any. If it is not valid, the updated issue object can be retrieved as:

   ```
   MutableIssue updatedIssue = updateResult.getIssue();
   ```

Deleting an issue

In this recipe, let us look at deleting an issue programmatically.

How to do it...

Let us assume that we have an existing issue object. For deletion as well, we will use the `IssueService` class. Following are the steps to do it:

1. Validate the delete operation on the issue using `IssueService`

   ```
   DeleteValidationResult deleteValidationResult = issueService.
   validateDelete(user, issue.getId());
   ```

   Here, the issue is the existing issue object that needs to be deleted.

2. If `deleteValidationResult` is valid, invoke the delete operation:

   ```
   ErrorCollection deleteErrors = issueService.delete(user,
   deleteValidationResult);
   ```

3. If the `deleteValidationResult` is invalid, handle the errors appropriately.

4. Confirm whether the deletion was successful by checking `deleteErrors`
   ErrorCollection.

   ```
   if (deleteErrors.hasAnyErrors()){
     Collection<String> errorMessages = deleteErrors.
   getErrorMessages();
     for (String errorMessage : errorMessages) {
       System.out.println(errorMessage);
     }
   } else {
     System.out.println("Deleted Succesfully!");
   }
   ```

Adding new issue operations

In this recipe, we will look at adding new operations to an issue. The existing issue operations include **Edit Issue**, **Clone Issue**, and so on, and most of the time, people tend to look for similar operations with variations or entirely new operations that they can perform on an issue.

Prior to JIRA 4.1, the issue operations were added using the Issue Operations Plugin Module (`http://confluence.atlassian.com/display/JIRADEV/Issue+Opera tions+Plugin+Module`). But since JIRA 4.1, new issue operations are added using **Web Item Plugin Module** (`http://confluence.atlassian.com/display/JIRADEV/Web+Item+Plugin+Module`).

A **Web Item Plugin** module is a generic module that is used to define links in various application menus. One such menu is the issue operations menu. We will see more about the web items module and how it can be used to enhance the UI, later in this book; so, in this recipe, we will only concentrate on using the web-item module to create issue operations.

Getting ready

Create a skeleton plugin using Atlassian Plugin SDK.

How to do it...

Creating a web item is pretty easy! All we need to do is to place it in the appropriate section. There are already defined web sections in JIRA and we can add more sections using the **Web Section** module, if needed.

Let us create a new operation that lets us administer the project of an issue when we are on the view issue page. All we need here is to add an operation that takes us to the **Administer Project** page. Following are the steps to create the new operation:

1. Identify the web section where the new operation should be placed.

   For issue operations, JIRA already has multiple web sections defined. We can add our new operation on any one of the sections. The following is a diagram from the Atlassian documentation detailing on each of the available web sections for the issue operations:

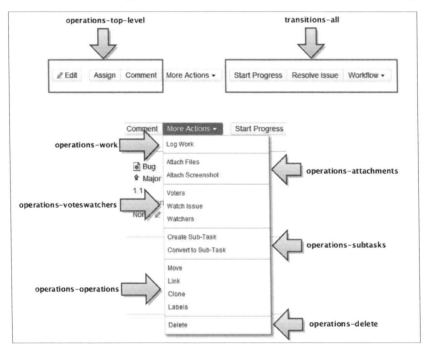

2. For example, if we want to add a new operation along with **Move**, **Link**, and so on, we need to add the new web item under the **operations-operations** section. If you are rather hoping to add it right at the top, along with **Edit**, **Assign**, and **Comment**, the section must be **operations-top-level**. We can reorder the operation using the `weight` attribute.

3. Define the web item module in the plugin descriptor with the section identified in the previous step! For our example, the module definition in `atlassian-plugin.xml` will look like the following:

```
<web-item key="manage-project" name="Manage Project"
section="operations-operations" weight="100">
   <label>Manage Project</label>
   <tooltip>Manages the Project  in which the issue belongs </
tooltip>
   <link linkId="manage-project-link">
      /secure/project/ViewProject.jspa?pid=${issue.project.id}
   </link>
</web-item>
```

As you can see, it has a unique `key` and a human-readable `name`. The section here is `operations-operations`. The `weight` attribute is used to reorder the operations as we saw earlier and here we use weight as 100 to put it at the bottom of the list.

The `label` is the name of the operation that will appear to the user. We can add a `tooltip` as well, which can have a friendly description of the operation. The next part, that is, `link` attribute, is the most important one as that links us to the operation that we want to perform. Essentially, it is just a link and hence you can use it to redirect to anywhere, the Atlassian site, for example.

In our example, we need to take the user to the *administer* project area. Luckily, in this case, we know the action to be invoked as it is an existing action in JIRA. All we need to do is to invoke the `ViewProject` action by passing the project ID as pid. The issue object is available on the view issue page as `$issue` and hence we can retrieve the project ID on the link as `${issue.project.id}`.

In cases where we need to do new things, we will have to create an action by ourselves and point the link to the same. We will see more about creating new actions and extending actions later in the book.

4. Package the plugin and deploy it.

How it works...

At runtime, you will see a new operation on the **View Issue** page on the **More Actions** drop-down menu, as shown in the next screenshot:

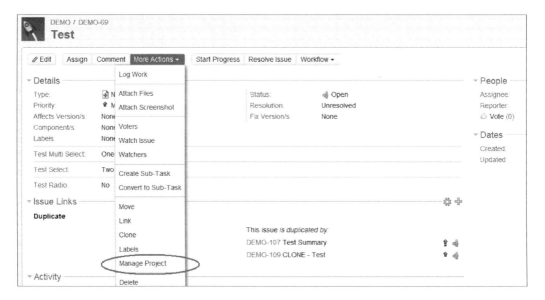

After clicking on the link, the **Administer Project** screen will appear, as expected. As you might notice, the URL is populated with the correct `pid` from the expression `${issue.project.id}`.

Also, just change the section or weight and see how the operation appears at various places on the screen!

There's more...

Prior to JIRA 4.1, The **Issue Operations** module was used in creating new issue operations. It is outside the scope of the book, though you can find the details in the Atlassian documentation at: `http://confluence.atlassian.com/display/JIRADEV/Issue+Operations+Plugin+Module`.

See also

- ▶ *Extending a Webwork action in JIRA*
- ▶ *Adding new Links in the UI*

Conditions on issue operations

When new operations are created, it is often a requirement to hide them or show them, based on the permissions or state of the issue or something else. JIRA allows conditions to be added while defining the web items, and when the conditions are not satisfied, the web item won't show up!

In this recipe, we will lock down the new issue operation we created in the previous recipe to *Project Administrators* exclusively.

Getting ready...

Create the **Manage Project** issue operation, as explained in the previous recipe.

How to do it...

Following are the steps to add a new condition to an issue operation's web item:

1. Create the `condition` class. The class should implement the `com. atlassian.plugin.web.Condition` interface, but it is recommended to extend `com.atlassian.jira.plugin.webfragment.conditions. AbstractIssueCondition` when creating an issue condition.

    While extending `AbstractIssueCondition`, we will have to implement the `shouldDisplay` method, as shown here:

    ```
    public class AdminCondition extends AbstractIssueCondition {
      private final PermissionManager permissionManager;

      public AdminCondition(PermissionManager permissionManager) {
        this.permissionManager = permissionManager;
      }

      @Override
      public boolean shouldDisplay(User user, Issue issue, JiraHelper
    jiraHelper) {
            return this.permissionManager.hasPermission(Permissions.
    PROJECT_ADMIN, issue.getProjectObject(), user);
      }
    }
    ```

    Here, a `true` value is returned if the user has the `PROJECT_ADMIN` permission on the project. That is all we need on the `condition` class.

2. Include the `condition` in the web item.

```
<web-item key="manage-project" name="Manage Project"
section="operations-operations" weight="100">
  <label>Manage Project</label>
  <tooltip>Manages the Project  in which the issue belongs </
tooltip>
  <link linkId="manage-project-link">
    /secure/project/ViewProject.jspa?pid=${issue.project.id}
  </link>
  <condition class="com.jtricks.conditions.AdminCondition"/>
</web-item>
```

It is possible to invert a condition by using the invert flag, as shown:

```
<condition class="com.jtricks.conditions.AdminCondition"
invert="true"/>
```

Condition elements can also take optional parameters, as shown:

```
<condition class="com.atlassian.jira.plugin.webfragment.
conditions.JiraGlobalPermissionCondition">
    <param name="permission">sysadmin</param>
</condition>
```

The parameters can be retrieved in the `condition` class by overriding the `init(Map params)` method. Here, `params` is a map of string key/value pairs that hold these parameters, in which case, the Map will have permission as the key, and the value passed (sysadmin in the example) can be accessed using the key and can then be used in passing or failing the condition.

For example, the following code in the conditions class will get you the appropriate permission type.

```
int permission = Permissions.getType((String) params.
get("permission"));
// Permissions.SYSTEM_ADMIN in this case
```

It is also possible to combine multiple conditions using the `conditions` element. `conditions` element will have multiple condition elements connected through logical AND (default) or OR condition.

For example, if we want to make our example operation available to both project administrators as well JIRA System Administrators, we can do it using an OR condition, as shown:

```
<conditions type="OR">
  <condition class="com.atlassian.jira.plugin.webfragment.
conditions.JiraGlobalPermissionCondition">
    <param name="permission">sysadmin</param>
  </condition>
  <condition class="com.jtricks.conditions.AdminCondition"/>
</conditions>
```

3. Package the plugin and deploy it.

How it works...

Once the plugin is deployed, we can go and check the operation on the View Issue Page, as we did in the previous chapter. If you are a Project Administrator (or a JIRA's system admin, depending on which condition you used), you will see the operation. If the user doesn't have the permissions, the operation won't be shown.

For example, if we added a **Manage Project** issue operation and limited it only to project admin, and a **New Manage Project** operation, and limited it to project admin or JIRA's system admin, a logged in **Project Admin** would see both the operations, but a logged in **Admin** will see only the latter operation as shown in the following screenshot:

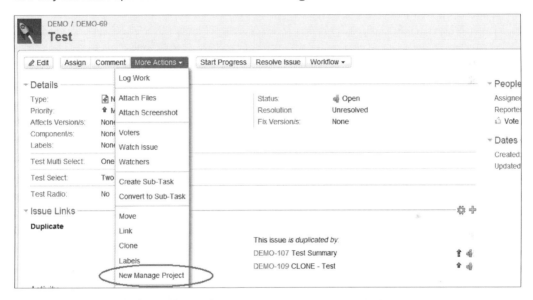

Working with attachments

Attachments feature is a useful feature in JIRA, and it sometimes helps to manage the attachments on an issue through the JIRA APIs. In this recipe, we will learn how to work with attachments using the JIRA API.

There are three major operations that can be done on attachments - Create, Read, and Delete. We will see each of them in this recipe.

Getting ready...

Make sure the attachments are enabled in your JIRA instance. You can do this from **Administration | Global Settings | Attachments**, as mentioned at `http://confluence.atlassian.com/display/JIRA/Configuring+File+Attachments`.

How to do it...

All the operations on the attachments can be performed using the `AttachmentManager` API. The `AttachmentManager` can be retrieved either by injecting it in the constructor or from the `ComponentManager` class, as shown:.

```
AttachmentManager attachmentManager = ComponentManager.
getInstance().getAttachmentManager();
```

Creating an attachment

An attachment can be created on an issue using the `createAttachment` method on the `AttachmentManager`, as shown:

```
ChangeItemBean changeBean = attachmentManager.createAttachment(new
File(fileName), newFileName, "text/plain", user, issue.
getGenericValue());
```

The following are the arguments:

- ▶ The `fileName` here needs to be the full path to the file on the server. You can also create a File object by uploading from the client machine, depending on the requirement.

- ▶ `newFileName` is the name with which the file will be attached to the issue, and it can be different from the original filename.

- ▶ The third parameter is the `contentType` of the file. In this case, we are uploading a text file and hence the content type is text/plain.

- ▶ `user` is the user who is attaching the file

- ▶ `issue` is the issue to which the file will be attached

If you also want to set a list of properties on an attachment as a key/value pair and create the attachment on a specific **time**, it can be done using the overloaded method `createAttachment`, which takes two extra parameters: `attachmentProperties`, a Map containing the key/value properties and `createdTime` which is of type `java.util.Date`.

These properties will be stored in the database using `PropertySet`.

Reading attachments on an issue

`AttachmentManager` has a method to retrieve the list of attachments, of type `com.atlassian.jira.issue.attachment.Attachment`, available on an issue. The following is how we do it:

```
List<Attachment> attachments = this.attachmentManager.
getAttachments(issue);
for (Attachment attachment : attachments) {
```

```
    System.out.println("Attachment: "+attachment.getFilename()+"
attached by "+attachment.getAuthor());
}
```

The object attachment holds all the information of the attachment, including any properties set during the creation of the attachment.

Deleting an attachment

All you need to do here is to retrieve the attachment object that needs to be deleted and invoke the `deleteAttachment` method on `AttachmentManager`.

```
    this.attachmentManager.deleteAttachment(attachment);
```

Here, attachment is an attachment that can be retrieved using the getAttachment(id) method or by iterating on the list of attachments retrieved above.

There's more...

`AttachmentManager` also has other useful methods like `attachmentsEnabled()`, `isScreenshotAppletEnabled()`, `isScreenshotAppletSupportedByOS()`, and so on, to check whether the respective functionality is enabled or not.

Check out: `http://docs.atlassian.com/jira/latest/com/atlassian/jira/ issue/AttachmentManager.html` for a full list of available methods.

Time tracking and worklog management

Time tracking is one of the biggest pluses for any issue tracking system. JIRA's time tracking is highly configurable and gives plenty of options to manage the work done and the remaining time.

Even though the time tracking in JIRA can be done using the JIRA UI, many users want to do it from the customized pages or third-party applications or plugins. In this recipe, we will see how to do time tracking using the JIRA APIs.

Before we start, each of the operations on worklogs, namely, create, edit, or delete, have different modes. Whenever one of these operations is performed, we can adjust the remaining amount of work to be done in the following ways:

1. Let JIRA adjust the remaining work automatically.

    For example, if the remaining estimate is 2 hours and if we log 30 minutes, JIRA will automatically adjust the remaining estimate to 1 hour 30 minutes.

2. Enter a new remaining estimate time while performing the operations.

   For example, if the remaining estimate is 2 hours and if we log 30 minutes, we can force JIRA to change the remaining estimate to 1 hour (instead of the automatically calculated 1 hour 30 minutes).

3. Adjust the remaining estimate or in other words reduce a specific amount of time from the remaining estimate

   For example, if the remaining estimate is 2 hours and if we log 30 minutes, we can force JIRA to reduce the remaining estimate by 1 hour 30 minutes (instead of automatically reducing the logged 30 minutes). When we do that, the remaining estimate will come out to be 30 minutes.

4. Leave the remaining estimate as it is.

Getting ready...

Make sure time tracking is turned on as explained at `http://confluence.atlassian.com/display/JIRA/Configuring+Time+Tracking`. It can be enabled from the **Administration | Global Settings | Time Tracking** menu.

How to do it...

Worklogs in JIRA can be managed using the `WorklogService` class. It does all the major operations like creating worklogs, updating them, or deleting them, and that too, in all the four different modes we have seen earlier.

We will see how to create worklogs, or in other words, log work in the following four modes:

- ▶ Auto adjusting the remaining estimate
- ▶ Logging work and retaining the remaining estimate
- ▶ Logging work with a new remaining estimate
- ▶ Logging work and adjusting the remaining estimate by a value

Auto adjusting the remaining estimate

1. Create the JIRA Service Context for the user who is logging work.

   ```
   JiraServiceContext jiraServiceContext = new
   JiraServiceContextImpl(user);
   ```

2. Create a `WorklogInputParametersImpl.Builder` object to create the parameters needed for the worklog creation.

   ```
   final WorklogInputParametersImpl.Builder builder =
   WorklogInputParametersImpl.issue(issue).timeSpent(timeSpent).
   startDate(new Date()).comment(null).groupLevel(null).
   roleLevelId(null);
   ```

Here, the issue is the issue on which work is logged, and `timeSpent` is the time that we are going to log in. `timeSpent` is a String that represents the format in which time is entered in JIRA , that is, `*w *d *h *m` (representing weeks, days, hours, and minutes, where * can be any number).

`startDate` here can be the date from where the work has started. We can also optionally add comments and set the worklog visibility to certain groups or project roles! Set these parameters as null when the worklog is visible to all.

3. Create the `WorklogInputParameters` object from the builder and validate it using the `WorklogService`.

   ```
   WorklogResult result = this.worklogService.validateCreate(jiraS
   erviceContext, builder.build());
   ```

4. Create the worklog using `WorklogService`.

   ```
   Worklog worklog = this.worklogService.createAndAutoAdjustRemain
   ingEstimate(jiraServiceContext, result, false);
   ```

   Here, as you can see, the method invoked is `createAndAutoAdjustRemainingEstimate`, which will create the worklog and automatically adjust the remaining estimate on the issue.

   The method takes as input the service context we created, the `WorklogResult` object after validating the input parameters, and a Boolean which will be used to dispatch an event, if needed. When the Boolean value is true, the **Work Logged On Issue** event is fired.

With this, the work will be logged on the issue.

Logging work and retaining the remaining estimate

Here, the first three steps are similar to what was discussed in the *Auto adjusting remaining estimate* section. The only difference is that the method invoked on `WorklogService` is `createAndRetainRemainingEstimate` instead of `createAndAutoAdjustRemainingEstimate`. The full code is as shown:

```
JiraServiceContext jiraServiceContext = new
JiraServiceContextImpl(user);
final WorklogInputParametersImpl.Builder builder =
WorklogInputParametersImpl.issue(issue).timeSpent(timeSpent).
startDate(new Date()).comment(null).groupLevel(null).
roleLevelId(null);
WorklogResult result = this.worklogService.validateCreate(jiraServ
iceContext, builder.build());
Worklog worklog = this.worklogService.createAndRetainRemainingEsti
mate(jiraServiceContext, result, false);
```

Logging work with a new remaining estimate

Here the first two steps are similar to what was discussed in the *Auto adjusting remaining estimate* section.

1. Create the JIRA Service Context for the user who is logging work.

```
JiraServiceContext jiraServiceContext = new
JiraServiceContextImpl(user);
```

2. Create a `WorklogInputParametersImpl.Builder` object to create the parameters needed for the worklog creation.

```
final WorklogInputParametersImpl.Builder builder =
WorklogInputParametersImpl.issue(issue).timeSpent(timeSpent)
.startDate(new Date()).comment(null).groupLevel(null).
roleLevelId(null);
```

3. Create the New Estimate Input Parameters from the Builder object.

```
final WorklogNewEstimateInputParameters params = builder.
newEstimate(newEstimate).buildNewEstimate();
```

Here, we specify the `newEstimate`, which is a String representation similar to `timeSpent`. The `newEstimate` will be set as the remaining estimate on the issue.

4. Create the `WorklogResult` from `WorklogNewEstimateInputParameters` using `WorklogService`:

```
WorklogResult result = this.worklogService.validateUpdateWithNewEs
timate(jiraServiceContext, params);
```

The result here will be an instance of `WorklogNewEstimateResult`, which will be used in the next step!

5. Create the worklog using `WorklogService`.

```
Worklog worklog = this.worklogService.createWithNewRemainingEs
timate(jiraServiceContext, (WorklogNewEstimateResult) result,
false);
```

Here, the method used is `createWithNewRemainingEstimate`, which sets the `newEstimate` as the remaining estimate on the issue, after logging the work using `timeSpent`! As you can see, the result object is converted to `WorklogNewEstimateResult`.

Logging work and adjusting the remaining estimate by a value

Here the process is much similar to the above. The only difference is that the `adjustmentAmount` method is used on Builder instead of `newEstimate` and `validateCreateWithManuallyAdjustedEstimate` is used on `WorklogService` to create the worklog. Also, the `WorklogResult` is an instance of `WorklogAdjustmentAmountResult`.

The code is as follows:

```
JiraServiceContext jiraServiceContext = new
JiraServiceContextImpl(user);
final WorklogInputParametersImpl.Builder builder =
WorklogInputParametersImpl.issue(issue).timeSpent(timeSpent).
startDate(new Date()).comment(null).groupLevel(null).
roleLevelId(null);
final WorklogAdjustmentAmountInputParameters params = builder.adju
stmentAmount(estimateToReduce).buildAdjustmentAmount();
WorklogResult result = worklogService.validateCreateWithManuallyAd
justedEstimate(jiraServiceContext, params);
Worklog worklog = this.worklogService.createWithManuallyAdjustedEs
timate(jiraServiceContext, (WorklogAdjustmentAmountResult) result,
false);
```

How it works...

Once we create or update the worklogs using the `WorklogService` API, the changes will be reflected on the issue under the **Work Log** tab, as shown in the following screenshot:

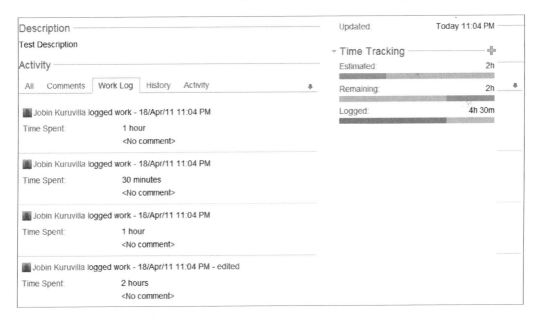

You can also see that the graphical representation of time tracking reflects these changes.

When a worklog is deleted, it appears on the **Change history** as shown:

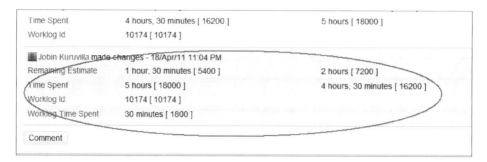

There's more

Updating worklogs

Updating worklogs is similar to the creating them in many ways. Here, we pass the ID of the `Worklog` object to be updated instead of the issue we pass while creating a worklog. And, of course, the methods invoked on `WorklogService` are different. The following is the code to update a given **Worklog** for the first mode where the remaining estimate is auto adjusted.

```
JiraServiceContext jiraServiceContext = new
JiraServiceContextImpl(user);
final WorklogInputParametersImpl.Builder builder =
WorklogInputParametersImpl.worklogId(worklog.getId()).
timeSpent(timeSpent).startDate(new Date()).comment(null).
groupLevel(null).roleLevelId(null);
WorklogResult result = this.worklogService.validateUpdate(jiraServ
iceContext, builder.build());
Worklog updatedLog = this.worklogService.updateAndAutoAdjustRemain
ingEstimate(jiraServiceContext, result, false);
```

As you can see, a *builder* is created by passing the worklog ID, which is unique across issues. The `WorklogResult` here is created using the `validateUpdate` method and the worklog is finally updated using the `updateAndAutoAdjustRemainingEstimate` method.

The other modes are also similar to how we created the worklogs. Let us quickly see how to update a worklog with a new remaining estimate:

```
JiraServiceContext jiraServiceContext = new
JiraServiceContextImpl(user);
final WorklogInputParametersImpl.Builder builder =
WorklogInputParametersImpl.worklogId(worklog.getId()).
timeSpent(timeSpent).startDate(new Date()).comment(null).
groupLevel(null).roleLevelId(null);
```

```
final WorklogNewEstimateInputParameters params = builder.
newEstimate(newEstimate).buildNewEstimate();
WorklogResult result = this.worklogService.validateUpdateWithNewEs
timate(jiraServiceContext, params);
Worklog updatedLog = this.worklogService.updateWithNewRemaining
Estimate(jiraServiceContext, (WorklogNewEstimateResult) result,
false);
```

The above looks pretty familiar, doesn't it? It is similar to creating a worklog with a new estimate, except that we call the respective update methods, as discussed before.

We can update a worklog by retaining the estimate and also adjust it by a specified amount of time from the remaining estimate in the same way.

Deleting worklogs

Deleting a worklog is slightly different and maybe easier than creating or updating one, as it doesn't involve building the input parameters.

Auto Adjusting remaining estimate

All we need here is the worklog ID and to create the JIRA Service Context. The code is as shown below:

```
JiraServiceContext jiraServiceContext = new
JiraServiceContextImpl(user);
WorklogResult worklogResult = worklogService.validateDelete(jiraServic
eContext, worklog.getId());
worklogService.deleteAndAutoAdjustRemainingEstimate(jiraServiceConte
xt, worklogResult, false);
```

Here, the `validateDelete` method takes the worklog ID as input and creates a `WorklogResult`, which is then used in the `deleteAndAutoAdjustRemainingEstimate` method.

Deleting a worklog and retaining the remaining estimate

This is done in much the same way as mentioned in the previous section, expect that the `deleteAndRetainRemainingEstimate` method is used instead of `deleteAndAutoAdjustRemainingEstimate`.

```
JiraServiceContext jiraServiceContext = new
JiraServiceContextImpl(user);
WorklogResult worklogResult = worklogService.validateDelete(jiraSe
rviceContext, worklog.getId());
worklogService.deleteAndRetainRemainingEstimate(jiraServiceConte
xt, worklogResult, false);
```

Deleting a worklog with a new remaining estimate

As mentioned before, we don't create the input parameters while deleting worklogs. Instead, the newEstimate is used to create WorklogResult, which is an instance of WorklogNewEstimateResult, while validating. The code is as follows:

```
JiraServiceContext jiraServiceContext = new
JiraServiceContextImpl(user);
WorklogResult worklogResult = worklogService.validateDeleteWithNew
Estimate(jiraServiceContext, worklog.getId(), newEstimate);
worklogService.deleteWithNewRemainingEstimate(jiraServiceContext,
(WorklogNewEstimateResult) worklogResult, false);Deleting a worklog
and adjusting the remaining estimate
```

This is also pretty much the same as mentioned in the previous section, except for the method names.

```
JiraServiceContext jiraServiceContext = new
JiraServiceContextImpl(user);
WorklogResult worklogResult = worklogService.validateDeleteWit
hManuallyAdjustedEstimate(jiraServiceContext, worklog.getId(),
adjustmentAmount);
worklogService.deleteWithManuallyAdjustedEstimate(jiraServiceContext,
(WorklogAdjustmentAmountResult) worklogResult, false);
```

Here, adjustmentAmount is the value that is used to increase the remaining estimate on the issue.

Working with comments on issues

In this recipe, we will see how to manage commenting on issues using the JIRA API.

How to do it...

JIRA uses the CommentService class to manage the comments on an issue. Let us have a look at all the three major operations—creating, editing, and deleting comments. We will also have a look at how to restrict the comment visibility to a specific group of people or to a project role.

Creating comments on issues

A comment can be added on to an issue as follows:

```
Comment comment = this.commentService.create(user, issue,
commentString, false, new SimpleErrorCollection());
```

Here, `commentString` is the comment we are adding, user is the user adding the comment, and issue is the issue on which the comment is added. The fourth argument is a boolean that determines whether an event should be dispatched or not. If it is true, an `Issue Commented` event is thrown.

Creating comments on an issue and restricting it to a project role or group

If we need to restrict the visibility of the comments, we need to use the overridden `create` method on the `CommentService` class that takes the role ID and group name along with the other attributes. Only one of them should be passed at one time.

In order to restrict the comment visibility to groups, the `Comment visibility` property under **General Configuration** should be set to **Groups & Project Roles**. The default is to allow restricting comments only for project roles.

For example, the comment can be restricted to a **group** as follows:

```
Comment comment = this.commentService.create(user, issue,
commentString, group, null, false, new SimpleErrorCollection());
```

In this group, `group` is the name of the group, and the fifth parameter (`null`) is the `roleId`.

Restricting to a **role** is done as follows:

```
Comment comment = this.commentService.create(user, issue,
commentString, null, roleId, false, new SimpleErrorCollection());
```

In this case, the `group` is `null` and `roleId` is the unique ID of the `ProjectRole` that we need to restrict the comment to.

The Boolean to dispatch events can be used in both cases.

Updating comments

Following are the steps to update a comment:

1. Create the `MutableComment` object from the comment to be updated

   ```
   MutableComment comm = this.commentService.
   getMutableComment(user, comment.getId(), new
   SimpleErrorCollection());
   ```

2. Modify the comment with the following statement:

   ```
   comm.setBody("New Comment");
   ```

   Here, we update the body of the comment, though we can also update other attributes like the author, group level, role level, and so on.

3. Update the comment using `CommentService`:

```
this.commentService.update(user, comm, false, new
SimpleErrorCollection());
```

Deleting comments

A comment can be deleted as shown:

```
this.commentService.delete(new JiraServiceContextImpl(user), comment,
false);
```

`comment` is the comment object to be deleted.

Programming Change Logs

Tracking changes to an issue is very important. JIRA stores all the changes that are done on an issue as change logs along with the information of who made the change and when. Sometimes, when we do custom development, we will have to update the **Change History** by ourselves when something changes on the issue by our plugin.

Change Histories are logged as change groups which are a group of one or more change items made by a user at any one time. Each change item will be a change made on any single field.

In this recipe, we will see how to add change logs on an issue using the JIRA API.

How to do it...

Each change item in JIRA is created as a `ChangeItemBean`. `ChangeItemBean` can be of two different types—one for **system** fields where the field type is `ChangeItemBean.STATIC_FIELD` and another for **custom** fields where the field type is `ChangeItemBean.CUSTOM_FIELD`.

The following are the steps to add a Change History.

1. Create a `ChangeItemBean` for the change that needs to be recorded for every item that is changed.

```
ChangeItemBean changeBean = new ChangeItemBean(ChangeItemBean.
STATIC_FIELD, IssueFieldConstants.SUMMARY, "Old Summary", "New
Summary");
```

Here, the first attribute is the `fieldType` and the second one is the name of the field. For system fields of type `ChangeItemBean.STATIC_FIELD`, the name can be retrieved from `IssueFieldConstants` class. For example, `IssueFieldConstants.SUMMARY` represents the issue summary.

The third and fourth arguments are the *old value* and the *new value* of the field respectively.

As we know, some of the JIRA fields have an id value and a String value. For example, the issue Status has the status name and the corresponding status ID. In such cases, we can use an overridden constructor that also takes the old id and new id as shown below.

```
ChangeItemBean changeBean = new ChangeItemBean(ChangeItemBean.
STATIC_FIELD, IssueFieldConstants.STATUS,"1", "Open", "3", "In
Progress");
```

For custom fields, we use the field type `ChangeItemBean.CUSTOM_FIELD` and the custom field name. Everything else is same.

```
ChangeItemBean changeBean = new ChangeItemBean(ChangeItemBean.
CUSTOM_FIELD, "My Field",  "Some Old Value", "Some New Value");
```

It is worth noting that the field name can be manipulated to give any value when the `fieldType` is `ChangeItemBean.CUSTOM_FIELD`. It is probably a useful feature when you want to programmatically add change logs that are not directly relates to a field. Say, for adding a subtask!

```
ChangeItemBean changeBean = new ChangeItemBean(ChangeItemBean.
CUSTOM_FIELD, "Some Heading", "Some Old Value", "Some New Value");
```

2. Create a change holder and add the change items in to it.

```
IssueChangeHolder changeHolder = new DefaultIssueChangeHolder();
changeHolder.addChangeItem(changeBean);
```

3. Create and store the `changelog` using the items in the `changeHolder` using `ChangeLogUtils` class.

```
GenericValue changeLog = ChangeLogUtils.createChangeGroup(user,
issue, issue, changeHolder.getChangeItems(),  false);
```

Here **user** is the user making the change. The second and third arguments are the original issue and the issue after changes. You can give both the same if the change items are explicitly created and added to `changeHolder`.

But if we are modifying an issue using the setter methods, an easier way might be to pass the original issue object along with the modified issue object (object after setter methods are invoked) and set the last argument as `true` which determines whether a list of change items needs to be generated from the before and after objects. In that case, we don't need to explicitly create `changeItems` and hence the third argument can be an empty list. We can still pass additional `changeItems` if needed as the third argument in which case both the passed `changeItems` and generated `changeItems` (from issue before and after modification) will be created!

How it works...

Once the change logs are added, they will appear in the issues change log panel, as shown in the following screenshot:

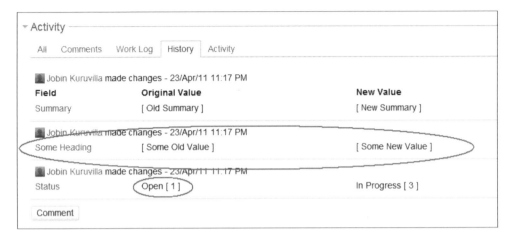

Notice that the highlighted *change log* is added even though there is no field named **Some Heading**. Also, see how both the ID and name are shown for the **Status** field!

Programming issue links

Issue linking is another important feature in JIRA. It helps us to define the relationship between issues. In this recipe, we will see how to create links between issues and to break them using the JIRA APIs!

Before we start, an issue link type has an inward and an outward description. For every issue link, there will be a source issue and a destination issue. From a source issue, we can look up the destination issues by looking up the outward links. Similarly, from a destination issue, we can look up the source issues by looking up inward links.

Getting Ready...

Make sure the Issue Linking feature is turned ON in JIRA and valid link types are created. This can be done from **Administration | Global Settings | Issue Linking**, as explained at `http://confluence.atlassian.com/display/JIRA/Configuring+Issue+Linking`.

How to do it...

Issue Links are managed in JIRA with the help of the `IssueLinkManager` class. The following are the steps to create an issue link between two given issues:

1. Get the `IssueLinkType` object for the link type we are going to create. This can be retrieved using the `IssueLinkTypeManager` class. The `IssueLinkTypeManager` class can be retrieved from the `ComponentManager` or can be injected in the constructor.

    ```
    IssueLinkTypeManager issueLinkTypeManager = ComponentManager.
    getInstance().getComponentInstanceOfType(IssueLinkTypeManager.
    class);
    IssueLinkType linkType = issueLinkTypeManager.getIssueLinkTypesByN
    ame("Duplicate").iterator().next();
    ```

    Here we are getting the `Duplicate` issue link type. Even though the `getIssueLinkTypesByName` method returns a Collection, there will be only one link with the same name.

2. Create the issue link using the `IssueLinkManager` class. The `IssueLinkManager` class can also be retrieved from the `ComponentManager` class or injected in the constructor.

    ```
    IssueLinkManager issueLinkManager = ComponentManager.
    getInstance().getIssueLinkManager();
    issueLinkManager.createIssueLink(sourceIssue.getId(), destIssue.
    getId(), linkType.getId(), null, user);
    ```

    Here, we pass the source and destination issue IDs, in the order mentioned, along with the link type ID. The fourth parameter is the sequence, which is of type `long`, used to order the links on the user interface. `user` is the user who is performing the link action.

There's more...

Let's now see how to delete them or just display links.

Deleting Issue Links

Following are the steps:

1. Retrieve the `IssueLinkType`, as we did earlier:

    ```
    IssueLinkTypeManager issueLinkTypeManager = ComponentManager.
    getInstance().getComponentInstanceOfType(IssueLinkTypeManager.
    class);
    IssueLinkType linkType = issueLinkTypeManager.getIssueLinkTypesByN
    ame("Duplicate").iterator().next();
    ```

2. Get the `IssueLink` to be deleted using the `IssueLinkManager` class.:

```
IssueLink issueLink = issueLinkManager.getIssueLink(sourceIssue.
getId(), destIssue.getId(), linkType.getId());
```

3. Here the `sourceIssue` and `destIssue` are the source and destination issues, respectively.

4. Delete the Link using the `IssueLinkManager` class.

```
issueLinkManager.removeIssueLink(issueLink, user);
```

Retrieving Issue Links on an issue

We can retrieve the inward or outward links on an issue or all the linked issues using different methods on the `IssueLinkManager` class.

All inward links can be retrieved as shown:

```
List<IssueLink> links = issueLinkManager.getInwardLinks(issue.
getId());
for (IssueLink issueLink : links) {
  System.out.println(issueLink.getIssueLinkType().getName()+": Linked
from "+issueLink.getSourceObject().getKey());
}
```

Here, `issue` is the destination object and we are getting all the inward issue links and displaying the source issue key.

Similarly, outward links can be retrieved as shown:

```
links = issueLinkManager.getOutwardLinks(issue.getId());
for (IssueLink issueLink : links) {
  System.out.println(issueLink.getIssueLinkType().getName()+": Linked
to "+issueLink.getDestinationObject().getKey());
}
```

Here, issue is the source object and we are getting all the outward issue links and displaying the destination issue key.

All the linked issues can be retrieved in a single method as shown:

```
LinkCollection links = this.issueLinkManager.getLinkCollection(issue,
user);
Collection<Issue> linkedIssues = links.getAllIssues();
```

Validations on issue linking

There are scenarios that we might come across where we need to do extra validations while linking. In this recipe, we will quickly look at adding some extra validations by extending the existing link issue action in JIRA.

Getting Ready...

Create a Skeleton plugin using Atlassian Plugin SDK. It is recommended to read the *Extending JIRA actions* recipe before proceeding.

How to do it...

As we have seen while extending JIRA actions, all we need to do here is to create a new webwork action that extends the existing JIRA action and override the required method. In this specific case, will be overriding the doValidation() method to do some extra validation.

Let us, for example, consider that we want to restrict linking to all issues of type **New Feature**. Following are the steps to do the same.

1. Add a new webwork module in the atlassian-plugin.xml with a new action class and the same alias as JIRA's link action, LinkExistingIssue. Once we do that, the new action class will be executed while linking issues.

```
<webwork1 key="jtricks-link-issue-details" name="JTricks Link
Issue Details" >
  <actions>
    <action name="com.jtricks.JTricksLinkExistingIssue"
alias="LinkExistingIssue">
    <view name="error">/secure/views/issue/linkexistingissue.jsp</
view>
    <view name="input">/secure/views/issue/linkexistingissue.jsp</
view>
    </action>
  </actions>
</webwork1>
```

2. Create the new class extending the existing action class.

```
public class JTricksLinkExistingIssue extends LinkExistingIssue {
   ...
}
```

3. Override the `doValidation()` method to add extra validation.

```
@Override
protected void doValidation() {
  super.doValidation();
  // Custom Validation
}
```

4. Add the custom validation as appropriate. In our example, we throw an error if any of the issues selected for linking is of type **New Feature**. The selected issues can be found using the `getLinkKey()` method, which returns a String array of selected issue keys.

```
List<String> invalidIssues = new ArrayList<String>();
for (String key : getLinkKey()) {
  MutableIssue issue = this.issueManager.getIssueObject(key);
  if (issue.getIssueTypeObject().getName().equals("New
Feature")) {
    invalidIssues.add(key);
  }
}
if (!invalidIssues.isEmpty()) {
  addErrorMessage("Linking not allowed to New Features:" +
getString(invalidIssues));
}

private String getString(List<String> invalidIssues) {
  StringBuffer invalidIssue = new StringBuffer("{ ");
  for (String key : invalidIssues) {
    invalidIssue.append(key + " ");
  }
  invalidIssue.append("}");
  return invalidIssue.toString();
}
```

5. As you can see, all we do here is check for the issue key and mark it as invalid if the issue type is **New Feature**. If invalid, we then throw an error for those invalid keys.

6. Package the plugin and deploy it.

We can use the same approach to add extra validations.

 An action can be overridden only once. Care must be taken not to override it again in another plugin (might be a third-party plugin) as only one will be picked up.

How it works...

Let us consider linking to three existing issues, out of which, two are **New Features**. Once the plugin is deployed, we will see an error as shown:

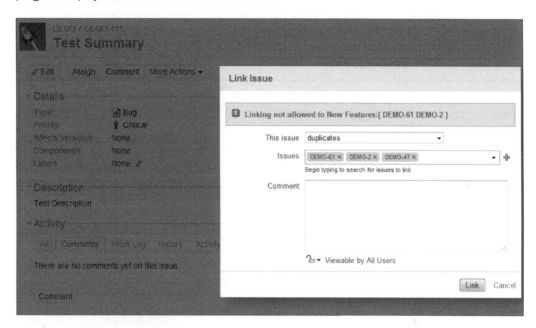

See also

▶ *Extending a Webwork action in JIRA*

Discarding fields while cloning

Cloning of issues in JIRA is an easy way to replicate an existing issue. While cloning, a new issue is created exactly similar to the original issue with identical values for all its fields except for a few special ones. The special ones include `created date`, `updated date`, `issue key`, `status`, and so on.

But, in addition to the special fields JIRA has chosen, we might want to ignore a few other fields while cloning an issue. How about a unique custom field? We surely don't want to replicate it while cloning?

Here is an easy way to discard any such fields while cloning an issue.

Getting ready...

Create a Skeleton plugin using Atlassian Plugin SDK. It is recommended to read the *Extending JIRA actions* recipe before proceeding.

How to do it...

As we have seen while extending JIRA actions in the previous recipe, all we need to do here is to create a new webwork action that extends the existing JIRA Clone action and overrides the required method. In this specific case, will be overriding the `setFields()` method to remove the cloning of the specific fields we are interested in!

Let us, for example, say that we want to avoid cloning a unique number field named `Test Number`. Following are the steps to follow:

1. Add a new webwork module in the `atlassian-plugin.xml` with a new action class and the same alias as JIRA's clone action, `CloneIssueDetails`. Once we do that, the new action class will be executed while cloning issues.

    ```
    <webwork1 key="jtricks-link-issue-details" name="JTricks Link
    Issue Details" >
      <actions>
        <action name="com.jtricks.JTricksCloneIssueDetails"
    alias="CloneIssueDetails">
            <view name="input">/secure/views/cloneissue-start.jsp</view>
            <view name="error">/secure/views/cloneissue-start.jsp</view>
        </action>
      </actions>
    </webwork1>
    ```

2. Create the new class extending the existing action class.

    ```
    public class JTricksCloneIssueDetails extends CloneIssueDetails{
      ...
    }
    ```

3. Override the `setFields ()` method to set a `null` value for the fields we do not want to clone.

    ```
    @Override
    protected void setFields() throws FieldLayoutStorageException {
      super.setFields();
      // Set null values for interested fields here
    }
    ```

4. Add the code to set `null` values. In our example, we set null value for the Test Number custom field.

```
CustomField customField = customFieldManager.getCustomFieldObjectB
yName("Test Number");
getIssueObject().setCustomFieldValue(customField, null);
```

Here we get the cloned issue using the method `getIssueObject` and set the null value for the custom field. Don't forget to use the `getCustomFieldObject` method by passing the custom field ID if the field name is not unique!

If we want to set null values for a system field like fix for versions, the method is the same.

```
getIssueObject().setFixVersions(null);
```

5. Package the plugin and deploy it.

 An action can be overridden only once. Care must be taken not to override it again in another plugin (might be a third-party plugin) as only one will be picked up.

How it works...

Once the clone operation is invoked, the new action we have created will be executed. The clone operation creates a new issue object and copies the values to its fields from the original issue. This is done in the `setFields` method.

It is only logical to override this method and set `null` values for fields we do not want to clone. As shown above, the `setFields` method from the super class, which is the JIRA's in-built class, is first executed. Once the method is executed, the new issue object, which can be retrieved using the method `getIssueObject`, has all the values populated. We just reset some of the values by setting them to `null`.

See also

▶ *Extending a Webwork action in JIRA*

JavaScript tricks on issue fields

JIRA provides a lot of options to manage the various fields on an issue. Field configuration schemes, screen schemes, and so on, help the JIRA admins to show or hide fields, mark them as mandatory, and so on, differently for different issue types and projects.

Irrespective of how configurable these schemes are, there are still areas where we need to perform custom development. For example, if we need to show or hide fields, based on the values of another field, then JIRA doesn't have any in-built options to do so.

Then, what is the best way to deal with this? It is always possible to create a new composite custom field that can have multiple fields driven by each other's behavior. But probably an easier way—that doesn't need developing a plugin—is to drive this using JavaScript. And to make things better, JIRA offers jQuery library that can be used to write neat JavaScript code!

However, using JavaScript to handle field behavior can create problems. It limits the behavior to the browser, it is client side and is dependent on whether JavaScript is enabled or not. But given its advantages and ease of use, most users prefer to do it. In this recipe, we will see a small example of using JavaScript to show or hide the values of a custom field based on the issue's priority value!

How to do it...

Let us assume that we have a custom field named **Why Critical?**. The field should be shown only if the priority of the issue is **Critical**.

Following are the simple steps to achieve it using JavaScript:

1. Write the JavaScript to achieve the functionality.

    In our example, we need to show the **Why Critical** field only when the priority is Critical. Let us write the JavaScript for these purposes as an example!

    a. Identify the ID value for priority. We can get it by looking at the URL while editing the priority or from the JIRA database by looking at the `priority` table.

    b. Identify the ID of the custom field. We can get this also in a similar fashion, either by looking at the URL while editing the custom field or from the `customfield` table!

    c. Write the JavaScript to show or hide the field depending on the priority value. Here, we use the JIRA's jQuery library, which has a predefined namespace `AJS`, a short name for Atlassian JavaScript!

```
<script type="text/javascript">
(function($){
  $(document).ready(function(){
    var priority = document.getElementById('priority');
    hideOrShow(priority.value);
    priority.onchange=function() {
      hideOrShow(priority.value);
    };
  });
```

```
     function hideOrShow(priorityVal){
        if (priorityVal == '2'){
          AJS.$("#customfield_10170").closest('div.field-
group').show();
        } else {
          AJS.$("#customfield_10170").closest('div.field-
group').hide();
        }
      }
    })(AJS.$);
    </script>
```

d. Here 10170 is the `id` of the `customfield` and hence `customfield_10170` represents the unique custom field ID! Also, 2 is the ID of the priority system field.

In the example, we created a page load event where the script looks at the priority value and sets the visibility of the div surrounding the custom field as hidden or shown.

The following part captures the on load event of the page where custom field is in edit mode.

```
(function($){
$(document).ready(function(){
    ...
   });
}) (AJS.$);
```

And the following code shows the field, if priority is 2.

```
AJS.$("#customfield_10170").closest('div.field-group').
show();
```

For every other priority value, the closet `div` surrounding field is hidden.

2. Add the above JavaScript to the description of the custom field.

The field behavior will be effective on the next reload after the JavaScript is added on to the field description.

How it works...

Whenever the field is rendered under the velocity view in the edit mode, the field description is executed along with all the JavaScript code in there!

Once the script is added in the relevant field configuration screen, the field will not appear for priority values other than **Critical**, as shown in the next screenshot:

Here, the **Priority** is **Major** (value 3), and hence the field **Why Critical?** is not available. But the moment the priority is changed to **Critical**, we can see the field appearing back on the page.

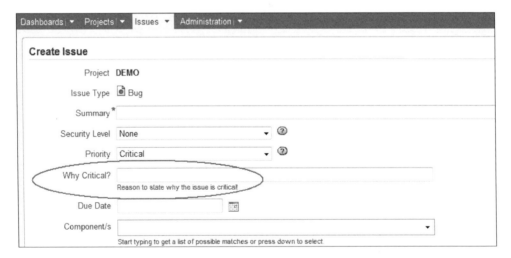

The JavaScript can now be modified to do a lot of other useful stuff! Don't forget to modify the scripts according to your needs, specifically your browser and your version of JIRA.

8
Customizing the UI

In this chapter, we will cover:

- ▶ Changing the basic look and feel
- ▶ Adding new web sections in the UI
- ▶ Adding new web items in the UI
- ▶ Adding conditions for web fragments
- ▶ Creating new velocity context for web fragments
- ▶ Adding a new drop-down on the top navigation bar
- ▶ Dynamic creation of web items
- ▶ Adding new tabs in the **View Issue** screen
- ▶ Adding new tabs in the **Browse Project** screen
- ▶ Creating the **Project Tab Panel** using fragments
- ▶ Adding new tabs in the **Browse Version** screen
- ▶ Adding new tabs in the **Browse Component** screen
- ▶ Extending a webwork action to add UI elements
- ▶ Displaying dynamic notifications/warnings on issues
- ▶ Re-ordering issue operations in the **View Issue** page
- ▶ Re-ordering fields in the **View Issue** page

Introduction

One of the good things about JIRA is that it has a simple but powerful user interface. A lot has changed between 3.13.x and 4.1.x in terms of the user interface, and it still continues to be one that keeps the users happy and plugin developers interested.

While the existing JIRA interface works for many people, there are cases where we need to modify bits and pieces of it, add new UI elements, remove some, and so on.

Normally, when we think of modifying a web application's user interface, the first thought that comes to our mind is to go and modify the JSPs, VMs, and many others involved. While it is true, in some cases, for JIRA as well, a lot of the user-interface changes can be introduced without even touching the JIRA code. JIRA helps us to do that with the help of a number of UI-related plugin modules.

In this chapter, we will be looking at various recipes for enhancing the JIRA UI with the various plugin modules available, and also, in some cases, by modifying the JSPs or other files involved.

Note that the look and feel can be changed to a big extent only by modifying the CSS files and other templates involved. But here we are talking about adding new web fragments, such as new sections and links, in the various parts of the UI without actually modifying the core JIRA files or with little modification of them. If we modify the JIRA files, it should be noted that maintaining the files over various JIRA versions, enabling or disabling of the changes, and so on, would be very difficult and worth considering!

Changing the basic look and feel

As mentioned earlier, any big changes to the look and feel of JIRA can be achieved only by modifying the CSS files, JSPs, templates, and other tools involved. But JIRA lets its administrators make slightly simpler changes like changing the logo, coloring scheme, and so on, with some simple configurations. In this recipe, we will see some examples on how easy it is to make those changes.

There are mainly four things that can be configured to change JIRA's appearance:

- ▶ **Logo**: Understandably, this is one thing everyone wants to change.
- ▶ **Colors**: JIRA has a nice theme of colors revolving around a theme of blue. But we can easily change these colors to suit our taste or rather the company's taste!
- ▶ **Gadget colors**: For each gadget in JIRA, we can set a different color chosen from a predefined set of colors. We can easily change the predefined list of colors through simple configuration.

▶ **Date and Time formats**: The Date and Time formats in JIRA could be modified easily to suit our needs, provided it is a valid format supported by Java's SimpleDateFormat (http://download.oracle.com/javase/1.4.2/docs/api/java/text/SimpleDateFormat.html).

How to do it...

The following are the steps to make changes to the basic JIRA look and feel.

1. Log in to JIRA as an administrator.

2. Navigate to **Administration | Global Settings | Look and Feel**.

3. Click on **Edit Configuration**.

4. Make the changes as appropriate:

    a. **Logo**: Bundle your new logo as part of the JIRA WAR or drop it under the JIRA installation under the images folder or another valid directory. Refer to the new logo's URL as a relative path to your new logo within the JIRA installation directory.

    For example, /images/logo/mynewlogo.png will refer to the mynewlogo.png image under the images/logo folder. Enter the new logo width or height as suitable.

    b. **Colors**: Specify the hexadecimal notations (HEX values) of the interested colors if the color scheme needs to be changed.

    c. **Gadget colors**: Here also, specify the hexadecimal notations (HEX values) of the interested colors so that gadget users can pick from the new set of colors.

    d. **Date and Time formats**: Enter the new Date and Time formats, provided it is a valid format supported by Java's SimpleDateFormat (http://download.oracle.com/javase/1.4.2/docs/api/java/text/SimpleDateFormat.html).

5. Click on **Update**.

Repeat the cycle until the desired result is achieved. We can always get back to the defaults by clicking on **Reset Defaults** while editing the configurations.

With some simple changes, the JIRA UI can look a lot different from how it normally looks. The following screenshot is a small example:

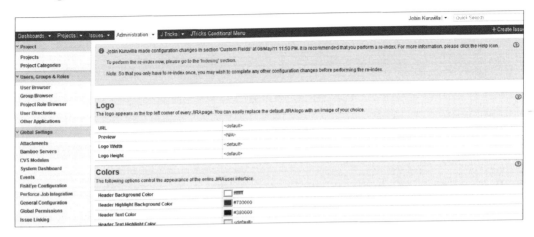

In this case, the **View issue** page will look like the following screenshot:

This is a small, yet powerful change!

Adding new web sections in the UI

A web *fragment* is a link or a section of links at a particular location of the JIRA web interface. It can be a menu in JIRA's top navigation bar, a new set of issue operations, or a new section in the **Admin UI** section.

There are two types of plugin modules to add new web fragments in JIRA, namely, the **Web Section** plugin module and the **Web Item** plugin module. A **Web Section** is a collection of links that is displayed together at a particular location of the JIRA user interface. It maybe a group of buttons on the issue operations bar or a set of links separated by lines.

In this recipe, we will see how to add a new web section to JIRA.

How to do it...

The following are the steps to add a new web section into JIRA:

1. Identify the *location* where the new sections should be added.

    JIRA has a lot of identified locations in its user interface and it lets us add new web sections in any of these locations. A complete list of the available locations can be found at `http://confluence.atlassian.com/display/JIRA/Web+Fragments`.

2. Add the new `web-section` module into the `atlassian-plugin.xml`.

    ```
    <web-section key="jtricks-admin-section" name="JTricks Section"
    location="system.admin" i18n-name-key="webfragments.admin.jtricks.
    section" weight="900">
      <label>J Tricks</label>
      <description>J Tricks Section Descitption</description>
      <tooltip>J Tricks - Little JIRA Tricks</tooltip>
    </web-section>
    ```

3. As with all other plugin modules, it has unique module `key`. Here, the two other important attributes of the `web-section` element are `location` and `weight`. `location` defines the location in the UI where the section should appear and `weight` defines the order in which it should appear.

    In the above example, location is `system.admin`, which will create a new web section under the administration screen, just like the existing sections: **Project**, **Global Settings**, and so on.

4. The `web-section` module also has a set of child elements. The `condition` or `conditions` element can be used to define conditions, one or more, details of which we will see in the following recipes. The `context-provider` element can be used to add a new context provider which will then define the velocity context for the web section. `label` is what will be displayed to the user. `param` is another element that can be used to define key/value parameters and is handy if we want to use additional custom values from the UI. The `resource` element can be used to include resource files like JavaScript or CSS files and the `tooltip` element will provide a tooltip for the section. `label` is the only mandatory element.

Elements such as `label` and `tooltip` can have optional key value parameters, as shown in the following code:

```
<label key="some.valid.key">
  <param name="param0">$somevariable</param>
</label>
```

As you can see in the example, label takes a `key/value` parameters where the value is dynamically populated from a velocity variable. The `param` will be passed to the text as {0} and will substitute that position in the label. Here, the parameters allow one to insert values into the `label` using Java's `MessageFormat` syntax, the details of which can be found at `http://download.oracle.com/javase/7/docs/api/java/text/MessageFormat.html`. Parameter names must start with `param` and will be mapped in alphabetical order to the substitutions in the format string, that is, `param0` is {0}, `param1` is {1}, `param2` is {2}, so on and so forth.

5. Deploy the plugin.

How it works...

Once the plugin is deployed, we can see that a new section is created in the Admin screen of JIRA, as shown in the following screenshot. The web item is explained in detail in the next recipe.

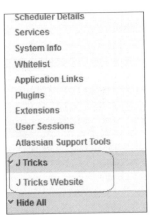

We can add the section at many different places just by changing the `location` attribute. If we change the location alone to `opsbar-operations`, the new section will appear on the **View issue** page, as shown in the next screenshot.

The web item's section attribute must be changed to match the new location as well, that is, `opsbar-operations/jtricks-admin-section`.

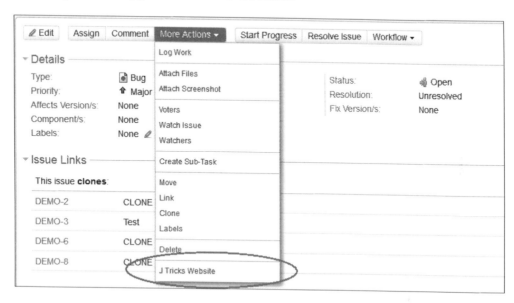

Note that the web section label may not always be visible because in some cases the section is used to just group the links. For example, in the case of issue operations, the section is just used to group the links together as shown before.

See also

▶ *Adding new web items in the UI*

Adding new web items in the UI

A *web item* is a new link that can be added at various places in the JIRA UI. A link will typically go under a *web section*. A link can simply point to a URL or can be used to invoke an action. In this recipe, we will see how to add a new web item to JIRA.

How to do it...

The following are the steps to add a new web item into JIRA:

1. Identify the *web section* where the new link should be added.

2. We have already seen how to create a new web section. A link is then added into a section created as above or into a predefined JIRA section. We can add the link directly to a location if it is a **non-sectioned** one. For **sectioned** locations, it is the location **key**, followed by a slash ('/'), and the **key** of the web section in which it should appear.

   For example, if we want to place a link in the web section created before, the section element will have the value `system.admin/jtricks-admin-section`.

3. Add the new web item module into the `atlassian-plugin.xml`.

   ```
   <web-item key="jtricks-admin-link" name="JTricks Link"
   section="system.admin/jtricks-admin-section" i18n-name-
   key="webfragments.admin.jtricks.item" weight="10">
      <label>J Tricks Website</label>
      <link linkId="jtricks.admin.link">http://www.j-tricks.com</link>
   </web-item>
   ```

   A Web item module also has a unique `key`. The other two important attributes of a web-item are `section` and `weight`. `section` defines the web section where the link is placed, as mentioned above, and `weight` defines the order in which the link will appear.

   A web item also has all the elements of a web section: `condition/conditions`, `context-provider`, `description`, `param`, `resource`, and `toolitp`. In addition, a web item also has a `link` element that defines where the web item should link to. The link could be an action, a direct link, and so on, and can be created using velocity parameters dynamically, as shown in the examples below:

   ```
   <link linkId="create_link" absolute="false">/secure/
   CreateIssue!default.jspa</link>
   <link linkId="google_link">http://www.google.com</link>
   <link linkId="profile_link" absolute="false">/secure/ViewProfile.
   jspa?name=$user.name</link>
   ```

   In the third example, `user` is a variable available in the velocity context!

   An `icon` element is used when we need to add an icon alongside the link:

   ```
   <icon height="16" width="16">
      <link>/images/avatar.gif</link>
   </icon>
   ```

4. Deploy the plugin.

How it works...

Once the plugin is deployed, we can see that a new web item is shown in the web section we created previously under the **Admin** screen of JIRA.

We can add the item under various different places, just by changing the section attribute. We have seen an example while creating a new issue operation in the previous recipe.

See also

▶ *Adding new web sections in the UI*

Adding conditions for web fragments

As we saw in the previous recipes, adding a web fragment is pretty easy. However, the job doesn't stop with that always. In many cases, we would want to limit the web item based on a set of conditions.

For example, an **Edit Issue** link should only appear for people with edit permission on an issue. An admin link should appear only if the user is a JIRA Administrator. In this recipe, let us look at how we can implement conditions for displaying web fragments.

How to do it...

It is possible to add one or more conditions to a web section or a web item. In the latter case, the `conditions` element is used, in this case, a collection of `condition/conditions` elements and a `type` attribute. The type attribute is either the logical AND or OR.

For example, the following condition specifies that the user should have either the `admin` permission or `use` permission in a project before he/she can see the web fragment that has the following condition:

```
<conditions type="OR">
  <condition class="com.atlassian.jira.plugin.webfragment.conditions.
JiraGlobalPermissionCondition">
    <param name="permission">admin</param>
  </condition>
  <condition class="com.atlassian.jira.plugin.webfragment.conditions.
JiraGlobalPermissionCondition">
    <param name="permission">use</param>
  </condition>
</conditions>
```

Possible values of permission are `admin`, `use`, `sysadmin`, `project`, `browse`, `create`, `edit`, `scheduleissue`, `assign`, `assignable`, `attach`, `resolve`, `close`, `comment`, `delete`, `work`, `worklogdeleteall`, `worklogdeleteown`, `worklogeditall`, `worklogeditown`, `link`, `sharefilters`, `groupsubscriptions`, `move`, `setsecurity`, `pickusers`, `viewversioncontrol`, `modifyreporter`, `viewvotersandwatchers`, `managewatcherlist`, `bulkchange`, `commenteditall`, `commenteditown`, `commentdeleteall`, `commentdeleteown`, `attachdeleteall`, and `attachdeleteown`.

Let us consider a simple example of how to write a condition and display the web items based on it. In this example, we will display a web item in the top navigation bar if, and only if, the user has logged in and belongs to the `jira-developer` group. The following are the steps:

1. Write the `condition` class. The class should extend the `AbstractJiraCondition` class and override the following abstract method.

   ```
   public abstract boolean shouldDisplay(User user, JiraHelper
   jiraHelper);
   ```

2. In our example, all we need to check is that the user is not null and is a member of the group `jira-developers`. The class is implemented as follows:

   ```
   public class DeveloperCondition extends AbstractJiraCondition {
     @Override
     public boolean shouldDisplay(User user, JiraHelper jiraHelper) {
       return user != null && user.getGroups().contains("jira-
   developers");
     }
   }
   ```

3. Add the new condition class in the `web-item`:

   ```
   <web-item key="jtricks-condition-menu" name="JTricks Condition
   Menu" section="system.top.navigation.bar" weight="160">
     <description>J Tricks Web site with condition</description>
   ```

```
<label>JTricks Conditional Menu</label>
<tooltip>J Tricks Web site</tooltip>
<link linkId="jtricks-condition-menu">http://www.j-tricks.com</
link>
    <condition class="com.jtricks.conditions.DeveloperCondition"/>
</web-item>
```

As you can see, the section here is `system.top.navigation.bar`, which will place the new link on the Top Navigation bar. But the link will be visible only if the condition `DeveloperCondition` returns `true`.

We can easily invert a condition using the `invert` flag as follows:

```
<condition class="com.jtricks.conditions.DeveloperCondition"
invert="true"/>
```

This will display the link if the user is not logged in or not in the group of JIRA developers!

4. Deploy the plugin.

How it works...

Once the plugin is deployed, we can see that the new **JTricks Conditional Menu** is rendered in the Top Navigation bar only when the user is logged in and in the group of JIRA developers.

The following screenshot shows the dashboard of a user who is logged in and in the group of JIRA developers:

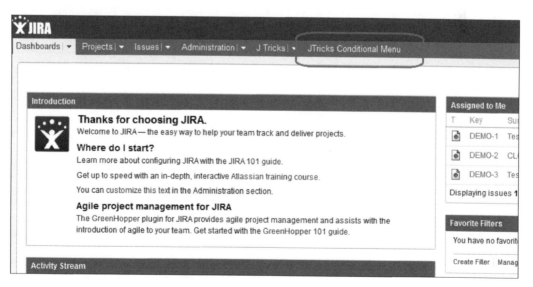

If the user is not logged in, the menu is not shown as seen in the following screenshot. In this case, we only have web items that don't have conditions defined for them!

Creating new velocity context for web fragments

As we have mentioned in the previous recipes, it is possible to add velocity variables while constructing a JIRA web fragment. JIRA supports a list of variables by default, which includes `user`, `req`, `baseurl`, and so on. The full list and the details of these variables can be found at `http://confluence.atlassian.com/display/JIRADEV/Web+Fragments#WebFragments-VelocityContext`.

In this recipe, we will see how to add more variables to the velocity context with the use of the `context-provider` element.

How to do it...

The `context-provider` element adds to the Velocity context available to the web section and web item modules. Only one `context-provider` can be added for an item. The following steps show how we can make use of a context provider:

1. Create the new `ContextProvider` class.

   The class must implement `com.atlassian.plugin.web.ContextProvider`. To make things easy, it is enough to extend the `AbstractJiraContextProvider` class and override the following abstract method in it:

   ```
   public abstract Map getContextMap(User user, JiraHelper
   jiraHelper);
   ```

The following is what the `class` looks like if you want to add the full name of the user as a separate variable in the velocity context.

```
public class UserContextProvider extends
AbstractJiraContextProvider {
  @Override
  public Map getContextMap(User user, JiraHelper helper) {
    return EasyMap.build("userName", user.getFullName());
  }
}
```

Please note that the `$user` variable is already available in the velocity context of web fragments and so the full name can be retrieved easily using `$user.getFullName()`. This is just a simple example of how to use the context providers.

2. Use the variable which is added into the velocity context appropriately while constructing the web section/item.

   In the example, let us create a new web section with the user's full name in the admin section with a single web item in it to link to the user's website.

```
<web-section key="jtricks-admin-context-section" name="JTricks
Context Section" location="system.admin" i18n-name-
key="webfragments.admin.context.jtricks.section" weight="910">
    <label>$userName</label>
    <context-provider class="com.jtricks.context.
UserContextProvider" />
</web-section>

<web-item key="jtricks-admin-context-link" name="JTricks Context
Link" section="system.admin/jtricks-admin-context-section" i18n-
name-key="webfragments.admin.context.jtricks.item" weight="10">
    <label>Website</label>
    <link linkId="jtricks.admin.context.link">http://www.j-tricks.
com</link>
</web-item>
```

   As you can see, the web section refers to `$userName` in its label.

3. Deploy the plugin.

How it works...

Once the plugin is deployed, we can see that the new web section is created under JIRA Admin UI, as shown in the following screenshot. The $userName variable is dynamically replaced by the current user's full name.

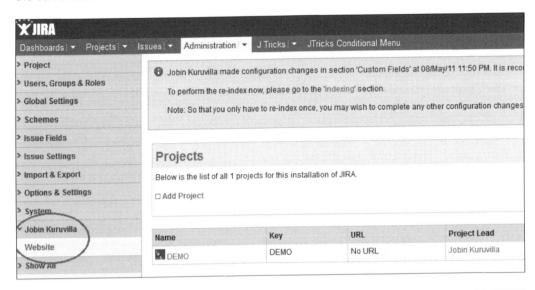

Adding a new drop-down menu on the top navigation bar

In this recipe, we will show how to use the web section and web-item modules quickly to add a new drop-down menu in JIRA's top navigation bar.

How to do it...

Here we need a *web item* first to be placed in the system's top navigation bar and then have a *web section* declared under it. The web section can then have a list of web items created under it which will then form the links on the drop-down menu.

Following are the steps to do it:

1. Create a new web item under the system's top navigation bar:

```
<web-item key="jtricks-menu" name="JTricks Menu" section="system.
top.navigation.bar" weight="150">
  <description>J Tricks Web site</description>
  <label>J Tricks</label>
```

```
<tooltip>J Tricks Web site</tooltip>
<link linkId="jtricks-menu">http://www.j-tricks.com</link>
</web-item>
```

As you can see, the section is `system.top.navigation.bar`. It can have a link that is pointed to somewhere, in this case, the JTricks' website. Here, an important thing to notice is that the `linkId` should be same as the `key`. In this case, both come under `jtricks-menu`.

2. Define a web section located under the above web item:

```
<web-section key="jtricks-section" name="JTricks Dropdown"
location="jtricks-menu" weight="200"></web-section>
```

Make sure the location is pointing to the `key` of the first web item which is also its `linkId`.

3. Now add the various web-items under the above web section.

```
<web-item key="jtricks-item" name="Jtricks Item" section="jtricks-
menu/jtricks-section" weight="210">
   <description>J Tricks Tutorials</description>
   <label>J Tricks Tutorials</label>
   <tooltip>Tutorials from J Tricks</tooltip>
   <link linkId="jtricks.link">http://www.j-tricks.com/tutorials</
link>
</web-item>
```

Note that the section is pointed to `jtricks-menu/jtricks-section`, which is similar to a localized section. Here `jtricks-menu` is the key for the first web-item and `jtricks-section` is the key for the previous web section.

4. Deploy the plugin.

How it works...

Once the plugin is deployed, we can see that the new web fragments are created in the top navigation banner. We have a web item, `JTricks Menu`, under which a list of links are grouped into a section, as shown in the following screenshot:

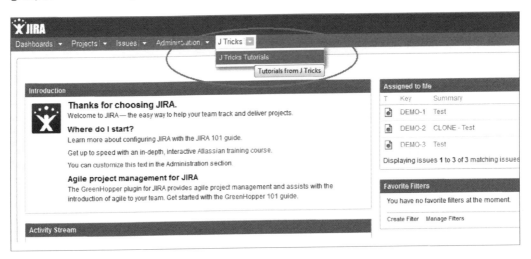

Dynamic creation of web items

We have now seen quite a few recipes on how to create web items and place them at different places in the UI. But in all the cases, we knew what links we needed. How about creating these links on the fly?

In this recipe, we will see how to create web items dynamically.

Getting ready

Create a new web item, **Favourites**, in the system top navigation bar, as discussed in the previous recipe.

How to do it...

Let us assume we want to create some links in the system top navigation bar. We have seen the same thing in the previous recipe, but that works only when we know the links in advance. Let us consider a new scenario where the user sees different sets of links when he/she is logged in and not logged in! Here the links change based on the user's status and hence need to be created dynamically.

The following is a step-by-step process to do the same:

1. Create a **Favourites** web section in the system top navigation bar.

```
<web-item key="favourites-menu" name="Favourites Menu"
section="system.top.navigation.bar" weight="900">
   <description>Favourites Menu</description>
   <label>Favourites</label>
   <tooltip>My Favourite Links</tooltip>
   <link linkId="favourites-menu">http://www.j-tricks.com</link>
</web-item>

<web-section key="favourites-section" name="Favourites Dropdown"
location="favourites-menu" weight="200">
</web-section>
```

Here, we did exactly what we saw in the previous recipe. A web-item is created in the top navigation bar under which a web section is created.

2. Define a **simple link factory** in the `atlassian-plugin.xml`. A Simple Link Factory defines a new link factory that creates the set of links dynamically. It always hangs off an already declared web section, `favourites-section` in our case.

```
<simple-link-factory key="favourites-factory" name="Favourites
Link Factory" section="favourites-menu/favourites-section"  i18n-
name-key="jtricks.favourites.factory" weight="10" lazy="true"
class="com.jtricks.web.links.FavouritesLinkFactory"/>
```

3. As you can see, a simple link factory has a unique `key` and it points to an already available `location`. In our case, the location is `favourites-menu/favourites-section`, which is declared in *Step 1*.

The most important attribute is the `class` attribute, `FavouritesLinkFactory`. Also, notice that the attribute `lazy` is declared as `true` to represent lazy loading.

Create the **simple link factory** class. The class should implement the `SimpleLinkFactory` interface, as shown:

```
public class FavouritesLinkFactory implements SimpleLinkFactory {

   public List<SimpleLink> getLinks(User user, Map<String, Object>
arg1) {
      ...
   }

   public void init(SimpleLinkFactoryModuleDescriptor arg0) {
   }
}
```

All we need to do is to implement two methods, getLinks and init. The init method needs to be implemented only when you need to initialize anything in your plugin. This will be invoked only once, that is, at JIRA startup.

The getLinks method is the actual method that we need to implement.

4. Implement the getLinks method. In this method, we need to return a collection of links that will be then displayed as a web-item under the section we defined earlier.

Each link we return is an instance of the SimpleLink class. A SimpleLink object is the Java representation of a web item we normally declare in the atlassian-plugin.xml. It has all the same attributes such as the label, title, iconUrl, style, url, and an accesskey.

The following is the method for our example:

```
public List<SimpleLink> getLinks(User user, Map<String, Object>
arg1) {
   List<SimpleLink> links = new ArrayList<SimpleLink>();

   if (user != null) {
      links.add(new SimpleLinkImpl("id1", "Favourites 1", "My
Favourite One", null, null, "http://www.google.com", null));
         links.add(new SimpleLinkImpl("id2", "Favourites 2", "My
Favourite Two", null, null, "http://www.j-tricks.com", null));
      } else {
         links.add(new SimpleLinkImpl("id1", "Favourite Link", "My
Default Favourite", null, null, "http://www.google.com", null));
      }
   return links;
}
```

Here, we just create different links based on whether the user is null or not. A user is null if he/she is not logged in. As you can see, each link has different attributes mentioned earlier.

5. Package the plugin and deploy it.

The links should now be created dynamically.

How it works...

Once the plugin is deployed, we can see that the new web fragments are created in the top navigation banner. If the user is not logged in, the **Favourites** menu is shown with the default link, as shown in the following screenshot:

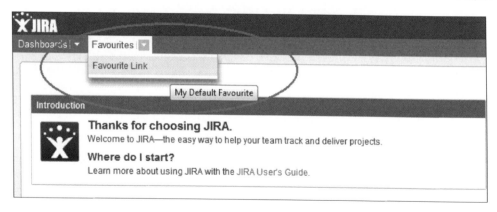

Once the user is logged in, he/she will see a different set of links, as per the getLinks method.

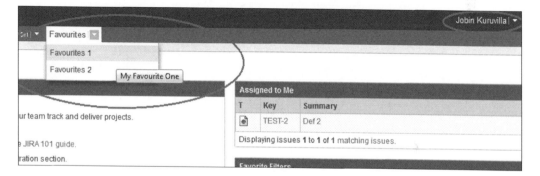

The same idea can be used to create dynamic links based on a different criterion, and of course, at various different places in the UI.

Adding new tabs in the View Issue screen

We have seen how to enhance the UI by adding new sections and links at various locations. In this recipe, we will see how to add a new tab panel under the view issue page, similar to the existing panels such as Comments, Change History, and so on.

Getting ready

Create a new skeleton plugin using the Atlassian Plugin SDK.

How to do it...

Adding a new tab panel to the **View Issue** page can be done by the **Issue Tab Panel** Plugin **Module**. Following are the steps to create a new issue tab panel that displays some static text with a greeting to the logged-in user.

1. Define the `Issue Tab Panel` in the `atlassian-plugin.xml`.

```
<issue-tabpanel key="jtricks-issue-tabpanel" i18n-name-
key="issuetabpanel.jtricks.name" name="Issue Tab Panel"
class="com.jtricks.JTricksIssueTabPanel">
   <description>A sample Issue Tab Panel</description>
   <label>JTricks Panel</label>
   <resource type="velocity" name="view" location="templates/issue/
issue-panel.vm" />
   <order>100</order>
   <sortable>true</sortable>
</issue-tabpanel>
```

   Here, the plugin module has a unique `key` and should define the `class` that implements the tab panel. It also has a list of elements, as explained as follows:

   a. `description`: A description of the tab panel

   b. `label`: A human-readable label for the panel

   c. `resource`: Defines the velocity template that renders the tab panel view

   d. `order`: Defines the order in which the panels will appear on the view issue page

   e. `sortable`: Defines whether the contents of the panel is sortable or not. For example, sorting comments or the change history elements.

2. Implement the `Issue Tab Panel` class.

   The class should extend the `AbstractIssueTabPanel` class, which in turn implements the `IssueTabPanel` interface. We need to implement the `showPanel` and `getActions` methods.

   a. Implement the `shownPanel` method to return `true` if the panel can be displayed to the user. This method can have complex logic to check whether the user can see the tab or not, but in the example we have, we just return `true`.

   ```
   public boolean showPanel(Issue issue, User remoteUser) {
      return true;
   }
   ```

   b. Implement the `IssueAction` classes that need to be returned in the `getActions` method. It is in the `Action` classes that we populate the velocity context to render the view and also return the time performed to facilitate sorting if `sortable = true`.

In the example, let us create a single `Action` class as follows:

```
public class JTricksAction extends AbstractIssueAction{
   private final JiraAuthenticationContext
authenticationContext;

   public JTricksAction(IssueTabPanelModuleDescriptor
   descriptor, JiraAuthenticationContext
   authenticationContext) {
      super(descriptor);
      this.authenticationContext = authenticationContext;
   }

   @Override
   public Date getTimePerformed() {
      return new Date();
   }

   @Override
   protected void populateVelocityParams(Map params) {
            params.put("user", this.authenticationContext.
getUser().getFullName());
   }
}
```

As you can see, the action class must extend the `AbstractIssueAction` class, which in turn implements the `IssueAction` interface.

In the `getTimePerformed` method, it just returns the current date. `populateVelocityParams` is the important method where the velocity context is populated. In our example, we just include the current user's full name with key name as `user`.

c. Implement the `getActions` method in the `Tab Panel` class to return a list of `IssueActions`. In our example, we just return a list that contains the new `JTricksAction`.

```
public List getActions(Issue issue, User remoteUser) {
   List<JTricksAction> panelActions = new
ArrayList<JTricksAction>();
   panelActions.add(new JTricksAction(descriptor,
authenticationContext));
   return panelActions;
}
```

Here, the `descriptor` is an instance variable of the super class. All we do here is create an instance of the `Action` class and return a list of such actions.

3. Create the view template in the location specified earlier.
   `Hey $user, sample Issue Tab Panel!` is all we need and the user here is populated into the context in the `Action` class.

4. Package the plugin and deploy it.

How it works...

Once the plugin is deployed, a new tab panel will appear in the **View Issue** page, as shown in the following screenshot.

As you can see, the greeting message there is populated using the velocity context and the attributes in it.

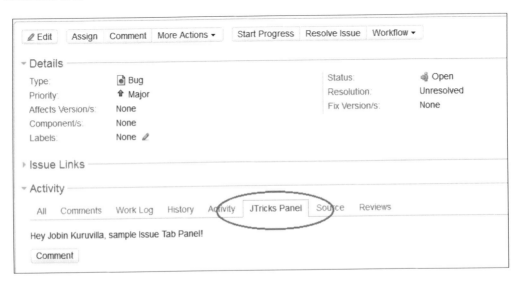

Adding new tabs in the Browse Project screen

In this recipe, we will see how to add a new tab in the **Browse Project** screen.

Getting ready

Create a new skeleton plugin using Atlassian Plugin SDK.

How to do it...

The following are the steps to create a new project tab panel:

1. Define the `Project Tab Panel` in the `atlassian-plugin.xml`.

```xml
<project-tabpanel key="jtricks-project-panel" i18n-name-
key="projectpanels.jtricks.name" name="JTricks Panel" class="com.
jtricks.JTricksProjectTabPanel">
    <description>A sample Project Tab Panel</description>
    <label>JTricks Panel</label>
    <order>900</order>
    <resource type="velocity" name="view" location="templates/
project/project-panel.vm" />
</project-tabpanel>
```

Here, the plugin module has a unique `key` and should define the `class` that implements the tab panel. It also has a list of elements, as explained as follows:

   a. `description`: A description of the tab panel

   b. `label`: A human-readable label for the panel

   c. `resource`: Defines the velocity template that renders the tab panel view

   d. `order`: Defines the order in which the panels will appear on the browse project screen.

2. Implement the `Project Tab Panel` class.

   The class should extend the `AbstractProjectTabPanel` class, which in turn implements the `ProjectTabPanel` interface. We need to implement only the `showPanel` method.

   The `showPanel` method should return `true` if the panel can be displayed to the user. This method can have complex logic to check whether the user can see the tab or not, but in the example we have, we just return `true`.

```java
public boolean showPanel(Issue issue, User remoteUser) {
    return true;
}
```

3. Create the view template in the location specified earlier. The template we defined is as follows:

```
Sample Project Tab Panel from <a href="http://www.j-tricks.
com">J Tricks</a>
```

   If we need extra velocity parameters in this context, it can be populated in the `Project Tab Panel` class by overriding the `createVelocityParams` method.

4. Package the plugin and deploy it.

How it works...

Once the plugin is deployed, a new tab panel will appear in the **Browse Project** page, as shown in the following screenshot:

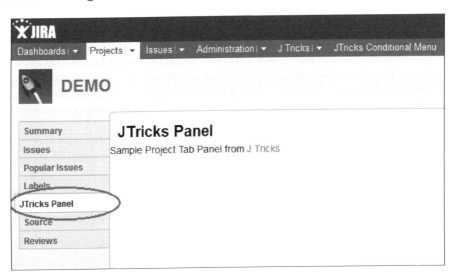

Creating Project Tab Panel using fragments

We have seen how to create a new `Project Tab Panel` in the previous recipe. While this works in most cases, sometimes we would like to create the nice fragmented view in JIRA 4.1+. Here, each project tab panel has a list of fragments organized in two columns. We can create the fragments and order them so that they appear in a formatted way on clicking the new tab panel.

In this recipe, we will see how to create the project tab panel using fragments. Before we start, there are a couple of things worth mentioning.

1. We need to use the same package structure, `com.atlassian.jira.plugin.projectpanel.impl`, to create the fragment class, as we need to override the protected methods in it.

2. The components used in creating the fragments are not available in the OSGI v2.0 plugins, and hence we have chosen to go with a v1.0 plugin.

How to do it...

Following are the steps to create a fragmented `Project Tab Panel`.

1. Add the project tab panel module in `atlassian-plugin.xml`.

```
<project-tabpanel key="jtricks-project-fragment-panel" i18n-
name-key="projectpanels.fragments.jtricks.name" name="JTricks
Frag Panel" class="com.atlassian.jira.plugin.projectpanel.impl.
JTricksFragProjectTabPanel">
    <description>A sample Project Tab Panel with fragments
    </description>
    <label>JTricks Fragments Panel</label>
    <order>910</order>
</project-tabpanel>
```

The attributes and elements are similar to a normal `Project Tab Panel`, except that it doesn't have a view velocity resource defined. The HTML here is constructed with the help of fragments.

2. Create the fragments needed in the project panel. Let us assume we need two fragments, `FragmentOne` and `FragmentTwo`, for our example.

   Each Fragment must extend the `AbstractFragment` class. We need to override three methods for a fragment.

   a. `getId`: It defines the ID of the fragment, which will also be the name of the velocity template used to render this fragment.

   b. `getTemplateDirectoryPath`: It returns the path where the velocity template is placed.

   c. `showFragment`: It defines whether the fragment is visible to the user or not.

   A fourth method, `createVelocityParams`, can be overridden if we need to pass extra parameters to the velocity context. Following is how `FragmentOne` looks:

```
public class FragmentOne extends AbstractFragment{

    protected static final String TEMPLATE_DIRECTORY_PATH =
    "templates/project/fragments/";
    public FragmentOne(VelocityManager velocityManager,
ApplicationProperties applicationProperites,
JiraAuthenticationContext jiraAuthenticationContext) {
        super(velocityManager, applicationProperites,
jiraAuthenticationContext);
    }

    public String getId() {
        return "fragmentone";
    }
```

```
    public boolean showFragment(BrowseContext ctx) {
      return true;
    }

    @Override
    protected String getTemplateDirectoryPath() {
      return TEMPLATE_DIRECTORY_PATH;
    }

    @Override
    protected Map<String, Object> createVelocityParams(BrowseCont
ext ctx) {
      Map<String, Object> createVelocityParams = super.
createVelocityParams(ctx);
      createVelocityParams.put("user", ctx.getUser().
getFullName());
      return createVelocityParams;
    }
}
```

Here the velocity template will be `fragmentone.vm`, placed under `templates/project/fragments/`. The fragment is always shown, but this can be modified to include complex logic. We also add a new variable, `user`, to the context which then holds the full name of the current user. Note that user variable is already in the context, but this is just for an example.

`FragmentTwo` will be similar, as shown in the next few lines of code:

```
public class FragmentTwo extends AbstractFragment {
  protected static final String TEMPLATE_DIRECTORY_PATH =
"templates/project/fragments/";
  public FragmentTwo(VelocityManager velocityManager,
ApplicationProperties applicationProperites,
JiraAuthenticationContext jiraAuthenticationContext) {
     super(velocityManager, applicationProperites,
jiraAuthenticationContext);
    }
  public String getId() {
    return "fragmenttwo";
    }
  public boolean showFragment(BrowseContext ctx) {
    return true;
    }
  @Override
  protected String getTemplateDirectoryPath() {
    return TEMPLATE_DIRECTORY_PATH;
    }
}
```

Here, the velocity template will be `templates/project/fragments/` `fragmenttwo.vm`. Note that we don't override the `createVelocityParams` method here as we don't need any extra parameter in the context.

3. Create the fragent-based project tab panel class. In our example, the class is `JTricksFragProjectTabPanel`. The class must extend the `AbstractFragmentBasedProjectTabPanel` class. We need to implement three methods in this class:

   a. `getLeftColumnFragments`: This returns a list of `ProjectTabPanelFragment` classes that form to the left column of the panel.

   b. `getRightColumnFragments`: This returns a list of `ProjectTabPanelFragment` classes that forms to the right column of the panel.

   c. `showPanel`: This determines whether the panel can be shown or not.

   The class will look like the following:

```
public class JTricksFragProjectTabPanel extends
AbstractFragmentBasedProjectTabPanel {
   private final FragmentOne fragmentOne;
   private final FragmentTwo fragmentTwo;
   public JTricksFragProjectTabPanel(VelocityManager
velocityManager, ApplicationProperties applicationProperites,
JiraAuthenticationContext jiraAuthenticationContext) {
      this.fragmentOne = new FragmentOne(velocityManager,
applicationProperites, jiraAuthenticationContext);
      this.fragmentTwo = new FragmentTwo(velocityManager,
applicationProperites, jiraAuthenticationContext);
   }

   @Override
   protected List<ProjectTabPanelFragment> getLeftColumnFragment
s(BrowseContext ctx) {
      final List<ProjectTabPanelFragment> frags = new ArrayList<P
rojectTabPanelFragment>();
      frags.add(fragmentOne);
      return frags;
   }
   @Override
   protected List<ProjectTabPanelFragment> getRightColumnFragmen
ts(BrowseContext ctx) {
      final List<ProjectTabPanelFragment> frags = new ArrayList<P
rojectTabPanelFragment>();
      frags.add(fragmentTwo);
      return frags;
```

```
        }

        public boolean showPanel(BrowseContext ctx) {
          return true;
        }
}
```

Here, we just construct the fragment objects and return them to the appropriate column list.

4. Create the velocity templates for the fragments.

    In our example, `fragmentone.vm` looks like the following:

    ```
    <div class="mod-header">
      <h3>Fragment 1</h3>
    </div>
    <div class="mod-content">
      <ul class="item-details">
        <li>Welcome, $user!</li>
        <li>This is fragment 1.</li>
      </ul>
    </div>
    ```

    Notice the use of `$user`, which was populated in the velocity context of the `FragmentOne` class. Also, the various `div` elements are used for the UI conformance.

    Similarly, `fragmenttwo.vm` is as follows:

    ```
    <div class="mod-header">
      <h3>Fragment 2</h3>
    </div>
    <div class="mod-content">
      <ul class="item-details">
        <li>This is fragment 2!!</li>
      </ul>
    </div>
    ```

    The only difference is that we don't use the `velocity` variable here.

5. Package the plugin and deploy it.

How it works...

Once the plugin is deployed, a new fragment-based tab panel will appear in the **Browse Project** page, as shown in the following screenshot:

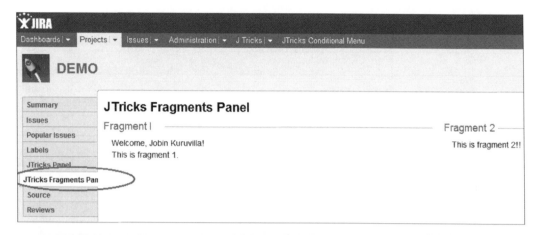

Adding new tabs in the Browse Version screen

In this recipe, we will see how to add a new tab in the **Browse Version** screen. This screen holds details of a particular version in JIRA.

Getting ready

Create a new skeleton plugin using **Atlassian Plugin SDK**.

How to do it...

The following are the steps to create a new version tab panel. It is much similar to creating a new project tab panel, except for the obvious changes in the files and keywords involved.

1. Define the Version Tab Panel in the atlassian-plugin.xml.

   ```
   <version-tabpanel key="jtricks-version-panel" i18n-name-
   key="versionpanels.jtricks.name" name="jtricks Version Panel"
   class="com.jtricks.JTricksVersionTabPanel">
     <description>A sample Version Tab Panel</description>
     <label>JTricks Panel</label>
     <order>900</order>
   ```

```
<resource type="velocity" name="view" location="templates/
version/version-panel.vm" />
</version-tabpanel>
```

Here, the plugin module has a unique `key` and should define the `class` that implements the tab panel. It also has a list of elements, as explained below:

    a. `description`: A description of the tab panel

    b. `label`: A human-readable label for the panel

    c. `resource`: Defines the velocity template that renders the tab panel view

    d. `order`: Defines the order in which the panels will appear on the Browse Version Screen.

2. Implement the `Version Tab Panel` class.

    The class should extend the `GenericTabPanel` class, which in turn would implement the `TabPanel` interface. We need to implement only the `showPanel` and `createVelocityParams` methods, the latter only if we need to add extra variables into the velocity context.

    The `showPanel` method should return true if the panel can be displayed to the user. This method can have complex logic to check whether the user can see the tab or not, but in the example we have, we just return true.

```
public boolean showPanel(Issue issue, User remoteUser) {
   return true;
}
```

    Let us just override the createVelocityParams method to add a new variable, user to the velocity context.

```
@Override
protected Map<String, Object> createVelocityParams(BrowseVersionCo
ntext context) {
   Map<String, Object> createVelocityParams = super.
createVelocityParams(context);
   createVelocityParams.put("user", context.getUser().
getFullName());
   return createVelocityParams;
}
```

    This variable will now be available on the view template that we are using.

3. Create the view template in the location specified in the plugin descriptor. Let us just create a simple template with a greeting to the current user as follows:

    Welcome $user, This is your new Version Tab!

    Note that we have used the `$user` variable that we populated in the previous step.

4. Package the plugin and deploy it.

How it works...

Once the plugin is deployed, a new tab panel will appear in the **Browse Version** page, as shown in the next screenshot:

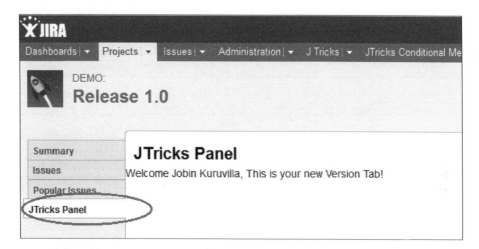

Adding new tabs in the Browse Component screen

In this recipe, we will see how to add a new tab in the **Browse Component** screen. This screen holds details of a particular component in JIRA, and the process of adding a new tab is much similar to adding a new version tab or project tab panel.

Getting ready

Create a new skeleton plugin using **Atlassian Plugin SDK**.

How to do it...

The following are the steps to create a new component tab panel.

1. Define the Component Tab Panel in the atlassian-plugin.xml.

   ```
   <component-tabpanel key="jtricks-component-panel" i18n-name-
   key="componentpanels.jtricks.name" name="jtricks Component Panel"
   class="com.jtricks.JTricksComponentTabPanel">
   ```

```
<description>A sample Component Tab Panel</description>
<label>JTricks Panel</label>
<order>900</order>
<resource type="velocity" name="view" location="templates/
component/component-panel.vm" />
</component-tabpanel>
```

As in the case of a version tab panel, component tab panel also has a unique key and should define the `class` that implements the tab panel. It also has a list of elements, as explained below:

a. `description`: A description of the tab panel

b. `label`: A human-readable label for the panel

c. `resource`: Defines the velocity template that renders the tab panel view

d. `order`: Defines the order in which the panels will appear on the Browse Component Screen.

2. Implement the `Component Tab Panel` class.

The class should extend the `GenericTabPanel` class, which in turn implements the `ComponentTabPanel` interface. We need to implement only the `showPanel` method and `createVelocityParams` method, the latter only if we need to add extra variables into the velocity context.

The `showPanel` method should return true if the panel can be displayed to the user. This method can have complex logic to check whether the user can see the tab or not, but in the example we have, we just return true.

```
public boolean showPanel(Issue issue, User remoteUser) {
    return true;
}
```

As in the previous recipe, let us override the `createVelocityParams` method to add a new variable, `user`, to the velocity context.

```
@Override
protected Map<String, Object> createVelocityParams(BrowseVersionCo
ntext context) {
    Map<String, Object> createVelocityParams = super.
createVelocityParams(context);
    createVelocityParams.put("user", context.getUser().
getFullName());
    return createVelocityParams;
}
```

This variable will now be available on the view template that we are using.

3. Create the view template in the location specified in the plugin descriptor. Let us create a simple template, as in the previous recipe, as follows:

   Welcome $user, This is your new Component Tab!

   Note that we have used the $user variable, which we populated in the previous step.

4. Package the plugin and deploy it.

How it works...

Once the plugin is deployed, a new tab panel will appear in the Browse component page, as shown in the following screenshot:

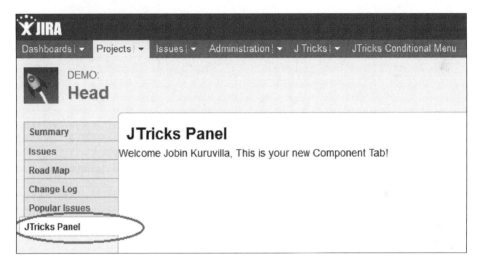

Extending a webwork action to add UI elements

In the second chapter, we have seen how to extend a webwork action. In this recipe, let us build on it and see how we can add more UI elements to an existing JIRA form.

Getting ready

Create a skeleton plugin using Atlassian plugin SDK .

How to do it...

Let us consider a simple example for explaining this. The clone issue operation in JIRA creates a copy of the original issue with the value of almost all of its fields copied across, barring few fields like issue key, created date, updated date, estimates, number of votes, and so on.

What if we want to copy across the number of votes on the issue as well? Let us say we want to add a checkbox on the clone issue form, leaving the decision to the user whether to copy the votes across or not. If the user selects the checkbox, votes will be copied across and if not, the cloned issue will be created with 0 votes as it happens in JIRA by default. This example will give a rough idea on adding new UI elements on JIRA forms and using them in the action classes.

The following is the step-by-step process that can be used to implement our example:

1. Override the JIRA web action for `CloneIssue` by creating an entry for it in the `atlassian-plugin.xml`.

   ```
   <webwork1 key="clone-issue" name="Clone Issue with new UI
   elements" class="java.lang.Object">
     <description>Sample Webwork action with extended UI elements</
   description>
     <actions>
       <action name="com.jtricks.web.action.
   ExtendedCloneIssueDetails" alias="CloneIssueDetails">
         <view name="input">/secure/views/extended-cloneissue-start.
   jsp</view>
         <view name="error">/secure/views/extended-cloneissue-start.
   jsp</view>
       </action>
     </actions>
   </webwork1>
   ```

   As we have seen in *Chapter 2, Understanding Plugin Framework*, the alias of the action remains the same as that of the `Clone Issue` action. We have gone for a custom class `ExtendedCloneIssueDetails` that extends the JIRA action class `CloneIssueDetails`.

   Here, we also use a copy of the original JSP, named as `extended-cloneissue-start.jsp`, just to keep track of the modified files. It is entirely possible to modify directly on the JIRA-supplied `cloneissue-start.jsp`.

2. Create the new action class extending the original action class. It is also possible to create an entirely new action class, but extending the original action will be easier as it leaves us with the task of only adding the extra bits that are needed.

   ```
   public class ExtendedCloneIssueDetails extends CloneIssueDetails {

       public ExtendedCloneIssueDetails(ApplicationProperties
   applicationProperties, PermissionManager permissionManager,
   IssueLinkManager issueLinkManager, IssueLinkTypeManager
   ```

```
issueLinkTypeManager, SubTaskManager subTaskManager,
AttachmentManager attachmentManager, FieldManager fieldManager,
IssueCreationHelperBean issueCreationHelperBean, IssueFactory
issueFactory, IssueService issueService) {
  super(applicationProperties, permissionManager,
issueLinkManager, issueLinkTypeManager, subTaskManager,
attachmentManager, fieldManager, issueCreationHelperBean,
issueFactory, issueService);
    }
  ...
}
```

3. Declare a variable for the new field we are going to add in the Clone Issue form. The variable name will be same as the name of the UI element.

    The variable that we declare should match the type of the UI element. For example, a checkbox will have a Java Boolean as the variable type.

    ```
    private boolean cloneVotes = false;
    ```

    Different UI elements are mapped to different Java types like text fields to Java String, number fields to Long, and so on.

4. Create getters and setters for the new field.

    ```
    public boolean isCloneVotes() {
      return cloneVotes;
    }

    public void setCloneVotes(boolean cloneVotes) {
      this.cloneVotes = cloneVotes;
    }
    ```

    These getter/setter methods will be used to get values to and from the JSPs.

5. Add the new UI element into the JSP. In our case, the JSP is `extended-cloneissue-start.jsp`, which is a copy of `cloneissue-start.jsp`. The UI element that we add should follow the rules of the templates used in the version of JIRA we are using. This is important as the UI keeps changing between versions.

    As in JIRA 4.3, the new checkbox can be added as follows:

    ```
    <page:applyDecorator name="auifieldgroup">
      <aui:checkbox label="'Clone Votes?'" name="'cloneVotes'"
    fieldValue="'true'" theme="'aui'">
        <aui:param name="'description'">
          <ww:text name="'Clone the votes on the original issue?'"/>
        </aui:param>
      </aui:checkbox>
    </page:applyDecorator>
    ```

    Note that the checkbox field has the same `name` as that of the class variable in the Action class. The rest of the code revolves around the decorator to use, attributes and elements to be passed, and so on.

6. Capture the checkbox value in the action class when the form is submitted. The value can be retrieved in the class using the getter method. We can now do all the things that we want using the checkbox value.

   In this case, if the cloneVotes checkbox is checked, the votes field should be copied across from the original issue to the cloned one. As we have seen in the previous chapter while discarding field values during cloning, we can override the `setFields` method to do that.

```
@Override
protected void setFields() throws FieldLayoutStorageException {
  super.setFields();
  if (isCloneVotes()) {
    getIssueObject().setVotes(getOriginalIssue().getVotes());
  }
}
```

   The important bit here is that the checkbox value is passed across to the action class behind the scenes and we are using the same to decide whether to copy the votes' values across.

7. Package the plugin, deploy it, and see it in action. Don't forget to copy the modified JSP file to the `/secure/views` folder.

An action can be overridden only once. Care must be taken not to override it again in another plugin (might be a third party one), as only one will be picked up.

How it works...

Once the plugin is deployed and the JSP file is copied across to the right location, we can find the modified UI while cloning an issue. The form will have the new field, **Clone Votes?**, as shown in the following screenshot:

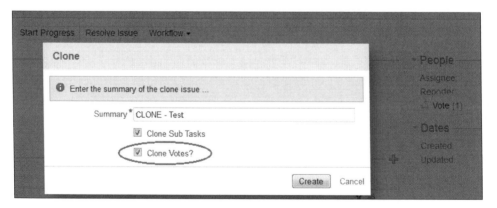

Note that the issue we are cloning has one vote on it. If the cloneVotes field is checked, the cloned issue will have the votes on it, as shown in the following screenshot:

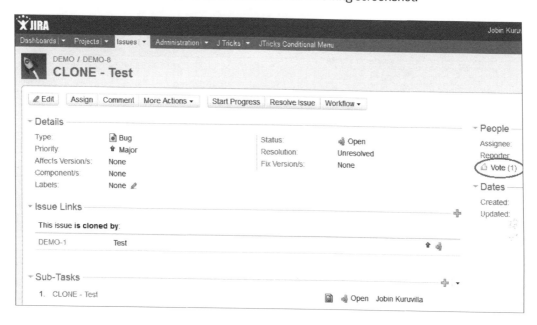

A similar approach can be used to add any new fields into the JIRA forms and use the fields in the action classes, as required. You can find more information about the various elements and its attributes by looking at the `webwork.tld` file, residing in the `WEB-INF/tld/` folder.

See also

▶ *Extending a webwork action in JIRA*

Displaying dynamic notifications/warnings on issues

JIRA has an interesting feature, the Announcement Banner, which can be used to make announcements to its user community via JIRA itself. But sometimes, it isn't enough to satisfy all its users. Power users of JIRA sometimes want to see warnings or notifications while they are viewing an issue based on some attributes of the issue.

In this recipe, we will see how to add a warning or error message on an issue based on whether the issue has subtasks or not!

Getting ready

Create a Skeleton plugin using Atlassian Plugin SDK. Here also, as in the previous recipe, the core logic is in extending the JIRA action and modifying the existing JSP files.

How to do it...

The following are the steps to display warnings/errors based on the number of subtasks on a standard issue type.

1. As in the previous recipe, extend the JIRA action (in this case, View action) by adding a webwork module in `atlassian-plugin.xml`.

   ```
   <webwork1 key="view-issue" name="View Issue with warning"
   class="java.lang.Object">
     <description>View Issue Screen with Warnings</description>
       <actions>
         <action name="com.jtricks.web.action.ExtendedViewIssue"
   alias="ViewIssue">
           <view name="success">/secure/views/issue/extended-
   viewissue.jsp</view>
           <view name="issuenotfound">/secure/views/issuenotfound.
   jsp</view>
           <view name="permissionviolation">/secure/views/
   permissionviolation.jsp</view>
             <command name="moveIssueLink" alias="MoveIssueLink">
               <view name="error">/secure/views/issue/viewissue.jsp</
   view>
             </command>
         </action>
       </actions>
   </webwork1>
   ```

2. Override the action class `ViewIssue` with `ExtendedViewIssue`, mentioned above, and add a public method to check whether the issue has any subtasks or not. Make sure the method is public so that it can be invoked from the JSP.

   ```
   public boolean hasNoSubtasks(){
      return !getIssueObject().isSubTask() && getIssueObject().
   getSubTaskObjects().isEmpty();
   }
   ```

3. It just checks whether the issue is a subtask or not and returns `true` if it is a standard `issuetype` and has no subtasks of its own.

4. Modify the `extended-viewissue.jsp` file to add a warning at the top, if the issue has no subtasks. Here we add a condition to check if the public method returns `true`, and if so, the warning is added, as shown below:

```
<ww:if test="/hasNoSubtasks() == true">
  <div class="aui-message warning">
    <span class="aui-icon icon-warning"></span>
    The Issue has no Subtasks!  - WARNING
  </div>
</ww:if>
```

5. As you can see, we have used the JIRA styles to add a warning icon and a warning div container.

6. Package the plugin and deploy it to see it in action.

How it works...

Once the plugin is deployed, if a standard issue has no subtasks, the user will see a warning, as shown below, if the warning code was added immediately after the summary field.

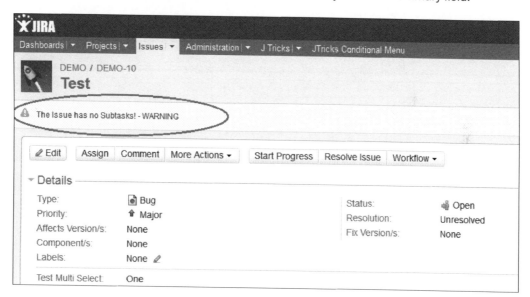

Just by modifying the CSS to add error styles, the message will appear as shown:

```
<ww:if test="/hasNoSubtasks() == true">
  <div class="aui-message error">
    <span class="aui-icon icon-error"></span>
    The Issue has no Subtasks! - ERROR
  </div>
</ww:if>
```

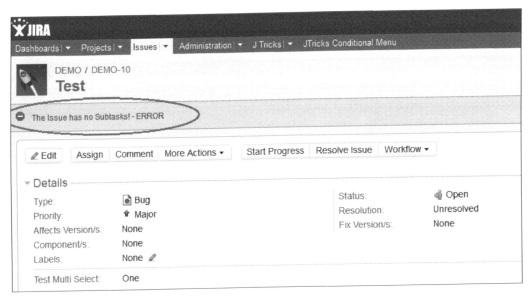

See also

▶ *Extending a webwork action in JIRA*

Re-ordering Issue Operations in the View Issue page

In the previous chapter, we have seen how to create new issue operations. All the existing issue operations in JIRA have a predefined order associated with it. Currently, in JIRA, the actions are ordered as shown in the following screenshot:

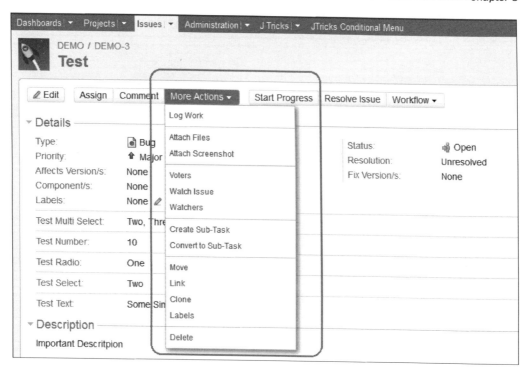

In this recipe, we will see how we can reorder those actions with out actually doing any coding! For example, let us assume we want to move **Delete** option to first in the list and then move the subtask operations up the chart!

How to do it...

Following is the step-by-step process to reorder the issue operations:

1. Go to the `system-issueoperations-plugin.xml` residing under the `WEB-INF/classes` folder. This is the file where all the issue operations are defined.

2. Modify the `weight` attribute on the relevant plugin modules to order them.

   `weight` is the attribute that defines the order of JIRA web fragments. Issue operations post JIRA 4.1.x are stored as web fragments and hence are reordered using weight.

   Prior to JIRA 4.1, issue operations were defined using Issue Operations plugin module instead of `web-items`. In those modules, the `order` attribute was used to define the ordering, which is an equivalent to the current `weight` attribute.

   Lower the `weight`, and the item will appear first.

3. Save the file and restart JIRA.

How it works...

In our example, we wanted the Delete operation to appear first. As 10 is the lowest weight value by default, if we give a weight of 5 to the `delete` web section, that is, `operations-delete`, it will appear first in the list, as shown below. Similarly, we can reorder every other action, as we have done for the subtask operations as well.

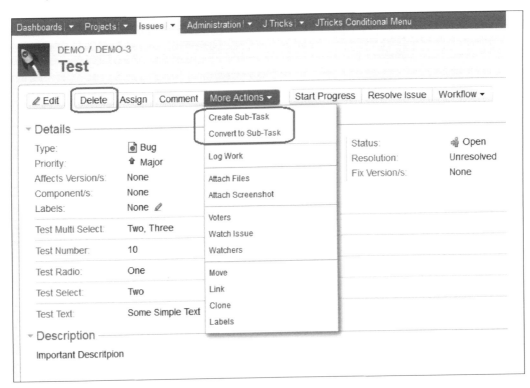

See also

▶ *Adding new Issue Operations*

Re-ordering fields in the View Issue page

It is always difficult to satisfy everyone in a big user community and that is what has happened with JIRA's view issue page. While some people love it, some think there are simple improvements possible, resulting in huge customer satisfaction.

One such thing is the layout of the view issue page. While it is neatly organised in terms of the code, the order in which they appear seems to be a strong contender for change in many cases.

For example, in the view issue page, the summary of the issue is followed by standard issue fields like Status, Priority, versions, components, and so on. It is then followed by the custom fields and then comes the description of the issue. This can sometimes be a pain, for example, in cases where description is the most important field.

Following is how the view issue page looks when you have a large custom field:

As you can see, the `Test Free Text` field has a huge value and the `description` field is not present anywhere on the screen. In this recipe, we will see how we can re-order some of the things.

How to do it...

As we saw in the previous recipe, the view issue action makes use of `/secure/views/issue/viewissue.jsp`. If we closely look at the JSP, it is neatly arranged by placing the different section of fields in different JSPs. For example, custom fields, description, attachments, linking, subtasks, and so on, all have different dedicated JSPs and are ordered in a manner that works for most.

If we want to make `description` the very first field on the view issue page, we can do that by just moving the JSP rendering description, that is, `issue_descriptiontable.jsp,` higher up in the order.

The page will then appear like this:

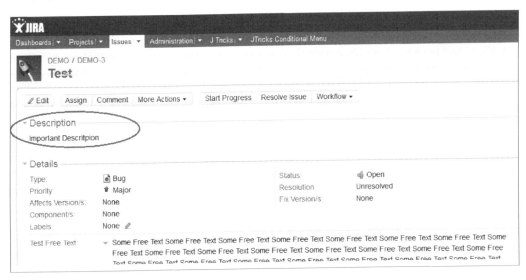

We can even wrap the custom fields in a separate div with the appropriate CSS classes, as shown in the following screenshot. Make sure you don't duplicate the values.

```
<div id="details-module" class="module toggle-wrap">
  <div class="mod-header">|
     <h3 class="toggle-title">Custom Fields</h3>
   </div>
  <div class="mod-content">
     <jsp:include page="/includes/panels/issue/view_customfields.
jsp" />
   </div>
</div>
```

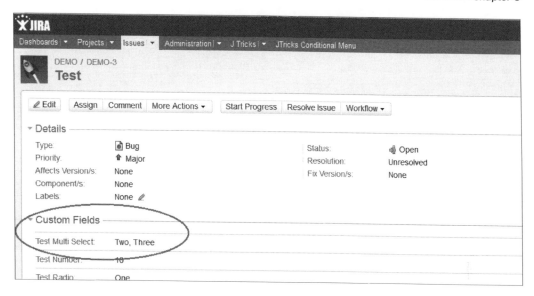

Similarly, we can reorder the other UI fragments on JIRA's **View Issue** page as well!

9
Remote Access to JIRA

In this chapter, we will cover:

- ▶ Creating a SOAP client
- ▶ Creating an issue via SOAP
- ▶ Working with custom fields and SOAP
- ▶ Attachments and SOAP
- ▶ Work logs and time tracking via SOAP
- ▶ Commenting on an issue via SOAP
- ▶ User and Group Management via SOAP
- ▶ Progressing an issue in workflow using SOAP
- ▶ Managing versions via SOAP
- ▶ Administration methods in SOAP API
- ▶ Deploy a SOAP service in JIRA
- ▶ Deploy a XML-RPC service within JIRA
- ▶ Writing a Java XML-RPC client
- ▶ Exposing services and data entities as REST APIs
- ▶ Writing Java client for REST API

Introduction

We have seen various ways to enhance the JIRA functionality in the previous chapters, but how do we communicate with JIRA from another application? What are the various methods of integrating third-party applications with JIRA? Or in simple words, how does JIRA expose its functionalities to the outside world?

JIRA exposes its functionalities via **REST**, **SOAP**, or **XML/RPC** interfaces. Only a handful of the full JIRA functionality is exposed via these interfaces but JIRA also lets us extend these interfaces. In this chapter, we will learn how to communicate with JIRA using these interfaces and add more methods into these interfaces by developing plugins. The focus of this chapter is more on SOAP with examples for other interfaces as well. The core principle for all the interfaces is the same.

There are quite a lot of methods in SOAP, most of which can be understood well from the API at `http://docs.atlassian.com/software/jira/docs/api/rpc-jira-plugin/latest/com/atlassian/jira/rpc/soap/JiraSoapService.html`. But there are some methods that need better understanding and those are the ones we will concentrate on in this chapter leaving the rest to the readers.

SOAP is usually the most preferred method of remote access but Atlassian is slowly moving towards REST as the preferred mode. A more detailed explanation of these interfaces can be found at: `http://confluence.atlassian.com/display/JIRADEV/JIRA+RPC+Services`.

Creating a SOAP client

As mentioned previously, SOAP is currently the preferred mode of remote access in JIRA though Atlassian is slowly moving towards REST. SOAP has the most number of methods compared to REST or XML/RPC and is probably used the most in the plugins that we find around us. In this recipe, we will start with the basics and see how we can write a simple SOAP client.

Getting ready

Install Maven2 and configure a Java development environment. Make sure the RPC plugin is enabled in JIRA and the **Accept remote API calls** option is turned ON at **Administration | Global Settings | General Configuration**.

How to do it...

The following are the steps to create a JIRA SOAP client:

1. Download the latest demo SOAP client distribution from the Atlassian public repository at: `http://svn.atlassian.com/svn/public/atlassian/rpc-jira-plugin/tags/`. This contains a Maven 2 project configured to use Apache Axis, and a sample Java SOAP client, which creates test issues at `http://jira.atlassian.com`.

2. Modify the `jira.soapclient.jiraurl` property in the `pom.xml` to point to your JIRA instance, the instance you want to connect to. By default, it points to `http://jira.atlassian.com`.

3. Download the WSDL file of the instance you want to connect to. You can find the WSDL file under the `/src/main/wsdl` location. If it is not there, or if you want to download the WSDL afresh, run the following command:

    ```
    mvn -Pfetch-wsdl -Djira.soapclient.jiraurl=http://{your_jira_
    instance}/
    ```

4. This will download the WSDL from the configured JIRA instance (as in *Step 2*) to `/src/main/wsdl/`. Skip the `jira.soapclient.jiraurl` property to download the Atlassian JIRA WSDL.

5. Create the client JAR. We can do this by running the following command to generate the sources from the WSDL and create the SOAP client:

    ```
    mvn -Pbuildclient
    ```

6. This will generate a JAR file with all the necessary classes required. There is a second JAR file created with the dependencies (such as the axis) embedded in it. The latter will do a world of good if you are executing it from an environment without axis and other dependencies already configured in it.

7. Write the client program. Let us go with the simplest approach in this recipe, that is, to create a simple standalone Java class in Eclipse. Start by creating an Eclipse project by running the following command:

    ```
    mvn eclipse:eclipse
    ```

> You can alternatively try other IDEs or even run from the command prompt, whichever is convenient. Make sure you add the client JAR created in *Step 4* in the classpath. All set to write a simple program that just logs into our JIRA instance. From now on, it is just another web service invocation as detailed in the following steps.

8. Create the standalone Java class.

9. Get the SOAP service locator:

```
JiraSoapServiceServiceLocator jiraSoapServiceLocator = new
JiraSoapServiceServiceLocator();
```

10. Get the SOAP service instance from the locator by passing the URL of your JIRA instance:

```
JiraSoapService jiraSoapService = jiraSoapServiceLocator.
getJirasoapserviceV2(new URL(your_url));
```

11. Start accessing the methods using the SOAP service instance. For example, the log in can be done as follows:

```
String token = jiraSoapService.login(your_username, your_
password);
```

The token retrieved here is used for all the other operations instead of logging in every time. You can see the token as the first argument in all other operations.

12. With that, our SOAP Client is ready. Let us just try getting an issue using the key and print its key and ID to prove that this stuff works!

```
RemoteIssue issue = jiraSoapService.getIssue(authToken, ISSUE_
KEY);
System.out.println("Retrieved Issue:"+issue.getKey()+" with
Id:"+issue.getId());
```

You will find the output printed with the issue key and ID.

Hopefully, this gives you a fair idea to get started with your first SOAP client! There is a lot more you can do with the SOAP client some of which we will see in the coming recipes.

Creating an issue via SOAP

In the previous recipe, we have seen how to create a SOAP client. We also saw how to use the client to connect to the JIRA instance and perform the operations, by taking 'browsing an issue' as an example. In this recipe, we will see how to create an issue using SOAP API.

Getting ready

Create a JIRA SOAP client as mentioned in the previous recipe.

How to do it...

Following are the steps to create an issue with the standard fields populated on it:

1. As mentioned in the previous recipe, get the JIRA SOAP service stub and log in to the box:

```
JiraSoapServiceServiceLocator jiraSoapServiceLocator = new
JiraSoapServiceServiceLocator();
JiraSoapService jiraSoapService = jiraSoapServiceLocator.
getJirasoapserviceV2(new URL(your_url));
String authToken = jiraSoapService.login(userName, password);
```

2. Create an instance of `RemoteIssue`:

```
RemoteIssue issue = new RemoteIssue();
```

3. Populate the standard fields on the `RemoteIssue` as appropriate:

```
issue.setProject(PROJECT_KEY);
issue.setType(ISSUE_TYPE_ID);
issue.setSummary("Test Issue via my tutorial");
issue.setPriority(PRIORITY_ID);
issue.setDuedate(Calendar.getInstance());
issue.setAssignee("");
```

Make sure the `PROJECT_KEY`, `ISSUE_TYPE_ID`, `PRIORITY_ID`, and so on, are all valid values in your JIRA instance. `ISSUE_TYPE_ID` and `PRIORITY_ID` are IDs and not the name of the issue type and priority.

4. Set the components on the issue. An issue can have multiple components and hence we need to set an array of `RemoteComponent` objects as shown in the following block of code:

```
RemoteComponent component1 = new RemoteComponent();
component1.setId(COMPONENT_ID1);
RemoteComponent component2 = new RemoteComponent();
component2.setId(COMPONENT_ID2);
issue.setComponents(new RemoteComponent[] { component1, component2
});
```

We can have as many components as we want, provided the `id` instances are valid component IDs in the project we are creating the issue. Here, `id` is the unique ID you will find for the component when we browse a component, as shown in the following screenshot:

5. Set the **Fix for Versions** or **Affected Versions** similar to how we set the components:

```
RemoteVersion version = new RemoteVersion();
version.setId(VERSION_ID);
RemoteVersion[] remoteVersions = new RemoteVersion[] { version };
issue.setFixVersions(remoteVersions);
```

Again, `VERSION_ID` the unique ID of the version and can be found while browsing the version as we did with components.

6. Invoke the create issue operation on the soap client by passing the authentication token and the `RemoteIssue` object we constructed.

```
RemoteIssue createdIssue = jiraSoapService.createIssue(authToken,
issue);
```

7. The issue should now be created and its details like the ID are available on the returned `RemoteIssue` object, which can be printed as follows:

```
System.out.println("\tSuccessfully created issue " + createdIssue.
getKey() + " with ID:" + createdIssue.getId());
```

How it works...

This is just a classic example of invoking a web service from a Java application using Axis2. Once the Java client is written as explained before, we can run the same and the issue will be created in the instance we have referenced in the client.

Following is a screenshot of an issue created in the TEST project at `http://jira.atlassian.com`.

As you can see, the issue gets populated with all the fields we have set on the `RemoteIssue` object.

Working with custom fields and SOAP

We have seen how to create an issue with its standard fields. In this recipe, we will deal with custom fields—**create**, **update,** and **read** their values.

Getting ready

As in the previous recipe, create a JIRA SOAP client.

How to do it...

As mentioned earlier, we will see the creation, updating, and browsing of custom field values separately in this recipe.

Creating an issue with custom field values

Creating an issue with custom fields is pretty similar to creating issues with components or versions. All the custom fields are set on the issue using a single method `setCustomFieldValues`, which takes an array of `RemoteCustomFieldValue` objects.

The following steps explain how it's done:

1. Identify the custom fields that need to be set on the issue and find their IDs. The ID of a custom field is of the form `customfield_[id]` where `[id]` is the database ID of the custom field. This ID can be determined from the database, or by editing a custom field in the admin interface, and copying its ID from the URL, as shown in the following screenshot:

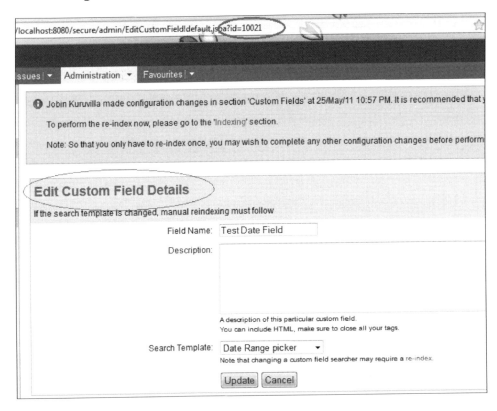

2. Create a `RemoteCustomFieldValue` for each of the custom fields identified. `RemoteCustomFieldValue` can be created as follows:

```
RemoteCustomFieldValue customFieldValue = new
RemoteCustomFieldValue(CUSTOM_FIELD_KEY, "", new String[] {
CUSTOM_FIELD_VALUE1, CUSTOM_FIELD_VALUE2 });
```

The values that we pass—`CUSTOM_FIELD_VALUE1`, `CUSTOM_FIELD_VALUE2`, and so on—should be valid for the field or else will result in validation errors in the server. For single-value custom fields, the array will consist only of a single value. The second attribute takes a `parentKey` value that is used only for multidimensional fields such as Cascading select lists. For single-value and multi-value fields like select lists, multi select, and so on, the `parentKey` will be an empty string.

For example, `RemoteCustomFieldValue` is constructed for a cascading select as follows:

```
RemoteCustomFieldValue customFieldValue = new
RemoteCustomFieldValue(CUSTOM_FIELD_KEY_2, "PARENT_KEY", new
String[] { CUSTOM_FIELD_VALUE_2 });
```

The parent key will be used to construct the full key of the custom field. For example, a cascading select will have the full custom field key as `customfield_10061:1` where `customfield_10061` is the key of the parent and `:1` indicates the first child. In fact, the following two represent the same thing:

```
RemoteCustomFieldValue customFieldValue = new RemoteCustomFieldVal
ue("customfield_10061", "1", new String[] { "Some Val" });
```

```
RemoteCustomFieldValue customFieldValue = new RemoteCustomFieldVal
ue("customfield_10061:1", null, new String[] { "Some Val" });
```

3. Set the array of all the custom field values on the issue.

```
RemoteCustomFieldValue[] customFieldValues = new
RemoteCustomFieldValue[] { customFieldValue1, customFieldValue2 };
issue.setCustomFieldValues(customFieldValues);
```

4. Create the issue as usual:

```
RemoteIssue createdIssue = jiraSoapService.createIssue(authToken,
issue);
```

Updating custom fields on an issue

Updating a custom field is much similar. However in the `updateIssue` method, it takes an array of `RemoteFieldValue` which could be a standard field or a custom field. In the case of a custom field, we should set the ID of the custom field (full ID if it's a multidimensional field as `RemoteFieldValue` doesn't take a parent key!) and an array of String values as shown next:

```
RemoteFieldValue[] actionParams = new RemoteFieldValue[] { new
RemoteFieldValue(CUSTOM_FIELD_KEY, new String[] { CUSTOM_FIELD_VALUE
}) };
```

The issue can now be updated as follows:

```
RemoteIssue updatedIssue = jiraSoapService.updateIssue(authToken,
ISSUE_KEY, actionParams);
```

Here, `ISSUE_KEY` is the key of the issue to be updated.

Note that the same `updateIssue()` method is used for updating standard fields as well but the only difference is that the `key` used in `RemoteFieldValue` will be the key of the standard field. The key of the standard field can be found from the `IssueFieldConstants` class.

Browsing custom fields on an issue

Custom fields on an issue can be retrieved using the `getCustomFieldValues` method on `RemoteIssue`. It can then be printed as follows:

```
RemoteCustomFieldValue[] cfValues = issue.getCustomFieldValues();
for (RemoteCustomFieldValue remoteCustomFieldValue : cfValues) {
  String[] values = remoteCustomFieldValue.getValues();
  for (String value : values) {
    System.out.println("Value for CF with Id:" +
  remoteCustomFieldValue.getCustomfieldId() + " -" + value);
  }
}
```

Here, `remoteCustomFieldValue.getValues()` returns an array of String representation of the custom field value.

Attachments and SOAP

In this recipe, we will see how to add attachments on an issue via SOAP and browse existing attachments.

Getting ready

As in the previous recipes, create a JIRA SOAP client. Also, make sure attachments are enabled on the JIRA instance.

How to do it...

Since JIRA4, attachments are added into an issue using `addBase64EncodedAttachmentsToIssue` method where as pre JIRA4 `addAttachmentsToIssue` method was used. The latter is still available though it is deprecated. There is also a known issue with the latter where it fails on large attachments.

Following are the steps to add attachments on an issue using `addBase64EncodedAttachmentsToIssue` method:

1. Create a File object using the path of the file to be uploaded. The file should be accessible via a valid URL.

   ```
   File file = new File("var/tmp/file.txt");
   ```

   The path should be valid in the context.

2. Read the contents of file into a Byte array:

```
// create FileInputStream object
FileInputStream fin = new FileInputStream(file);

/*
 * Create byte array large enough to hold the content of the file.
 * Use File.length to determine size of the file in bytes.
 */
fileContent = new byte[(int) file.length()];

/*
 * To read content of the file in byte array, use int read(byte[]
 * byteArray) method of java FileInputStream class.
 */
fin.read(fileContent);
fin.close();
```

3. Create an encoded String from the Byte array using the BASE64Encoder.

```
String base64encodedFileData = new BASE64Encoder().
encode(fileContent);
```

4. Do *Step 1* to *Step 3* for all the attachments that need to be uploaded and create a String array of the all the encoded data. In our case, we have only one:

```
String[] encodedData = new String[] { base64encodedFileData };
```

5. Use the encodedData in the addBase64EncodedAttachmentsToIssue method.

```
boolean attachmentAdded = jiraSoapService.addBase64EncodedAtta
chmentsToIssue(authToken, ISSUE_KEY, new String[] { "test.txt"
}, encodedData);
```

where ISSUE_KEY is the key of the issue where the files are attached and the String array (third argument) holds the names using which the attachments will be stored on issue.

The addAttachmentsToIssue method will also work and is similar to the one mentioned earlier, except that we don't encode the data. Instead of sending the files as a String array of encoded data, this method needs sending the files as an array of Byte arrays. Following are the steps:

1. Read the file into a Byte array as before:

```
File file = new File(filePath);
FileInputStream fin = new FileInputStream(file);
fileContent = new byte[(int) file.length()];
fin.read(fileContent);
fin.close();
```

2. Create an array of these Byte arrays and add the read files into it:

```
byte[][] files = new byte[1][];
files[0] = fileContent;
```

3. You can read as many files as you want and each will be read as a Byte array and will be added into files array.

4. Invoke the `addAttachmentsToIssue` method:

```
boolean attachmentAdded = jiraSoapService.addAttachmentsToIssue(au
thToken, ISSUE_KEY, new String[] {"test.txt" }, files);
```

Browsing the attachments on an issue can be done using the `getAttachmentsFromIssue` method. It returns an array of `RemoteAttachment` objects from which the details, such as name, `id`, and so on, can be retrieved. We can then construct the URL to the attachment using the information retrieved. Following are the steps:

1. Get the array of `RemoteAttachment` objects:

```
RemoteAttachment[] attachments = jiraSoapService.getAttachments
FromIssue(authToken, ISSUE_KEY);
```

Here, `ISSUE_KEY` is the key of the issue we are browsing.

2. Information about the attachment can be read from the `RemoteAttachment` object

```
System.out.println("Attachment Name:" + remoteAttachment.
getFilename() + ", Id:"+ remoteAttachment.getId());
```

The URL of the attachment on the JIRA instance can be constructed as follows:

```
System.out.println("URL: "+ BASE_URL+ "/secure/attachment/"
+ remoteAttachment.getId() + "/"+ remoteAttachment.
getFilename());
```

Here, `BASE_URL` is the JIRA's base URL including context path.

Worklogs and time tracking via SOAP

Time tracking in JIRA is a great feature that allows the users to track the time they spent on a particular issue. It lets the users to log the work as and when they spend time on an issue and JIRA will keep track of the original estimated time, actual time spent, and the remaining time. It also lets the users to adjust the remaining time to be spent on the issue, if needed!

While JIRA has a great user interface to let users log the work they are doing there at times, like when integrating with the third-party products, it is necessary to log the work using SOAP. In this recipe, we will see logging work using the SOAP API.

Getting ready...

As shown in the previous recipes, create a JIRA SOAP client. Also, make sure that time tracking is enabled on the JIRA instance.

How to do it...

There are different methods available to log work on an issue depending on what we need to with the remaining estimate on the issue. In all the cases, we need to create a `RemoteWorklog` object that holds the details of the work we are logging. The following are the steps:

1. Create the `RemoteWorklog` object with the details as required:

    ```
    RemoteWorklog worklog = new RemoteWorklog();
    worklog.setTimeSpent("1d 3h");
    worklog.setComment("Some comment!");
    worklog.setGroupLevel("jira-users");
    worklog.setStartDate(new GregorianCalendar(2011, Calendar.MAY,
    10));
    ```

    Note that the `setStartDate()` method takes a `Calendar` object as opposed to the `Date` object mentioned in the Javadocs.

2. Use the appropriate method to add the previous worklog. For example, if you want to automatically adjust the remaining estimate on the issue, we can use the `addWorklogAndAutoAdjustRemainingEstimate` method:

    ```
    RemoteWorklog work = jiraSoapService.addWorklogAndAutoAdjustRemain
    ingEstimate(authToken, ISSUE_KEY, worklog);
    System.out.println("Added work:" + work.getId());
    ```

3. If you want to retain the remaining estimate, use `addWorklogAndRetainRemainingEstimate`:

    ```
    RemoteWorklog work = jiraSoapService.addWorklogAndRetainRemainingE
    stimate(authToken, ISSUE_KEY, worklog);
    ```

4. If you want to add a new remaining estimate, use `addWorklogWithNewRemainingEstimate`.

    ```
    RemoteWorklog work = jiraSoapService.addWorklogWithNewRemainingEst
    imate(authToken, ISSUE_KEY, worklog, "1d");
    ```

5. This will add the work done as `1d 3h` and will reset the remaining estimate to `1d` (1 day) no matter how much the original estimate was.

How it works...

In the first step, we used the setter methods to populate the fields. As you might have guessed, the most important field is `timeSpent` which specifies a time duration in JIRA duration format, representing the time spent working on the worklog. In our example, we have used `1d 3h` which is translated to 1 day and 3 hours.

As in the previous code, we can also specify a `startDate` for the logged work, `groupLevel`, or `roleId`, which are used to restrict the visibility of the logged work and add a comment. Note that the ID shouldn't be set on the object as it will be automatically generated when the worklog is added on the issue. Also, the visibility can be set only for a group or for a role, not for both.

There's more...

Updating and deleting worklogs works in the same way using the following methods:

- `updateWorklogAndAutoAdjustRemainingEstimate`
- `updateWorklogAndRetainRemainingEstimate`
- `updateWorklogWithNewRemainingEstimate`
- `deleteWorklogAndAutoAdjustRemainingEstimate`
- `deleteWorklogAndRetainRemainingEstimate`
- `updateWorklogWithNewRemainingEstimate`

The following is an example for an update and a delete call:

```
jiraSoapService.updateWorklogWithNewRemainingEstimate(authToken, work,
"1d");
jiraSoapService.deleteWorklogAndRetainRemainingEstimate(authToken,
work.getId());
```

All the existing worklogs on an issue can be browsed using `getWorklogs` method that returns an array of `RemoteWorklog` objects.

Commenting on an issue via SOAP

In this recipe, we will see how to manage comments on an issue.

Getting ready

Create a JIRA SOAP client as mentioned in the first recipe.

How to do it...

Adding a comment on an issue using SOAP can be done as follows:

1. Create a `RemoteCommentobject` and set the necessary fields using the setter methods.

    ```
    final RemoteComment comment = new RemoteComment();
    comment.setBody(COMMENT_BODY);
    //comment.setRoleLevel(ROLE_LEVEL); // Id of your project role
    comment.setGroupLevel(null); // Make it visible to all
    ```
    Note that the ID shouldn't be set on the object as it will be generated automatically when the comment is created on the issue. Also, the visibility can be set only for a group or for a role, not for both at the same time.

2. Add the comment to the issue:

    ```
    jiraSoapService.addComment(authToken, ISSUE_KEY, comment);
    ```

    Comments on an issue can be retrieved using the `getComments` method, which returns an array of `RemoteComment` objects.

    ```
    RemoteComment[] comments = jiraSoapService.getComments(authToken,
    ISSUE_KEY);
    for (RemoteCommentremoteComment : comments) {
        System.out.println("Comment:" + remoteComment.getBody() + "
    written by " + remoteComment.getAuthor());
    }
    ```

A comment can be edited using the `editComment` operation but we should check if we have the edit permission or not by using the `hasPermissionToEditComment` method as shown next:

```
// Check permissions first
if (jiraSoapService.hasPermissionToEditComment(authToken, comment)) {
    comment.setBody(COMMENT_BODY + " Updated");
    comment.setGroupLevel("jira-users");
    jiraSoapService.editComment(authToken, comment);
}
```

Deleting a comment is not exposed via SOAP yet!

User and group management via SOAP

Let us now have a look at the user and group management using SOAP. This is really useful when the users and groups need to be managed from a third-party application.

Getting ready

Create a SOAP client as mentioned in the previous recipes.

How to do it...

Creating a group and user are pretty straightforward. The following is how we do it once the client is created:

```
//Create group jtricks-test-group
RemoteGroup group = jiraSoapService.createGroup(authToken, "jtricks-
test-group", null);
//Create user jtricks-test-user
RemoteUser user = jiraSoapService.createUser(authToken, "jtricks-test-
user", "password", "Test User", "support@j-tricks.com");
```

Here, the first snippet creates a group with name `jtricks-test-group`. The third argument is a `RemoteUser` who can be added to the group as the first user when the group is created. We can leave it as null if the group has to be created empty.

The second snippet creates a user with the relevant details, such as `Name`, `Password`, `Full Name`, and `Email`.

A user can be added to a group as follows:

```
jiraSoapService.addUserToGroup(authToken, group, user);
```

Here, group and user are `RemoteGroup` and `RemoteUser` objects respectively.

An existing user or group can be retrieved as follows:

```
RemoteUser user = jiraSoapService.getUser(authToken, "jtricks-test-
user");
RemoteGroup group = jiraSoapService.getGroup(authToken, "jtricks-test-
group");
```

The users in a group can be retrieved from the `RemoteGroup` object as shown next:

```
RemoteUser[] users = group.getUsers();
for (RemoteUser remoteUser : users) {
    System.out.println("Full Name:"+remoteUser.getFullname());
}
```

Deleting a user or group is also straightforward as shown next:

```
//Delete User.
jiraSoapService.deleteUser(authToken, user1.getName());
//Delete Group.
jiraSoapService.deleteGroup(authToken, group1.getName(), group.
getName());
```

Here, swapGroup identifies the group to change the comment and work log visibility to.

Progressing an issue in workflow using SOAP

This is something everyone wants to do when JIRA is integrated with third-party applications. The status of an issue needs to be changed for various use cases and the right way to do this is to progress the issue through its workflow.

Progressing will move the issue to the appropriate statuses and will fire the appropriate post functions and events. In this recipe, we will see how to do the same.

Getting ready

As usual, create a SOAP client if you have not already done so.

How to do it...

JIRA exposes the method, `progressWorkflowAction` to progress an issue through its workflow. The following are the steps to do it:

1. Identify the ID of the action that we should execute from the current state. For every issue status, there is a step associated with it and there are zero or more transitions to the other steps in the workflow.

   The action ID can be identified from the workflow screen within brackets alongside the transition name, as shown in the following screenshot:

View Workflow Steps — jira

This shows all of the steps for **jira**.

Not editable because workflow is **Active**.

☐ View all workflows.
☐ View all statuses.

Step Name (id)	Linked Status	Transitions (id)	Operations
Open (1)	🖐 Open	*Start Progress* (4) >> In Progress *Resolve Issue* (5) >> Resolved *Close Issue* (2) >> Closed	View Properties
In Progress (3)	🖐 In Progress	*Stop Progress* (301) >> Open *Resolve Issue* (5) >> Resolved	View Properties

The previous screenshot shows the JIRA default workflow and the action ID for **Resolve Issue** from **Open** status is **5**. Note that the same action from different states can have a different ID if they are not sharing the common actions. So, it is important that we identify the action ID before proceeding to *Step 2*.

You might have to store these action IDs on the client side when implementing a full-fledged application as JIRA doesn't expose a method to retrieve action ID based on the current *state*.

The ID can also be retrieved from the XML by looking up the `action` element:

```
<action id="5" name="Resolve Issue" view="resolveissue">
```

A workflow can be exported to XML from the **Administration | Workflows** screen by clicking on the XML link.

2. Identify the set of fields that need to be modified during the transition and create a `RemoteFieldValue` object for each of them. You can only modify those fields that are available on the workflow transition.

   In our example, we use the JIRA default workflow's **Resolve Issue** action and it has the **Resolve Screen** associated with it. We have the fields **Assignee** and **Resolution** on the screen and hence we can create the `RemoteFieldValue` objects for them as follows:

```
RemoteFieldValue field1 = new RemoteFieldValue("resolution", new
String[] { "3" });
RemoteFieldValue field2 = new RemoteFieldValue("assignee", new
String[] { "jobinkk" });
```

   The `RemoteFieldValue` takes the ID and an array of String values representing the value we need to set. In our example, the fields are single value fields and hence the array has only a single element. Multidimensional fields such as cascade fields should have the fully qualified ID as we have seen earlier in this chapter while updating custom fields. The full list of standard field IDs can be found at the `IssueFieldConstants` class. Any fields that are not in the transition screen will be ignored.

3. Execute the `progressWorkflowAction` using these attributes.

```
RemoteIssue updatedtissue = jiraSoapService.progressWorkflowAct
ion(authToken, ISSUE_KEY, "5", new RemoteFieldValue[] { field1,
field2 });
```

   Before we wind up this recipe, the current status on an issue can be found from the `RemoteIssue` object using the `getStatus` method.

```
System.out.println("Progressed "+updatedtissue.getKey()+ " to " +
updatedtissue.getStatus() + " status!");
```

Managing versions via SOAP

We have seen how to add versions as a fix for versions or affected versions on an issue. But how do we create those versions using SOAP? In this recipe, we will see how to create versions in a project and manage them!

Getting ready

As usual, create the SOAP client.

How to do it...

A new version can be added into a project as follows:

1. Create a `RemoteVersion` object with the necessary details:

```
RemoteVersion remoteVersion = new RemoteVersion();
remoteVersion.setName("Test Release");
remoteVersion.setReleaseDate(new GregorianCalendar(2011, Calendar.
MAY, 10));
remoteVersion.setSequence(5L);
```

Here, the `sequence` defines the order in which the version will appear in the version list.

2. Create the version using `addVersion` method:

```
RemoteVersion createdVersion = jiraSoapService.
addVersion(authToken, "TST", remoteVersion);
System.out.println("Created version with id:"+createdVersion.
getId());
```

where `TST` is the project key in which the new version is created.

Once a version is created, you can release the version using `releaseVersion` method. It takes a `RemoteVersion` as an input and needs the released flag to be set on it.

```
createdVersion.setReleased(true);
jiraSoapService.releaseVersion(authToken, "TST", createdVersion);
```

The same method can be used to `unrelease` a version. All you need to do is to set the `released` flag to `false`!

If the `released` flag is set to `true` and the version is already released, an error is thrown. This is the same case while trying to `unrelease` a version that is not yet released.

Archiving a version works similar to releasing a version. Here, the archived flag is passed as an argument instead of setting the released flag. Also, here the version name is used instead of a `RemoteVersion` object.

```
// Archives version with name "Test release" in project with key JRA
jiraSoapService.archiveVersion(authToken, "JRA", "Test Release",
true);
```

All the versions in a project can be retrieved using the `getVersions` method, which returns an array of `RemoteVersion` objects.

```
RemoteVersion[] versions = jiraSoapService.getVersions(authToken,
"JRA");
```

Administration methods in SOAP API

Before we wind up the various useful methods in SOAP API, we can have a look at the administration methods. In this recipe, we will be concentrating on some methods revolving around the creation of projects and permissions. Remaining methods are an easy read once you have a fair idea on the ones we are discussing in this recipe.

Getting ready

Create the SOAP client as we discussed in the previous recipes.

How to do it...

We can have a look at the journey of creating a permission scheme, creating a project using it and adding some users into the project roles. Other schemes used during creation of the project like notification scheme and issue security scheme are not supported via SOAP.

Following are the steps for our journey:

1. Create the new Permission scheme:

    ```
    RemotePermissionScheme permScheme = jiraSoapService.createPermissi
    onScheme(authToken, "Test P Scheme", "Test P Description");
    ```

    Here, we use the `createPermissionScheme` method to create a new permission scheme by passing the authentication token, a name, and a description. Note that we can instead get an existing permission scheme from the list retrieved using the `getPermissionSchemes` method.

2. Add relevant permissions to the newly created permission scheme using the `addPermissionTo` method. This step is relevant only if we are creating a new permission scheme:

```
RemotePermissionScheme modifiedPermScheme = jiraSoapService.
addPermissionTo(authToken, permScheme, adminPermission, user);
```

Here, `adminPermission` should be a `RemotePermission` which is in the list of `RemotePermission` objects retrieved using `getAllPermissions` method. For example, the **Administer Project** permission can be obtained as follows:

```
RemotePermission[] permissions = jiraSoapService.
getAllPermissions(authToken);
RemotePermission adminPermission = null;
for (RemotePermission remotePermission : permissions) {
  if (remotePermission.getPermission().equals(23L)) {
    adminPermission = remotePermission;
    break;
  }
}
```

Here, `23L` is the ID of the **Administer Project** permission. The IDs of other permissions can be found at `com.atlassian.jira.security.Permissions` class.

The final argument to `addPermissionTo` method is a `RemoteEntity`, which can be a `RemoteUser` or a `RemoteGroup` object. We have seen accessing users and groups via SOAP in the previous recipes. In our example, we get a user by name as follows:

```
RemoteUser user = jiraSoapService.getUser(authToken, "jobinkk");
```

3. Create the project using `createProject` method:

```
RemoteProject project = jiraSoapService.createProject(authToken,
"TEST", "Test Name", "Test Description", "http://www.j-tricks.
com", "jobinkk", permScheme, null, null);
```

The following are the arguments:

token	**- Authentication Token**
key	**- Project Key**
name	**- Project Name**
description	**- Project Description**
url	**- URL of the project**
lead	**- Project Lead**
permissionScheme	**- Permission Scheme for the project of type RemotePermissionScheme**
notificationScheme	**- Notification Scheme for the project of type RemoteScheme**
issueSecurityScheme	**- Issue Security Scheme for the project of type RemoteScheme**

For the schemes, we use the newly created permissions schemes and leave the other two as null. We can specify a specific notification scheme or issue security scheme with a `RemoteScheme` object created by populating the correct ID of the relevant schemes.

4. Add an actor to the newly created Project:

```
jiraSoapService.addActorsToProjectRole(authToken, new String[] {
"jobinkk" }, adminRole, project, "atlassian-user-role-actor");
```

Here, the `addActorsToProjectRole` method takes an array of actors (only `jobinkk` in this case), the role to which the actor should be added, project we have created, and the type of the actor.

The project role can be retrieved using the role ID as shown :

```
RemoteProjectRoleadminRole = jiraSoapService.
getProjectRole(authToken, 10020L);
```

The actor type can either be `atlassian-user-role-actor` or `atlassian-group-role-actor` depending on whether the actor we have added in the array is a user or a group.

We should now have the project created with the new permission scheme and with the member(s) we added to the relevant roles.

How it works...

Once the method is executed, we can find the project created as follows:

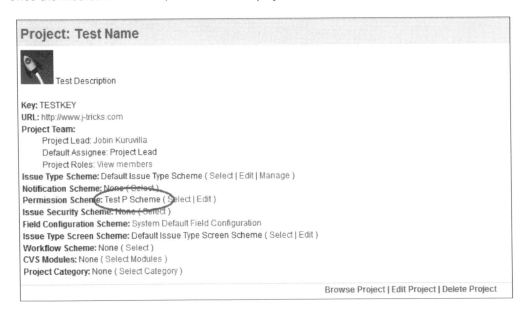

Project: Test Name

Test Description

Key: TESTKEY
URL: http://www.j-tricks.com
Project Team:
    Project Lead: Jobin Kuruvilla
    Default Assignee: Project Lead
    Project Roles: View members
Issue Type Scheme: Default Issue Type Scheme (Select | Edit | Manage)
Notification Scheme: None (Select)
Permission Scheme: Test P Scheme (Select | Edit)
Issue Security Scheme: None (Select)
Field Configuration Scheme: System Default Field Configuration
Issue Type Screen Scheme: Default Issue Type Screen Scheme (Select | Edit)
Workflow Scheme: None (Select)
CVS Modules: None (Select Modules)
Project Category: None (Select Category)

Browse Project | Edit Project | Delete Project

The new permission scheme is created as shown in the following screenshot:

Edit Permissions — Test P Scheme

On this page you can edit the permissions for the "Test P Scheme" permission scheme.

☐ Grant permission
☐ View all permission schemes

Project Permissions	Users / Groups / Project Roles	Operations
Administer Projects Ability to administer a project in JIRA	☒ Single User (jobinkk) (Delete)	☐ Add
Browse Projects Ability to browse projects and the issues within them.		☐ Add
View Version Control Ability to view Version Control commit information for issues.		☐ Add

Issue Permissions	Users / Groups / Project Roles	Operations
Create Issues Ability to create issues.		☐ Add
Edit Issues Ability to edit issues.		☐ Add
Schedule Issues Ability to set or edit an issue's due date.		☐ Add
Move Issues Ability to move issues between projects or between workflows of the same project (if applicable). Note the user can only move issues to a project he or she has the create permission for.		☐ Add

Here only one permission is added, that is to administer the project. We can add the rest in a similar fashion.

Similarly, the project members are added as shown in the following screenshot:

Manage Project Role Membership for Project: Test Name

On this page you can manage project role membership for the Test Name project.

Role	Users	Groups
Administrators A project role that represents administrators in a project	Jobin Kuruvilla Edit	jira-administrators Edit
Developers A project role that represents developers in a project	*None selected.* Edit	jira-developers Edit
Users A project role that represents users in a project	*None selected.* Edit	jira-users Edit

As you can see, the default actors will be part of the membership in addition to the one we have added!

There are lot of other useful methods in the SOAP API which can be found at: `http://docs.atlassian.com/software/jira/docs/api/rpc-jira-plugin/latest/com/atlassian/jira/rpc/soap/JiraSoapService.html`.

Make sure you look at the right Java Docs for your version of JIRA!

Deploy a SOAP service in JIRA

So far we have seen various methods to perform various operations in JIRA via SOAP. But what about operations that are not supported by SOAP? That little something which prevents you from integrating your JIRA with your third-party app? Here is where the **RPC Endpoint Plugin Module** is useful.

The RPC End Point Plugin module lets us deploy new SOAP and XML-RPC end points within JIRA. The new end points added will not be a part of the existing WSDL. Instead, they are available on a new URL and hence you will have to access both the web services if you want to access the new methods and other existing methods.

In this recipe, we will see how to deploy a new SOAP end point to perform a new operation.

Getting ready

Create a skeleton plugin using Atlassian Plugin SDK. As I write this, PRC plugin is still v1, so make sure to create a v1 plugin if `https://jira.atlassian.com/browse/JRA-22596` isn't resolved yet!

Also, make sure **Accept Remote API Calls** option is turned on under **Administration | General Configurations**.

How to do it...

Let us create a SOAP RPC plugin to expose a new method, `getProjectCategories`, that retrieves all the project categories in the JIRA instance This is a simple method but will hopefully help us in covering all the basics of creating a new SOAP RPC end point.

1. Add the RPC plugin dependency in the `pom.xml` to get hold of the existing RPC classes. Change the version accordingly.

```
<dependency>
  <groupId>atlassian-jira-rpc-plugin</groupId>
  <artifactId>atlassian-jira-rpc-plugin</artifactId>
  <version>3.13-1</version>
  <scope>provided</scope>
</dependency>
```

This JAR is a part of the JIRA installation. So, if your maven build fails looking for the JAR, just navigate to `WEB-INF/lib` folder and install the JAR into your local maven repository as follows:

```
mvn install:install-file -DgroupId=atlassian-jira-rpc-plugin
-DartifactId=atlassian-jira-rpc-plugin -Dversion=3.13-1
-Dpackaging=jar -Dfile=atlassian-jira-rpc-plugin-3.13-1.jar
```

2. Declare the new RPC service in the `atlassian-plugin.xml`.

```
<rpc-soap key="jtricks-soap-service" name="JTricks SOAP Service"
class="com.jtricks.JTricksSoapServiceImpl">
  <description>JTricks SOAP service.</description>
  <service-path>jtricksservice</service-path>
  <published-interface>com.jtricks.JTricksSoapService</published-
interface>
</rpc-soap>
```

Here, the SOAP RPC plugin module has a unique `key` and it declares a new `interface` for your SOAP module and an implementation `class` for it. In this case, we have `JTricksSoapService` and `JTricksSoapServiceImpl`. The service path `jtricksservice` defines where in the URL namespace the services will be published and will appear in the URL of the WSDL.

3. Create a **Component Plugins** module for this new class to avoid the client getting a null pointer exception:

```
<component key="jtricks-soap-component" name="JTricks SOAP
Component" class="com.jtricks.JTricksSoapServiceImpl">
  <interface>com.jtricks.JTricksSoapService</interface>
</component>
```

4. Declare the new method in the interface as shown:

```
public interface JTricksSoapService {
   String login(String username, String password);
   // Method to return Project Categories
   RemoteCategory[] getProjectCategories(String token) throws
RemoteException;
}
```

As you can see we have added a method `getProjectCategories` that returns an array of `RemoteCategory` objects. We have added a login method as well so that we can test this by accessing just the new WSDL.

5. Create the `RemoteCategory` bean. Make sure the new bean extends `AbstractNamedRemoteEntity` class. The bean should have all the required attributes with getters and setters defined for it. `AbstractNamedRemoteEntity` already exposes the field name and hence will be available for `RemoteCategory`. We will add a new field `description`.

```
public class RemoteCategory extends AbstractNamedRemoteEntity {
   private String description;

   public RemoteCategory(GenericValue value) {
     super(value);
     this.description = value.getString("description");
   }
```

```
    public void setDescription(String description) {
      this.description = description;
    }

    public String getDescription() {
      return description;
    }
  }
```

As you can see, the constructor takes a `GenericValue` and sets the description from it. In the super class, `AbstractNamedRemoteEntity`, name is set likewise.

6. Implement the `getProjectCategories` method in the implementation class:

```
public RemoteCategory[] getProjectCategories(String token) throws
RemoteException {
  validateToken(token);

  Collection<GenericValue> categories = projectManager.
getProjectCategories();
  RemoteCategory[] remoteCategories = new
RemoteCategory[categories.size()];

  int i = 0;
  for (GenericValue category : categories) {
    remoteCategories[i++] = new RemoteCategory(category);
  }
  return remoteCategories;
}
```

Here, all we do is to get the collection of project categories and return an array of `RemoteCategory` objects initialized using the category `GenericValue` objects. Note that the `getProjectCategories()` method is deprecated from JIRA 4.4 and it is advised to use `getAllProjectCategories()` method that returns a Collection of `ProjectCategory` objects instead of the `GenericValue`.

If you have noticed, we validate the *token* first before returning the categories. The validation is done as follows:

```
private void validateToken(String token) {
  try {
    User user = tokenManager.retrieveUser(token);
  } catch (RemoteAuthenticationException e) {
    throw new RuntimeException("Error Authenticating!,"+e.
toString());
  } catch (RemotePermissionException e) {
    throw new RuntimeException("User does not have permission for
this operation,"+e.toString());
  }
}
```

We retrieve the user using the token and throws the appropriate error if the token is not valid. The `ProjectManager` and `TokenManager` classes can be injected in the constructor as shown:

```
public JTricksSoapServiceImpl(ProjectManagerprojectManager,
TokenManagertokenManager) {
    this.projectManager = projectManager;
    this.tokenManager = tokenManager;
}
```

Note that from JIRA 4.4, `retrieveUserNoPermissioncheck` method should be used instead of `retrieveUser` as some JIRA instances may want to allow anonymous access. Individual methods will do the permission checks.

7. Implement the `login` method to return the token.

```
public String login(String username, String password) {
    try {
        return tokenManager.login(username, password);
    } catch (RemoteAuthenticationException e) {
        throw new RuntimeException("Error Authenticating!,"+e.
toString());
    } catch (com.atlassian.jira.rpc.exception.RemoteException e) {
        throw new RuntimeException("Couldn't login,"+e.toString());
    }
}
```

It simply uses `TokenManager` to return a _token_ created from the username and password.

Compile the plugin and deploy it. As it is v1, make sure the plugin is dropped into the `WEB-INF/lib` folder.

How it works...

Once the plugin is deployed, the new WSDL should be available at: `{your_jira_url}/rpc/soap/jtricksservice?WSDL`.

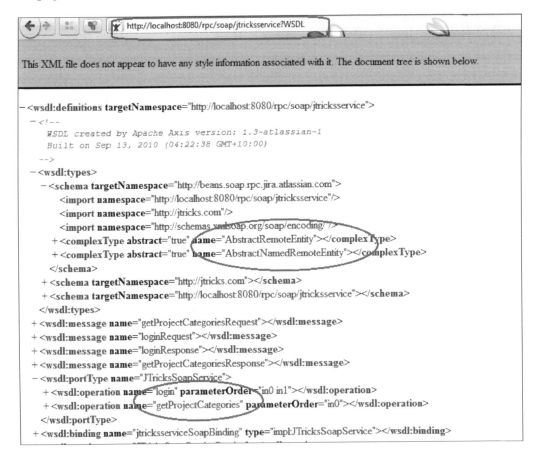

As you can see, the new methods that we exposed via the interface are now visible in the WSDL file at the circled locations in the previous screenshot.

Deploy a XML-RPC service within JIRA

In the previous recipe, we have seen how to deploy a SOAP service within JIRA. In this one, we will see how to deploy a XML-RPC service.

Create a skeleton plugin using Atlassian Plugin SDK. Here again, we are developing a v1 plugin. So, make sure the `atlassian-plugin.xml` doesn't have the Version 2 attribute in it.

And yes, make sure **Accept Remote API Calls** option is turned **ON**, as in the previous recipe.

How to do it...

As in the case of SOAP plugin, let us expose a new method, `getProjectCategories`, that retrieves all the project categories in the project. The following are the steps:

1. Add the RPC plugin dependency in the `pom.xml` to get hold of the existing RPC classes. Change the version accordingly:

    ```
    <dependency>
        <groupId>atlassian-jira-rpc-plugin</groupId>
        <artifactId>atlassian-jira-rpc-plugin</artifactId>
        <version>3.13-1</version>
        <scope>provided</scope>
    </dependency>
    ```

2. Declare the new RPC service in the `atlassian-plugin.xml`:

    ```
    <rpc-xmlrpc key="xmlrpc" name="JTricks XML-RPC Services"
    class="com.jtricks.XmlRpcServiceImpl">
        <description>The JTricks sample XML-RPC services.</description>
        <service-path>jtricks</service-path>
    </rpc-xmlrpc>
    ```

    Here, we define a class, `XmlRpcServiceImpl` and a `service-path`. The service path, jtricks, is used to access the new methods in place of the default `jira1` path used in accessing the existing methods.

3. Create an interface for the class, with `XmlRpcServiceImpl` named as `XmlRpcService` and define the new methods in it.

    ```
    public interface XmlRpcService {
        String login(String username, String password) throws Exception;
        Vector getprojectCategories(String token);
    }
    ```

    As before, we have a `login` method as well. If you have noticed, the return type of the `getprojectCategories` method is a `Vector` instead of an array of `RemoteCategory` objects.

All the methods in the RPC interface should return a `Vector` if it is returning a list of objects and a `HashTable` if it is returning a single object (`GenericValue`). The Vector will be made of one or more `Hashtables` each representing a `GenericValue` in the list.

4. Define the `RemoteCategory` as defined in the previous recipe. We will create a `Vector` from an array of `RemoteCategory` objects to return the project category details:

```
public class RemoteCategory extends AbstractNamedRemoteEntity {
  private String description;

  public RemoteCategory(GenericValue value) {
    super(value);
    this.description = value.getString("description");
  }

  public void setDescription(String description) {
    this.description = description;
  }

  public String getDescription() {
    return description;
  }
}
```

5. Implement the `XmlRpcServiceImpl` class. The `getprojectCategories` method is implemented as follows:

```
public Vector getprojectCategories(String token) {
  validateToken(token);

Collection<GenericValue> categories = projectManager.
getProjectCategories();
  RemoteCategory[] remoteCategories = new
RemoteCategory[categories.size()];

  int i = 0;
  for (GenericValue category : categories) {
    remoteCategories[i++] = new RemoteCategory(category);
  }
  return RpcUtils.makeVector(remoteCategories);
}
```

Here we create an array of `RemoteCategory` objects and then create a Vector from it using the `RpcUtils` utility class. The class, behind the scenes, converts the array of `RemoteCategory` objects into a Vector of `Hashtables`, each `Hashtable` representing a `RemoteCategory`.

If we want to return a single `RemoteCategory` object instead of an array, we should return it as a `Hashtable` constructed as follows:

```
RpcUtils.makeStruct(remoteCategory);
```

As mentioned earlier, use the `getAllProjectCategories` method from JIRA4.4. Implement the `login` and `validateToken` methods, as discussed in the previous recipe.

6. Compile the plugin and deploy it. As it is v1, make sure the plugin is dropped into the `WEB-INF/lib` folder.

How it works...

Once the plugin is deployed, the new methods can be accessed using the new service path as `jtricks.getprojectCategories`. More details about how to access an XML-RPC method can be found in the next recipe.

See also

▶ *Writing a Java XML-RPC client*

Writing a Java XML-RPC client

In the previous recipes, we saw how to create a SOAP client and use it to connect to JIRA from an external third-party application. We have also seen ways of exposing new methods in JIRA through SOAP and XML-RPC interfaces. In this recipe, we will see how to invoke an XML-RPC method from a client application written in Java.

The Javadocs for XML-RPC client can be found at: `http://docs.atlassian.com/software/jira/docs/api/rpc-jira-plugin/latest/com/atlassian/jira/rpc/xmlrpc/XmlRpcService.html`.

Getting ready

Make sure **Accept Remote API Calls** option is turned **ON** in JIRA under **Administration | Global Settings**.

How to do it...

Let us try to retrieve the list of projects using XML-RPC service deployed within JIRA. Following are the steps:

1. Create a Maven2 project and add the dependency for `Apache2 xml-rpc` libraries.

```
<dependency>
  <groupId>xmlrpc</groupId>
  <artifactId>xmlrpc</artifactId>
  <version>1.1</version>
</dependency>
```

Note that the version of `xml-rpc` libraries we have used in this recipe is Version 1.1.

2. Create a Java client. In this example, we will create a standalone Java class with all the libraries in the `classpath`.

3. Instantiate the `XmlRpcClient` object:

```
XmlRpcClientrpcClient = new XmlRpcClient(JIRA_URI + RPC_PATH);
```

Here, the `JIRA_URI` is the URI of your JIRA instance, `http://jira.atlassian.com`, for example, `RPC_PATH` will be `/rpc/xmlrpc`, which will be the same even for new methods exposed via plugins. In this case, the full path will be: `http://jira.atlassian.com/rpc/xmlrpc`.

Note that we are using XML-RPC v2 here. Check out the syntax for the version you are using!

4. Log in to JIRA by invoking the `login` method as shown:

```
// Login and retrieve logon token
Vector loginParams = new Vector(2);
loginParams.add(USER_NAME);
loginParams.add(PASSWORD);
String loginToken = (String) rpcClient.execute("jira1.login",
loginParams);
System.out.println("Logged in: " + loginToken);
```

As you can learn from the Javadocs, the method expects a username and password, which are passed into the execute method on the client as a Vector object. The first argument is the method name which is preceded with the namespace under which the methods are exposed. In this case, it is `jira1` and is equivalent to the service path we have seen in the previous recipe. The full method name will hence become `jira1.login`.

In the case of the `login` method, the return object is an authentication token which is a String object.

5. Retrieve the list projects using the `getProjectsNoSchemes` method:

```
// Retrieve projects
Vector loginTokenVector = new Vector(1);
loginTokenVector.add(loginToken);
List projects = (List) rpcClient.execute("jira1.
getProjectsNoSchemes",  loginTokenVector);
```

Here again, we need to send a `Vector` as input along with the method name, in this case, with the authentication token in the `Vector`. If we need to invoke a method that needs a complex object in scenarios like creating an issue, we should create a `HashTable` with the input parameters as key/value pairs and add it into the `Vector`.

The return type in this case is type cast into a `List`. This will be a `List` of map objects, each map representing a `RemoteProject` with the details of the project in it as key/value pairs. For example, the name of the project can be accessed from the map using the key name, as shown in the next step.

6. Retrieve the details of projects from the list. Details will be the attributes of the project published with the getter/setter methods in the `RemoteProject` object, such as name, lead, and so on.

```
for (Iterator iterator = projects.iterator(); iterator.hasNext();)
{
  Map project = (Map) iterator.next();
  System.out.println(project.get("name") + " with lead " +
project.get("lead"));
}
```

As mentioned in the previous step, the details can be retrieved as key/value pairs from the Map objects representing a project. This same logic applies to all XML-RPC methods where complex objects are retrieved as Maps with key/value pairs in it.

7. Log out from JIRA:

```
Boolean bool = (Boolean) rpcClient.execute("jira1.logout",
loginTokenVector);
```

Here the output is converted to Boolean as the method returns a Boolean.

8. If we try to get the list of categories using the new method exposed in the previous recipe, the code will look similar to the following:

```
// Retrieve Categories
Vector loginTokenVector = new Vector(1);
loginTokenVector.add(loginToken);
List categories = (List) rpcClient.execute("jtricks.
getprojectCategories", loginTokenVector);
```

```
for (Iterator iterator = categories.iterator(); iterator.
hasNext();) {
  Map category = (Map) iterator.next();
  System.out.println(category.get("name"));
}
```

Note that the method name here is prefixed with jtricks as it is the service path used in the RPC Endpoint Plugin Module. Everything else works the same.

Expose services and data entities as REST APIs

Now that we have seen how to expose JIRA functionalities via SOAP and XML-RPC interfaces, it is time to move to REST APIs. Similar to the RPC Endpoint Plugin Module Type, JIRA also has a REST Plugin module type using which services or data can be exposed to the outside world.

In this recipe, we will see how to expose the getProjectCategories method we have used as examples in the previous recipes using the REST interface.

Getting ready

Create a skeleton plugin using Atlassian Plugin SDK. The plugin should be v2 for it to work.

How to do it...

Following is a step-by-step procedure to create a REST plugin to expose the getProjectCategories method.

1. Add the maven dependencies require for REST to the pom.xml file:

    ```
    <dependency>
      <groupId>javax.ws.rs</groupId>
      <artifactId>jsr311-api</artifactId>
      <version>1.0</version>
      <scope>provided</scope>
    </dependency>
    <dependency>
      <groupId>javax.xml.bind</groupId>
      <artifactId>jaxb-api</artifactId>
      <version>2.1</version>
      <scope>provided</scope>
    </dependency>
    <dependency>
      <groupId>com.atlassian.plugins.rest</groupId>
      <artifactId>atlassian-rest-common</artifactId>
      <version>1.0.2</version>
    ```

```
  <scope>provided</scope>
</dependency>
<dependency>
  <groupId>javax.servlet</groupId>
  <artifactId>servlet-api</artifactId>
  <version>2.3</version>
  <scope>provided</scope>
</dependency>
```

Note that all the dependencies are of scope provided as they are already available in the JIRA runtime.

2. Add the REST plugin module into the `atlassian-plugin.xml`.

```
<rest key="rest-service-resources" path="/jtricks" version="1.0">
  <description>Provides the REST resource for the tutorial
plugin.</description>
</rest>
```

Here, the path and version defines the full path where the resources will be available only after the plugin is deployed. In this case, the full path will become `BASE_URL/rest/jtricks/1.0/` where `BASE_URL` is the JIRA base URL.

Define the data that will be returned to the client. JAXB Annotations are used to map these objects to XML and JSON formats.

In our example, the `getCategories` method should return a List of Category objects and hence we need to define a Categories object and a Category object, the former containing a List of the latter. For both the objects, we should use the Annotations.

3. Define the `Category` object as follows:

```
@XmlRootElement
public static class Category{
  @XmlElement
  private String id;

  @XmlElement
  private String name;

  public Category(){
  }

  public Category(String id, String name) {
    this.id = id;
    this.name = name;
  }
}
```

Make sure the annotations are used properly. The `@XmlRootElement` annotation maps a class or an Enum type to an XML element and is used for the categories in this case. `@XmlElement` maps a property or field to an XML Element. Other annotations available are `@XmlAccessorType` and `@XmlAttribute` used for controlling whether fields or properties are serialized by default and mapping a property or field to an XML Attribute respectively.

 The details can be read at: `http://jaxb.java.net/nonav/jaxb20-pfd/api/javax/xml/bind/annotation/package-summary.html`.

Make sure a public non-argument constructor is available so as to render the output properly when accessed via the direct URL. Also, note that only the annotated elements will be exposed via the REST API.

4. Define the `Categories` object:

```
@XmlRootElement
public class Categories{
  @XmlElement
  private List<Category> categories;

  public Categories(){
  }

  public Categories(List<Category> categories) {
    this.categories = categories;
  }
}
```

Same rules apply here as well.

5. Create the `Resource` class. On the package level or the class level or the method level, we can have `@Path` annotations to define the path where the resource should be available. If it is available on all the levels, the final path will be a cumulative output.

This means that if you have `@Path("/X")` at package level, `@Path("/Y")` at class level, and `@Path("/Z")` at method level, the resource is accessed at:

```
BASE_URL/rest/jtricks/1.0/X/Y/Z
```

Different methods can have different paths to differentiate between each other. In our example, let us define a path `/categories` at class level:

```
package com.jtricks;
...............
```

```
@Path("/category")
public class CategoryResource {
    ..................
}
```

6. Write the method to return the `Categories` resource:

```
@GET
@AnonymousAllowed
@Produces({ MediaType.APPLICATION_JSON, MediaType.APPLICATION_XML
})
public Response getCategories() throws SearchException {
Collection<GenericValue> categories = this.projectManager.
getProjectCategories();
   List<Category> categoryList =  new ArrayList<Category>();
   for (GenericValue category : categories) {
     categoryList.add(new Category(category.getString("id"),
category.getString("name")));
   }
   Response.ResponseBuilder responseBuilder = Response.ok(new
Categories(categoryList));
   return responseBuilder.build();
}
```

As you can see, the method doesn't have a `@Path` annotation and hence will be invoked at the URL, `BASE_URL/rest/jtricks/1.0/category`. Here, we normally construct a `Categories` object with a simple bean class and then use the `ResponseBuilder` to create the response.

The `@GET` annotation mentioned earlier denotes that the class method will handle requests for a GET HTTP message.

 Other valid annotations include POST, PUT, DELETE, and so on, and can be viewed in detail at:

http://jsr311.java.net/nonav/javadoc/javax/ws/rs/package-summary.html.

`@AnonymousAllowed` indicates that the method can be called without supplying user credentials. `@Produces` specifies the content types the method may return. The method can return any type if this annotation is absent. In our case, the method must return an XML or JSON object.

Two other useful annotations are: `@PathParam` and `@QueryParam`. `@PathParam` maps a method variable to an element in the `@Path` whereas `@QueryParam` maps a method variable to a query parameter.

The following is how we use each of them:

@QueryParam

Following is an example of how @QueryParam is used:

```
@GET
@AnonymousAllowed
@Produces({ MediaType.APPLICATION_JSON, MediaType.APPLICATION_XML
})
public Response getCategories(@QueryParam("dummyParam") String
dummyParam) throws SearchException {
  System.out.println("This is just a dummyParam to show how
parameters can be passed to REST methods:"+dummyParam);
................
                    return responseBuilder.build();
}
```

Here, we take a query parameter named dummyParam, which can then be used within our method. The resource will then be accessed as follows: BASE_URL/rest/jtricks/1.0/category?dummyParam=xyz.

In this case, you will see that the value xyz is printed into the console.

@PathParam

```
@GET
@AnonymousAllowed
@Produces({ MediaType.APPLICATION_JSON, MediaType.APPLICATION_
XML })
@Path("/{id}")
public Response getCategoryFromId(@PathParam("id") String id)
throws SearchException {
  GenericValue category = this.projectManager.
getProjectCategory(new Long(id));  Response.
ResponseBuilderresponseBuilder = Response.
ok(new Category(category.getString("id"), category.
getString("name")));
  return responseBuilder.build();
}
```

Let us say we want to pass the ID of a category as well in the path and get the details of that Category alone; we can use the PathParam here as shown earlier. In that case, the URL to this method will be as shown:

```
BASE_URL/rest/jtricks/1.0/category/10010
```

Here, 10010 is the category ID passed into the previously described method as id.

When query parameters are used, the resource will not be cached by a proxy or your browser. So if you are passing in an ID to find some information about some sort of entity, then use a path parameter. This information will then be cached.

7. Package the plugin and deploy it.

How it works...

If you have deployed the plugin with both the `getCategories()` method and `getCategoryFromId()` method seen earlier, the list of categories can be retrieved at the URL: `BASE_URL/rest/jtricks/1.0/category`, as shown in the following screenshot:

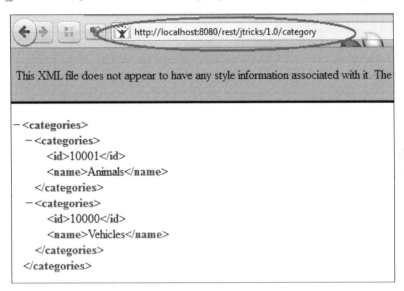

The details of a particular category can be retrieved using the ID in the path, `BASE_URL/rest/jtricks/1.0/category/10001` for example, as shown in the next screenshot:

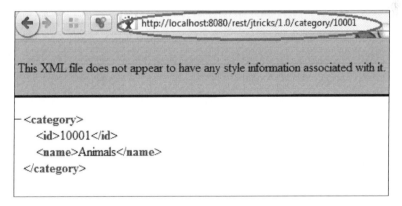

Atlassian has published some guidelines at: `http://confluence.atlassian.com/display/REST/Atlassian+REST+API+Design+Guidelines+version+1`, which is a very useful read before developing your production version of REST service plugin. Check out: `http://confluence.atlassian.com/display/REST/REST+API+Developer+Documentation` for more details.

Writing Java client for REST API

In this recipe, we will quickly see how we can create a Java client to communicate with JIRA using the REST APIs.

Getting ready

Make sure **Accept Remote API Calls** option is turned **ON** in JIRA under **Administration | Global Settings**.

How to do it...

In order to connect to JIRA using REST APIs, Atlassian has developed a JIRA REST Java Client Library, called JRJC in short. It provides a thin layer of abstraction on top of the REST API and related HTTP(S) communication and gives a domain object model to represent the JIRA entities, such as issues, priorities, resolutions, statuses, users, and so on. The REST API and the JRJC Library are in alpha phase and are quickly evolving! The status of the library can be viewed at: `https://studio.atlassian.com/wiki/display/JRJC/Home`.

We will be using JRJC to connect to our JIRA instance using the standalone Java program. Following are the steps:

1. Create a Maven project and add the JRJC dependency to the `pom.xml` file.

    ```
    <dependency>
      <groupId>com.atlassian.jira</groupId>
      <artifactId>jira-rest-java-client</artifactId>
      <version>0.2.1</version>
    </dependency>
    ```

    Make sure you use the appropriate version of JRJC. All the versions can be found in the maven repository under `https://maven.atlassian.com/public/com/atlassian/jira/jira-rest-java-client/`. If you are not using Maven, the full dependencies are listed in the Atlassian documentation at `https://studio.atlassian.com/wiki/display/JRJC/Project+Dependencies`.

2. Create a Java project by running `maven eclipse:eclipse` if you are using Maven or create the project using your favorite IDE and add all dependencies listed earlier in the class path. Once done, create a standalone Java class.

3. Create a connection to the JIRA server

    ```
    JerseyJiraRestClientFactory factory = new
    JerseyJiraRestClientFactory();
    URI uri = new URI("http://localhost:8080/jira");
    JiraRestClient jiraRestClient = factory.createWithBasicHttpAuthent
    ication(uri, "username", "password");
    ```

Here, we instantiate the `JerseyJiraRestClientFactory` and use the `createWithBasicHttpAuthentication` method to instantiate the REST client by passing the username and password.

RESTful architecture promotes stateless connection and hence there is no notion of the user session. This means the credentials will be send back and forth in plain text, just encoded with `Base64`, for each request and so it is not safe to use it outside a firewall or company network.

4. Initiate the `ProgressMonitor`. All REST remote calls take this as a parameter. As per Atlassian docs, first, it serves as a clear marker of a remote call and second, in the future, they plan to make this interface capable of reporting the progress and cancelling (where possible) the remote requests taking too much time.

As of now, we initiate it as follows:

```
NullProgressMonitor nullProgressMonitor = new
NullProgressMonitor();
```

Retrieve the appropriate client needed for the operation. The `jiraRestClient` exposes a set of clients, such as `IssueRestClient`, `ProjectRestClient`, `SearchClient`, and so on, each one exposing the related set of operations. In this example, we will try to retrieve an issue and hence will go for the `IssueRestClient`:

```
IssueRestClient issueRestClient = jiraRestClient.
getIssueClient();
```

5. Retrieve the issue details and print it. Alternatively, perform the required operation as appropriate:

```
Issue issue = issueRestClient.getIssue("TST-10",
nullProgressMonitor);
System.out.println(issue);
```

Here, the issue is `com.atlassian.jira.rest.client.domain.Issue`!

Various other operations can be performed on the issue, details of which can be found in the Javadocs at `http://docs.atlassian.com/jira-rest-java-client/0.2.1/apidocs/com/atlassian/jira/rest/client/IssueRestClient.html`.

For example, we can vote on the issue as follows:

```
issueRestClient.vote(issue.getVotesUri(), nullProgressMonitor);
```

The API for this is available at `http://docs.atlassian.com/jira-rest-java-client/0.2.1/apidocs/com/atlassian/jira/rest/client/IssueRestClient.html`.

Some operations are a little more complex. For example, in order to progress the issue through its workflow, you will need the appropriate transition ID, the fields needed during the transition, and optionally a comment. We can do it as follows:

1. Get the available transitions from the issue.

    ```
    Iterable<Transition> transitions = issueRestClient.
    getTransitions(issue.getTransitionsUri(), nullProgressMonitor);
    ```

2. Find the relevant transition by name or ID as follows:

    ```
    private static Transition getTransitionByName(Iterable<Transition>
    transitions, String transitionName) {
      for (Transition transition : transitions) {
        if (transition.getName().equals(transitionName)) {
          return transition;
        }
      }
      return null;
    }
    ```

3. Create a list of fields needed during the transition. This can be empty if the fields are not mandatory:

    ```
    Collection<FieldInput>fieldInputs = Arrays.asList(new
    FieldInput("resolution", "Done"));
    ```

    Create a `Comment` object if needed:

    ```
    Comment.valueOf("New comment");
    ```

4. Transition the issue as follows:

    ```
    issueRestClient.transition(issue.getTransitionsUri(), new Transi
    tionInput(startProgressTransition.getId(), fieldInputs, Comment.
    valueOf("New comment")),nullProgressMonitor);
    ```

5. You will see that the issue is progressed in the workflow by executing the transition we selected.

Similarly, the various methods can be executed using the appropriate clients. Given the fact that JIRA REST API is evolving so quickly, JRJC has a lot of potential and is worth investing time in.

10
Dealing with a Database

In this chapter, we will cover:

- ▶ Extending JIRA DB with custom schema
- ▶ Accessing DB entities from plugins
- ▶ Persisting plugin information in JIRA DB
- ▶ Using Active Objects to store data
- ▶ Accessing JIRA configuration properties
- ▶ Getting database connection for JDBC calls
- ▶ Migrating a custom field from one type to another
- ▶ Retrieving issue information from a database
- ▶ Retrieving custom field details from a database
- ▶ Retrieving permissions on issues from a database
- ▶ Retrieving workflow details from a database
- ▶ Updating issue status in a database
- ▶ Retrieving users and groups from a database
- ▶ Dealing with Change history in a database

Introduction

We have already seen in *Chapter 2, Understanding Plugin Framework*, that JIRA uses the Ofbiz suite's Entity Engine module to deal with database operations.

OfBiz stands for Open For Business and the OfBiz Entity Engine is a set of tools and patterns used to model and manage entity-specific data.

As per the definition from the standard entity-relationship modeling concepts of RDBMS, an entity is a piece of data defined by a set of fields and a set of relations to other entities.

In JIRA, these entities are defined in two files, `entitygroup.xml` and `entitymodel.xml`, both residing in the `WEB-INF/classes/entitydefs` folder. `entitygroup.xml` stores the entity names for a previously-defined group. If you look at the file, you will see that, the default group in JIRA is named `default`; you will find the same defined in the entity configuration file, which we will see in a moment. `entitymodel.xml` holds the actual entity definitions, details of which we will see in the recipes.

The entity configuration is defined in `entityengine.xml`, residing in the `WEB-INF/classes` folder. It is in this file that the `datasource`, transaction factory, and so on, are defined. The content of this file varies based on the database that we use and the application server. For example, the `datasource` definition will be as follows, when the database is MySQL and application server is `tomcat`:

```
<datasource add-missing-on-start="true" check-fk-indices-on-
start="false" check-fks-on-start="false" check-indices-on-start="true"
check-on-start="true" field-type-name="mysql" helper-class="org.
ofbiz.core.entity.GenericHelperDAO" name="defaultDS" use-foreign-key-
indices="false" use-foreign-keys="false">
        <jndi-jdbc jndi-name="java:comp/env/jdbc/JiraDS" jndi-server-
name="default"/>
</datasource>
```

More about connecting to various other databases can be read at `http://confluence.atlassian.com/display/JIRA/Connecting+JIRA+to+a+Database`.

For other application servers, the `jndi-server` attribute in the `jndi-jdbc` element varies, as follows:

▶ Orion format: <jndi-jdbc jndi-server-name="default" jndi-name="jdbc/JiraDS"/>

▶ JBoss format: <jndi-jdbc jndi-server-name="default" jndi-name="java:/JiraDS"/>

▶ Weblogic format: <jndi-jdbc jndi-server-name="default" jndi-name="JiraDS"/>

The `transaction-factory` tag is defined as follows:

```
<transaction-factory class="org.ofbiz.core.entity.transaction.
JNDIFactory">
        <user-transaction-jndi jndi-name="java:comp/env/UserTransaction"
jndi-server-name="default"/>
        <transaction-manager-jndi jndi-name="java:comp/env/
UserTransaction" jndi-server-name="default"/>
  </transaction-factory>
```

The entity definition XMLs are referenced in the file using the `entity-group-reader` and `entity-model-reader` attributes that point to `entitygroup.xml` and `entitymodel.xml`, respectively.

```
<entity-model-reader name="main">
<resource loader="maincp" location="entitydefs/entitymodel.xml"/>
</entity-model-reader>
<entity-group-reader name="main" loader="maincp" location="entitydefs/
entitygroup.xml"/>
```

The delegator element is also defined in this file, as follows:

```
<delegator entity-group-reader="main" entity-model-reader="main"
name="default">
        <group-map datasource-name="defaultDS" group-name="default"/>
</delegator>
```

The field type mapping XMLs for different databases are also defined in this file. An example of this is:

```
<field-type loader="maincp" location="entitydefs/fieldtype-mysql.xml"
name="mysql"/>
```

Read more about configuring `entityengine.xml` at `http://www.atlassian.com/software/jira/docs/latest/entityengine.html` and about entity modeling concepts at `http://ofbiz.apache.org/docs/entity.html`.

In the recipe, *Extending JIRA DB with custom schema*, we will also see glimpses of the JIRA database architecture, which is also explained in detail at `http://confluence.atlassian.com/display/JIRADEV/Database+Schema`.

Extending JIRA DB with custom schema

Now that we know that JIRA scheme definitions are maintained in `WEB-INF/classes/entitydefs/entitygroup.xml` and `entitymodel.xml`, let us have a look at extending the existing scheme definitions. How would you extend the JIRA scheme if you want to add one or two custom tables into JIRA? Is it just about creating the new tables in our database? We will see that in this recipe.

How to do it...

JIRA uses the schema definitions entered in the `WEB-INF/classes/entitydefs/entitygroup.xml` and `entitymodel.xml` files. It makes use of these files not only to validate and create the schema but also during import and export of the JIRA Data backup. JIRA also uses these entity definitions to read and write to a database, using OfBizDelegator (`http://docs.atlassian.com/jira/latest/com/atlassian/jira/ofbiz/OfBizDelegator.html`), details of which we will see in the upcoming recipes.

The following are quick steps to add a new table into the JIRA schema. Let us assume we are adding a table to hold the details of an employee.

1. Identify an entity name for the table. This could be the same as the table name or different from it. This name will be used in the XML backups and also by the OfBizDelegator to read or write data.

   In our example, let us choose `Employee` as the entity name.

2. Modify the `WEB-INF/classes/entitydefs/entitygroup.xml` file to include the new entity group definition:

   ```
   <entity-group group="default" entity="Employee"/>
   ```

   Here, the `group` attribute refers to the group name the delegator is associated with. You can find it in the `WEB-INF/classes/entityengine.xml`, as shown:

   ```
   <delegator name="default" entity-model-reader="main" entity-group-
   reader="main">
     <group-map group-name="default" datasource-name="defaultDS"/>
   </delegator>
   ```

   The `entity` attribute holds the name of the entity.

3. Modify the `WEB-INF/classes/entitydefs/entitymodel.xml` file to include the new entity definition:

   ```
   <entity entity-name="Employee" table-name="employee" package-
   name="">
     <field name="id" type="numeric"/>
     <field name="name" type="long-varchar"/>
     <field name="address" col-name="empaddress" type="long-
   varchar"/>
     <field name="company" type="long-varchar"/>

     <prim-key field="id"/>
     <index name="emp_entity_name">
       <index-field name="name"/>
     </index>
   </entity>
   ```

Here, the `entity-name` attribute holds the name of the entity we have used in *Step 2*. The `table-name` holds the name of the table; it is optional and will be derived from `entity-name`, if not present. `package-name` can be used if you want to organize and structure the entities' definitions into different packages.

The `entity` element contains one field element for each column in the table that needs to be created. The `field` element has a `name` attribute that holds the name of the field. If the column name of the field is different, the `col-name` attribute can be used, as in the case with employee address. If `col-name` is missing, the name of the field is used. The next important attribute is `type`. In our example, `id` is `numeric` whereas `name` and `address` are `long-varchar`.

These type definitions of a field are mapped to the appropriate column type for each database type. The `field-type` mappings are stored under `WEB-INF/classes/entitydefs/` and is declared in `entityengine.xml`, as shown next:

```
<field-type name="oracle10g" loader="maincp" location="entitydefs/
fieldtype-oracle10g.xml"/>
```

If you look inside `fieldtype-oracle10g.xml`, you will notice that `numeric` is mapped to `NUMBER(18,0)` and `long-varchar` is mapped to `VARCHAR2(255)`. You can find out the various mappings and even the related Java data type from the same file.

The `prim-key` element is used to define the primary key constraint for the table, as shown previously. In our case, `id` is the primary key. It is mandatory to name the primary key as `id` for all the new tables we are creating.

The `index` element creates a DB index for the field specified for that table. We can specify the index name and the group of the fields that needs to be indexed underneath it.

You can also define the relationship between entities using the element `relation` as shown next:

```
<relation type="one" title="Parent" rel-entity-name="Company">
  <key-map field-name="company" rel-field-name="id"/>
</relation>
```

Here, we are adding a relationship between the `Employee` entity and `Company` entity by saying an employee can have only one company. In the above case, `Employee` should have a field `company` that points to the `id` field of a company's record. In other words, the `company` field in an employee's record will be the foreign key to the company's record.

More details of entity definition can be found at `http://ofbiz.apache.org/docs/entity.html#Entity_Modeling`.

4. Restart JIRA after the changes are made.

How it works...

When JIRA is restarted with the previous changes, you will notice that a warning message appear in the logs during startup, as shown next:

```
Database configuration OK

    Database Configuration
    Loading entityengine.xml from              : file:/C:/Jobin/Softwares/JI
RA/JIRA-Enterprise-4.3.3/atlassian-jira/WEB-INF/classes/entityengine.xml
    Entity model field type name               : mysql
    Entity model schema name                   :
    Database Version                           : MySQL - 5.5.13
    Database Driver                            : MySQL-AB JDBC Driver - mysq
l-connector-java-5.1.10 ( Revision: $(svn.Revision) )
    Database URL                               : jdbc:mysql://127.0.0.1:3306
/jiradb?useUnicode=true&characterEncoding=UTF8
    Database JNDI address                      : java:comp/env/jdbc/JiraDS

2011-06-24 23:09:03,614 main WARN       [core.entity.jdbc.DatabaseUtil] Entity "E
mployee" has no table in the database
2011-06-24 23:09:05,341 main INFO       [atlassian.jira.startup.JiraStartupLogger
]
```

Once JIRA recognizes that there is no table corresponding to the new entity name **employee** in the database; it will create one, as shown:

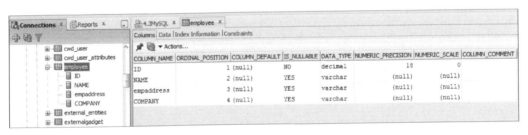

Even the index information is stored, as shown:

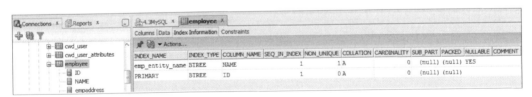

If you want to add a new column to an existing table, you can add a field definition, as we saw earlier and, on restarting JIRA, the table will be updated to include the column.

You will notice an error message in the JIRA logs if the database has a table, or a column in the table, that doesn't have a valid entity or field definition in the `entitymodel.xml`.

Care must be taken to update the `entitygroup.xml` and `entitymodel.xml` files when JIRA is upgraded or else the changes will be lost.

Accessing DB entities from plugins

We have seen how the various entities in the JIRA database are defined and how we can introduce new entities. In this recipe, we will see how we can read and write data from the database using these entity definitions.

How to do it...

JIRA exposes the OfBizDelegator (`http://docs.atlassian.com/jira/latest/com/atlassian/jira/ofbiz/OfBizDelegator.html`) component, which is a wrapper around `org.ofbiz.core.entity.DelegatorInterface`, to communicate with its database using the Ofbiz layer.

You can get hold of an instance of `OfBizDelegator` by injecting it in the constructor or from ComponentManager, as follows:

```
OfBizDelegator delegator = ComponentManager.getInstance().getComponent
InstanceOfType(OfBizDelegator.class);
```

Reading from a database

We can read from the database using the various methods exposed via the above delegator class. For example, all the records in the employee table we defined in the previous recipe can be read as:

```
List<GenericValue> employees = delegator.findAll("Employee");
```

Here, the `findAll` method takes the entity name (not the table name) and returns a list of `GenericValue` objects, each representing a row in the table. The individual fields can be read from the object using the name of the field (not `col-name`), as follows:

```
Long id = employees.get(0).getLong("id");
String name = employees.get(0).getString("name");
```

The data type to which the field should be converted can be found from the `field-type` mapping XML we saw in the previous recipe.

We can read data from a database, when certain conditions are satisfied, using the findByAnd method:

```
List<GenericValue> employees = delegator.findByAnd("Employee",
EasyMap.build("company","J-Tricks"));
```

This will return all the records where company name is J-Tricks. You can enforce more complex conditions using the findByCondition method and select only the interested fields, as follows:

```
List<GenericValue> employees = this.delegator.
findByCondition("Employee", new EntityExpr("id",EntityOperator.
GREATER_THAN,"15000"), EasyList.build("id","name"));
```

Here, we find all employee records with ID greater than 15000 and we retrieve only the ID and name of the employees.

findListIteratorByCondition (http://docs.atlassian.com/jira/latest/
com/atlassian/jira/ofbiz/OfBizDelegator.html#findListIteratorByCondi
tion%28java.lang.String,%20org.ofbiz.core.entity.EntityCondition,%20
org.ofbiz.core.entity.EntityCondition,%20java.util.Collection,%20
java.util.List,%20org.ofbiz.core.entity.EntityFindOptions%29)

This method can be used to add more options like the orderBy clause, EntityFindOptions, where conditions, having conditions, and so on, as follows:

```
OfBizListIterator iterator = this.delegator.findListIteratorByCo
ndition("Employee", new EntityExpr("id",EntityOperator.GREATER_
THAN,"15000"), null, UtilMisc.toList("name"), UtilMisc.toList("name"),
new EntityFindOptions(true, EntityFindOptions.TYPE_SCROLL_INSENSITIVE,
EntityFindOptions.CONCUR_READ_ONLY, true));
List<GenericValue> employees = iterator.getCompleteList();
iterator.close();
```

Here, we search for all records with the ID greater than 15000. We don't have a having condition in this case and, so, we will leave it null. The next two arguments specify that only the name field needs to be selected and the records should be ordered by the name field. The last argument specifies the EntityFindOptions. Here, we define the EntityFindOptions with four arguments including TYPE_SCROLL_INSENSTITVE and CONCUR_READ_ONLY. The first true is for specifyTypeAndConcur and the last true is for distinct select.

If specifyTypeAndConcur is true, the following two parameters will be used to specify resultSetType and resultSetConcurrency. If false, the default values of the JDBC driver will be used. In the above case, specifyTypeAndConcur is true and, hence, resultSetType is taken as TYPE_SCROLL_INSENSITIVE and resultSetConcurrency is taken as CONCUR_READ_ONLY. More about this and the possible values can be found at http://download.oracle.com/javase/tutorial/jdbc/basics/retrieving.html.

As discussed before, the last true in the `EntityFindOptions` constructor is for selecting distinct values. Apparently, this is the only way to do a distinct select using Entity Engine. You will find more information about this in the entity engine cookbook at `http://www. opensourcestrategies.com/ofbiz/ofbiz_entity_cookbook.txt`.

Don't forget to close the iterator, as shown in the previous code snippet.

Writing a new record

Creating a new record in a table using OfBizDelegator is pretty easy, as shown next:

```
GenericValue newEmployee = this.delegator.
createValue("Employee",EasyMap.build("name","Some Guy",
"address","Some Address",  "company","J-Tricks"));
```

Make sure you don't provide the ID, as it is automatically generated. Also, the missing fields in the map will be set to `null`. Data for all the mandatory fields should be provided so as to avoid errors.

Updating a record

Writing a record is done by retrieving the record, modifying the values, and using the `store()` method. For example, we can retrieve a record with ID `12000` and modify it, as follows:

```
GenericValue employee = delegator.findByAnd("Employee",    EasyMap.
build("id","12000")).get(0);
employee.setString("name","New Name");
employee.store();
```

More useful methods can be found in the Java docs at `http://docs.atlassian.com/ jira/latest/com/atlassian/jira/ofbiz/OfBizDelegator.html`.

Persisting plugin information in JIRA DB

While developing plugins, we come across many scenarios where we need to store specific information about the plugins, be it configuration detail or metadata for entities. How can we do this without creating a custom schema and going through the pain of editing entity definitions? In this recipe, we will how we can make use of JIRA's existing framework to store information specific to the plugins we develop.

JIRA uses Open symphony's `PropertySet` framework to store properties in the database. These properties are a set of key/value pairs and are stored against any entity that the user wants. The key of the property is always a String value; the value can be: String, Long, Date, Boolean, or Double. We have already seen how JIRA uses it in *Chapter 2, Understanding Plugin Framework*. In this recipe, we will see we can use `PropertySet` to store our custom data.

How to do it...

Suppose that we need to store a Boolean value in the database as part of our plugin's configuration and read it later; here are the steps to follow to do it:

1. Get an instance of `PropertySet`, using `PropertiesManager`:

   ```
   PropertySet propertySet = PropertiesManager.getInstance().
   getPropertySet();
   ```

   From JIRA 4.3 onwards, the `PropertiesManager.getInstance()` method is deprecated. Instead, you can inject the `PropertiesManager` into the constructor, using dependency injection, or retrieve it from `ComponentManager`, as follows:

   ```
   PropetySet propertySet =  ComponentManager.
   getComponent(PropertiesManager.class).getPropertySet();
   ```

2. Persist the Boolean property using the `setBoolean` method:

   ```
   propertySet.setBoolean("mt.custom.key1", new Boolean(true));
   ```

   Similarly, String, Long, Double, and Date values can be stored using the respective methods.

3. The property that is stored can be retrieved at any point, as follows:

   ```
   Boolean key = propertySet.getBoolean("mt.custom.key1");
   ```

However, how do we store a more complex structure, such as a property, to an existing entity? Let us say we want to store the address of a user. JIRA stores the user information against the entity `OSUser`, as follows:

1. Retrieve the ID of the user entity we are going to store the address against. For example, if there is a user `jobinkk`, we can find the ID of the user from the `OSUser` entity that corresponds to the `userbase` table in JIRA. Let us assume the ID is `10032`.

2. Get an instance of `PropertySet`, using `PropertySetManager`, by passing the details of the entity we got:

   ```
   HashMap entityDetails = new HashMap();
   entityDetails.put("delegator.name", "default");
   entityDetails.put("entityName", "OSUser");
   entityDetails.put("entityId", 10032L);
   PropertySet userProperties = PropertySetManager.
   getInstance("ofbiz", entityDetails);
   ```

Here, we create a map with the entity name, that is, `OSUser`, and the ID of the user, that is, `10032`. We also pass the delegator name as defined in the `entityengine.xml`, under the `WEB-INF/classes` folder, which is the default in this case. We then retrieve the `PropertySet` instance from `PropertySetManager`, using `ofbiz` as the key.

3. The values can be set as before, depending on the type of the field. In this case, we will have more than one key for state, country, and so on:

```
userProperties.setString("state", "Kerala");
userProperties.setString("country", "India");
```

This will then be stored in the appropriate tables.

4. We can retrieve these values later by creating the `PropertySet` in a similar manner and using the getter methods:

```
System.out.println("Address:" + userProperties.
getString("state")+", "+userProperties.getString("country"));
```

How it works...

When a property is set using `PropertySet` instantiated from `PropertiesManager` as we did in the case of the Boolean values, it gets stored in the **propertyentry** table with the `ENTITY_NAME` as **jira.properties** and `ENTITY_ID` as **1**. It will also have a unique ID, which will then be used to store the value in the **propertynumber**, **propertystring**, **propertytext**, or **propertydate** tables, depending on the data type we used.

In our case, the **propertyentry** table is populated with values, as shown next:

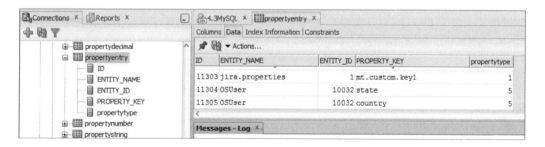

The first one is the Boolean property we added whereas the second and third are the user properties.

Boolean values get stored as numbers (0 or 1) and hence, the **propertyentry** table stores the **propertytype** as **1**, which denotes a number value. There is a corresponding entry in the **propertynumber** table, with ID **11303**, for the Boolean property, as shown:

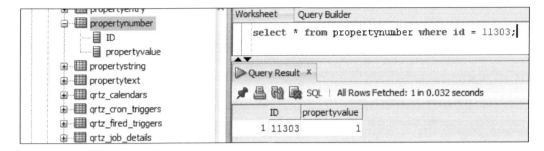

In our example, the **Boolean** is set to **true** and, hence, the **propertynumber** stores the value **1**. If set to `false`, it will store **0**.

In the case of address, the entity is **OSUser** and it has an **entityId** of **10032**. We have seen two rows with IDs **11304** and **11305**, each with **propertytype** as **5**, which denotes String values. Because they are String values, they are stored in the **propertystring** table, as shown in the following screenshot:

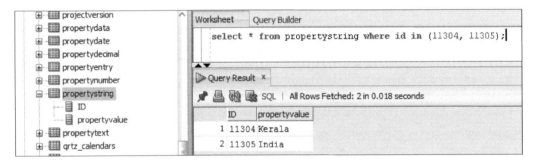

Hopefully, this gives a fair idea about how we can store attributes against an existing entity record.

The good thing about the usage of `propertySet` is that we don't need to create an extra scheme or entity definition and these properties are exported in the backup XML when JIRA data is exported. So, all configurations stored like this will be retained when the data is imported back into another JIRA instance.

Using active objects to store data

Active objects represent a technology recently used by JIRA to allow per-plugin storage. This gives the plugin developers a real protected database where they can store the data belonging to their plugin and which other plugins won't be able to access. In this recipe, we will see how we can store an address entity in the database using active objects.

You can read more about active objects at `http://java.net/projects/activeobjects/pages/Home`.

Getting ready

Create a skeleton plugin using Atlassian Plugin SDK.

How to do it...

In order to understand it better, let us look at the simple 'address entity' example that we used in the previous recipe. This will also help in an easy comparison with `PropertySet`, if desired Follow the ensuing steps to use active objects in the plugin:

1. Include the active objects dependency in `pom.xml`. Add the appropriate `ao` version:

    ```
    <dependency>
        <groupId>com.atlassian.activeobjects</groupId>
        <artifactId>activeobjects-plugin</artifactId>
        <version>${ao.version}</version>
        <scope>provided</scope>
    </dependency>
    ```

2. Include the active objects plugin artifacts, under the `maven-jira-plugin` configuration, in the `pom.xml` file as shown:

    ```
    <plugin>
     <groupId>com.atlassian.maven.plugins</groupId>
     <artifactId>maven-jira-plugin</artifactId>
     <version>3.0.6</version>
     <extensions>true</extensions>
     <configuration>
      <pluginArtifacts>
       <pluginArtifact>
        <groupId>com.atlassian.activeobjects</groupId>
        <artifactId>activeobjects-plugin</artifactId>
        <version>${ao.version}</version>
       </pluginArtifact>
       <pluginArtifact>
    ```

```
    <groupId>com.atlassian.activeobjects</groupId>
    <artifactId>activeobjects-jira-spi</artifactId>
    <version>${ao.version}</version>
   </pluginArtifact>
  </pluginArtifacts>
  <productVersion>${jira.version}</productVersion>
  <productDataVersion>${jira.data.version}</productDataVersion>
 </configuration>
</plugin>
```

3. Add the active objects plugin module to the Atlassian plugin descriptor:

```
<ao key="ao-module">
  <description>The configuration of the Active Objects service</description>
  <entity>com.jtricks.entity.AddressEntity</entity>
</ao>
```

As you can see, the module has a unique key and it points to an entity we are going to define later, AddressEntity in this case.

4. Include a component-import plugin to register ActiveObjects as a component in the atlassian-plugin.xml previous with the above module:

```
<component-import key="ao" name="Active Objects components"
interface="com.atlassian.activeobjects.external.ActiveObjects">
  <description>Access to the Active Objects service</description>
</component-import>
```

5. Define the entity to be used for data storage. The entity should be an interface and should extend the net.java.ao.Entity interface. All we need to do in this entity interface is to define getter and setter methods for the data that we need to store for this entity.

For example, we need to store the name, city and country as part of the address entity. In this case, the AddressEntity interface will look like the following:

```
public interface AddressEntity extends Entity{
  public String getName();
  public void setName(String name);

  public String getState();
  public void setState(String state);

  public String getCountry();
  public void setCountry(String country);
}
```

By doing this, we have setup the entity to facilitate the storage of all the three attributes. We can now create, modify, or delete the data using the `ActiveObjects` component. The component can be instantiated by injecting it into the constructor.

```
private ActiveObjects ao;

public ManageProperties(ActiveObjects ao) {
   this.ao = ao;
}
```

A new row can be added to the database using the following piece of code:

```
AddressEntity addressEntity =  ao.create(AddressEntity.class);
addressEntity.setName(name);
addressEntity.setState(state);
addressEntity.setCountry(country);
addressEntity.save();
```

Details can be read either using the `id`, which is the primary key, or by querying the data using a `net.java.ao.Query` object. Using ID is as simple as is shown next:

```
AddressEntity addressEntity = ao.get(AddressEntity.class, id);
```

The `Query` object can be used as follows:

```
AddressEntity[] addressEntities = ao.find(AddressEntity.class, Query.
select().where("name = ?", name));
for (AddressEntity addressEntity : addressEntities) {
   System.out.println("Name:"+addressEntity.getName()+",
State:"+addressEntity.getState()+", Country:"+addressEntity.
getCountry());
}
```

Here, we are querying for all records with a given name.

Once you get hold of an entity by either means, we can edit the contents simply by using the setter method:

```
addressEntity.setState(newState);
addressEntity.save();
```

Deleting is even simpler!

```
ao.delete(addressEntity);
```

Hopefully, that gives a fair introduction to active objects.

How it works...

Behind the scenes, separate tables are created in the JIRA database for every entity that we add. The active objects service interacts with these tables to do the work.

If you see the database, a table of the name AO_{SOME_HEX}_MY_OBJECT is created for every entity named MyObject belonging to a plugin with key com.example.ao.myplugin, where:

- ► AO is a common prefix
- ► SOME_HEX is a set of the first six characters of the hexadecimal value of the hash of the plugin key com.example.ao.myplugin
- ► MY_OBJECT is the upper-case translation of the entity class name MyObject

For every attribute with getter method, getSomeAttribute defined in the entity interface, a column is created in the table with the name SOME_ATTRIBUTE using the Java Beans naming convention—separating the two words by an underscore and keeping them both in upper case.

In our **AddressEntity** example, we have the following table, **ao_d6b86e_address_entity**, created:

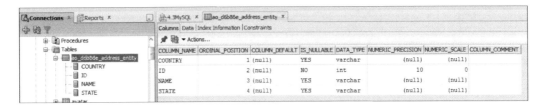

And, for our example, the data is stored as shown next:

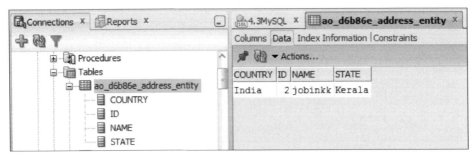

Accessing JIRA configuration properties

We have seen how to use `PropertySet` to store details of plugins in the previous recipes. In this recipe, we will see how we can access the JIRA configuration properties using `PropertySet`.

How to do it...

There are lot of global configurations settings in JIRA which are configured using Administration menus. More on the various options can be read at `http://confluence. atlassian.com/display/JIRA/Configuring+Global+Settings`. Where does JIRA store this information and how do we access it?

All these configuration properties, such as, settings under **General Configuration**, **Base URL**, **Attachments path**, **license info**, and more, are stored in the `propertyset` tables we saw earlier. They are stored against a virtual entity, `jira.properties`. This is the same virtual entity that is used when the `PropertySet` is retrieved using `PropertiesManager`, as we saw while persisting plugin information.

Here, all the property key entries are stored in the `propertyentry` table, with `jira.properties` as the entity name and `entityid` as 1. The `propertytype` for each property varies, depending on what is stored against it. For example, `jira.option. allowattachments` is a flag and hence is stored in the `propertynumber` table, with a value of either 0 or 1.

In this case, the `propertytype` is 1, denoting the number `value`. `jira.path.index`, on the other hand, stores a String that holds the index path and will have 5 as `propertytype`. Here the value is stored in `propertystring` table.

All the properties can be accessed using the following SQL command:

```
select * from propertyentry where ENTITY_NAME='jira.properties';
```

If you want to see only String properties and their values, you can get it using the command:

```
select PROPERTY_KEY, propertyvalue from propertyentry pe, propertystring
ps where pe.id=ps.id and pe.ENTITY_NAME='jira.properties' and
propertytype='5';
```

If you want to search for a specific property, you can do that using the following command:

```
select PROPERTY_KEY, propertyvalue from propertyentry pe, propertynumber
pn where pe.id=pn.id and pe.ENTITY_NAME='jira.properties' and
pe.PROPERTY_KEY='jira.option.allowattachments';
```

Note that the appropriate property table should be used, `propertynumber` in this case!

The same things can be achieved in a plugin, as follows:

1. Retrieve the `PropertySet` object:

   ```
   PropertySet propertySet = PropertiesManager.getInstance().
   getPropertySet();
   ```

   As said before, from JIRA 4.3, the `PropertiesManager.getInstance()` method has been deprecated. Instead, you can inject the `PropertiesManager` in the constructor using dependency injection or retrieve it from `ComponentManager`, as shown:

   ```
   PropetySet propertySet =  ComponentManager.
   getComponent(PropertiesManager.class).getPropertySet();
   ```

2. All property keys can be retrieved as follows:

   ```
   Collection<String> keys = propertySet.getKeys();
   ```

3. Similarly, all the properties of a specific type can be accessed as:

   ```
   Collection<String> stringKeys = propertySet.getKeys(5);
   ```

4. The value of a particular key can be accessed as follows:

   ```
   String attachmentHome = propertySet.getString("jira.path.
   attachments");
   ```

   ```
   boolean attachmentsAllowed = propertySet.getBoolean("jira.option.
   allowattachments");
   ```

Getting database connection for JDBC calls

It is not always feasible to use **OfBizDelegator** to get all the details that we need. What if we need to execute a complex query in the database via JDBC? In this recipe, we will see how we can retrieve the database connection that is defined in `entityengine.xml`.

How to do it...

The database connection lookup is pretty simple if you are familiar with JDBC. Follow these quick steps to retrieve a connection:

1. Create a `javax.naming.InitialContext` object:

   ```
   InitialContext cxt = new InitialContext();
   ```

2. Retrieve the database information from the entity configurations using `EntityConfigUtil`:

   ```
   DatasourceInfo datasourceInfo = EntityConfigUtil.getDatasourceInfo
   ("defaultDS");
   ```

Here, `defaultDS` is the name of the data source defined in `entityengine.xml`.

3. Retrieve the `jndi-name` string from the `DataSourceInfo` object:

```
String jndiName = datasourceInfo.jndiJdbcElement.getAttribute (
"jndi-name" );
```

4. Use `jndi-name` to look up the `javax.sql.DataSource` object:

```
DataSource ds = ( DataSource ) cxt.lookup ( jndiName );
```

5. Create the `java.sql.Connection` object from the DataSource:

```
Connection conn = ds.getConnection();
```

6. Once you get the connection, it is similar to any other JDBC calls. Create your statements or prepare statements and execute them.

As I write this, JIRA 4.3 is being released, and getting a connection is going to be much simpler. Just do the following:

```
Connection conn = new DefaultOfBizConnectionFactory().getConnection();
```

Simple, isn't it?

`DataSourceInfo` can be accessed as follows:

```
DatasourceInfo datasourceInfo = new DefaultOfBizConnectionFactory().
getDatasourceInfo();
```

Over to you, to write the JDBC calls wisely!

Migrating a custom field from one type to another

Custom fields in JIRA are of different types—text fields, select lists, number fields, and so on. We might come across scenarios where we need to change the type of a field but without losing all the data we have entered until then! Is possible to do that? It is, to a certain extent. In this recipe, we will see how to do it.

The type of a field can only be changed via the database, as the UI doesn't support that. But, it won't be possible with all the field types. For example, it isn't possible to convert a text field to a number field because all the values that the field already has may not be number fields. However, the reverse is possible, because all number values can be treated as text values. Similarly, you can convert a select field to a text field but you cannot convert a multi-select field to a text field because a multi-select has multiple values, each with a separate row in the `customfieldvalue` table.

So, the first step is to identify whether the conversion is feasible, by looking at the source and target types. If it is feasible, we can go on and modify the type, as described in this recipe.

How to do it...

The following steps outline how to modify the type of custom field if the source and target types satisfy the condition we discussed earlier:

1. Stop the JIRA instance.

2. Connect to the JIRA DB as the JIRA user.

3. Modify the custom field key in the `customfield` table by executing the SQL script as shown:

   ```
   update customfield set customfieldtypekey = 'com.atlassian.jira.
   plugin.system.customfieldtypes:textfield' where cfname = 'Old
   Number Value';
   ```

   Here, the type of the custom field named **'Old Number Value'** is changed to text field. Make sure that the custom field name is unique; if not, use custom field ID in the `where` condition.

4. Modify the searcher key similarly, with an appropriate searcher. In the previous case, we need to modify the searcher value to text searcher, as shown:

   ```
   update customfield set customfieldsearcherkey = 'com.atlassian.
   jira.plugin.system.customfieldtypes:textsearcher' where cfname =
   'Old Number Value';
   ```

5. Commit the changes and disconnect.

6. Start JIRA.

7. Do a complete reindexing of the JIRA instance by going to **Administration | System | Indexing**.

The custom field should now be modified to a text field from the old number field. Add or update values and search them to verify the change.

Retrieving issue information from a Database

Information about an issue is scattered around in multiple tables in the JIRA database. However, a good starting point is the `jiraissue` table, which is where the issue record is stored. It has foreign keys referencing other tables and, at the same time, the issue ID is referenced in few other tables.

The following diagram captures the important tables that the `jiraissue` table has a parent relationship with:

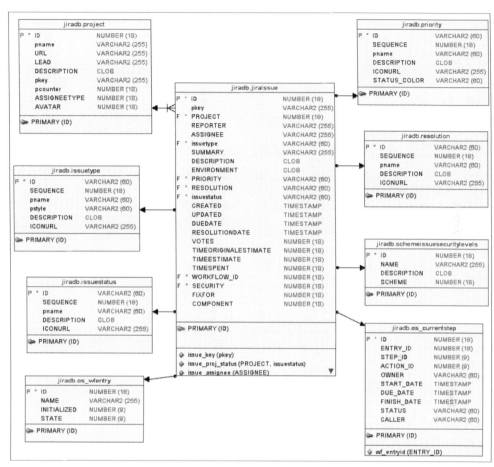

As you can see, critical information about an issue, such as, the project, issue type, status, priority, resolution, security level, workflow, and so on, are all stored in the respective tables but are referenced from the `jiraissue` table, using a foreign key. The foreign key points to the ID of the other tables in all cases, but there are no foreign key constraints enforced on any of these tables.

Similarly, the following diagram shows the tables that the `jiraissue` table has a child relationship with:

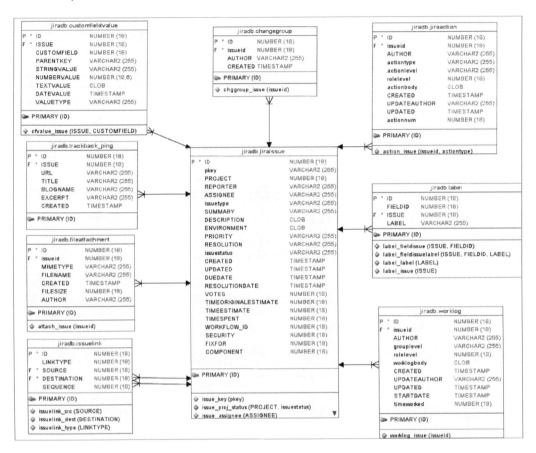

Here, the tables `customfieldvalue`, `changegroup`, `jiraaction`, `label`, `worklog`, `fileattachment`, `issuelink`, `trackback_ping`, and so on, have a foreign key with the name `issueid` or `issue` (or source or destination) pointing to the relevant issue's ID.

In this recipe, we will learn how to access some of the issue's information with the help of the previous diagrams.

How to do it...

When there is a parent-child relationship between tables, we can do a join operation to get most of the information we are looking for. For example, all the issues along with their project names can be retrieved by the following query:

```
select ji.id, ji.pkey, pr.pname from jiraissue ji inner join  project pr
on ji.project = pr.id;
```

Here we do an inner join on the condition that the project's ID is the same as the project column value in the `jiraissue` table.

Similarly, all the comments on an issue can be retrieved by the following query:

```
select ji.pkey, ja.actionbody, ja.created, ja.author from jiraissue ji
left join jiraaction ja on ji.id = ja.issueid;
```

In the example, we retrieve the comments on issues with their author and created date. The same approach can be used with all tables in the previous diagrams.

There's more...

Accessing version and component information on an issue is slightly different. Even though you see the `fixfor` and `component` columns in the `jiraissue` table, they are not used anymore!

Each issue can have multiple versions or components and hence there is a `join` table between the `jiraissue` and `version/component` tables, called `nodeassociation`. The `source_node_entity` will be the `ISSUE` and the `source_node_id` represents the issue ID. The `sink_node_entity` will be **Component** or **Version**, in this case, and `sink_node_id` will hold the ID of the respective component or version.

There is a third column, `association_type`, which will be `IssueFixVersion`, `IssueVersion`, or `IssueComponent` for fixes for versions, affected versions or components respectively.

We can access the components of an issue as follows:

```
select ji.pkey, comp.cname from nodeassociation na, component comp,
jiraissue ji where comp.id = na.sink_node_id and ji.id = na.source_
node_id and na.association_type = "IssueComponent" and ji.pkey =
'DEMO-123';
```

Here, `DEMO-123` is the issue. We can also retrieve the affected versions and fix versions in a similar fashion.

Retrieving custom field details from a database

In the previous recipe, we have seen how to retrieve the standard fields of an issue from the database. In this recipe, we will see how to retrieve the custom field details of an issue.

All the custom fields in JIRA are stored in the `customfield` table, as we have seen while modifying the custom field types. Some of these custom fields, such as, select fields, multi-select fields, and so on, can have different options configured and they can be found in the `customfieldoption` table.

For each custom field, there can be a set of contexts configured. These contexts specify the projects or a list of issue types the field is associated with. For each such context, an entry is made in the `fieldconfigscheme` with a unique ID. For each `fieldconfigscheme`, there will be entries in the `configurationcontext` and `fieldconfigschemeissuetype` tables, `configurationcontext` holding the projects the field is associated with in the relevant context, and `fieldconfigschemeissuetype` holding the issue types the field is associated with! For fields, such as Select and Multi Select, there can be different options configured for different contexts and this can be found from the `customfieldoption` table, using the `customfildconfig` column, which points to the respective row in the `fieldconfigscheme` table.

There must always be a record in `configurationcontext` and `fieldconfigschemeissuetype` for each configuration scheme. If the scheme isn't restricted to any projects or issue types, the `project` and `issuetype` columns of the respective tables should be `NULL`.

For individual issues, the value(s) of the custom fields are stored in the `customfieldvalue` table with a reference to the `jiraissue` and `customfield` tables. For multi-value fields, such as multiple select, multiple checkboxes, and so on, there will be multiple entries in the `customfieldvalue` table.

We capture this information in a simple diagram like the following:

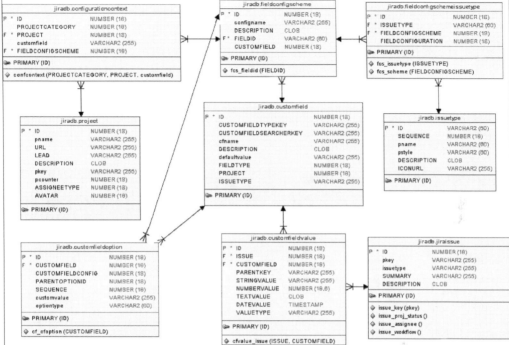

How to do it...

Once a custom field is added, the details of the field can be retrieved from the `customfield` table with this simple query:

```
select * from customfield where cfname = 'CF Name';
```

If it is a field with multiple options, such as the select field, the options can be retrieved using a simple join, as shown next:

```
select cf.id, cf.cfname, cfo.customvalue from customfield cf inner join
customfieldoption cfo on cf.id = cfo.customfield where cfname = 'CF
Name';
```

The various field configurations can be retrieved from the `fieldconfigscheme` table, as follows:

```
select * from fieldconfigscheme where fieldid = 'customfield_12345';
```

Here, `12345` is the unique ID for the custom field.

The projects associated with a custom field can be retrieved as follows:

```
select project.pname from configurationcontext inner join project on
configurationcontext.project = project.id where fieldconfigscheme in
(select id from fieldconfigscheme where fieldid = 'customfield_12345');
```

When the project is NULL, the field is global and hence available for all projects!

Similarly, the issue types associated with the field can be retrieved as follows:

```
select issuetype.pname from fieldconfigschemeissuetype inner join
issuetype on fieldconfigschemeissuetype.issuetype = issuetype.id where
fieldconfigscheme in (select id from fieldconfigscheme where fieldid =
'customfield_12345');
```

Retrieving permissions on issues from a database

JIRA is quite powerful in enforcing permissions on issues. There are quite a lot of configuration options in controlling who can do what. All these revolve around two different schemes in JIRA, **Permission Scheme** and **Issue Security Scheme**.

Permission Scheme enforces project-level security whereas Issue Security Scheme enforces issue-level security. It is possible for you to grant access to view issues in a project and yet hide some of those issues from the user. However, the reverse is not possible, that is, one cannot grant access to certain selected issues when the user originally didn't have access to view the issues in the project.

The various tables involved in storing permission information in the JIRA database, along with the relations between them, can be depicted as follows:

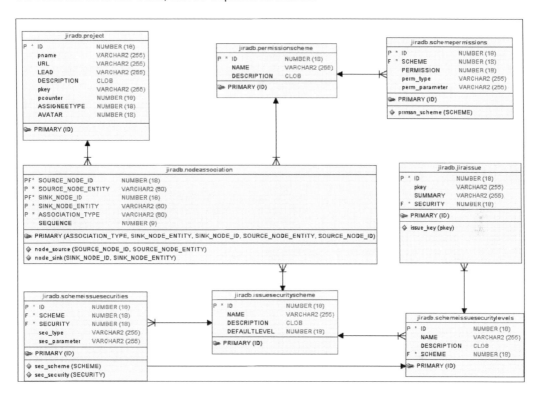

As you can see here, both the Permission Schemes and Issue Security Schemes are related to a project via the `nodeassociation` table. Here, the **SOURCE_NODE_ENTITY** is **Project** and the corresponding **SOURCE_NODE_ID** holds the ID of the project. The **SINK_NODE_ENTITY** is `PermissionScheme` or `IssueSecurityScheme` depending on the scheme type. **SINK_NODE_ID** will point to the appropriate scheme. The **ASSOCIATION_TYPE** is `ProjectSheme`, in both the cases.

For each of the permission schemes, there are multiple permissions predefined, such as, **Administer Project**, **Browse Project**, **Create Issues**, and so on. For each of these permissions, the `perm_type` and `perm_parameter` hold the type of the entity and its value that has the relevant permission. For example, the `perm_type` could be group, user, project role, and so on, and `perm_parameter` will be the group name, username, or the project role , respectively. Multiple permission types can be granted a single permission.

Similarly, issue security scheme holds a number of security levels that are stored in the `schemeissuesecuritylevels` table. Each of these security levels can have different entities in them, which are also defined using `type` and `parameter` values; in this case, the column names are `sec_type` and `sec_parameter`.

The Permission Scheme is enforced on an issue based on the project it resides in, whereas the security scheme is enforced by looking at the security level the issue is assigned. The security column in the `jiraissue` table holds this information.

Let us see how we can retrieve some of this information from an issue, based on the previous diagram.

How to do it...

It is fairly easy to find out the Permission Scheme associated with a project with the help of the `nodeassociation` table, as shown next:

```
select pr.pname, ps.name from nodeassociation na, project pr,
permissionscheme ps where pr.id = na.source_node_id and ps.id = na.sink_
node_id and na.association_type = 'ProjectScheme' and na.source_node_
entity = 'Project' and na.sink_node_entity = 'PermissionScheme';
```

Similarly, Issue Security Scheme can be retrieved as follows:

```
select pr.pname, iss.name from nodeassociation na, project pr,
issuesecurityscheme iss  where pr.id = na.source_node_id and iss.id =
na.sink_node_id and na.association_type = 'ProjectScheme' and na.source_
node_entity = 'Project' and na.sink_node_entity = 'IssueSecurityScheme';
```

The permissions parameters associated with a specific permission in a permission scheme, with an `id` value 9, can be easily retrieved as follows:

```
select sp.perm_type, sp.perm_parameter from schemepermissions sp inner
join permissionscheme ps on sp.scheme = ps.id where ps.id = 9 and
sp.permission = 23
```

Here, `sp.permission = 23` denotes `PROJECT_ADMIN` permission. The different permission types can be found in `com.atlassian.jira.security.Permissions` class. Here, the `perm_type` denotes whether the permission is granted to a group, user, or role; `perm_parameter` holds the name of the respective group, user, or role.

Similarly, queries can be written to retrieve information on the issue security schemes. For example, the security levels and the security type and parameters for each level in a issue security scheme can be retrieved as follows:

```
select iss.name, sisl.name, sis.sec_type, sis.sec_parameter
from issuesecurityscheme iss , schemeissuesecurities sis,
schemeissuesecuritylevels sisl where sis.scheme = iss.id and sisl.scheme
=iss.id;
```

Writing more complex queries is outside the scope of the book but, hopefully, the previous schema diagram and the sample SQL diagrams give enough information to start with!

Retrieving workflow details from a database

Other major information that people normally look for in the database is about workflows. What is the current status of an issue? How does one find out which workflow an issue is associated with? Where is the workflow XML stored in the database? In this recipe, we will take a quick tour of the tables related to workflows.

JIRA workflows, as we have seen in the previous chapters, have statuses, steps, and transitions. There is always a one-to-one mapping between status and step and they are always kept in sync. Then, there are transitions which will move the issue from one step to another and, hence, from one status to another.

The workflows themselves are stored as XML files in the `jiraworkflows` table. JIRA processes these XMLs using the OSWorkflow APIs to retrieve the necessary information for each transition, step, and so on. Any draft workflows are stored in the `jiradraftworkflows` table.

The `jiraissue` table holds the ID of its current status and the status details are stored in the `issuestatus` table. We can use the status ID in the `jiraissue` table to retrieve the corresponding details from the `issuestatus` table.

`jiraissue` also has another column, `workflow_id`, which points to the workflow the issue is associated with and the current step in the workflow the issue is in. The first bit of information, that is, the workflow an issue is associated with, is stored in the `os_wfentry` table. Here, the `workflow_id` will point to the ID column of the `os_wfentry` table. The second bit of information, that is, the current step associated with an issue, is stored in the `os_currentstep` table. Here, the `workflow_id` points to the `entry_id` column in the `os_currentstep` table.

So, for every issue, there is an entry in the `os_wfentry` and `os_currentstep` tables. And the relations are: `jiraissue.WORKFLOW_ID == OS_WFENTRY.ID` and `jiraissue.WORKFLOW_ID == OS_CURRENTSTEP.ENTRY_ID`.

There is another table `os_history` step, which holds all the history information of the steps an issue has gone through. Here, again, the `workflow_id` points to the `entry_id` column in the `os_historystep` table. From this table, we can retrieve information on how long an issue remained in a particular step or status.

The following schema diagram captures the important relations:

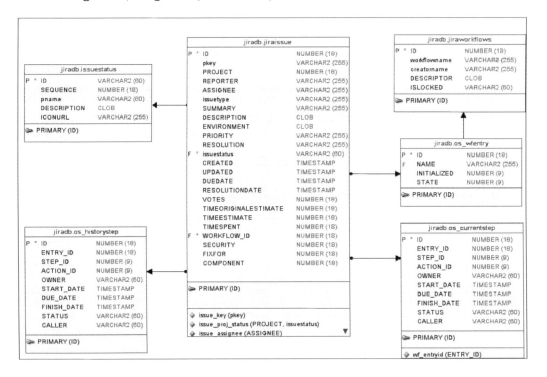

How to do it...

The status of an issue, `DEMO-123`, can be retrieved by a simple query, as shown next:

```
select istat.pname from issuestatus istat, jiraissue ji where istat.
id=ji.issuestatus and ji.pkey='DEMO-123';
```

The details of the workflow associated with an issue can be retrieved, as follows:

```
select * from os_wfentry where id=(select workflow_id from jiraissue
where pkey='DEMO-123');
```

You can retrieve the workflow XML for an issue using the following query:

```
select ji.pkey, wf.descriptor from jiraissue ji, jiraworkflows wf, os_
wfentry osw where ji.workflow_id = osw.id and osw.name = wf.workflowname
and ji.pkey='DEMO-123';
```

The current step associated with an issue can be retrieved as follows:

```
select * from os_currentstep where entry_id = (select workflow_id from
jiraissue where pkey = 'DEMO-123');
```

The history of workflow status (step) changes can be retrieved from the `os_historystep`, as shown:

```
select * from os_historystep where entry_id = (select workflow_id from
jiraissue where pkey = 'DEMO-123');
```

Updating issue status in a database

In this recipe, we will quickly see how to update the status of an issue in the JIRA database.

Getting ready

Go through the previous recipe to understand the workflow related tables in JIRA.

How to do it...

Refer to the follow steps to update the status of an issue in JIRA:

1. Stop the JIRA server.

2. Connect to JIRA database.

3. Update the `issuestatus` field in `jiraissue` table with the status you need:

   ```
   UPDATE jiraissue SET issuestatus = (select id from issuestatus
   where pname = 'Closed') where pkey = 'DEMO-123';
   ```

4. Modify the `step_id` in the `os_currentstep` table with the step ID linked to the status you used in the previous step. The `step_id` can be found in the workflow XML alongside the step name within brackets, as shown in the following screenshot:

Reopened (5)	🔧 Reopened	*Resolve Issue* (5) >> Resolved *Close Issue* (2) >> Closed *Start Progress* (4) >> In Progress	View Properties
Closed (6)	⚓ Closed	*Reopen Issue* (3) >> Reopened	View Properties

As you can see, the status **Closed** in the JIRA default workflow is linked to the **Closed** step with an `id` value 6. Now, the `step_id` can be updated as follows:

```
UPDATE os_currentstep SET step_id = 6 where entry_id = (select
workflow_id from jiraissue where pkey = 'DEMO-123');
```

Here, we modify the `step_id` in `os_currentstep` where the `entry_id` is the same as the `workflow_id` in the `jiraissue` table.

This is very important as the step and status should always be in sync. Updating the status alone will change it on the issue but will prevent further workflow actions on it.

5. Add entries in the `os_historystep` field if you want to keep track of the status changes. This is entirely optional. Leaving it out won't cause any issues except that the records won't be available for reporting at a later stage.

6. Update the `os_currentstep_prev` and `os_historystep_prev` tables accordingly. These tables hold the ID of the previous record. This is again optional.

7. Commit the changes and start JIRA.

8. Do a full re-index by going to **Administration** | **System** | **Indexing**.

Retrieving users and groups from a database

When external user management is not turned **ON**, we can find all the information about JIRA users and their groups from the database by running a few simple SQL queries. In this recipe, we will see the various tables involved.

In versions prior to JIRA 4.3, user information is stored in the `userbase` table, the group information is stored in the `groupbase` table, and the details of which users belong to which groups are stored in the `membershipbase` table.

In those versions, user properties are stored using `PropertySet`, as we have seen earlier in one of the recipes (where we added an address against a user). There will be an entry for the user in the `propertyentry` table with the `entity_name` as `OSUser` and `entity_id` as the ID of the user in the `userbase` table. Examples of properties stored are full name and e-mail address and they are stored as String values in the `propertystring` table.

There is another table, `userassociation`, that holds the information about watching an issue and voting on an issue. In this table, the `source_name` column holds the unique username and `sink_node_id` holds the ID of the issue. `sink_node_entity` has the value `Issue` and `association_type` has values `WatchIssue` or `VoteIssue`, depending on the operation.

From version 4.3 onwards, JIRA uses **Embedded Crowd** as its user management framework. Here, the users are stored in the `cwd_user` table, groups in the `cwd_group` table, and the membership details in the `cwd_membership` table. It is possible to have group-user membership or group-group membership in versions 4.3+, and this information is also stored in the `cwd_membership` table. Also, as opposed to the previous versions, there are separate tables for storing attributes—`cwd_user_attributes` to store user attributes and `cwd_group_attributes` to store group attributes.

JIRA versions 4.3+ also have the concept of user directories. A JIRA instance can have multiple directories and different directories can have the same name in it. The directory details are stored in the `cwd_directory` table and its attributes in the `cwd_directory_attribute` table. There are references in the `cwd_user` table and the `cwd_group` table, both with name `directory_id`, and pointing to the appropriate directory ID. The `cwd_directory_operation` table stores the available operations on a directory, based on user permissions.

When there are multiple users with the same name in different directories, JIRA will only recognize the user in the highest-priority directory. The priority is stored in the `directory_position` column.

The table relations prior to 4.3 are too simple to draw ER diagrams from, hence we will draw one for 4.3+ versions:

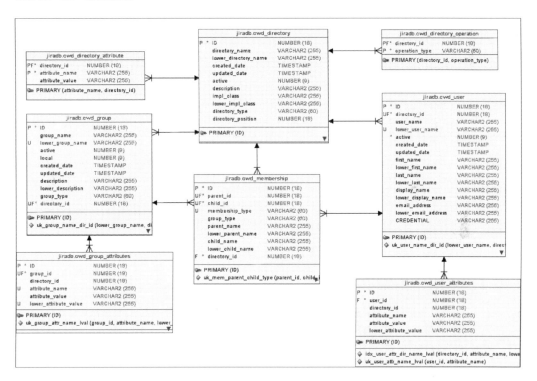

Watches and votes in JIRA versions 4.3+ work in the same way as in the previous versions.

How to do it...

With the simple layout of table structure, it is quite easy to list the users, groups or their relationships by directly accessing the database. For example, prior to version 4.3, we can find all users in a group by simply running:

```
select user_name from membershipbase where group_name = 'jira-
administrators';
```

In versions 4.3+, we can do the same, as follows:

```
select child_name from cwd_membership where parent_name='jira-
administrators' and membership_type = 'GROUP_USER' and directory_id = 1;
```

Here, we consider the directory as well, because we can have the same users and groups in different directories.

Prior to version 4.3, the properties like full name and e-mail are stored and accessed from `propertystring` table, as follows:

```
select pe.property_key, ps.propertyvalue from propertystring ps inner
join propertyentry pe on ps.id = pe.id  where pe.entity_name = 'OSUser'
and pe.entity_id = (select id from userbase where userbase.username =
'username');
```

In versions 4.3+, these attributes are part of the `cwd_user` table, but there can be other attributes stored in the `cwd_user_attributes` table, such as, last login time, invalid password attempts, and so on, which are accessed as shown in the command:

```
select attribute_name, attribute_value from cwd_user_attributes where
user_id = (select id from cwd_user where user_name = 'someguy' and
directory_id =1);
```

In all the versions, users watching an issue can be retrieved as follows:

```
select source_name from userassociation where association_type =
'WatchIssue' and sink_node_entity = 'Issue' and sink_node_id = (select id
from jiraissue where pkey='DEMO-123');
```

Similarly, all the issues watched by a user can be retrieved as:

```
select ji.pkey from jiraissue ji inner join userassociation ua on
ua.sink_node_id =  ji.id where ua.association_type = 'WatchIssue' and
ua.sink_node_entity = 'Issue' and ua.source_name = 'someuser';
```

It is the same for votes, except that the association type will be `VoteIssue`.

Dealing with Change history in a database

Before we wind up this chapter, let us touch up on the change history tables as well. Change histories on issues hold important information on what was changed and when. It is sometimes very useful for reporting and, sometimes, we find ourselves manually adding change histories in the database to keep record of the changes we made via SQL - for example, updating the status of an issue via SQL as we saw earlier in this chapter.

A set of changes happening on an issue at a single point of time are grouped together to form a change group. There is an entry for each such change group in the `changegroup` table, with the information about the issue on which the change is made, the user who makes the change, and the time at which the changes happened.

Then, there is an entry for each of those individual changes in the `changeitem` table, all pointing to the respective `changegroup`. The `changeitem` table holds information on what was actually changed—the old value and the new value. There can be both numerical and textual representation in some cases like status where there is a human-readable text (status name) as well as a unique ID (`status_id`). They are stored in `oldvalue` and `oldstring`, and `newvalue` and `newstring` respectively.

How to do it...

Let us have a look at both retrieving change histories and adding them. For a given issue, we can find out the all changes that happened on it using a simple join, as follows:

```
select  cg.author, cg.created, ci.oldvalue, ci.oldstring, ci.newvalue,
ci.newstring  from changegroup cg inner join changeitem ci on cg.id =
ci.groupid  where cg.issueid = (select id from jiraissue where pkey =
'DEMO-123') order by cg.created;
```

It is quite easy to modify this to filter out changes made by a user or during a particular period.

Now, let us quickly have a look at adding a new change on an issue via the database, as follows:

1. Stop the JIRA server.
2. Connect to the JIRA database.
3. Create an entry in the `changegroup` table, with the correct ID of the issue, author name, and created time.

   ```
   insert into changegroup values
   (12345,10000,'someguy','2011-06-15');
   ```

   Make sure the ID value (`12345`) is larger than the `max(ID)` in the table.

4. Insert a change item for this change group. Let us consider the status change we made in the earlier recipe:

```
insert into changeitem values (11111, 12345, 'jira','status','1','
Open','6','Closed');
```

5. Note that the `groupid` here is same as the ID attribute in *Step 3*. The third column holds the field type, which could be JIRA or custom. For all the standard JIRA fields, such as, `summary`, `status`, and so on, the field type is JIRA. For custom fields, we use the field type as `custom`.

   For fields such as `status`, there is a textual representation (the name) and there is a unique ID; hence, both `oldvalue` and `oldstring` columns are populated. The same is the case with the `newvalue` and `newstring` columns. For fields such as `Summary`, only the `oldstring` and `newstring` columns needs to be populated.

   Here, also make sure the `id(11111)` is larger than `max(id)` in the table.

6. Update the `sequence_value_item` table to hold a higher value in the `seq_id` column for the `ChangeGroup` and `ChangeItem` entities. In the previous case, we can give a value `12346` for `ChangeGroup` and `11112` for `ChangeItem`. Ofbiz normally allocates IDs in batches of ten, so the `SEQ_ID` is the next available ID, rounded up to the nearest value **10**, though adding 1 should be enough.

```
update sequence_value_item set seq_id = 12346 where seq_name =
'ChangeGroup';
```

```
update sequence_value_item set seq_id = 11112 where seq_name =
'ChangeItem';
```

 This step is required whenever a row is inserted into any of the JIRA tables. The `seq_id` value in the `sequence_value_item` table should be updated for the entity where the new row is added. The new sequence value should be atleast one more than the `max(id)` of the entity.

7. Commit the changes and start JIRA.

8. Re-index the JIRA instance by going to **Administration | System | Indexing**.

11
Useful Recipes

In this chapter, we will cover:

- ▶ Writing a service in JIRA
- ▶ Writing scheduled tasks in JIRA
- ▶ Writing listeners in JIRA
- ▶ Customizing e-mail content
- ▶ Redirecting to different page in webwork actions
- ▶ Adding custom behavior for user details
- ▶ Deploying a servlet in JIRA
- ▶ Adding shared parameters to Servlet Context
- ▶ Writing a ServletContextListener interface
- ▶ Using filters to intercept queries in JIRA
- ▶ Adding and importing components in JIRA
- ▶ Adding new module types to JIRA
- ▶ Enabling access logs in JIRA
- ▶ Enabling SQL logging in JIRA
- ▶ Overriding JIRA's default components in plugins
- ▶ Creating issues and comments from e-mail
- ▶ Internationalization in webwork plugins
- ▶ Sharing common libraries across v2 plugins
- ▶ Operations via direct HTML links

Introduction

So far, we have grouped the recipes under common themes as different chapters in this book. We have seen all the important themes but we still are left with some useful recipes and a handful of plugin modules that are not covered in the previous chapters.

In this chapter, we will look at some of those powerful plugin points and useful tricks in JIRA that are not covered in the earlier chapters. Not all of these recipes are related, but they are all useful in its own ways.

Writing a service in JIRA

A service that runs at regular intervals is a much wanted feature in any web application. It is more so if it is the one that can be managed with user-configured parameters and without having to reboot, and so on. JIRA offers a mechanism to add new services on to it that run at regular intervals after every start-up. It lets us do things related to JIRA and things independent of it. It lets us integrate with third-party applications. It lets us do wonders!

There are built-in services in JIRA. Export Service, POP Service, Mail Service, and so on, to name a few. In this recipe, we are going to see how we can add a custom service on to JIRA.

Getting ready

Create a skeleton plugin using Atlassian Plugin SDK. Note that the `atlassian-plugin.xml` file can be removed as it is not used in a service.

How to do it...

As opposed to the other JIRA plug-in modules, services don't need a plugin descriptor. Instead, it uses a configuration XML. It is typically a JAR file with the related classes, files and a configuration XML. Following are the steps to write a simple service that just prints something onto the server console:

1. Write the configuration XML. This is the most important part of a service. The following is a simple configuration XML:

```
<someservice id="jtricksserviceid">
  <description>My New Service</description>
  <properties></properties>
</someservice>
```

This is a simple configuration XML that doesn't take any properties. It has a root element and a unique ID both of which can be custom names of your pick. The root element we have is someservice and the ID is jtricksserviceid. The description, as the name suggests, is just a short description of the service. properties tag holds the different properties you want to associate with the service. These properties will be entered by the user while configuring the service. We will see more on that later.

2. Put the XML file under src/main/resources/com/jtricks/services.

3. Create the service class. The class clan be put under any package structure as it will be referenced with the fully qualified name when it is added in JIRA. The class should extend AbstractService, which implements JTricksService:

```
public class JTricksService extends AbstractService {
   . . .
}
```

4. Implement the mandatory methods in the service class. The following are the only ones that you need to implement:

```
public void run() {
   System.out.println("Running the JTricks service!!");
}

public ObjectConfiguration getObjectConfiguration() throws
ObjectConfigurationException {
   return getObjectConfiguration("MYNEWSERVICE", "com/jtricks/
services/myjtricksservice.xml", null);
}
```

Here run is the key method that is executed when the service runs at regular intervals.

The other key mandatory method is getObjectConfiguration(). We get the configurations from the XML we have written earlier (in *Step 1*) in this method. All we need to do here is to call the parent class' getObjectConfiguration method by passing three arguments. The first argument is a unique **ID** (which need not be same as the ID in the XML file). This ID is used as a key while saving the configurations internally. The second one is the **path** to the configuration XML file we wrote earlier, and the third argument is a **Map** using which you can add user parameters on to the object configuration.

 The third argument is mostly null in case of services as these user parameters are not used anywhere. It is meaningful in other places of JIRA, such as portlets, though not in the case of services.

5. Compile these two files in to a JAR and drop it under `WEB-INF/lib`.

6. Restart JIRA.

Now the service is ready. We can go to **Administration | System | Services** and add the new service with the appropriate delay. While adding the service, we need to use the fully qualified name of the service class. More about registering a service can be found at: `http://confluence.atlassian.com/display/JIRA/Services#Services-RegisteringaService` and is outside the scope of the book.

See also

▶ *Adding configurable parameters to a service*

Adding configurable parameters to a service

For a simple service as the one we just wrote, there is only one parameter that can be configured. It is the delay at which the service runs! What if we need to add more parameters? Let's say we want to add the tutorial name in the service which can be changed later if needed.

How to do it...

Following are the steps:

1. Modify the service configuration XML to include the configurable properties:

```
<someservice id="jtricksserviceid">
  <description>My New Service</description>
  <properties>
    <property>
      <key>Tutorial</key>
      <name>The tutorial you like</name>
      <type>string</type>
    </property>
  </properties>
</someservice>
```

Here, we have added a string property with the key: `Tutorial`.

2. Override the `init()` method in the service class to retrieve the new property.

```
@Override
public void init(PropertySet props) throws
ObjectConfigurationException {
  super.init(props);
  if (hasProperty(TUTORIAL)) {
```

```
        tutorial = getProperty(TUTORIAL);
    } else {
        tutorial = "I don't like tutorials!";
    }
}
```

Here, we retrieve the property `Tutorial` from the `PropertySet` in the `init` method.

3. Use the property as appropriately in the `run()` method. Here, let us just print the tutorial name:

```
@Override
public void run() {
    System.out.println("Running the JTricks service!! Tutorial? " +
    tutorial);
}
```

How it works...

The `init` method will be called whenever the service is configured or re-configured and the property values we entered on the JIRA Admin GUI are retrieved in this method for use in the `run()` method.

We can also optionally override the destroy method to do anything we want before the service is removed!

Once the service is deployed and added in the GUI, it prints **Running the JTricks service Tutorial? I don't like tutorials!** as the tutorial property is not configured yet.

```
Jul 11, 2011 11:36:00 PM org.apache.catalina.startup.Catalina start
INFO: Server startup in 30665 ms
2011-07-11 23:36:00,708 QuartzWorker-0 INFO ServiceRunner      Backup Service [jir
a.bc.dataimport.DefaultExportService] Finished saving the Active Objects Backup
2011-07-11 23:36:01,734 Modification Check:thread-1 INFO         [atlassian.jira.st
artup.JiraStartupLogger]

   Modifications

      Modified Files                            : jira-application.properties

      Removed Files                             : None

2011-07-11 23:40:50,755 http-8080-2 WARN jobinkk 1420x12x1 1jimvug 0:0:0:0:0:0:0:0
:1 /secure/admin/EditService!default.jspa [webwork.view.taglib.IteratorTag] Valu
e is null! Returning an empty set.
Running the JTricks service!! Tutorial? I don't like tutorials!
Running the JTricks service!! Tutorial? I don't like tutorials!
```

Go to the **Administration | System | Services** area, edit the service to enter a value under **The tutorial you like** field. Assuming you entered **JTricks Tutorials**, you will see some output as shown below:

```
Jul 11, 2011 11:36:00 PM org.apache.catalina.startup.Catalina start
INFO: Server startup in 30665 ms
2011-07-11 23:36:00,708 QuartzWorker-0 INFO ServiceRunner     Backup Service [jir
a.bc.dataimport.DefaultExportService] Finished saving the Active Objects Backup
2011-07-11 23:36:01,734 Modification Check:thread-1 INFO        [atlassian.jira.st
artup.JiraStartupLogger]

    Modifications

    Modified Files                              : jira-application.properties

    Removed Files                               : None

2011-07-11 23:40:50,755 http-8080-2 WARN jobinkk 1420x12x1 1jimvug 0:0:0:0:0:0:0
:1 /secure/admin/EditService!default.jspa [webwork.view.taglib.IteratorTag] Valu
e is null! Returning an empty set.
Running the JTricks service!! Tutorial? I don't like tutorials!
Running the JTricks service!! Tutorial? I don't like tutorials!
Running the JTricks service!! Tutorial? I don't like tutorials!
Running the JTricks service!! Tutorial? JTricks Tutorials
Running the JTricks service!! Tutorial? JTricks Tutorials
```

See also

▶ *Writing a service in JIRA*

Writing scheduled tasks in JIRA

Have you ever thought of running scheduled tasks within JIRA? Why do we need scheduled tasks when we have the JIRA Services? We have seen how to write a service in the previous recipe. But in spite of all the advantages we discussed so far, these services have a disadvantage. It always starts when JIRA is restarted and runs at regular intervals after that. So, if you have a service that does some heavy memory-intensive operation and if you restart JIRA in the middle of the day, you will suddenly find your instance's performance compromised! If it is scheduled to run every 24 hours, you will find the same service running in the middle of the day from then on until the next restart.

Scheduled tasks in JIRA are a good way to make sure all such operations happen at quite times, midnight, for example. In this chapter, we will write a simple scheduled task and see how easy that can be!

How to do it...

Let us write a simple scheduled task that prints a line in the console. Following are the steps:

1. Write a Java class that implements the `Quartz job` interface. JIRA internally uses Quartz for scheduling its tasks and so Quartz comes bundled within JIRA.

```
public class JTricksScheduledJob implements Job{

   . . .

}
```

2. Implement the `execute` method. This is the method that gets executed every time the job runs. Whatever we do in this method can be as simple as a one liner or as complex as initiating a nuclear explosion! Our scheduled job just prints a line to the console and hence the Java class that we write is as simple as follows:

```
public void execute(JobExecutionContext context) throws
JobExecutionException {
   System.out.println("Running the job at "+(new Date()).
toString());
   }
```

3. Package the class in a JAR file and deploy it under `WEB-INF/lib` folder.

4. Modify the `scheduler-config.xml` file under `WEB-INF/classes` folder to let JIRA know of our new scheduled task. JIRA stores all the information about scheduled tasks in this file:

   a. Define a job under the `<job>` tag as shown:

   ```
   <job name="JTricksJob" class="com.jtricks.
   JTricksScheduledJob" />
   ```

   b. Add a trigger that runs the `JTricksJob`. This is where we define the `cron` expression to run the job at defined timings:

   ```
   <trigger name="JTricksJobTrigger" job="JTricksJob"
   type="cron">
      <expression>0 0/2 * * * ?</expression><!-- run every 2
   minutes -->
   </trigger>
   ```

   c. The previous trigger schedules the job to run every two minutes. More details about writing a `cron` expression can be found at: `http://www.quartz-scheduler.org/docs/tutorial/TutorialLesson06.html`.

5. Restart JIRA.

How it works...

Once JIRA is restarted, the new job can be seen at the scheduler details page under **Administration | System | Scheduler Details**. We can also verify the next fire time for the task on the same page, as shown in the following screenshot:

Jobs

Name	Class		Attributes
GROUP: DEFAULT			
RefreshActiveUserCount	com.atlassian.jira.user.job.RefreshActiveUserCountJob		Volatile: TRUE Durable: TRUE Stateful: FALSE
ServicesJob	com.atlassian.jira.service.ServiceRunner		Volatile: TRUE Durable: TRUE Stateful: FALSE
JTricksJob	com.jtricks.JTricksScheduledJob		Volatile: TRUE Durable: TRUE Stateful: FALSE
OptimizeIndexes	com.atlassian.jira.issue.index.job.OptimizeIndexJob		Volatile: TRUE Durable: TRUE Stateful: FALSE

Triggers

Name	Job	Next Fire	Attributes
GROUP: DEFAULT			
RefreshActiveUserCountTrigger	DEFAULT.RefreshActiveUserCount	12/Jul/11 2:00 AM	Volatile: TRUE
ServicesTrigger	DEFAULT.ServicesJob	12/Jul/11 12:20 AM	Volatile: TRUE
JTricksJobTrigger	DEFAULT.JTricksJob	12/Jul/11 12:20 AM	Volatile: TRUE
OptimizeIndexesTrigger	DEFAULT.OptimizeIndexes	13/Jul/11 12:00 AM	Volatile: TRUE

And when the job runs, you will see the following printed in the console!

```
Jul 12, 2011 12:19:04 AM org.apache.coyote.http11.Http11Protocol start
INFO: Starting Coyote HTTP/1.1 on http-8080
Jul 12, 2011 12:19:04 AM org.apache.catalina.startup.Catalina start
INFO: Server startup in 30409 ms
2011-07-12 00:19:04,925 QuartzWorker-1 INFO ServiceRunner     Backup Service [jir
a.bc.dataimport.DefaultExportService] Finished saving the Active Objects Backup
2011-07-12 00:19:06,112 Modification Check:thread-1 INFO     [atlassian.jira.st
artup.JiraStartupLogger]

    Modifications _____

    Modified Files                             : jira-application.properties
  , scheduler-config.xml
    Removed Files                              : None

Running the job at Tue Jul 12 00:20:00 BST 2011
Running the job at Tue Jul 12 00:22:00 BST 2011
```

Writing listeners in JIRA

Listeners are very powerful features in JIRA. JIRA has a mechanism of throwing events whenever something happens on an issue, such as when creating an issue, updating an issue, progressing on the workflows, or in similar events. Using listeners, we can capture these events and do special things based on our requirements.

There are two different ways using which listeners can be implemented in JIRA. The old way of doing it is to extend the `AbstractIssueEventListener` class which in turn implements the `IssueEventListener` interface. The `AbstractIssueEventListener` class captures the event, identifies its type, and delegates the event to the appropriate method where it is handled. To write a new listener, all we need to do is to extend the `AbstractIssueEventListener` class and override the methods of interest!

The new way of doing it is to use the `atlassian-event` library. Here, we register the listener in the plugin descriptor and implement the listener with the help of `@EventListener` annotation.

Both ways are supported in JIRA now, though they have their own advantages and disadvantages. For example, it is possible to add properties for a listener in the old way. Adding properties is not supported in the new way but then the new way doesn't need any configuration as it is registered automatically. The new way, on the other hand, can be written as a fully fledged v2.0 plugin.

In this recipe, we will see how to write listeners in both the ways.

Getting ready

Create a skeleton plugin using Atlassian Plugin SDK.

How to do it...

Writing a listener in the old way, by extending `AbstractIssueEventListener`, is done as follows:

1. Create a listener class that extends the `AbstractIssueEventListener` class.

   ```
   public class OldEventListener extends AbstractIssueEventListener {
     ...
   }
   ```

2. Define the properties for the listener. This is an optional step, needed only if you need to define properties for the listener, which can then be used during execution. An example could be to enter the mail server details, if we have a listener that sends custom e-mail using a specific mail server when an event is fired.

   a. Override the `getAcceptedParams` method to return a String array of properties to be defined.

   ```
   @Override
   public String[] getAcceptedParams() {
     return new String[] { "prop 1" };
   }
   ```

b. Here, we define a property named `prop1`.

c. Override the `init` method and retrieve the property value entered by the user.

```
@Override
public void init(Map params) {
    prop1 = (String) params.get("prop 1");
}
```

d. The `init` method is invoked whenever a listener is configured or re-configured. Here, we just retrieve the property value and assigns it to a class variable for future use.

3. Override the appropriate listener methods. For example, an issue created event can be captured by overriding `issueCreated` method as shown next.

```
@Override
public void issueCreated(IssueEvent event) {
    Issue issue = event.getIssue();
    System.out.println("Issue " + issue.getKey() + " has been
created and property is:"+prop1);
}
```

Here, we just retrieve the issue that triggered the event—the issue that is newly created in this case—and just prints the details along with the listener property. We can write even more complex methods in this method. It is also possible to retrieve other things from the event like the change log details if there are any changes involved, for example, in case of `issueUpdated` event or when entering the comment using a transition.

Note that only a handful of events can be listened to like this and there are events like `project creation`, which do not throw an event at all! In such cases, you might want to extend the respective action and throw a custom event if needed. All the available events can be found at: `http://docs.atlassian.com/jira/latest/com/atlassian/jira/event/issue/IssueEventListener.html`.

4. An important method that is worth mentioning here is the `customEvent` method, which is invoked whenever a custom event is triggered. This happens for all the custom events configured by the user as mentioned in the next recipe. We can capture them as shown next:

```
@Override
public void customEvent(IssueEvent event) {
    Long eventTypeId = event.getEventTypeId();
    Issue issue = event.getIssue();
```

```
if (eventTypeId.equals(10033L)) {
    System.out.println("Custom Event thrown here for issue:" +
issue.getKey()+" and property is:"+prop1);
   }
}
```

Here, 10033 is the ID of the new event.

5. Package the class into a JAR file and deploy it under the `jira-home/plugins/installed-plugins` folder.

6. Restart JIRA

7. Configure the listener by going to **Administration | System | Listeners**.

    a. Enter name and the fully qualified class name and click on **Add**.

    b. Edit the listener to add properties if there are any!

A listener created in the new way, that is, using `@EventListener` annotation is written as follows:

1. Register the listener in `atlassian-plugin.xml`.

```
<component key="eventListener" class="com.jtricks.
NewEventListener">
  <description>Class that processes the new JIRA Event</
description>
</component>
```

Here the `class` attribute holds the fully qualified name of the listener class that we are going to write.

2. Import the `EventPublisher` component using `component-import` plugin module.

```
<component-import key="eventPublisher" interface="com.atlassian.
event.api.EventPublisher"/>
```

3. Write the listener class:

    a. Inject the `EventPublisher` component into the class and use the `register` method to self register as shown next:

```
public class NewEventListener {
    public NewEventListener(EventPublisher eventPublisher) {
        eventPublisher.register(this);
    }
}
```

b. Create methods to handle the events using `@EventListener` as shown in the following code:

```
@EventListener
public void onIssueEvent(IssueEvent issueEvent) {
System.out.println("Capturing event with
ID:"+issueEvent.getEventTypeId()+" here");

    . . .
}
```

Note that the annotation can be used with any number of public methods in the class and all of them will be invoked when an event is fired in JIRA.

c. Handle the events appropriately.

```
@EventListener
public void onIssueEvent(IssueEvent issueEvent) {   System.
out.println("Capturing event with ID:"+issueEvent.
getEventTypeId()+" here");
    Long eventTypeId = issueEvent.getEventTypeId();
        Issue issue = issueEvent.getIssue();

    if (eventTypeId.equals(EventType.ISSUE_CREATED_ID)) {
        System.out.println("Issue "+issue.getKey()+" has been
created");
            } else if (eventTypeId.equals(10033L)) {
            System.out.println("Custom Event thrown here for
issue:"+issue.getKey());
            }
}
```

Here, as we can see, the event ID is checked and then handled as appropriate. First, we handled the issue created event and then the custom event.

4. Package the plugin and deploy it under the `jira-home/plugins/installed-plugins` folder.

How it works...

In both the cases, the listener works exactly the same way once configured. Note that the configuration is applicable only for the old way and when done the listener can be seen under **Administration | System | Listeners** as follows:

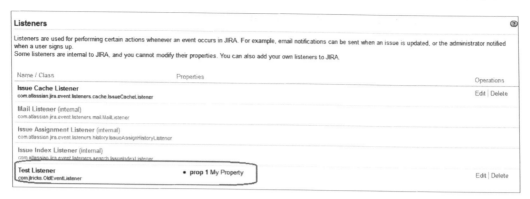

Note that there is the property **prop 1** configured in the listener.

When the event is fired in JIRA, listeners capture them and the appropriate methods are invoked. The old one will print the issue key along with the property name. The new one works the same way, except that there is no property value.

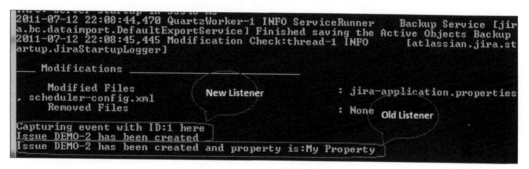

It is possible to add properties to the listener even in the new way but that needs a separate configuration screen to capture and maintain the properties.

There's more...

It is possible that the plugin maybe disabled and re-enabled by the Administrators while the service is still running. The constructor is invoked when the listener is initially loaded at JIRA startup but we might want to handle the enabling or disabling of plugins separately as they are not captured in the constructor.

Handling, enabling, and disabling of plugins

Atlassian plugins are implemented as Spring dynamic modules, and the `atlassian-plugin.xml` is transformed into a Spring XML bean configuration before it is actually loaded by the product. In case of listeners, Event Listener will become a Spring bean and hence we can apply the Spring interfaces—`InitializingBean` and `DisposableBean`—to capture the creation and destruction of the bean. In our case, the code is modified as follows:

```
public class NewEventListenerModified implements InitializingBean,
DisposableBean {
  private final EventPublisher eventPublisher;
  public NewEventListenerModified(EventPublisher eventPublisher) {
    this.eventPublisher = eventPublisher;
  }
  @EventListener
  public void onIssueEvent(IssueEvent issueEvent) {
    System.out.println("Capturing event with ID:" + issueEvent.
getEventTypeId() + " here");
    Long eventTypeId = issueEvent.getEventTypeId();
    Issue issue = issueEvent.getIssue();
    if (eventTypeId.equals(EventType.ISSUE_CREATED_ID)) {
      System.out.println("Issue " + issue.getKey() + " has been
created");
    } else if (eventTypeId.equals(10033L)) {
      System.out.println("Custom Event thrown here for issue:" +
issue.getKey());
    }
  }
  public void afterPropertiesSet() throws Exception {
    eventPublisher.register(this);
  }

  public void destroy() throws Exception {
    eventPublisher.unregister(this);
  }
}
```

As you can see, the registering and un-registering happens in methods `afterPropertiesSet` and `destroy` events respectively. These methods are invoked during the creation/destruction of the bean and that effectively handles enabling/disabling of the plugin.

Don't forget to add the `spring-beans` JAR in the project build path in this case to avoid compilation issues! Alternatively, the following dependency can be added in the `pom.xml`:

```
<dependency>
          <groupId>org.springframework</groupId>
          <artifactId>spring-beans</artifactId>
          <version>2.5.6</version>
          <scope>provided</scope>
</dependency>
```

Customizing e-mail content

We have already seen how JIRA throws various events when something happens and how we can handle these events to things ourselves. One such handling of these events includes sending e-mail notifications to users based on the notification schemes that are setup in JIRA. But what if we don't like the default content of JIRA notifications? What if we just want a different wording or maybe even amend the e-mail content?

In this recipe, we will see how we can customize the e-mail content that is sent as a notification when an event is thrown in JIRA.

How to do it...

JIRA has a set of e-mail templates written using velocity that is rendered when a notification is sent. For each event, a template is configured within JIRA and that template is used when the event is thrown. We can either create new templates and edit the events to use these new templates or modify the existing templates and leave the events as they are!

In both the cases, the steps are pretty much similar and are as follows:

1. Identify the event for which the notification needs to be changed. The event could be an existing JIRA event such as `Issue Created` and `Issue Updated` or the custom event that the JIRA administrator has created.

2. Find the template mapped to the event.

   For each event, be it system-based or custom, there is a template associated to it. We cannot change the templates associated with a system event. For example, an `Issue Updated` event is associated with `Issue Updated` template. We can, however, choose any template for the custom events we have added.

3. The e-mail template mapping for the chosen template can be found at `atlassian-jira/WEB-INF/classes/email-template-id-mappings.xml`. In this file, we can find many templates associated to each event. For example, `Issue Updated` event has the following entry:

```
<templatemappings>
  ...
  <templatemapping id="2">
    <name>Issue Updated</name>
    <template>issueupdated.vm</template>
    <templatetype>issueevent</templatetype>
  </templatemapping>
  ...
</templatemappings>
```

4. Here, we can add new mappings if we are adding new templates as follows:

```
<templatemappings>
  ...
  <templatemapping id="20">
    <name>Demo Event</name>
    <template>demoevent.vm</template>
    <templatetype>issueevent</templatetype>
  </templatemapping>
  ...
</templatemappings>
```

Make sure the `id` we use here is unique in the file.

5. Identify the template to be edited if we are customizing an existing template or add a new template with the name mentioned in the `email-template-id-mappings.xml` file.

   Email templates are stored under two different locations within JIRA one for HTML mails and another for Text mails. The templates for those can be found at `WEB-INF/classes/templates/email/html` and `WEB-INF/classes/templates/email/text` respectively. In addition to these, the subject of the e-mail can be found under `WEB-INF/classes/templates/email/subject`.

   Note that the name of the template is the same in all the three places. In our example, the name of the template being edited is `issueupdated.vm` and hence if we need to only modify the subject, we just need to modify the `WEB-INF/classes/templates/email/subject/issueupdated.vm` file. Similarly, HTML or text content can be edited at `WEB-INF/classes/templates/email/html/issueupdated.vm` or `WEB-INF/classes/templates/email/text/issueupdated.vm` respectively.

   If we are adding the template, `demoevent.vm` in our case, we need to create three templates one for each subject, HTML body and text body, all with the same name put under the respective folders.

6. Restart JIRA after editing the templates appropriately.

How it works...

After, a template is newly added and JIRA is restarted, we can associate it with the custom events we have created. When the notification is sent, JIRA will use the updated or newly added templates to render the e-mail content.

There's more...

It is possible to add more information about an issue, such as custom fields in the notification e-mails by editing the relevant velocity templates.

Advanced Customization—adding custom field information

All the VM templates have got the $issue object in the velocity context along with other variables that are elaborated at: http://confluence.atlassian.com/display/ JIRADEV/Velocity+Context+for+Email+Templates. It is fairly easy to use this to retrieve the contents on an issue while generating the e-mail content.

For example, $issue.summary will retrieve the issue summary and you can see it in the e-mail subject rendered using WEB-INF/classes/templates/email/subject/ issueupdated.vm. Similarly, other information on the issue can be easily accessed. For example, custom field details can be accessed as follows:

```
$issue.getCustomFieldValue($customFieldManager.getCustomFieldObject("c
ustomfield_10010"))
```

Here, 10010 is the unique ID for the custom field.

You can see various other examples of formatting at: http://confluence.atlassian. com/display/JIRADEV/Adding+Custom+Fields+to+Email.

Redirecting to different page in webwork actions

This recipe covers a very simple concept in JIRA web actions. While writing plugins, we often come across scenarios where we need to navigate to a new page such as a Dashboard or to browse a new project or view another issue after the action is executed. JiraWebActionSupport provides a simple method for doing this, which we will see in this recipe.

How to do it...

What if we want to navigate to the Dashboard instead of rendering a success view when an action is executed? What if we can't directly link it from the JSP page or the velocity template because we want to perform something in the action class before we redirect?

All you need here is to return getRedirect(URL) in the action class's doExecute method (or the appropriate method)! This method will redirect to the specified location when the action method is successfully finished. If there are any errors, it will go to the error page as the getRedirect() method returns Action.ERROR in that case.

You can force redirect to the URL even if there are errors by using `forceRedirect(URL)` instead of `getRedirect()` method. It doesn't clear the return URL and will always go to the redirect URL.

For example, if we need to return to Dashboard when SUCCESS, we can do it as follows:

```
@Override
protected String doExecute() throws Exception {
    System.out.println("Action invoked. Doing something important before
redirecting to Dashboard!");
    return getRedirect("/secure/Dashboard.jspa");
}
```

Replacing `getRedirect` with `forceRedirect` will take the user to Dashboard irrespective of the result.

Adding custom behavior for user details

In JIRA, you can see that the user details are formatted with the full name and a link to the users' profile within the application. For example, when the issues are displayed in the issue navigator, the assignee and reporter are displayed as follows:

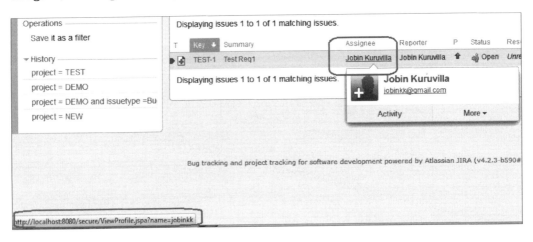

But what if we want to change how the user details are displayed? Say, if we want to display the user avatar alongside? Or, if we want to display their usernames with an external link, like a link to their Twitter profile?

JIRA provides the User Format plugin module to serve this purpose. Using this module, we can define different formats in which the user will be displayed and use them within the existing JIRA displays or within out-custom plugins.

Getting ready

Create a skeleton plugin using the Atlassian Plugin SDK.

How to do it...

In this recipe, let us try to create a new user profile that will display the username (instead of full name) with a link to their twitter profile to add some spice! The following are the steps to do it:

1. Add the user-profile module in to the `atlassian-plugin.xml`:

   ```
   <user-format key="twitter-format" name="Twitter User Format"
   class="com.jtricks.TwitterUserFormat" system="true">
     <description>User name linking to twitter</description>
   <type>twitterLink</type>
     <resource type="velocity" name="view" location="templates/
   twitterLink.vm"/>
   </user-format>
   ```

   As with other plugin modules, user profile module also has a unique **key**. It then points to the **class** that will be used by the user formatter, `TwitterUserFormat` in this case.

   The `type` element holds the unique profile type name that will be used while formatting the user. Following are the types existing in JIRA by default as on 4.4 version: `profileLink`, `fullName`, `profileLinkSearcher`, `profileLinkExternal`, `profileLinkActionHeader`, `fullProfile`.

   The `resource` element points to the velocity template to be used for rendering the view, `twitterLink.vm` in this case.

2. Create the formatter class in the previous step. The class should implement the `UserFormat` interface.

   ```
   public class TwitterUserFormat implements UserFormat {
     private final UserFormatModuleDescriptor moduleDescriptor;

     public TwitterUserFormat(UserFormatModuleDescriptor
   moduleDescriptor){
       this.moduleDescriptor = moduleDescriptor;
     }
   }
   ```

   Here, we inject `UserFormatModuleDescriptor` into the class as it will be used in rendering the velocity template, as shown in the next step.

3. Implement the required methods. We will have to implement the two overridden **format** methods.

   The first method takes a `username` and `id` where the `username` is the name of the user, which can also be *null*, and `id` is an extra argument that can be used to pass an extra context to the renderer. Ideally, an implementation might include this ID in the rendered output such that it can be used for test assertions. An example of how the ID is used can be found in displaying the assignee in the column view (`/WEB-INF/classes/templates/jira/issue/field/assignee-columnview.vm`) where the ID is assignee.

   We are not going to use ID in the example, but the method is implemented as follows:

   ```
   public String format(String username, String id) {
      final Map<String, Object> params = getInitialParams(username,
   id);
      return moduleDescriptor.getHtml(VIEW_TEMPLATE, params);
   }
   ```

   where the `getInitialParams` just populates the `params` map with the username as shown:

   ```
   private Map<String, Object> getInitialParams(final String
   username, final String id) {
      final Map<String, Object> params = MapBuilder.<String, Object>
   newBuilder().add("username", username).toMutableMap();
      return params;
   }
   ```

   We can populate the map with as many things as needed if we want to render the user details in some other way!

   The second method takes `username`, `id`, and a `map` pre-populated with extra values to add more to the context! The method is implemented as follows:

   ```
   public String format(String username, String id, Map<String,
   Object> params) {
      final Map<String, Object> velocityParams =
      getInitialParams(username, id);
      velocityParams.putAll(params);
      return moduleDescriptor.getHtml(VIEW_TEMPLATE, velocityParams);
   }
   ```

   The only difference is that the extra context is also populated into `params` map.

   In both cases, the `moduleDescriptor` renders the velocity template, defined by the name `VIEW_TEMPLATE` or "view".

4. Write the velocity template that uses the context populated in `params` map in the previous step to display the user information:

   ```
   #if ($username)
      #set ($quote = '"')
   ```

```
    #set($author = "<a id=${quote}${textutils.
htmlEncode($username)}${quote} href=${quote}http://twitter.com/#!/
${username}${quote}>$textutils.htmlEncode($username)</a>")
#else
    #set($author = $i18n.getText('common.words.anonymous'))
#end
${author}
```

In our example, we just display the username as it is with a link `http://twitter.com/#!/${username}` that will point to the twitter account with that username. Note that the `quote` variable is assigned a double quotation mark inside a single quotation mark. Single quotation here is the velocity syntax and double quotation is the value. It is used to construct the URL where encoded name, href value, and so on are placed between quotes!

Don't forget to handle the scenario when the user is null. In our case, we just display the name as Anonymous when the user is null.

5. Package the plugin and deploy it.

How it works...

Once the plugin is deployed, the new user profile, `twitterLink` in this case, can be used in various places in JIRA where appropriate. For example, the `assignee-columnview.vm` can be modified to include `twitterLink` profile instead of the default `profileLink` as follows:

```
#if($assigneeUsername)
    #if ($displayParams && $displayParams.nolink)
        $userformat.formatUser($assigneeUsername, 'fullName',
'assignee')
    #else
        <span class="tinylink">$userformat.
formatUser($assigneeUsername, 'twitterLink', 'assignee')</span>
    #end
#else
    <em>$i18n.getText('common.concepts.unassigned')</em>
#end
```

When you do that, the assignee column in issue navigator will appear as follows with a link to the user's Twitter account:

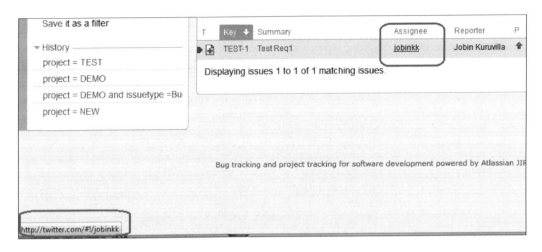

We can also use the new profile in the plugins to render user details just by invoking the `formatUser` as follows:

```
$userformat.formatUser($username, 'twitterLink', 'some_id')
```

Or:

```
$userformat.formatUser($username, 'twitterLink', 'some_id',
$someMapWithExtraContext)
```

Deploying a servlet in JIRA

We all know how useful a servlet is! JIRA provides an easy way to deploy a JAVA servlet with the help of the Servlet Plugin module. In this recipe, we will see how to write a simple servlet and access it in JIRA.

Getting ready

Create a skeleton plugin using the Atlassian Plugin SDK.

How to do it...

The following are the steps to deploy a JAVA servlet in JIRA:

1. Include the servlet plugin module in the `atlassian-plugin.xml`. The Servlet plugin module allows the following set of attributes:

    a. `class`: It is the servlet Java class and it must be a subclass of `javax.servlet.http.HttpServlet`. This attribute is mandatory.

    b. `disabled`: It indicates whether the plugin module should be disabled or enabled by default. By default, the module is enabled.

    c. `i18n-name-key`: The localization key for the human-readable name of the plugin module.

    d. `key`: It represents the unique key for the plugin module. This attribute is mandatory.

    e. `name`: It is the human-readable name of the servlet.

    f. `system`: It indicates whether this plugin module is a system plugin module or not. Only available for non-OSGi plugins.

    The following are the child elements supported:

    a. `description`: The description of the plugin module.

    b. `init-param`: Initialization parameters for the servlet, specified using `param-name` and `param-value` subelements, just as in `web.xml`. This element and its child elements may be repeated.

    c. `resource`: Resources for this plugin module. This element may be repeated.

    d. `url-pattern`: The pattern of the URL to match. This element is mandatory and may be repeated.

    In our example, let us use only the mandatory fields and some example init-params as shown:

```
<servlet name="Test Servlet" key="jtricksServlet" class="com.
jtricks.JTricksServlet">
    <description>Test Servlet</description>
    <url-pattern>/myWebsite</url-pattern>
    <init-param>
        <param-name>siteName</param-name>
        <param-value>Atlassian</param-value>
    </init-param>
    <init-param>
        <param-name>siteAddress</param-name>
        <param-value>http://www.atlassian.com/</param-value>
    </init-param>
</servlet>
```

Here `JTricksServlet` is the servlet class where as `/myWebsite` is the URL pattern. We are also passing a couple of `init` params: `siteName` and `siteAddress`.

2. Create a `servlet` class. The class must extend `javax.servlet.http.HttpServlet`.

```
public class JTricksServlet extends HttpServlet {
  ...
}
```

3. Implement the necessary methods:

   a. We can retrieve the `init` params in the `init` method as shown next:

```
@Override
public void init(ServletConfig config) throws
ServletException {
  super.init(config);
  authenticationContext = ComponentManager.getInstance().
  getJiraAuthenticationContext();   siteName = config.
  getInitParameter("siteName");
  siteAddress = config.getInitParameter("siteAddress");
}
```

   The `init()` method is invoked every time the servlet is initialized and this happens when the servlet is first accessed. `init()` method is also invoked when the servlet is first accessed after the plugin module is disabled and enabled back.

   As you can see, the `init` params we defined in the servlet plugin module can be accessed here from the `ServletConfig`. Here, we also initialize the `JiraAuthenticationContext` so that we can use it to retrieve the logged-in user details in the servlet. Similarly, we can initialize any JIRA components here.

   b. Implement the `doGet()` and/or `doPost()` methods to do what needs to be implemented. For the example, we will just use the `init` params to create a simple HTML page and print a line to the console.

```
@Override
protected void doGet(HttpServletRequest req,
HttpServletResponse resp) throws ServletException,
IOException {
  resp.setContentType("text/html");
  PrintWriter out = resp.getWriter();

  User user = authenticationContext.getUser();   out.
  println("Welcome " + (user != null ? user.getFullName() :
  "Anonymous"));
```

```
out.println("<br>Invoking the servlet...");
out.println("<br>My Website : <a href=\"" + siteAddress +
"\">" + siteName + "</a>");

doSomething();

out.println("<br>Done!");
}

private void doSomething() {
  System.out.println("Invoked servlet at " + (new Date()));
}
```

The `authenticationContext` retrieves the current username as mentioned earlier. From JIRA 4.3, `getLoggedInUser()` method is used to retrieve the current user and `getDisplayName()` gets the user's full name.

4. Package the plugin and deploy it.

How it works...

Once deployed, the servlet will be accessible at the URL: `http://yourserver/jira/plugins/servlet/${urlPattern}`. In our case, the URL is `http://yourserver/jira/plugins/servlet/myWebsite`.

When the servlet is accessed at `/plugins/servlet/myWebsite`, the output is as shown in the following screenshot:

Adding shared parameters to Servlet Context

In the previous recipe, we saw how to deploy a servlet and how to make use of the init params. What if we have a set of servlets or servlet filters or context listeners that make use of the same parameters? Do we really need to initialize them in all the plugin modules?

In this recipe, we will see how we can use the Servlet Context Parameter plugin module to share parameters across servlets, filters, and listeners.

Getting ready

Create a skeleton plugin using the Atlassian Plugin SDK.

How to do it...

All we need to do is to define the shared parameters to add a `servlet-context-param` module for each shared parameter in the `atlassian-plugin.xml`.

For example, a parameter with key `sharedText` can be defined as follows:

```
<servlet-context-param key="jtricksContext">
  <description>Shares this param!</description>
  <param-name>sharedText</param-name>
  <param-value>This is a shared Text</param-value>
</servlet-context-param>
```

Make sure the module has a unique key. Here, the parameter name is `sharedText` and it has a value **This is a shared Text**. Once the plugin is packaged and deployed, the parameter **sharedText** is available across servlets, filters, and listeners.

In a servlet, we can access the parameter in the `init` method as follows:

```
@Override
public void init(ServletConfig config) throws ServletException {
  super.init(config);
  String sharedText = config.getServletContext().
getInitParameter("sharedText");
}
```

How it works...

Once the shared text is retrieved, we can use it anywhere like while constructing the HTML

```
out.println("<br>Shared Text:"+sharedText);
```

The servlet will be now printing that as well, as shown in the following screenshot:

Writing a Servlet Context Listener

We have seen how to write servlets. How about writing a context listener for the same? This will come in handy if you want to integrate with frameworks that use context listeners for initialization.

Getting ready

Create a skeleton plugin using the Atlassian Plugin SDK.

How to do it...

Following are the steps to write a simple context listener:

1. Include the `servlet-context-listener` module in the `atlassian-plugin.xml`.

   ```
   <servlet-context-listener name="Test Servlet Listener"
   key="jtricksServletListener" class="com.jtricks.
   JTricksServletListener">
     <description>Listener for Test Servlet</description>
   </servlet-context-listener>
   ```

   Here, we have a unique module key and a class that is the servlet context listener's Java class.

2. Write the servlet context listener's class. The class must `javax.servlet.ServletContextListener`:

   ```
   public class JTricksServletListener implements
   ServletContextListener{       ...
   }
   ```

3. Implement the context listener methods as appropriate. For example, we just print some statements to the console:

   ```
   public void contextDestroyed(ServletContextEvent event) {  System.
   out.println("Test Servlet Context is destroyed!");
   }

   public void contextInitialized(ServletContextEvent event) {
   System.out.println("Test Servlet Context is initialized!");
   }
   ```

   The details of the context that is initialized or destroyed can be found from the `ServletContextEvent` object.

4. Package the plugin and deploy it.

How it works...

The `contextInitialized` method is not invoked at application startup. Instead, it is invoked the first time a servlet or filter in the plugin is accessed after each time it is enabled.

```
Jul 17, 2011 5:24:29 PM org.apache.coyote.http11.Http11Protocol start
INFO: Starting Coyote HTTP/1.1 on http-8080
Jul 17, 2011 5:24:29 PM org.apache.catalina.startup.Catalina start
INFO: Server startup in 94082 ms
Test Servlet Context is initialized!
Invoked servlet at Sun Jul 17 17:25:22 BST 2011
Running the job at Sun Jul 17 17:26:00 BST 2011
2011-07-17 17:26:03,673 Modification Check:thread-1 INFO       [atlassian.jira.st
artup.JiraStartupLogger]
```

Similarly the `contextDestroyed` method is invoked every time the plugin module containing a servlet or filter is disabled.

Using filters to intercept queries in JIRA

Servlet filters provide a powerful mechanism to intercept queries and do wise things such as profiling, monitoring, content generation, and so on. It works exactly like any normal Java servlet filter and JIRA provides the **Servlet Filter Plugin Module** to add them using plugins. In this recipe, we will learn about how to use filter to intercept certain queries to JIRA and how we can utilize them!

As with other servlet plugin modules, a `servlet-filter` plugin module also has a unique `key` and a `class` associated with it. The `name` attribute holds the human-readable name of the filter and `weight` indicates the order in which the filter will be placed in the filter chain. The higher the weight, the lower the filter's position.

There is another important attribute `location` that denotes the position of the filter in the application's filter chain. Following are the four possible values for the location:

- ▶ `after-encoding`: Very top of the filter chain in the application, but after any filters which ensure the integrity of the request.
- ▶ `before-login`: Before the filter that logs in the user.
- ▶ `before-decoration`: Before the filter which does Sitemesh decoration of the response.
- ▶ `before-dispatch`: At the end of the filter chain, before any servlet or filter which handles the request by default.

The `weight` attribute is used in conjunction with `location`. If two filters have the same location, then they are ordered based on the weight attribute.

`init-param` as usual takes the initialisation parameters for the filter.

`url-pattern` defines the pattern of the URL to match. This element can be repeated and the filter will be invoked for all the URLs matching any of the patterns specified. Unlike a servlet URL, the `url-pattern` here matches `${baseUrl}/${url-pattern}`. The pattern can use wild chars `*` or `?`, the former matching zero or many characters, including directory slashes and the latter matching zero or one character.

`dispatcher` is another element that determines when the filter is invoked. You can include multiple dispatcher elements with values `REQUEST`, `INCLUDE`, `FORWARD`, or `ERROR`. If not present, the filter will be invoked in all cases.

Getting ready

Create an skeleton plugin using the Atlassian Plugin SDK.

How to do it...

Let us try to intercept all the issue views, which has the URLs of the format `${baseUrl}/browse/*-*` and log them. The following are the step-by-step procedure to write a filter and implement the given logic.

1. Add the **Servlet Filter** plugin module into `atlassian-plugin.xml`.

   ```
   <servlet-filter name="Browse Issue Filter"
   key="jtricksServletFilter" class="com.jtricks.
   JTricksServletFilter" location="before-dispatch" weight="200">
           <description>Filter for Browse Issue</description>
           <url-pattern>/browse/*-*</url-pattern>
           <init-param>
               <param-name>filterName</param-name>
               <param-value>JTricks Filter</param-value>
           </init-param>
   </servlet-filter>
   ```

   Here `JTricksServletFilter` is the filter class and we have added the filter before dispatch. In our example, `url-pattern` will be `/browse/*-*` as the URL to browse an issue is of the form `${baseUrl}/browse/*-*`. We can use different URL patterns as required in our context.

2. Create the `Filter` class. The class should implement `javax.servlet.Filter`:

   ```
   public class JTricksServletFilter implements Filter {
     ...
   }
   ```

3. Implement the appropriate Filter methods:

```java
public void destroy() {
  System.out.println("Filter destroyed!");
}

public void doFilter(ServletRequest req, ServletResponse res,
FilterChain chain) throws IOException, ServletException {
  HttpServletRequest request = (HttpServletRequest) req;

  // Get the IP address of client machine.
  String ipAddress = request.getRemoteAddr();

  // Log the user details, IP address , current timestamp and URL.
  System.out.println("Intercepted in filter, request by user:"
  + authenticationContext.getUser().getFullName()  + " from IP
  " + ipAddress + " at " + new Date().toString() + ". Accessed
  URL:"+request.getRequestURI());

  chain.doFilter(req, res);
}

public void init(FilterConfig config) throws ServletException {
  System.out.println("Initiating the filter:"+config.getInitParamete
  r("filterName"));
  authenticationContext = ComponentManager.getInstance().
  getJiraAuthenticationContext();
}
```

Here, the `init` method is invoked when the filter is initialized, that is, the first time it is accessed after the plugin is enabled. In this method, we can retrieve the `init-param` instances defined or parameters defined using Servlet Context Parameter plugin module. In the previous code snippet, use `getLoggedInUser()` to retrieve logged user from JIRA 4.3+ and use `getDisplayName()` to retrieve the user's full name in that case.

The `destroy` method is invoked whenever a filter is destroyed.

The `doFilter` is the method which is invoked every time the URL matches the `url-pattern`. Here, we are just printing the IP address and user details requesting the **View Issue** page and logs the time but we can do many things like logging, using the data for profiling or monitoring, so on and so forth.

4. Package the plugin and deploy it.

How it works...

Whenever the URL in JIRA matches the `url-pattern`, the respective filter is invoked. This can be of huge help when you want to do specific things when a particular operation in JIRA is performed, or if you want to monitor who is doing what and when, or something else based on a specific URL.

```
Jul 19, 2011 7:52:44 PM org.apache.catalina.startup.Catalina start
INFO: Server startup in 33270 ms
2011-07-19 19:52:44,303 QuartzWorker-1 INFO ServiceRunner      Backup Service [jir
a.bc.dataimport.DefaultExportService] Finished saving the Active Objects Backup
2011-07-19 19:52:45,408 Modification Check:thread-1 INFO      [atlassian.jira.st
artup.JiraStartupLogger]

___ Modifications _____

    Modified Files                              : jira-application.properties

    Removed Files                               : None

Test Servlet Context is initialized!
Initiating the filter:JTricks Filter
Intercepted in filter, request by user:Jobin Kuruvilla from IP 0:0:0:0:0:0:0:1 a
t Tue Jul 19 19:52:59 BST 2011. Accessed URL:/browse/DEMO-1
Intercepted in filter, request by user:Jobin Kuruvilla from IP 0:0:0:0:0:0:0:1 a
t Tue Jul 19 19:53:12 BST 2011. Accessed URL:/browse/DEMO-2
Intercepted in filter, request by user:Jobin Kuruvilla from IP 0:0:0:0:0:0:0:1 a
t Tue Jul 19 19:53:23 BST 2011. Accessed URL:/browse/DEMO-1
```

With our code in the example, the details are printed, as shown in the previous screenshot, whenever an issue is viewed.

Adding and importing components in JIRA

JIRA has a component system that has so many Service classes and Manager classes that are registered in PicoContainer and are available for use by the core classes and plugins alike. It makes sense sometimes to add custom components to that component system that can then be used with the other modules in the same plugin or shared by other plugins.

In this recipe, we will see how we can add a new component in JIRA and how we can consume that from within the plugin and from a separate plugin.

Getting ready

Create a Skeleton plugin using Atlassian Plugin SDK. For the example, we will use the `RedirectAction` webwork module used in the previous recipe.

How to do it...

First, let us see how we can define a component and use them in the different modules within the same plugin. In our example, we will define a sample component and use the methods exposed by it in the `RedirectAction`. Following are the steps:

1. Create an interface with the required method definitions. The component will expose these methods when used elsewhere:

```
package com.jtricks.provider;

public interface MyComponent {
  public void doSomething();
}
```

2. Create the implementation class and implement the methods.

```
public class MyComponentImpl implements MyComponent{
  private final JiraAuthenticationContext authenticationContext;

  public MyComponentImpl(JiraAuthenticationContext
authenticationContext) {
    this.authenticationContext = authenticationContext;
  }

  public void doSomething() {
    System.out.println("Hey "+authenticationContext.getUser().
getFullName()+",  Sample method to check Components");
  }
}
```

In the implementation class, we can inject the JIRA components as usual and use them for various things. Here, we inject `JiraAuthenticationContext` to retrieve the current user details just to print a personalized message!

3. Declare the component in the `atlassian-plugin.xml` file using the Component Plugin module.

```
<component key="myComponent" name="My Component" class="com.
jtricks.provider.MyComponentImpl">
  <interface>com.jtricks.provider.MyComponent</interface>
</component>
```

Here, the component module has a unique key and a class attribute that points to the Implementation class. The element interface points to the component interface we created in *Step 1*.

Our component is now ready and available to use within the other plugin modules. For example, we can use this component in the RedirectAction class we saw earlier, as follows:

```
public class RedirectAction extends JiraWebActionSupport {
  private final MyComponent myComponent;

  public RedirectAction(MyComponent myComponent) {
    this.myComponent = myComponent;
  }

  @Override
  protected String doExecute() throws Exception {
    System.out.println("Execute the method in component!");
    this.myComponent.doSomething();
    System.out.println("Succesfully executed. Go to dashboard");
    return getRedirect("/secure/Dashboard.jspa");
  }
}
```

Here, the component is injected in the constructor as we normally do with a JIRA component (remember the `JiraAuthenticationContext` in the component itself!) and invoke the exposed method, `doSomething` in this case, where appropriate.

Exposing components to other plugins

When we create the components as discussed earlier, they remain private and are available only within the plugin even though we can expose these components to other plugins.

The following are the two things you need to do to expose a component:

1. Declare the component as public.
2. Export the packages required for the plugin so that they are available to the other plugins.

The following are the steps in detail to do the same:

1. Create the interface and implementation class as before.
2. Declare the component in the `atlassian-plugin.xml` using the Component Plugin module as a public component. For this, we use the public attribute on the component module, as shown in the following code:

```
<component key="myComponent" name="My Component" class="com.
jtricks.provider.MyComponentImpl" public="true">
  <interface>com.jtricks.provider.MyComponent</interface>
</component>
```

Export the packages using `bundle-instructions` element under `plugin-info` in `atlassian-plugin.xml`. This is done as follows:

```
<plugin-info>
  <description>Adding and importing components to JIRA</
  description>  <version>2.0</version>
  <vendor name="JTricks" url="http://www.j-tricks.com/" />
  <bundle-instructions>
    <Export-Package>com.jtricks.provider</Export-Package>
  </bundle-instructions>
</plugin-info>
```

Note that the `Export-Package` element exports `com.jtricks.provider` package that holds the interface and implementation class. More about bundle instructions can be found at: `http://confluence.atlassian.com/display/PLUGINFRAMEWORK/ Creating+your+Plugin+Descriptor#CreatingyourPluginDescriptor- {{bundleinstructions}}element`.

With that, the component is now ready and available to other plugins.

Importing public components

In order to use the public components in other plugins, we will have to first import them using the `component-import` plugin module. The module is entered in `atlassian-plugin.xml` as follows:

```
<component-import key="myComponent">
    <interface>com.jtricks.provider.MyComponent</interface>
</component-import>
```

Now, the component is available as if it is created within the plugin itself. The `RedirectAction` class will look exactly the same in the new plugin as well if we want to use the component there.

Using service properties in components

It is also possible to define a Map of properties for a public component which can then be used while importing the components with other plugins. It uses the `service-properties` element to define the properties which has child elements named entry and have key & value attributes. For example, a dictionary service can have the service properties defined with the language as key, as shown in the following code snippet:

```
<component key="dictionaryService" class="com.myapp.
DefaultDictionaryService" interface="com.myapp.DictionaryService">
    <description>Provides a dictionary service.</description>
    <service-properties>
        <entry key="language" value="English" />
    </service-properties>
</component>
```

It is now possible to use the `filter` attribute on the `component-import` module to import component only if the service matches the filter. For example, the dictionary service that has English as the language can be imported as follows:

```
<component-import key="dictionaryService" interface="com.myapp.
DictionaryService"  filter="(language=English)" />
```

How it works...

When a component is installed, it generates the `atlassian-plugins-spring.xml`. Spring Framework configuration file, transforming Component Plugin modules into Spring bean definitions. The generated file is stored in a temporary plugin JAR file and installed into the framework. If the `public` attribute is set to 'true', the component will be turned into an OSGi service under the covers, using **Spring Dynamic** modules to manage its lifecycle.

Component imports also generate the `atlassian-plugins-spring.xml` Spring Framework configuration file and transforms the Import Plugin Module to OSGi service references using Spring Dynamic modules. The imported component will have its bean name set to the component import key.

In both cases, it is possible to write our your own Spring configuration file, stored under the folder META-INF/spring in the plugin JAR.

More details about Component Plugin module and Component Import plugin module can be found in the Atlassian documentation at: `http://confluence.atlassian.com/display/`
`PLUGINFRAMEWORK/Component+Plugin+Module` and
`http://confluence.atlassian.com/display/JIRADEV/`
`Component+Import+Plugin+Module` respectively.

Adding new module types to JIRA

So far, we have seen a lot of useful plugin module types in JIRA. Custom field module type, webwork module type, servlet module type, and so on. But is it possible to add a custom module type in JIRA, one that can then be used to create different modules?

JIRA provides the Module Type plugin module using which we can add new module types dynamically to the plugin framework. In this recipe, we will see how we can add such a new plugin module type and use it to create different modules of that type.

Getting ready

Create a Skeleton plugin using Atlassian Plugin SDK.

How to do it...

Let us consider the same example Atlassian have used in their online documentation, that is, to create a new dictionary plugin module which can then be used to feed a dictionary service used by other plugins or modules.

Following are the steps to define a new plugin module type:

1. Add the module type definition in the `atlassin-plugin.xml` file.

    ```
    <module-type key="dictionary" class="com.jtricks.
    DictionaryModuleDescriptor" />
    ```

    Here, the key must be unique and will be used as the root element when defining the modules of this type. The class points to the `ModuleDescriptor` class that is instantiated when a new plugin module of this type is found.

    Other useful attributes of this module type includes `name` that holds a human readable name, `i18n-name-key` to hold the localization key for the human-readable name, `disabled` to indicate if the plugin module is disabled by default or not and `system` to indicate whether this plugin module is a system plugin module or not (available only for non-OSGi). You can also have an optional `description` as a child element.

2. Create an interface that can be used in the `ModuleDescriptor` class. This interface will have all the methods needed for the new module. For example, in the dictionary, we need a method to retrieve the definition of a given text and hence we can define the interface as follows:

    ```
    public interface Dictionary {
       String getDefinition(String text);
    }
    ```

    The new modules of this particular type will ultimately implement this interface.

3. Create the module descriptor class. The class must extend the `AbstractModuleDescriptor` class and should use the interface we created as the generic type.

    ```
    public class DictionaryModuleDescriptor extends AbstractModuleDesc
    riptor<Dictionary> {
       ...
    }
    ```

4. Implement the `getModule` method to create the module.

```
public class DictionaryModuleDescriptor extends AbstractModuleDesc
riptor<Dictionary> {
  public DictionaryModuleDescriptor(ModuleFactory moduleFactory) {
    super(moduleFactory);
  }

  public Dictionary getModule() {
    return moduleFactory.createModule(moduleClassName, this);
  }
}
```

Here, we have used the `ModuleFactory` to create a module of this type.

5. Define the attributes and elements that will be used in the new module type and retrieve them in the `init` method. For a dictionary, we need at least one attribute, that is the `language`, to differentiate the various dictionary modules. Let us name that attribute as `lang` and retrieve it in the `init` method. The class will now look similar to the following block of code:

```
public class DictionaryModuleDescriptor extends AbstractModuleDesc
riptor<Dictionary> {
  private String language;

  public DictionaryModuleDescriptor(ModuleFactory moduleFactory) {
    super(moduleFactory);
  }

  @Override
  public void init(Plugin plugin, Element element) throws
PluginParseException {
    super.init(plugin, element);
    language = element.attributeValue("lang");
  }

  public Dictionary getModule() {
    return moduleFactory.createModule(moduleClassName, this);
  }

  public String getLanguage() {
    return language;
  }
}
```

The `init` method takes as argument, `com.atlassian.plugin.Plugin` and `org.dom4j.Element`, the latter holding the module element. We have retrieved the 'lang' attribute here and assigned it to a local variable which has a getter method that can be used to get the language value in other plugins/modules.

We can have more attributes or child elements as required by the new module type.

6.   With that, the new plugin module is now ready. We can now write new modules of the type dictionary.

Creating modules using the new module type

The new module types will be as simple as the following:

```
<dictionary key="myUSEnglishDictionary" lang="us-english" class="com.jtricks.dictionary.USDictionary" />
<dictionary key="myUKEnglishDictionary" lang="uk-english" class="com.jtricks.dictionary.UKDictionary" />
```

Note that the root element is the same as the module types' key, **dictionary** in this case. Each has its own unique `key` and has the `lang` attribute we defined earlier. Each has a class which will implement the Dictionary interface appropriately. For example:

```
public class USDictionary implements Dictionary {
  public String getDefinition(String text) {
    if (text.equals("JIRA")){
      return "JIRA in San Fransisco!";
    } else {
      return "What are you asking? We in US don't know anything other
than JIRA!!";
    }
  }
}

public class UKDictionary implements Dictionary {
  public String getDefinition(String text) {
    if (text.equals("JIRA")){
      return "JIRA in London!";
    } else {
      return "What are you asking? We in UK don't know anything other
than JIRA!!";
    }
  }
}
```

Using the new modules created

Once the new modules are defined, `myUSEnglishDictionary` and `myUKEnglishDictionary` in our example, we can use these in other plugin modules. For example, if we want to use them in a servlet module to find the definition of JIRA in both the dictionaries, it can be done using the following steps:

1. Get all the enabled modules that use the dictionary module descriptor.

   ```
   List<DictionaryModuleDescriptor> dictionaryModuleDescriptors =
   pluginAccessor.getEnabledModuleDescriptorsByClass(DictionaryModule
   Descriptor.class);
   ```

   Here, `pluginAccessor` can be retrieved as follows:

   ```
   PluginAccessor pluginAccessor = ComponentManager.getInstance().
   getPluginAccessor();
   ```

   It can also be used to retrieve all the enabled modules that uses the given module descriptor class as shown in the code.

2. For each `DictionaryModuleDescriptor`, `getLanguage()` method will retrieve the value of the `lang` attribute and `getModule()` will retrieve the respective Dictionary implementation class. For example, JIRA definition for `uk-english` can be retrieved as follows:

   ```
   private String getJIRADescription(String key) {
       // To get all the enabled modules of this module descriptor  Li
   st<DictionaryModuleDescriptor> dictionaryModuleDescriptors =
   pluginAccessor.getEnabledModuleDescriptorsByClass(DictionaryModule
   Descriptor.class);
       for (DictionaryModuleDescriptor dictionaryModuleDescriptor :
   dictionaryModuleDescriptors){
           if (dictionaryModuleDescriptor.getLanguage().equals(key)){
               return dictionaryModuleDescriptor.getModule().
   getDefinition("JIRA");
           }
       }
       return "Not Found";
   }
   ```

   Here, the key that is passed will be `uk-english`.

How it works...

If we use a servlet to display all the definitions of the word JIRA in all the dictionaries deployed, US and UK in our case, it will appear as follows:

Enabling access logs in JIRA

Access logs are a good way to find out who is doing what in your JIRA instance. In this recipe, we will see how we can turn on access logging in JIRA.

How to do it...

As of JIRA 4.1, the list of users who are currently accessing JIRA can be found from **Administration | System | User Sessions** menu. But if you need more detailed information about who is doing what, access logging is the way to go.

In JIRA 4.x, enabling access logs can be done via the administration screen by going to **Administration | System | Logging & Profiling** as shown in the following screenshot:

We can turn **ON HTTP** and **SOAP** access logs separately as shown. There is an additional option to turn ON HTTP dump log and SOAP dump log as well. For HTTP, we can also include images in the HTTP access logs.

All these logs are disabled by default and if enabled via GUI, it will be disabled again on next restart.

In order to enable them permanently, we can switch them ON in the `log4j.properties` file residing under `WEB-INF/classes` folder under the section, **Access logs,** as shown next:

```
log4j.logger.com.atlassian.jira.soap.axis.JiraAxisSoapLog  = ON,
soapaccesslog
log4j.additivity.com.atlassian.jira.soap.axis.JiraAxisSoapLog = false
log4j.logger.com.atlassian.jira.soap.axis.JiraAxisSoapLogDump  = ON,
soapdumplog
log4j.additivity.com.atlassian.jira.soap.axis.JiraAxisSoapLogDump =
false
log4j.logger.com.atlassian.jira.web.filters.accesslog.AccessLogFilter
= ON, httpaccesslog
log4j.additivity.com.atlassian.jira.web.filters.accesslog.
AccessLogFilter = false
log4j.logger.com.atlassian.jira.web.filters.accesslog.
AccessLogFilterIncludeImages = ON, httpaccesslog
log4j.additivity.com.atlassian.jira.web.filters.accesslog.
AccessLogFilterIncludeImages = false
log4j.logger.com.atlassian.jira.web.filters.accesslog.
AccessLogFilterDump = ON, httpdumplog
log4j.additivity.com.atlassian.jira.web.filters.accesslog.
AccessLogFilterDump = false
```

Enabling Access logs prior to JIRA 4.x

Prior to JIRA 4.x, Access logs had only a single entry in the `log4j.properties` file and we could enable it by changing the log level from WARN to INFO as shown next:

```
log4j.category.com.atlassian.jira.web.filters.AccessLogFilter = INFO,
console, filelog
log4j.additivity.com.atlassian.jira.web.filters = false
```

The same option can be enabled from WARN to INFO on the GUI as well but it will be retained only till the next restart just like it is in 4.x.

How it works...

Once turned ON, the SOAP access logs will be written to `atlassian-jira-soap-access.log`, SOAP dump logs to `atlassian-jira-soap-dump.log`, HTTP access logs to `atlassian-jira-http-access.log` and HTTP dump logs to atlassian-jira-http-dump.log files, everything residing under the `logs` folder.

You can find detailed information in the access logs, similar to the following:

```
0:0:0:0:0:0:0:1 23x14x1 jobinkk [20/Jul/2011:00:23:43 +0100]
"GET /secure/AdminSummary.jspa HTTP/1.1" 200 89148 466 "http://
localhost:8080/secure/Dashboard.jspa" "Mozilla/5.0 (Windows NT 6.1;
WOW64; rv:5.0) Gecko/20100101 Firefox/5.0" "xdtgfh"
0:0:0:0:0:0:0:1 23x15x1 jobinkk [20/Jul/2011:00:23:50 +0100] "GET
/secure/admin/ViewLogging.jspa HTTP/1.1" 200 7521 724 "http://
localhost:8080/secure/AdminSummary.jspa" "Mozilla/5.0 (Windows NT 6.1;
WOW64; rv:5.0) Gecko/20100101 Firefox/5.0" "xdtgfh"
0:0:0:0:0:0:0:1 23x16x1 jobinkk [20/Jul/2011:00:23:55 +0100] "POST /
secure/admin/WebSudoAuthenticate.jspa HTTP/1.1" 302 - 273 "http://
localhost:8080/secure/admin/ViewLogging.jspa" "Mozilla/5.0 (Windows NT
6.1; WOW64; rv:5.0) Gecko/20100101 Firefox/5.0" "xdtgfh"
```

It is also possible to change the individual log file's name or path in the `log4j.properties` by modifying the appropriate properties. For example, the SOAP access log file can be written to `/var/log/soap-access.log` by modifying `log4j.appender.soapaccesslog.File` property as follows:

```
log4j.appender.soapaccesslog.File=/var/log/soap-access.log
```

Enabling SQL logging in JIRA

Similar to access logs, another useful piece of logging, especially when debugging an issue, is SQL logging. In this recipe, we will see how to turn on SQL logging.

How to do it...

SQL logging cannot be turned ON from the user interface. Instead, it can be turned ON in the `WEB-INF/classes/log4j.properties` file as we have seen with access logs. In this case, the logging entry to be modified is as follows:

```
log4j.logger.com.atlassian.jira.ofbiz.LoggingSQLInterceptor = ON,
sqllog
log4j.additivity.com.atlassian.jira.ofbiz.LoggingSQLInterceptor =
false
```

```
log4j.logger.com.atlassian.jira.security.xsrf.
XsrfVulnerabilityDetectionSQLInterceptor = ON, xsrflog
log4j.additivity.com.atlassian.jira.security.xsrf.
XsrfVulnerabilityDetectionSQLInterceptor = false
```

The latter logs the SQL queries executed for Xsrf vulnerability detection.

How it works...

Once turned **ON**, the SQL logs will be written to `atlassian-jira-sql.log` file under logs folder.

You can find details of numerous SQLs executed as follows:

```
2011-07-20 00:39:31,061 http-8080-6 jobinkk 39x31x1 1ogij3g /secure/
EditIssue!default.jspa 0ms "SELECT ID, ENTITY_NAME, ENTITY_ID,
PROPERTY_KEY, propertytype FROM PUBLIC.propertyentry WHERE ENTITY_
NAME='IssueType' AND ENTITY_ID='3'"
2011-07-20 00:39:31,063 http-8080-6 jobinkk 39x31x1 1ogij3g /secure/
EditIssue!default.jspa call stack ...

   at com.opensymphony.module.propertyset.ofbiz.OFBizPropertySet.
getKeys(OFBizPropertySet.java:82)  at com.atlassian.jira.propertyset.
PropertySetCache.bulkLoad(PropertySetCache.java:313)at com.atlassian.
jira.propertyset.JiraCachingPropertySet.init(JiraCachingPropertySet.
java:789)  at com.opensymphony.module.propertyset.PropertySetManager.
getInstance(PropertySetManager.java:58)  at com.opensymphony.module.
propertyset.PropertySetManager.getInstance(PropertySetManager.java:31)
```

As in the case of Access logs, the SQL log file path can be changed by modifying `log4j.appender.sqllog.file` property as follows:

```
log4j.appender.sqllog.File=/var/log/sql.log
```

Overriding JIRA's default components in plugins

JIRA uses **PicoContainer** as a central object factory. Picocontainer is responsible for instantiating objects and resolving their constructor dependencies. Within JIRA a lot of Manager, Service, and Utility classes are already registered with Picocontainer. The registration happens in `ComponentRegistrar` class' `registerComponents()` method and these classes can be retrieved via **dependency injection** or using `ComponentManager` class' getter methods or the `getComponentInstanceOfType()` method.

While it is true that most of the plugins can work with these already-registered components and the new ones created using Component Plugins module, sometimes the need arises to override an existing component registered within JIRA. In this recipe, we will see how to do that.

Getting ready

Create a skeleton plugin using Atlassian Plugin SDK. The plugin must be v1.

How to do it...

The overriding of existing components in JIRA is also done using the **Component Plugins** module. But you must note that the plugin must be v1 and should be deployed under `WEB-INF/lib` folder for the overriding to work. Following are the simple, yet powerful, steps:

1. Identify the component that we need to extend and find out the interface associated with it. For example, let us try to override the default JIRA `SubTaskManager`. The interface in this case will be `com.atlassian.jira.config.SubTaskManager`.

2. Add a component plugin module in the `atlassian-plugin.xml` with the interface in *Step 1*:

```
<component key="subtaskManager" name="My Subtask Manager"
class="com.jtricks.MySubtaskManager">
   <interface>com.atlassian.jira.config.SubTaskManager</interface>
</component>
```

   As usual, the component module has a unique **key** and an optional **name**. Here, the class points to the new component's implementation class.

3. Create the implementation class used in the component plugin module, `com.jtricks.MySubtaskManager` in this case.

   We will need to implement all the methods in the SubTaskManager interface but it is entirely up to us how to implement them. It will be a lot easier if we just need to manipulate only a few methods in them because in that case we can choose to extend the default implementation class in JIRA and override only the methods we are interested in!

   For simplicity, let us assume we need to only modify the `createSubTaskIssueLink` operation in `SubTaskManager` to do some extra bit. For this, we can create the `MySubtaskManager` by extending `com.atlassian.jira.config.DefaultSubTaskManager`, the default implementation class in JIRA, and override the `createSubTaskIssueLink` method:

```
public class MySubtaskManager extends DefaultSubTaskManager {
   public MySubtaskManager(ConstantsManager constantsManager,
IssueLinkTypeManager issueLinkTypeManager,  IssueLinkManager
issueLinkManager, PermissionManager permissionManager,
```

```
ApplicationProperties applicationProperties,
CollectionReorderer collectionReorderer, IssueTypeSchemeManager
issueTypeSchemeManager, IssueManager issueManager) {
    super(constantsManager, issueLinkTypeManager,
issueLinkManager, permissionManager, applicationProperties,
collectionReorderer, issueTypeSchemeManager, issueManager);
    }

  @Override
  public void createSubTaskIssueLink(GenericValue parentIssue,
GenericValue subTaskIssue, User remoteUser)     throws
CreateException {
System.out.println("Creating Subtask link in overriden component
using GenericValue!");
    super.createSubTaskIssueLink(parentIssue, subTaskIssue,
remoteUser);
    }
}
```

In our example, let us just print a line to the logs but we can do harder things here!

4. Package the plugin and deploy it under `WEB-INF/lib`.

How it works...

When JIRA is started, all the default components that are registered with **PicoContainer** are loaded first. But when the plugins are loaded, if there is a component module that uses the same interface and a different implementation class; this class will be registered for that interface. In our example, `MySubtaskManager` is registered instead of `DefaultSubTaskManager` class.

 This method fails in case of some Manager classes, possibly because of the order in which the classes are loaded. You might want to see the next section in such scenarios!

After overriding `SubTaskManager` as discussed before, we will see the message printed into the server logs every time a subtask is created, as shown in the following screenshot:

```
2011-07-20 10:07:23,221 main INFO      [atlassian.jira.scheduler.JiraSchedulerLa
uncher] JIRA Scheduler started.
Jul 20, 2011 10:07:23 AM org.apache.coyote.http11.Http11Protocol start
INFO: Starting Coyote HTTP/1.1 on http-8080
Jul 20, 2011 10:07:23 AM org.apache.catalina.startup.Catalina start
INFO: Server startup in 26253 ms
Creating Subtask link in overriden component using GenericValue!
Creating Subtask link in overriden component using GenericValue!
```

There's more...

While overriding a component, using the **Component Plugins** module is the recommended way, the same thing can be done in a couple of other ways.

Overriding by modifying JIRA code

For people who have modified the JIRA Source distribution, overriding the component can be done in a single line. After creating the new component—implementing the interface that we want to override—we can modify the `registerComponents` method in `com.atlassian.jira.ContainerRegistrar` class to include the new class instead of the default class.

For example, `SubTaskManager` can be overridden by replacing:

```
register.implementation(PROVIDED, SubTaskManager.class,
DefaultSubTaskManager.class);
```

With:

```
register.implementation(PROVIDED, SubTaskManager.class,
MySubtaskManager.class);
```

Note that components can either by `INTERNAL` meaning that they will be available only to JIRA itself or `PROVIDED` in which case they will also be available to `plugins2` plugins.

Overriding by extending PicoContainer

Prior to JIRA 4.3, there was a provision in JIRA to extend the PicoContainer and register the custom components in the extended PicoContainer. The following is how it was done:

1. Create a new `PicoContainer` class that implements `ContainerProvider` interface.

   ```
   public class MyContainerProvider implements ContainerProvider{
       ...
   }
   ```

2. Implement the `getContainer` method that builds a container from the parent and includes the new registrations. For our earlier example, the class will look similar to the following block of code:

   ```
   public class MyContainerProvider implements ContainerProvider{
       private DefaultPicoContainer container;

       public PicoContainer getContainer(PicoContainer parent){
           if (container == null)
               buildContainer(parent);
           return container;
       }
   ```

```
    private void buildContainer(PicoContainer parent){
        this.container = new DefaultPicoContainer(new
ProfilingComponentAdapterFactory(), parent);
    container.registerComponentImplementation(SubTaskManager.class,
MySubtaskManager.class);
    }
}
```

Here, `MySubtaskManager` will be created exactly the same way.

3. Register the new container provider in the `jira-application.properties` file, residing at `atlassian-jira/WEB-INF/classes` folder, using the key `jira.extension.container.provider`.

   ```
   jira.extension.container.provider = com.jtricks.
   MyContainerProvider
   ```

4. Deploy the JAR file with the new container class and component class under `WEB-INF/lib` folder and restart JIRA.

This works in JIRA 4.3 as well though deprecated. From 4.4, it still works but the `jira.extension.container.provider` property must be added in `jpm.xml` file instead of `jira-application.properties`. The property will be added as follows:

```
<property>
    <key>jira.extension.container.provider</key>
    <default-value>com.jtricks.MyContainerProvider</default-value>
    <type>string</type>
    <user-editable>true</user-editable>
</property>
```

Creating issues and comments from e-mail

It is possible to automatically create issues or comments in JIRA based on incoming e-mail messages. This feature is very useful in scenarios such as helpdesks where the users normally send an e-mail to a designated e-mail address and the support team works on issues raised such as this one!

Once configured correctly, any new e-mail that comes in will create a corresponding issue in JIRA and the replies to the e-mail notifications on that issue will be created as comments on that issue. It is also possible to attach documents on the issue by attaching them on the e-mail provided attachments that are enabled in JIRA. If external user management is not enabled, it is still possible to create a user account—if they don't already have an account.

In this recipe, we will see how we can configure JIRA to enable this feature.

How to do it...

The following are the steps to enable issue creation from e-mail.

1. Create an e-mail account on the server—typically, one e-mail account for each JIRA project. This mailbox should be accessible via POP, IMAP, or on the local file system. JIRA will periodically scan this mailbox and create issues or comments based on the e-mail.

2. Navigate to JIRA's **Administration | Global Settings | Mail Servers**

3. Click on **Configure new POP / IMAP mail server** link.

4. Enter the details for the POP or IMAP mail server created in *Step 1* and click on **Add**.

5. Verify the details on the **Mail Servers** page and modify if needed.

6. Navigate to JIRA **Administration | System | Services**.

7. Add a new service with the following details:

   a. **Name**: Name of the service

   b. **Class**: Pick one from the list of Built-in services. `com.atlassian.jira.service.services.pop.PopService` for example.

   c. **Delay**: Choose a delay for the service to run and scan the mails.

8. Adding the service will take you to the **Edit Service** page. Populate the details as follows and update:

   a. **Handler** : Select **Create Or Comment Handler** from the drop down box

   b. **Handler Parameters**: This is the most important part where we specify the parameters that will be used while creating the issue. Following are the list of important parameters:

▶ `project`: Key of the project where the issue should be created

▶ `issuetype`: Unique ID of the `issuetype`. For example, if we want the issue to be created as a Bug, provide `issuetype` as 1.

▶ `createusers`: if set to true, accounts will be created for new senders.

▶ `reporterusername`: Can be used to create issue with the specified reporter when the sender does not match with an existing user.

▶ `notifyusers`: Only used if `createusers` is true. Indicates whether users should get a mail notification for the new accounts created.

▶ `ccassignee`: If set, the new issue will be assigned to a matching user in To field or in Cc field if no one matches in To field.

- ▶ `bulk`: Determines how to handle "bulk" e-mails. Values possible are:
  - ❏ `ignore`: Ignore the e-mail and do nothing.
  - ❏ `forward`: Forward the e-mail to the address set in the "Forward Email" text field.
  - ❏ `delete`: Delete the e-mail permanently.
- ▶ `catchemail`: If added, JIRA will process only e-mails sent to this address. It is used when there are multiple aliases for the same e-mail inbox.
- ▶ `stripquotes`: If enabled, it strips previous messages from replies.
  - a. Forward e-mail: Error notifications and un-handled e-mails (used in conjunction with bulk forward handle parameter) will be forwarded to this address.
  - b. Uses SSL: Select SSL if used.
  - c. Server: Select the e-mail server for this service. It will be the one we added in *Step 2* to *Step 4*.
  - d. Port: It is the port to connect to. Leave blank if default.

JIRA is now configured to receive mails to the newly added mailbox.

How it works...

The service we have setup here scans the mailbox every **n** minutes as configured in the delay and picks up the new incoming messages. When a new message is received, JIRA scans through the subject to see if there are any mentions of an already existing issue. If there is one, the e-mail is added as a comment on the mentioned issue with the e-mail body as the comment text. If there is no mention of an issue in the subject, JIRA still checks whether the e-mail is a reply to another e-mail that already created an issue or not. If so, the e-mail body is again added as a comment on that issue. This is done by checking the `in-reply-to` header in the e-mail.

If JIRA still couldn't find any matching issues, a new issue is created in the project and of type configured in the handle parameters. The e-mail subject will become the issue, summary and e-mail body, the description.

Any attachments on an e-mail, new, or replies, will be added as attachments on the issue.

More information about the creation of issues and comments from an e-mail can be found at `http://confluence.atlassian.com/display/JIRA/Creating+Issues+and+Comments+from+Email`.

It is also worth checking the plugin exchange for plugins with extended mail handlers that are capable of adding more details on the issue while creation like custom field values. Some of them have far better filtering mechanisms as well.

Internationalization in webwork plugins

We have seen in the earlier chapters how to write webwork plugins to create new or extended JIRA actions. In this recipe, we will see how we can personalize the messages in these plugins using **internationalization** and **localization**.

As Wikipedia puts it:

> *"Internationalization and localization are means of adapting computer software to different languages, regional differences and technical requirements of a target market. Internationalization is the process of designing a software application so that it can be adapted to various languages and regions without engineering changes. Localization is the process of adapting internationalized software for a specific region or language by adding locale-specific components and translating text."*

The terms internationalization and localization are abbreviated to **i18n** where **18** stands for the number of letters between the first **i** and last **n** in internationalization!

How to do it...

Internationalization in a webwork plugin is achieved with the help of a resource bundle with the same name as the action that it is associated with. Following are the steps to enable it in a JIRA webwork plugin:

1. Create a `properties` file with the same name as that of the action class under the same package structure under `src/main/resources` folder in the plugin.

    For example, if we consider the `RedirectAction` example in the previous recipes, the property file will be `RedirectAction.properties` residing under `src/main/resources/com/jtricks` folder.

2. Add the key value pair of properties that needs to be used in action as follows:

    `good.bye=Good Bye`

    Here, `good.bye` is the key that will be used and will be same across all language `properties` files. The value here "Good Bye" will be used for the default locale but will have the equivalent translations in the other language property files.

3. Create `properties` files in the same folder for other required languages in the following format: `${actionName}_${languageCode}_${countryCode}.properties`. For example, if we need to personalize the above action for UK and US and French users, following will be the property filenames:

    `RedirectAction_en_US.properties`
    `RedirectAction_en_UK.properties`
    `RedirectAction_fr_FR.properties`

4. Add the property `good.bye` in each of the property files with the appropriate translation as the values. For example, a property with value Good Bye in the English property file will have value `revoir` in French!

   ```
   good.bye=Good Bye (in RedirectAction_en_UK.properties)
   good.bye=revoir (in RedirectAction_fr_FR.properties)
   ```

5. In the action class, use `getText(key)` method to retrieve the appropriate message. Keep in mind that the action `class` extends the `JiraWebActionSupport` class which implements the getText method!

   For example, the value Good Bye can be printed to users in different locales in their own language as follows:

   ```
   System.out.println(getText("good.bye"));
   ```

This magic however is broken in v2 plugins and there is already an issue reported with Atlassian at `https://jira.atlassian.com/browse/JRA-23720`. The workaround is to override the `getTexts` method as follows in the action class:

```
@Override
public ResourceBundle getTexts(String bundleName) {
   return ResourceBundle.getBundle(bundleName, getLocale(), getClass().
getClassLoader());
}
```

Here we get the `ResourceBundle` using the class loader of the action class and that fixes the above issue in v2 plugins!

Before we wind up, if you need to get the `i18N` texts in the velocity templates, following are the steps:

1. Add the property files as before.

2. Add the resource entry in the `atlassian-plugin.xml` as follows:

   ```
   <resource name="common-18n" type="i18n" location="com.jtricks.
   RedirectAction"/>
   ```

   Here, the resource points to the property file with the package and name (omitting the country or language code).

3. Use `$i18n` object to retrieve the property values as follows:

   ```
   $i18n.getText("good.bye")
   ```

Sharing common libraries across v2 plugins

We have already explored creating both v1 and v2 plugins throughout this book. One major difference between v1 and v2 plugins is that the v1 plugins has got access to all the libraries and classes available in the application class path whereas v2 plugins can't access them.

For example, the v1 plugins can access some common utility classes by dropping the JAR file with those classes in the `WEB-INF/lib` or adding those classes under `WB-INF/classes`. But that won't work with v2 plugins as they need the JAR files embedded with them under `MET-INF/lib` or the classes embedded in them. How will we handle this scenario when there is a utility class that we need to share across a few v2 plugins? Should we embed the class in all the plugins? The answer is no, and in this recipe, we will see how we can share those utility classes across v2 plugins by creating an OSGi bundle.

Getting ready

Create a skeleton plugin using Atlassian Plugin SDK.

How to do it...

Let us assume we have a Number utility class that does summation and multiplication of integer numbers. What should we do if we want to make this class available in all the v2 plugins? The following are the steps:

1. Create the Utility class under the correct package:

   ```
   package com.jtricks.utilities;

   public class NumberUtility {
     public static int add(int x, int y) {
       return x + y;
     }
   }
   ```

2. Export the classes that needs to be shared so that it is visible to other v2 plugins. This step is very important.

   Even though it is a simple utility class, we need the atlassian-plugin.xml for this step. We can use the `bundle-instructions` under `plugin-info` element in the `atlassian-plugin.xml` for exporting selected packages to other plugins/bundles.

   The bundle-instructions element allows child elements.

   Export-Package: To export selected packages from the plugin to be shared across other plugins

   Import-Package: Tom import only selected packages into a plugin. By default it imports all the exported packages from other plugins.

   In this case, we need to modify the atlassian-plugin.xml to export our utility class and this can be done as follows:

   ```
   <plugin-info>
     <description>Shared Utilities</description>
     <version>2.0</version>
   ```

```
<vendor name="JTricks" url="http://www.j-tricks.com/" />
<bundle-instructions>
  <Export-Package>com.jtricks.utilities</Export-Package>
</bundle-instructions>
</plugin-info>
```

3. It is possible to export only selected versions and choose not to export certain packages. More details on this can be found at `http://www.aqute.biz/Bnd/Bnd`.

4. Optionally, we can use the **Import-Package** element to import the above exported package. By default, it will anyways be imported and hence this step can be omitted. However it will be useful when you want to import only selected packages or make the import mandatory etc. Again, the details can be found in the above link.

5. Package the plugin and deploy it as a v2 plugin.

Now the utility class is available to all the other v2 plugins. When developing, the other plugins should have this class in the classpath which can be achieved by adding the above plugin as a dependency in the `pom.xml` with scope as provided.

```
<dependency>
    <groupId>com.jtricks</groupId>
    <artifactId>utility-plugin</artifactId>
    <version>1.0</version>
    <scope>provided</scope>
</dependency>
```

When we do that, the above method, add, can be invoked as if the class is within the same plugin. For example, the `RedirectAction` class may have the method as follows:

```
@Override
protected String doExecute() throws Exception {
    System.out.println("Action invoked. Doing something important
before redirecting to Dashboard!");
    System.out.println("Sum:"+NumberUtility.add(3, 5));
    return getRedirect("/secure/Dashboard.jspa");
}
```

Operations using direct HTML links

It probably make sense to wind up this book by giving a little tip on how we can do powerful operations in JIRA by a simple click on a link, either from your e-mail or a from a web form or from within JIRA itself!

Almost all the actions can be encoded into a single URL provided we have the right parameters to invoke those actions. Make no mistake, it has its own disadvantages because it will override all the pre-processing, validations, and so on, in place in some cases.

The URL that performs the action is constructed in the following manner:

`${baseUrl}/secure/${action}?${arguments}`

where `baseUrl` is the JIRA base url, `action` is the webwork action to be executed and `arguments` is the URL encoded arguments needed for the action. The arguments are constructed as key value pairs separated by `&`. Each key value pair will be of the form `key=value` and must comply with HTML link syntax—that is, all characters must be escaped. Let us see in detail.

How to do it...

Let us consider a simple example to start with, i.e. creating issues. Creating an issue has four stages.

- ► Going to initial create screen
- ► Selecting the project and `issuetype` and clicking on **Next**
- ► Entering all the details on the issue
- ► Clicking on **Submit** with details

We can execute each of these in single steps provided we know the details in advance. For the example, let us take `http://localhost:8080/` as the base URL for the JIRA instance.

1. Going to initial create issue screen can be done via the URL:

   `http://localhost:8080/secure/CreateIssue!default.jspa`

   Note that the recent `project` and `issuetype` are pre-selected when you access this link because that is the JIRA default behavior. But what if we want to pre-select some other project? All we need is to add the parameters `pid` in the URL as follows:

   `http://localhost:8080/secure/CreateIssue!default.jspa?pid=10100`

2. If we need to go to the second step directly by selecting the project and issuetype, just add the `issuetype` parameter as well into the URL separated by `&`.

   `http://localhost:8080/secure/CreateIssue!default.jspa?pid=10100&issuetype=1`

3. If we need to pre-populate create issue dialogue in one click, enter all the details in the URL as shown with the action name as `CreateIssueDetails!init.jspa`

   `http://localhost:8080/secure/CreateIssueDetails!init.jspa?pid=10100&issuetype=1&priority=1&summary=Emergency+Bug&reporter=jobinkk`

Note that all the mandatory fields should be populated to avoid validation errors. The above example also shows how the URL is encoded to comply with HTML syntax by replacing space in the summary with a +. i.e. Emergency Bug is written as Emergency+Bug which can also be written as Emergency%20Bug.

4. And if we want to create the issue in one click with the details above, use `CreateIssueDetails` action instead of `CreateIssueDetails!init`

   ```
   http://localhost:8080/secure/CreateIssueDetails.jspa?pid=10100&
   issuetype=1&priority=1&summary=Emergency+Bug&reporter=jobinkk
   ```

   Hopefully that gives as idea about how the operation can be executed via direct links. Make sure the user is logged or Anonymous issue creation is turned on when the above link are clicked.

But how do we find out what is the action class involved or what are the parameters to be passed?

This you can do easily from the browser URL if the request uses GET method. Create an issue with project and `issuetype` selected (case 2 above) is an example as shown next:

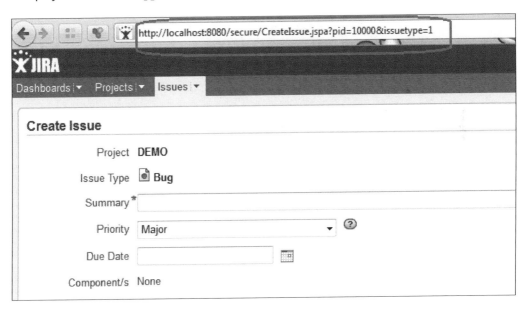

When the request is **POST** as in case 4, we can find out the action name from the URL but the parameters needs to be worked out from what is posted when the action is executed. There are multiple ways to do it and an easy way out of them will be to use the browser capabilities. For example, using **Firebug** with Mozilla Firefox will get you the parameters posted when an action is executed as shown below:

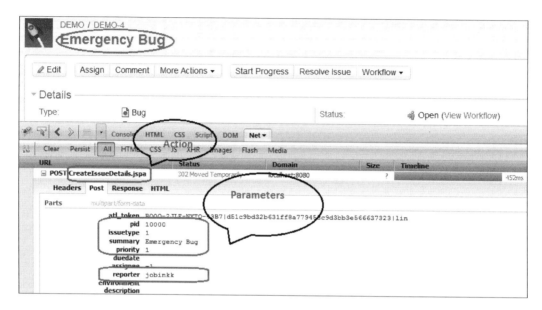

Here we can see the parameters pid, issuetype, priority, summary and reporter getting submitted in the **POST** section. Also, we can see the action name. Once you get the list of parameters, we can user them in the URL with appropriate values separated by & as we saw in *Step 4*.

This technique opens up lot of possibilities. For example, we can easily automate the submission of these URLs that we have constructed using command-line tools like wget or curl. Read about these more at: http://confluence.atlassian.com/display/ JIRA/Creating+Issues+via+direct+HTML+links And: http://confluence. atlassian.com/display/JIRACOM/Automating+JIRA+operations+via+wget.

Index

Symbols

A

O

object configurable parameters, for reports
153-160

OfBiz
about 27, 346
URL, for entity modeling 27

OfBizDelegator 348, 351, 362

OfBiz Entity Engine 27, 30, 346

Open For Business. *See* **OfBiz**

OpenSocial 28, 138

OpenSymphony documentation 26

operator 190

option.getChildOptions() method 72

option.getValue() method 72

OptionsManager class 71

OR condition 232

orderable element 106

orderBy clause 352

Orion format 346

OSGI bundles 68

OSGI platform
URL 36

OSGi plugins 41

OSUser 27

OSWorkflow 27, 92

other modules, JIRA
about 34
keyboard-shortcut 34
module-type 34
resource 34
servlet 34
servlet-context-listener 34
servlet-context-param 34
servlet-filter 34
user-format 34
web-resource 34

P

param attribute 44

param attribute, plugin-info element 35

passesCondition method 96, 99

path argument 383

permissions
retrieving, on issues from database 370-373

**permissions, based on workflow status 118,
119**

Permission Scheme 370

PicoContainer
about 411, 423
extending 426

pie chart
creating, in JIRA 160-164

PieChartGenerator class 161

plugin
issue, creating from 222-224

plugin descriptor 8

plugin development process, JIRA 8, 9

plugin-info element
about 35
application-version attribute 35
bundle-instructions attribute 36
description attribute 35
param attribute 35
vendor attribute 35
version attribute 35

plugin information
persisting, in JIRA DB 353-356

plugin key 8, 9

plugin modules types, JIRA
about 31
action and components 33
custom fields 32
links and tabs 33
other 34
remote invocation 33
reporting 32
searching 32
workflows 32

plugins
about 7
components, exposing to 413
converting, from v1 to v2 41, 42
DB entities, accessing from 351
JQL query, parsing in 210
resources, adding into 43, 44
web resources, adding into 45, 46

**plugins-version attribute, atlassian-plugin ele-
ment 35**

pom.xml file 13, 15, 51, 336

POP Service 382

Thank you for buying
JIRA Development Cookbook

About Packt Publishing

Packt, pronounced 'packed', published its first book "*Mastering phpMyAdmin for Effective MySQL Management*" in April 2004 and subsequently continued to specialize in publishing highly focused books on specific technologies and solutions.

Our books and publications share the experiences of your fellow IT professionals in adapting and customizing today's systems, applications, and frameworks. Our solution-based books give you the knowledge and power to customize the software and technologies you're using to get the job done. Packt books are more specific and less general than the IT books you have seen in the past. Our unique business model allows us to bring you more focused information, giving you more of what you need to know, and less of what you don't.

Packt is a modern, yet unique publishing company, which focuses on producing quality, cutting-edge books for communities of developers, administrators, and newbies alike. For more information, please visit our website: www.PacktPub.com.

About Packt Enterprise

In 2010, Packt launched two new brands, Packt Enterprise and Packt Open Source, in order to continue its focus on specialization. This book is part of the Packt Enterprise brand, home to books published on enterprise software – software created by major vendors, including (but not limited to) IBM, Microsoft and Oracle, often for use in other corporations. Its titles will offer information relevant to a range of users of this software, including administrators, developers, architects, and end users.

Writing for Packt

We welcome all inquiries from people who are interested in authoring. Book proposals should be sent to author@packtpub.com. If your book idea is still at an early stage and you would like to discuss it first before writing a formal book proposal, contact us; one of our commissioning editors will get in touch with you.

We're not just looking for published authors; if you have strong technical skills but no writing experience, our experienced editors can help you develop a writing career, or simply get some additional reward for your expertise.

JIRA 4 Essentials

ISBN: 978-1-84968-172-8   Paperback: 352 pages

Track bugs and issues and manage your software development projects

1. Successfully manage issues and track your projects using JIRA

2. Model business processes using JIRA Workflows

3. Ensure only the right people get access to your data, by using user management and access control in JIRA

4. Packed with step-by-step instruction, screenshots, and practical examples

Java EE 6 with GlassFish 3 Application Server

ISBN: 978-1-849510-36-3   Paperback: 488 pages

A practical guide to install and configure the GlassFish 3 Application Server and develop Java EE 6 applications to be deployed to this server

1. Install and configure the GlassFish 3 Application Server and develop Java EE 6 applications to be deployed to this server

2. Specialize in all major Java EE 6 APIs, including new additions to the specification such as CDI and JAX-RS

3. Use GlassFish v3 application server and gain enterprise reliability and performance with less complexity

Please check **www.PacktPub.com** for information on our titles

[PACKT] enterprise ✖
professional expertise distilled

[PACKT]
PUBLISHING

EJB 3.1 Cookbook

ISBN: 978-1-84968-238-1   Paperback: 436 pages

Enterprise JavaBean 3.1 - Build real world EJB solutions
with a collection of simple but incredibly effective
recipes

1. Build real world solutions and address many
   common tasks found in the development of
   EJB applications

2. Manage transactions and secure your EJB
   applications

3. Master EJB Web Services

4. Part of Packt's Cookbook series: Comprehensive
   step-by-step recipes illustrate the use of Java to
   incorporate EJB 3.1 technologies

Oracle APEX 4.0 Cookbook

ISBN: 978-1-84968-134-6   Paperback: 328 pages

Over 80 great recipes to develop and deploy fast,
secure, and modern web applications with Oracle
Application Express 4.0

1. Create feature-rich web applications in APEX 4.0

2. Integrate third-party applications like Google Maps
   into APEX by using web services

3. Enhance APEX applications by using stylesheets,
   Plug-ins, Dynamic Actions, AJAX, JavaScript, BI
   Publisher, and jQuery

4. Hands-on examples to make the most out of the
   possibilities that APEX has to offer

Please check **www.PacktPub.com** for information on our titles

Made in the USA
Lexington, KY
16 January 2015